MINJIAN

GLOBAL CHINESE CULTURE

GLOBAL CHINESE CULTURE

David Der-wei Wang, Editor

Michael Berry, *Speaking in Images: Interviews with Contemporary Chinese Filmmakers*

Sylvia Li-chun Lin, *Representing Atrocity in Taiwan: The 2/28 Incident and White Terror in Fiction and Film*

Michael Berry, *A History of Pain: Literary and Cinematic Mappings of Violence in Modern China*

Alexa Huang, *Chinese Shakespeares: A Century of Cultural Exchange*

Shu-mei Shih, Chien-hsin Tsai, and Brian Bernards, editors, *Sinophone Studies: A Critical Reader*

Andrea Bachner, *Beyond Sinology: Chinese Writing and the Scripts of Culture*

Jie Li, *Shanghai Homes: Palimpsests of Private Life*

Michel Hockx, *Internet Literature in China*

Lily Wong, *Transpacific Attachments: Sex Work, Media Networks, and Affective Histories of Chineseness*

MINJIAN

The Rise of China's Grassroots Intellectuals

SEBASTIAN VEG

Columbia University Press

New York

Columbia University Press gratefully acknowledges the generous support for this book provided by a member of our Publisher's Circle in honor of Ms. Monica Shu-ping Chen Yü.

Columbia University Press wishes to express its appreciation for assistance given by the Chiang Ching-kuo Foundation for International Scholarly Exchange and the Council for Cultural Affairs in the publication of this series.
Columbia University Press
Publishers Since 1893
New York Chichester, West Sussex
cup.columbia.edu

Paperback edition, 2021

Cataloging-in-Publication Data available from the Library of Congress

ISBN 978-0-231-19140-1 (cloth)
ISBN 978-0-231-19141-8 (pbk.)
ISBN 978-0-231-54940-0 (electronic)

Cover design: Chang Jae Lee
Cover image: Qiu Zhijie, *From Huaxia to China*, 2015, Ink on paper, Courtesy of the artist

Contents

Acknowledgments *vii*

Introduction 1

1. Grassroots Intellectuals: Theoretical and Historical Perspectives 26

2. Wang Xiaobo and the Silent Majority: Redefining the Role of Intellectuals After Tiananmen 52

3. *Minjian* Historians of the Mao Era: Commemorating, Documenting, Debating 84

4. Investigating and Transforming Society from the Margins: The Rise and Fall of Independent Cinema 123

5. Professionals at the Grassroots: Rights Lawyers, Academics, and Petitioners 164

6. Journalists, Bloggers, and a New Public Culture 204

Conclusion 247

Appendix: Minibiographies of Thirty Minjian *Intellectuals* *255*

Notes *261*

Index *335*

Acknowledgments

This book was researched and written in various stages over the last decade, during which time I have benefited immensely from the support and generosity of a great number of people.

Firstly I would like to thank friends and colleagues in Beijing, Shanghai, Chengdu, Kunming, and elsewhere in China who shared their insights, precious time, and material with me, in particular Ai Xiaoming, Chan Koonchung, Guo Yuhua, David Kelly, Lei Yi, Ma Li, Shao Yanjun, Sun Yu, Wang Bing, Wang Hongwei, Wang Hui, Wu Si, Wu Wenguang, Xiao Haisheng, Xu Jilin, Xu Zhiyuan, Yan Lianke, Yu Jian, Yu Jianrong, Zhang Enhe, Zhang Yihe, and many others whom I interviewed or corresponded with more sporadically. Special thanks are due to Wang Qinbo, who introduced me to Wang Xiaobo; to Laurent and Annette for their hospitality; and to Pierre Martin for his companionship during my research trips to Beijing.

Hong Kong, where I lived from 2006 to 2015, was an extraordinary place to conduct research on contemporary China, and I am grateful to colleagues in the French Centre for Research on Contemporary China (CEFC), The University of Hong Kong, and around town for their encouragement and many stimulating discussions. In particular I would like to thank Nicholas Bequelin, Jean-Philippe Béja, Michel Bonnin, Jean-Pierre Cabestan, Chan Kinman, Edmund Cheng, Cheung Lik-kwan, Frank Dikötter, Jean-François Huchet, Theodore Huters, Lucas Klein, Leo Ou-fan Lee, Lin Pei-yin, Gina Marchetti, Aurore Merle, William Nee, Pan Lü, Judith Pernin, Eva Pils, Roseann Rife, Ilaria Maria Sala, Christoph Steinhardt, Teng Biao, Kristof Van den Troost, Esther Yau, Winnie Yee, Samson Yuen, Zeng Jinyan, and Yinde Zhang, as well as our much-missed colleagues Esther Cheung and PK Leung (Yasi). I can conceive of no better place for academic work than the stimulating interdisciplinary environment of the CEFC (especially the late evening sessions in Wanchai) and its incomparable staff, including Alfred Aroquiame, Adeline Chiu, Florent Chevallier, Heipo Leung, Hugo Petit, Romain Warnault, Henry Wu, and Miriam Yang. As editor and publisher of *China Perspectives*, I further benefited greatly from the many ground-breaking contributions on contemporary China we published over the years, many of which have found their way into the notes of this book.

Beyond Hong Kong, my work has time and again benefited from the critical interest and intellectual generosity of friends and colleagues in various corners of the world and of the contemporary China field, in particular Geremie Barmé, Timothy Cheek, Gloria Davies, Rogier Creemers, Frederik Green, Hung Ho-fung, Seio Nakajima, Fumiaki Ozaki, Nicolai Volland, Wang Chaohua, and Jeffrey Wasserstrom. A special thank you is due to friends who follow contemporary China in Taiwan, especially Frank Muyard and Wu Jieh-min.

The finalization of the manuscript took place after my return to Paris to take up a position at the EHESS (School for Advanced Studies in Social Sciences), where I enjoyed discussions with an engaging set of colleagues within and beyond China studies, especially Antoine Lilti, Gisèle Sapiro, Philippe Roussin, and Isabelle Thireau, who all contributed to helping me work out the framework of this study. I also particularly want to thank those graduate students who, throughout the seminars I offered on topics related to this project, raised critical questions and comments.

I was lucky to be able to present this book project at different stages and on various occasions: I am grateful for invitations and critical comments from Robin McNeal and Nick Admussen at Cornell University; Andy Nathan, Ying Qian, and Robbie Barnett at Columbia University; David Ownby, Timothy Cheek, Joshua Fogel, and Mark McConaghy in Montréal; Gina Marchetti and Winnie Yee at HKU; Xu Jilin at East China Normal University (who organized an extremely fruitful discussion on *minjian*); Daniel Leese at the University of Freiburg; and Masahisa Suzuki and Takahiro Nakajima at Tokyo University.

I would like to express my deep gratitude to David Der-wei Wang for his unfailing support for this project as series editor, as well as to the three anonymous reviewers.

Wendy Larson, whose pioneering work on Wang Xiaobo was instrumental in sparking my own interest in his writings, took the time to read the entire manuscript and send several pages of detailed comments, which made me feel a little less apprehensive about publishing this book. Eva Pils also read several chapters and provided material related to Gongmeng from her collection. I am deeply thankful to both of them.

Finally I would like to thank my family—my mother, Anja; my father, Ervin, who passed away just at the inception of this project; and my brother, Nicholas—for their support and (sometimes bemused) encouragement for all my projects.

I would like to thank Qiu Zhijie for allowing me to use his evocative painting *From Huaxia to China* for the cover of this book and Ian Johnson for helping track him down.

A section of chapter 2 appeared previously in the chapter "Literary and Documentary Accounts of the Great Famine: Challenging the Political System and the Social Hierarchies of Memory," in Sebastian Veg, ed., *Popular Memories of the Mao Era: From Critical Debate to Reassessing History* (Hong Kong: Hong Kong University Press, 2019). Another paragraph of chapter 2 is adapted from "Debating the Memory of the Cultural Revolution in China Today," Modern Chinese Literature and Culture Online Series, August 2016. An early version of a section of chapter 3 was published as "Opening Public Spaces," *China Perspectives*, no. 1 (2010): 4–10. I would like to thank Hong Kong University Press, Modern Chinese Literature and Culture, and the French Centre for Research on Contemporary China respectively for allowing me to reuse this material.

MINJIAN

Introduction

Over the past quarter of a century, Chinese society has undergone a series of deep structural shifts, not least in the sphere of intellectuals and public discourses. Marketization of cultural production in the 1990s created a new category of metropolitan media and marginalized traditional academia. The Internet, blogs, social media, and smartphones created new spaces for intervention and debate as well as for surveillance and control. Digital video equipment empowered groups of grassroots video journalists and artists, who created a self-contained subculture of independent film production. Local languages and heritage experienced a revival around the country, led by local activists. Popular religion experienced a noted resurgence. Although the political system continued to resist reform, society diversified in astonishing ways: as professions gained a foothold through economic reforms, grassroots lawyers and nongovernmental organizations (NGOs) increasingly worked with disenfranchised communities on concrete projects. Information technologies played an important role in linking together participants engaged in different activities. These phenomena were also accompanied by reflexive discourses produced by the actors engaged in them. The present study is devoted to these discourses and how they implicitly or explicitly redefine the position of intellectuals in postreforms China.

Indeed, since the crackdown on the democracy movement of 1989 and the subsequent boost of economic reforms in 1992, a palpable change has been observed in the status and role of intellectuals in China. Whereas throughout the twentieth century intellectuals defined themselves through a posture of responsibility for the affairs of the nation and the state, in the past twenty-five years this notion of responsibility has been questioned as elitist, intellectual discourse has been displaced by the development of commercial media, and the centrality of the reference to the nation-state has come to be seen as problematic. Positions have become more diverse and more complex. In the early twentieth century, despite breaking with Confucianism and the imperial system, the figure of the May Fourth intellectual committed to improving the nation through science and democracy in fact showed strong continuities with the role and ethics of traditional literati. This figure found its final incarnation in the enlightenment revival of the 1980s and its culmination in the democracy movement of 1989. The perceived failure of that movement no doubt contributed to calling into question the role played by intellectuals in society and politics.

Beginning in the 1990s, intellectuals' positions changed in several important ways:

1. With the retreat of the controlling state and the advance of the private economy, intellectuals were no longer exclusively affiliated with state work units (universities, writers' associations, state media), and their sources of income became more diverse. New professional categories appeared, and specializations deepened: intellectuals were no longer only academics but also independent lawyers, journalists, filmmakers, editors, and amateur or citizen historians.

2. In the aftermath of the Tiananmen crackdown, many writers, journalists, academics, and filmmakers questioned the "grand narratives" of modernization and democracy, which had cemented the elite consensus over the conveniently vague notion of "reform" in the 1980s, buttressed by a belief in the existence of "correct theories" that could be formulated and employed to solve China's problems.[1] Although the pro-democracy movement had reached broad segments of society, many intellectuals, both critically self-reflecting on what had gone wrong and anticipating how to continue their work in a context of increased state control, took issue with the elitist bias of the democracy movement, both in the themes that it promoted and in its own organization on the square. Many now shifted their interests toward concrete problems, often associated with people situated not at the center but at the margins of society: petitioners, migrant workers, people infected with HIV-AIDS, unrehabilitated victims of Maoist persecutions. In a seminal essay published in *Orient* (*Dongfang* 東方) magazine[2] in August 1996 and one of the inspirations of the present study, the fiction and essay writer Wang Xiaobo 王小波 described these people as the "silent majority."[3] Wang and later others now described these people as disenfranchised or "vulnerable groups" (*ruoshi qunti* 弱勢群體); the newfound interest in their

problems was underpinned by a different set of theoretical references—no longer enlightenment and democracy but Foucauldian critiques of modernization and disciplinary biopolitics. Although this trend is obviously closely connected to the specificities of society in the People's Republic of China (PRC) in the 1990s and 2000s, it also shows some similarities with what Michel Foucault termed the rise of the "specific intellectual" in Western societies, whose interventions are grounded in precise study of specific social problems, as opposed to the traditional "universal intellectual," but also distinct from the "experts" who advise the political elite.[4]

3. This trend led to a pluralization (*duoyuanhua* 多元化) of society and a diversification of modes of action and intervention. Writing and publishing remained important, but they were both stimulated and displaced by a broadening set of public forums: the semiautonomous "metropolitan press" (especially the Southern Media Group) and the Internet—blogs, microblogs, and social media—provided new public venues and at the same time erased the specificities of intellectual discourse. New forms of intervention appeared: independent documentary films and the festivals in which they were screened and discussed; alternative spaces where artists settled in close proximity to migrant-worker dormitories (Songzhuang, Caochangdi in Beijing); a growing number of NGOs, where academics often worked closely together with lawyers, members of "vulnerable groups," and documentary filmmakers. These NGOs later nurtured a group of rights-defense lawyers that began to grow from the early 2000s.

FROM PUBLIC INTELLECTUALS TO "BRICKSPERTS"

In the early 2000s, the Anglo-American notion of the "public intellectual" (*gonggong zhishifenzi* 公共知識分子) began to be hotly debated after a translation of Richard Posner's book *Public Intellectuals: A Study in Decline* was published in 2002.[5] Following *Prospect Magazine*'s special one hundredth issue on "Britain's top 100 public intellectuals" in July 2004,[6] *Southern People Weekly* (*Nanfang Renwu Zhoukan* 南方人物週刊) published a special issue in September listing fifty "influential public intellectuals" (and six deceased "emeriti"). Warning against idealizing intellectuals as spokespeople for justice, the editorial nonetheless pointed out the role of critics of state policy, such as Bertrand Russell, Albert Einstein, and, after 9/11, Susan Sontag. It defined the present as the era of "the most intellectuals and the least intellectuals": armadas of professors who, as in David Lodge's novels, "feverishly publish frothy monographs to bolster their own fame, but fail to see and remain silent in the face of the momentous and striking problems that affect the interests of the majority."[7] Quoting media interventions by the economist Wu Jinglian 吳敬璉 (on secret funds), economic historian Qin Hui 秦暉 (on farmer taxes), and the "three young doctors in law" in the Sun Zhigang 孫志剛 affair, the editors of *Southern People Weekly* proposed to define public intellectuals as being simultaneously "holders of academic or professional knowledge, activists who intervene in public discussions or affairs, and idealists endowed with critical spirit and willing to take on responsibility for justice." Although intellectuals have been marginalized by the market, the editors, recalling the "sense of higher mission" (*tian jiang jiang daren yu si ren ye* 天將降大任於斯人也) that defined intellectuals in the 1980s, called on them to take up their critical responsibility.[8] Shanghai intellectual historian Xu Jilin 許紀霖 subsequently became an eloquent proponent of the need for "public intellectuals" who could bridge the divide between the specific and the universal.

In reaction, the notion of "public" was predictably targeted in a violent attack by the official press, through a commentary first published in the Shanghai newspaper *Liberation Daily* (*Jiefang Ribao* 解放日報) and reprinted in the *People's Daily* (*Renmin Ribao* 人民日報), which highlighted that intellectuals could not be "independent" but always had to defend the interests of a class. In the Chinese context, this class could only be the working class embodied in the party.[9] This criticism was reportedly picked up in Central Document no. 29 issued by the Central Committee on November 11.[10]

Over the past decade, with the exacerbation of both media commodification and political instrumentalization of knowledge (which often go hand in hand), the notion of the "public intellectual" has been increasingly criticized and even rejected. Readers critical of the perceived "liberal" bias of the Chinese media like to use the abbreviation *gong zhi* 公知 as a derogatory term: the equivalent of "media intellectual" (it might be rendered in somewhat Orwellian English as "pubint"). Even some liberal intellectuals reject the notion of the "public intellectual," such as the feminist scholar Ai Xiaoming 艾曉明 in an interview: "The reputation of public intellectuals stinks. . . . Has China ever had public intellectuals? I don't think so. In the feudal era there was an educated class but it was to serve power. Then came the May Fourth Movement. But few paid attention to the independence of intellectuals.... The Communists established a government and in the 1950s Mao declared intellectuals to be the stinking ninth class or as living as parasites [*siti bu qin, wugu bu fen* 四體不勤，五穀不分]. So how can you talk of public intellectuals?"[11]

Although in a special issue published in 2007 the liberal Guangzhou fortnightly *South Reviews* (*Nanfeng Chuang* 南風窗; literally "Southern Window") noted that intellectuals were increasingly being criticized for being part of the new elite, the editorial still held out hopes that they could recover their traditional role as moral critics in a context defined by the party's new role as a "ruling party" open to all classes of society.[12] By contrast, in 2012 the same magazine published another special issue titled "Intellectuals in a Time of Conflicting Interests" that thoroughly investigated the turn against the notion of public intellectual. Some of the critiques written for this issue are disingenuous, such as that intellectuals, ever since May Fourth times, have suffered from a form of Stockholm syndrome that makes them take the side of foreign colonizers and imperialists against the Chinese people[13] or that the "pub-int" has become a fashionable discursive model (*gong zhi fan'r* 公知範兒) that mechanistically criticizes "the system" while venerating a highly abstract image of America.[14] Other contributions are more thoughtful. Xu Jilin deplores that the deideologization of academia has been accompanied by a loss of ethical and academic norms.[15]

The feature article by in-house journalist Shi Yong 石勇 provides the most thorough discussion. Shi begins with an ironic digression on a neologism that could be translated as "brickspert" (*zhuanjia* 磚家), a pun on the homonymous word for expert (*zhuanjia* 專家). A "brickspert" is a cultural luminary whose theories lack academic basis and who basically "specializes in talking nonsense" ("brick" may also refer to using theories as bricks to throw at other people).[16] An amusing illustration of the connotations of this notion can be found in a photomontage by the visual artist Yang Fudong 楊福東 titled *The First Intellectual*, which shows a man in a Western suit in the middle of a road poised to throw a brick. As Yang describes it, the man "has blood running down his face and wants to respond, but he doesn't know at whom he should throw the brick, he doesn't know if the problem stems from himself or society."[17] Shi describes the turn against public intellectuals as follows: "Because a few intellectuals became 'bricksperts,' elites or cynics, a lot of people began to think that they were not preventing the breakdown of society but had become whirring cogs in it." Second, Shi notes that Chinese society has changed in the sense that conflicting interests have replaced conflicting ideologies: when private entrepreneurs expropriate vulnerable groups, the conflict is not ideological. In this context, everyone has become a public "intellectual" or spokesperson for his or her own interests.[18] Academics have been provided with opportunities to convert knowledge into money; in this sense, they speak out for their own interests. Qin Hui has made a similar point: "China [in the 1990s] was no longer under the spell of a utopian craze, rather the process of primitive accumulation by exchanging power for advantage had replaced the hypocrisy of the virtuous 'ideal state' as the new reality; as I have argued, the debate about 'whether to split the family home' has already given way to the debate about 'how to split the family home.'"[19] Conversely, successful businessmen have developed a sideline as commentators on social media, in this way also advancing their own agendas.

Third, Shi notes that intellectuals have begun to mobilize (*xingdonghua* 行動化) rather than only to use words, which marks a significant change in role. However, he believes their role must change further. Referring to Zygmunt Bauman's concepts (which are further discussed in chapter 1), he argues that Chinese intellectuals must stop being "legislators" (or "literary youths [*wen qing* 文青]" who prescribe changes from the comfort of their armchair) and become "interpreters" or, as he prefers to call it, "clarifiers [*chengqingzhe* 澄清者]." In an era when everyone has become a public intellectual, academics have no advantage in "democratic quality" over Wukan villagers; however, they have the knowledge to clarify the obfuscations that hide conflicting interests. Therefore, they should spend less time making discourses more abstract and confusing (theorizing) and focus on clarifying social consequences of different ideas and agendas as well as exposing discourses that are logically incoherent. Shi sees this new task as an opportunity to regain the public's confidence.[20] This elusive new role, based on specific knowledge in the midst of competing interests, could provide intellectuals with a new legitimacy.

It should be noted that the political environment has not always followed the evolution of society. Ten years of relative opening from 1997, after Jiang Zemin 江澤民 consolidated power at the Fifteenth Congress, were followed by a decade of tightening control beginning in 2007, when the Olympics and various subsequent international events heightened the Chinese government's wariness, and further stepped up after 2012. However, the deeper trends, in particular the diversification of Chinese society, continue to develop and to adapt to the challenges of the political environment.

THE RISE OF *MINJIAN* INTELLECTUALS

The main argument of this study is that a new figure of the intellectual appeared in the 1990s, breaking with the universalist, enlightenment paradigm of the 1980s as well as with the older, traditional figure of the advising and dissenting literati. Intellectuals who came of age in the 1990s no longer indulged as frequently in sweeping discourses (*jiang da daoli* 講大道理) about culture, the nation, or democracy. Their legitimacy derived from their work with "vulnerable groups" and their shared experience with marginal realms of society. Liang Congjie 梁從誡, the son and grandson of two giants among China's elite intellectuals, founded the environmental NGO Friends of Nature (Ziran zhi you 自然之友) in 1993. As Yang Guobin wrote in an obituary, "When Liang Congjie left the comfort zone of using words to understand and change the world and turned instead to grassroots citizens organizing, he became a new type of intellectual, a public intellectual. In doing so, he changed the meaning of being an intellectual in China."[21] The civil society organizations and new commercial media that sprang up throughout the 1990s attracted the "best and brightest" of China's graduates. Even the defense of workers no longer took place through the discourse of class, as expressed by China's official trade unions and socialist ideology, which were mobilized by laid-off state-owned enterprise workers in the 1990s, but through a push to empower marginalized and disenfranchised migrants workers who enjoyed no status.[22] Redefining the strategic position between state and society that intellectuals had long sought to occupy, this displacement moved many intellectuals away from the symbolic center of society and toward the "unofficial" (*minjian* 民間) groups outside the borders of officialdom (*guanfang* 官方).[23] The present study proposes to call them "*minjian* intellectuals."

Minjian is one of the most difficult Chinese words to translate. Its literal meaning is "among the people," and it is most often translated either as "folk," as in "folk music" (*minjian yinyue* 民間音樂), or as "unofficial," as in "unofficial journals" (*minjian kanwu* 民間刊物).[24] Because the term *minjian* takes its meaning from the historical dichotomy of *min* (people) and *guan* (officials), in the PRC context it is associated with anything that is "outside the system" (*tizhi wai* 體制外)—that is, any person, group, or activity that is not connected to a work unit (*danwei* 單位) in the official urban administrative system. In this sense, intellectuals truly "outside the system" only really began to exist after the economic reforms of the early 1990s loosened the *danwei* system, and it became possible to earn an income in other ways: Wang Xiaobo was one of the first to do so. However, the border was always blurry because activities outside the system often relied on contacts within the system.[25] Today it has become even more unclear because many people combine activities inside and outside the "system"; for example, it is considered possible to be "inside the system" (*tizhi nei* 體制內) by virtue of a university teaching position but nonetheless work "outside the system" (*tizhi wai*) with disenfranchised communities.

In everyday speech, *minjian* often refers to a combination, to different degrees, of three characteristics of people or institutions: independence from state income (self-funded), lack of approval by the state system (unofficial), and a low social marker (nonelite or grassroots). However, the term *minjian* does not refer to an organized civil society in the sense of political theory, nor does it necessarily imply the conscience of acting as a citizen endowed with rights and duties.[26] Therefore, the present study avoids the notion of "citizen intellectuals" in favor of a more modest but less loaded translation in this context: "grassroots intellectuals." This notion effectively conveys the idea of "ordinary people," although it may somewhat overstate the case that these intellectuals are outside the social elite. Chapter 6 attempts to further refine this discussion by highlighting the residual elitism of bloggers or intellectuals who assert their antielite stance. Although the adjective "grassroots" does not entirely cover the three semantic components of *minjian*, it provides a good proxy for capturing the critique of elitism and fascination with official recognition by the state that informs the break with the previously dominant model.

In December 2010, the Guangzhou weekly *Time-News* (*Shidai Zhoubao* 時代週報), a commercial emanation of the Guangdong Publications Bureau, published a list of "100 influential personalities," divided into ten categories, among which were "cultural workers," "public intellectuals," opinion makers, and, for the first time in such a ranking, a group named *minjian renshi* 民間人士 (grassroots personalities).[27] Another interesting nonacademic endeavor, although it does not use the term *minjian*, is *For the Record* (*Lici cunzhao* 立此存照), a project by documentary producer and former architect Yang Weidong 楊衛東 to interview five hundred people on film and to publish the transcripts in book form.[28] Focusing on writers, artists, and academics outside the system, it documents different ideas about China's history, political system, and future development and includes many of the personalities discussed in the chapters here.

Some studies in English have begun to explore this development. David Kelly suggested in 2006 that the rise of citizens' movements and the new role of lawyers provided an opportunity for public intellectuals to define a new position for themselves.[29] William Callahan uses the term "citizen intellectuals" to refer to a group of people who work sometimes with and sometimes against the state, such as Ai Weiwei 艾未未 and Jia Zhangke 賈樟柯, tying citizenship to a notion of "social responsibility."[30] He argues that "civil society is being created in post-socialist China through the small-scale work of such individuals and informal groups."[31] Although this study shares some of Callahan's observations, "citizen" and "civil society" are terms too loaded with theoretical assumptions about citizens' rights and political consciousness to fit with the material presented in this book. The effects of the crackdown on civil society activities since 2012 suggest that the use of these terms may also be somewhat premature. Many scholars harbor doubts about the applicability of the notion of "civil society" (*gongmin shehui* 公民社會) to present-day China, arguing for the prevailing power of the state to organize society.[32] Although some of the individuals discussed in this book (in particular the rights lawyers) describe their activities as those of citizens (*gongmin*),[33] others view these activities as part of their everyday routine, which suggests these individuals might be more usefully analyzed in the normatively less charged framework of "*minjian* society" (*minjian shehui* 民間社會).

Ching Kwan Lee and You-tien Hsing, examining a variety of forms of "new social activism," note the difficulty of reconceptualizing the current state of Chinese society. In parallel to traditional conflicts of redistribution, they highlight the rise of new claims to recognition and representation. Even as redistributive conflicts seem to be increasingly articulated in terms of citizenship rather than class (in particular through the legal system), there has been an opposing trend of fragmentation into demands for recognition of different groups' moral status and identity as well as symbolic contestation of both state and market ideologies. Lee and Hsing highlight the polycentric and networked, bottom-up nature of the new activism, which is able to leverage global connections, the state's sensitivity to global norms, and the strategic role of the market in opening new spaces. In this conceptualization, social activists (*shehui huodongjia* 社會活動家) play a central role in articulating new or suppressed identity claims.[34] Similarly, although the field of religion is generally considered distinct from studies of intellectuals, we may note recent academic interest in the revival of popular (*minjian*) religions and beliefs since the 1990s.[35]

In a recent study, the scholar and activist Zeng Jinyan 曾金燕 has also put forward the notion of "citizen intelligentsia" (*gongmin zhishifenzi* 公民知識分子) in connection with the tradition of the Russian intelligentsia (*zhishi jieceng* 知識階層), seen as more critical and socially less elitist than Western intellectuals. She also echoes the traditional moral expectations of a Chinese intellectual in refusing to apply the term "intelligentsia" to most academics working in today's China. Quoting Immanuel Kant's essay "What Is Enlightenment?" she distinguishes the "superfluous people [*duoyu de ren* 多餘的人]" of Russian literature (intellectuals in "inner emigration" such as Yang Jiang 楊絳, exiles such as Gao Xingjian 高行健, individualists such as Wang Xiaobo, contemporary aesthetes such as the journalist Jia Jia 賈葭) from a small new group of "citizen activists," in particular feminists (e.g., Ai Xiaoming, Ye Haiyan 葉海燕), NGO workers (e.g., Guo Yushan 郭玉閃), and documentary filmmakers (e.g., Huang Wenhai 黃文海).[36] In relation to independent documentary film, Zeng notes the need for directors to be spokespeople without depriving the "subaltern" of their own voice: these "citizen intellectuals" are defined as a group with a new authorial attitude, a new mode of production, and a citizen identity.[37] Although Zeng uses the notion of "intelligentsia" to mitigate the normative implications of the term "citizen," it is preferable to avoid the latter term altogether.

The present study argues that grassroots intellectuals are less "obsessed with China" and their social responsibilities and devote more energy to concrete and daily problems. The notion of "grassroots intellectuals" also suggests looking more carefully at people and groups of people who are not well known, as well as at the spaces they operate in. Studies on Chinese intellectuals have long been dominated by elite debates ("liberals" versus "New Left") and controversies;[38] these discussions are not at the center of this project, which tries to argue that the terms of such debates have become increasingly detached from the evolution of Chinese society. As Zeng's study suggests, the erosion of the traditional model of the elite intellectual must also be considered in gendered terms: it is no surprise that, contrary to traditional studies of Chinese intellectuals, many of the grassroots intellectuals discussed here (as well as in Zeng's book) are women.[39] Although most elite academic intellectuals are men (reflecting a correlation between gender domination and the norms defining the political and social mainstream), women play a central role among *minjian* intellectuals.

The notion of *minjian* or "grassroots" intellectuals has historical precedents. Li Hsiao-t'i 李孝悌 sketches out three stages of how intellectuals understood their relationship with "the people" in modern times: in the late Qing, commoners were first envisaged as citizens, and scholars became interested in using popular artistic forms to "enlighten the people." In May Fourth times, the catchword "going to the people" (*dao minjian qu* 到民間去) led to an unprecedented scholarly interest in popular culture during the Folk Literature Movement.[40] Luo Zhitian 羅志田 argues that the New Culture Movement saw a shift from elite to "marginal" intellectuals, somewhat educated villagers who did not have the cultural capital to play a leading role in urban intellectual circles but were instrumental in disseminating the new culture because they were willing to engage in social activism.[41] However, as Li Hsiao-t'i notes, within less than a decade the term *minzhong* 民眾 (the "masses") began to be substituted for *minjian* and to be understood as the "proletariat" in a Marxist perspective, which led to a new form of elitism in which intellectuals, informed by "correct" ideology, made decisions about which forms of popular culture were legitimate or progressive and which were "feudal."[42]

More recently, Chinese-language scholarship has shown renewed interest in the historical arc of "*minjian* thought." Shanghai literary scholar Chen Sihe 陳思和 was the first to point out a "return to *minjian*" in post–Cultural Revolution literature as a "value" irreducible to socialist ideology or enlightenment discourse. Whereas, in his view, intellectuals had tried to "reform" the realm of *minjian* culture through ideology ever since May Fourth, the rise of "roots literature" in the 1980s reversed this trend, marking a retreat from ideology and from the use of the politicized modern vernacular language.[43] Predictably, the notion was rejected by the New Left political philosopher Gan Yang 甘陽, who criticized the notion that a conflict could exist between the state's interest and the people's interests.[44] Shanghai historian Zhu Xueqin 朱學勤 spearheaded endeavors to excavate and reconstruct the "*minjian* thought" of the Mao era under the layers of official ideology by using the notion of "*minjian* thought tribes" (*minjian sixiang cunluo* 民間思想村落) that formed after Lin Biao's 林彪 death in 1971. After the beginning of Reform and Opening, these groups spread into three different directions: some members became reformist officials within government, some went into academia, and a third group remained outside the system.[45] The story of underground journals of the late 1970s that led to the publication of *Today* (*Jintian* 今天) was documented in a book by Xu Xiao 徐曉, herself a participant in these groups. In a review in *Dushu* 讀書 (Reading), Sun Yu 孫郁 (a scholar of Chinese literature at People's University) pointed out the continuity between the so-called *tongren zazhi* 同仁雜誌 (self-published "circle" journals not intended for profit, inspired by the Meiji-era *dōjinshi*) in the May Fourth era, the *minjian* journals in the 1970s, and the return to a preoccupation with the individual, which reached its fullest literary expression with Wang Xiaobo.[46]

Peking University (PKU) literary historian Qian Liqun 錢理群 further expanded on the idea of "resistance of *minjian* thought" and formed the project to publish a three-volume compendium studying the main thinkers left out of the history books of the Mao era.[47] As he noted in an interview, "Originally I wanted to enter the academic system, but after June Fourth [1989] I felt that the university could not be a way out. So I decided to break down the door and break out, and I began writing [several books on why intellectuals decided to stay in the PRC in 1948]; they all brought me closer and closer to participation in reality."[48] Although Qian remained at PKU until retirement, he did not take on any administrative positions and continued his activities "outside the system." In his reassessment of twentieth-century intellectual history, *minjian* appears as a kind of hidden tradition.

TENTATIVE TYPOLOGY

For the purposes of the present study, intellectuals are defined by three main traits: they are individuals who have acquired specialized knowledge in a certain area of activity, who intervene regularly in the national public sphere (in the present case the mainland Chinese or at least the sinophone public sphere), and who discuss questions of general interest, including their own work and its relevance in a reflexive manner. Intellectuals were traditionally defined by their profession: in Pierre Bourdieu's view, intellectuals were mainly writers, academics, and artists.[49] In contemporary China, the notion of profession is problematic because it is bound up with the old work-unit (*danwei*) system: although the intellectuals examined in this study engage in academic, literary, artistic, journalistic, legal, and charity work, they do not define themselves through their professional, state-condoned status, as intellectuals did in previous times. Some—mostly academics—do still hold such a status and define themselves through it, but for those who enjoy no such status or associated prestige, their independently acquired knowledge and self-organized activities are more significant.

The present study characterizes *minjian* or grassroots intellectuals by four main traits, leaving aside the blurred border between "inside" and "outside" the system.

First, they are specific intellectuals in the sense of Foucault's definition: neither generalists (autonomous but not specialized) nor experts (specialized but not autonomous); they speak out publicly on the basis of their specific knowledge.[50] Second, they define their activity as intellectuals in connection with "vulnerable" or marginal groups of society. Third, what makes them intellectuals (rather than grassroots activists) is their public discourse, including their discourse on their own activities and status: for this discourse, they rely on the embryonic and always endangered public sphere that has appeared in China. Fourth, they define their own activity as being neither part of the state nor part of the market and in this way attempt to open space for a possible third sector.

Specific Intellectuals

A revealing recent evolution in China is the decline of the writer as the ultimate generalist and the figure of the universal intellectual. Fiction writers enjoyed a unique moral aura in the 1980s, which steadily declined in the 1990s, hence their smaller role in this study.[51] Viewed from Bourdieu's perspective, such academics or writers used their prestige or status to intervene in the public sphere on generalist topics. *Minjian* intellectuals instead rely on their specialized knowledge and specific experience. Fang Lizhi's 方勵之 interventions in the 1980s reflected his universalist commitment to human rights and freedoms rather than his knowledge as an astrophysicist.[52] (In contrast, Foucault mentions J. Robert Oppenheimer as the emblematic figure of the "specific intellectual" who intervenes not only on the authority of his position but on the basis of his specialized knowledge.[53]) Wang Xiaobo often used his academic research to write fiction, the most famous example being his research on sexuality, which appears in many forms in his stories and novels and is used to make interventions about the nature of power and oppression. Wang Xiaobo's particular preoccupation, also related to his research on sexuality and society in general, was to break with the moral role of the intellectual and promote axiological neutrality.

There are many examples of this trend. Yu Jianrong 于建嶸, a prominent *minjian* intellectual, speaks out primarily as an academic sociologist who has specialized in rural issues and inequality rather than on general problems of governance by virtue of his status. Echoing a famous May Fourth debate, Qin Hui suggests that abstract "isms" (*zhuyi* 主義) need to be grounded in the discussion of concrete "issues" (*wenti* 問題).[54] As David Kelly, elaborating on Qin's position, puts it, "Both market and state are capable of answering the needs of 'issues'; what must be avoided is the implementation of phony markets and symbolic state institutions that satisfy the claims of 'isms.'"[55] Theories can be fruitfully discussed only if the discussion is historicized and empirically grounded: "what is excessive now," Qin argues, "is not liberalism or social democracy, but oligarchy and populism. It is essential, therefore, to critique both oligarchy from a liberal standpoint and populism from a social-democratic standpoint."[56] Qin believes that speaking about "left" and "right" in the context of China is meaningless. For this reason, he intervenes in public debates mainly on the basis of his specialized knowledge as an economist and an economic historian.[57]

The rise of specialization and professionals in the 1990s has produced not only a group of "experts" working in government think tanks but also specialized lawyers, journalists, and academics working within grassroots society. The progress of "academic norms" has thus not only served a neo-Hegelian discourse of authority[58] but also fostered a group of academics with a more modest and specialized understanding of their role. Therefore, whereas many recent studies focus on the "experts" co-opted in state think tanks, this project focuses mainly on writers, documentary filmmakers, and academics who, despite their specialization, define their roles as being mainly outside the system (although they are sometimes also active within it).

Subaltern Intellectuals

The notions of *ruoshi qunti* (vulnerable, dominated, or disenfranchised groups) and *diceng* 底層 (lower ranks), both of which could also be translated as "subaltern" (sometimes rendered as *chenshu* 臣屬) or "subordinated," have created a new community of discourse with a new public. These two possible translations point toward two different intellectual traditions that may have influenced Wang Xiaobo's and others' thinking: "subordinate" comes from a Gramscian and ultimately a Marxian perspective, whereas "subaltern" shares the same origin but was nominalized and established as a concept in its own right in Gayatri Chakravorty Spivak's famous article "Can the Subaltern Speak?" and in the field of cultural studies.[59] While the intellectuals of the 1980s enjoyed a form of semiautonomy, it was made possible only through their organic ties with patrons within the establishment and a generally elitist understanding of their role, handed down through China's various traditions. In the present century, Chinese society has witnessed the rise of a group of journalists, academics, lawyers, and documentary filmmakers who define their action in connection with "vulnerable groups" the most prominent of which are petitioners, victims of Maoist persecutions, disenfranchised migrant workers, sex workers, or other parts of *minjian* society. In the past, this link between critical intellectuals and "the grass roots" has been a particularly threatening one for the Chinese state, which has always done everything possible to control it.[60] In a recent publication, Merle Goldman notes a similar change: "In the first decade of the twenty-first century, despite the continuing repression, there was a qualitative change in the thinking and actions of China's public intellectuals: they increasingly became independent political actors who were willing to join with other social groups in political action."[61]

Bourdieu, of course, notes that intellectuals, as part of the dominant class, always have an ambiguous relationship with the "dominated."[62] Lawyers, writers, journalists, and filmmakers who work with petitioners, sex workers, migrant laborers, and expropriated farmers blur and question this dichotomy. By placing her review of Bourdieu's book *La misère du monde* as the introduction to her collection of articles *Listening Closely to the Underclass*, Guo Yuhua 郭于華 implicitly defines this "underclass" by reference to the subjective experience of "suffering" (*misère*), which in Bourdieu's perspective establishes a "homology" between different social positions.[63]

A particularly interesting example is the status of victims of Maoism. The Cultural Revolution was brought to a close in the late 1970s and early 1980s by encouraging intellectuals to denounce the Gang of Four and to write "scar literature" commemorating the harsh treatment they had received at the hands of the "masses." However, intellectuals who wrote such narratives in the 1980s were also interested in regaining their place of privilege and forming a renewed symbiosis with the state. Qin Hui has described the narrative of the 1980s as one of "victimization of the elite" (*jingying shounan* 精英受難): intellectuals described themselves as persecuted by the "people," which fostered further hostility toward both the people (*chou min* 仇民) and democracy.[64] This hostility led to a persistent view among the intellectual elite that democracy could be equated with mob rule. To reconstruct a critical understanding of society, it is therefore necessary to reassess the question of the "subaltern" in the Mao and post-Mao eras. Many of the *minjian* writers carrying out independent research on the Mao era today—sociologists such as Guo Yuhua, poets such as Liao Yiwu 廖亦武, historians and citizen journalists such as Yang Jisheng 楊繼繩—highlight that under Mao's rule the "subaltern" groups of ordinary people suffered as much as or more severely than intellectuals. The social position of these investigators is not easy to classify.

Pluralizing the Public Sphere

Intellectuals are defined by public discourse, which relies on the existence of a public. Since the privatizations and economic reforms of the 1990s, the public sphere has become much more diverse, and a large spectrum of political positions can be discussed, which have been mapped out according to different criteria.[65] This study is not particularly focused on the factional disputes between the "New Left" and the liberals, which largely take place among social elites in the language of universal enlightenment intellectuals.[66] However, both sides have tried to pay attention to the new subaltern groups, whether through rights-defense work (liberals) or through neo-Marxist theory (the Left). The rise of a consumerist popular culture in the context of privatization and commercialization has also undeniably provided opportunities for expression of ideas—including in the political field—that would not have been acceptable in the elite context of the 1980s: the obvious example is the blogger and race car driver Han Han 韓寒, whose political microblogging attracted unprecedented numbers of readers until 2013.

The partial privatization of the publishing sector, with the growing practice of commercial resale of book numbers, has allowed a far greater diversity of publications. Digital video cameras have played a similar role in the film industry, enabling an unprecedented number of independent film directors to produce films and screen them in alternative venues, such as festivals, bookshops, and artist villages. The appearance of a commercial though state-controlled media sector, often backed by private entrepreneurs, has also provided new opportunities to journalists. The Southern Media Group, reduced to all but silence since 2013, pioneered the struggle for new spaces and provided opportunities for intellectuals to speak to a larger public. In this perspective, the list of fifty influential "public intellectuals" published by *Southern People Weekly* in 2004 cannot simply be dismissed as a star parade of "media intellectuals" but represents a kind of manifesto for the pluralization of the public sphere. The development of the Internet and social media has also posed significant challenges to state control, providing channels to connect urban intellectuals and rural petitioners, migrants workers, and other "disenfranchised groups." Finally, growing connections with the sinophone public sphere outside the mainland—in Hong Kong, Taiwan, and overseas—also provide new spaces as well as economic support to critical intellectuals in China. A striking visual image of the complexity and diversity of the new intellectual landscape is provided in Qiu Zhijie's 邱志傑 six-part scroll painting *From Huaxia to China* (2015), in which two rivers flow through a landscape of ideologies, institutions, and associations, with the Tianxia system at the far left, a huge Coliseum-type arena in the middle that seems to offer a composite image of the one-party-market system, and modern political ideologies on the right.[67]

Third Sector

Finally, despite the importance of privatization and commercialization, the new century has also witnessed the emergence of a third sector that can be defined as belonging neither to the state nor to the market. In the 1980s, the state was ubiquitous: even a prominent critic and dissident such as Liu Binyan 劉賓雁 joined the Writers' Association and even stood for election in December 1984–January 1985 (he was appointed vice president after receiving the second-largest number of votes after Ba Jin 巴金).[68] Today, institutions such as the Writers' Association still control important networks of patron–client relations but have become increasingly irrelevant to society at large: Han Han forcefully declared he would never join such an institution.[69] Conversely, although the private economy was largely seen as a positive influence and a force to promote reform and liberalization in the 1980s, after China's all-out marketization began in 1992, a group of intellectuals sought to keep an equal distance from both the state and the market: art, nonprofit activities such as NGO work and "citizen journalism" can all be associated, under certain conditions, with the "third sector" of disinterested social practices, which induce a form of marginality. These new intellectuals are neither government-connected experts working for the state nor dissidents contesting the symbolic center of power under the "civil society" paradigm (both oriented toward the state) nor "media intellectuals" whose ideas are subordinated to their work for the market, often as postmodern skeptics. Rather, they live in inexpensive artist or migrant-worker urban villages (*cheng zhong cun* 城中村) and seek to ground their own position and legitimacy in the marginalization that a large portion of the Chinese population has undergone under the post-Mao regime.

In this sense, it is important to note that professionalization is not always synonymous with commodification. Edward Gu 顧昕 and Merle Goldman note that the "professionalization" of intellectuals often leads to a profit-oriented "expert professionalism."[70] Zhao Yuezhi 趙月枝 describes journalists who have largely profited from growing corruption in the media sector and have become spokespeople for the interests of the new capitalist elite—she argues that former *Caixin* 財新 (Financial news) editor Hu Shuli 胡舒立 was protected by financial technocrats—or are instrumentalized as a safety valve and made to "reveal" scandals that have already been investigated by the state, while "tens of millions of Chinese workers and farmers are being displaced by the processes of capitalist development and globalization [and] are driven towards the margins of Chinese society."[71] These observations are no doubt true, but they neglect the appearance of a group of intellectuals who have devoted much of their energies to investigative work or to participating in social practices that the mainstream or state media neglect. In the aftermath of the blood-transfusion scandal in Henan in the 1990s and the SARS crisis in 2003, more and more NGOs sprang up around China devoted to issues such as health and pollution and were tolerated or encouraged to various degrees by the state, in particular the local state.[72] These organizations are neither involved in the sphere of economic profit nor part of the state apparatus, as sporadic crackdowns demonstrate. The intellectuals' turn to NGOs and concrete concerns also echoes Foucault's theory of a break with universalistic enlightenment discourses, which bear the mark of scientism, and the turn to dealing with specific problems of control and domination.[73]

WANG XIAOBO AND THE SILENT MAJORITY

One of the first texts to theorize the intellectuals' new position was Wang Xiaobo's essay "The Silent Majority," first published in *Orient* magazine in 1996. *Orient* was one of the important venues of new thinking in the 1990s: in his content analysis of articles published in 1995, Zhidong Hao 郝志東 highlights the sheer diversity of subjects in *Orient* in comparison with party publications as well as their topicality.[74] At this time, Wang Xiaobo (1952–1997) was a writer who had recently shot to fame after publishing *The Golden Age* in 1992, a novella about educated youth (*zhiqing* 知青) during the Cultural Revolution.[75] He had personally experienced rustication in Yunnan before being admitted to People's University in 1978. After marrying the sociologist Li Yinhe 李銀河 in 1980, he followed her to the University of Pittsburgh, where he enrolled in a master's degree program in East Asian studies from 1984 to 1988. He came into contact with Foucault's work through Li Yinhe's research on gender issues. After his return to Beijing in 1988, he taught sociology at PKU before moving to People's University to teach practical English in the Accounting Department. After the literary success of *The Golden Age*, he became virtually the first well-known writer to resign from his work unit and to strive to make a living as a "freelance writer" (*ziyou zhuan'gaoren* 自由撰稿人). The resignation and his early death from a heart attack in 1997 created a full-fledged "Wang Xiaobo myth" and made his work iconic. If the emblematic author of the 1990s was Wang Shuo 王朔, Wang Xiaobo became a seminal reference for the millennial generation, whose importance ironically became clear only after his death.[76]

Because of his freelance status outside any work unit and his irreverent attitude toward the sacred topics of Chinese literature (history, politics, culture), Wang was immediately classified as a *minjian* writer and thinker. As the literary scholar Xie Yong 謝泳 wrote in 1997,

> In any society there is a mainstream and a nonmainstream; outside the court [*miaotang* 廟堂], there is *minjian* society. From the viewpoint of intellectual history, people always discover in retrospect that *minjian* ideas have more value than the court, that heterodoxy encompasses new thoughts and new culture. This is a very simple logic. Yet previously we always looked down on *minjian* and even now we often overlook it.... The critical reception of Wang Xiaobo's writing reflects how the community of mainstream literary critics in China pay no attention to *minjian*.... Among those who passed a positive judgment on Wang Xiaobo's works, almost all have a *minjian* perspective.[77]

Wang's essay "The Silent Majority" brings together some important strands in the definition of *minjian* intellectuals, in particular their subaltern stance and public engagement. Wang begins with a sweeping critique of Chinese intellectuals, from traditional Confucians to May Fourth enlighteners and Maoist mouthpieces, who are defined by their unchanging propensity to speak out. Speaking out is always a way of exercising power, as Wang notes in reference to Foucault. During the Cultural Revolution, everyone was keen to speak out to denounce others and to emancipate humankind. Keeping silent, by contrast, was the only way to preserve humanity from the encroachment of politics. Taking a longer view, he compares Chinese intellectuals' propensity throughout the centuries to speak out (*shuo* 說) with a form of tax (*shui* 稅) that intellectuals pay to the state, a tax in his view also known as "taking responsibility for all under heaven" (*yi tianxia wei ji ren* 以天下為己任).[78] In this sense, "taking a stance" (*biaotai* 表態), or speaking out to support Maoist propaganda—he makes an ironic reference to the "spiritual atomic bomb" of Mao Zedong 毛澤東 thought—is not fundamentally different from the role of the Confucian intellectual. Chinese intellectuals have always been good taxpayers who do not need too much encouragement to pay their tribute to the state. In this context, there is no possibility to speak out "against" the state; as a consequence, the whole notion of public speech needs to be reinvented.

Wang contrasts the world of speech and power with the silence of ordinary people. He uses the term "vulnerable groups" (*ruoshi qunti*) to refer to the many "ordinary people" who have no way of speaking out. This term, whose patronizing overtones have also been criticized, later gave way to the more sociological and value-neutral notion of *diceng*, "lower strata" or "subordinate." The *ruoshi qunti* are united not by their sense of class belonging but by a shared sense of disenfranchisement, of not having a say in society. Specifically referring to Li Yinhe's and his sociological work on sex workers and male homosexuals, Wang argues that the entire Chinese society is made up of such "vulnerable groups," not unlike those whom Foucault called "marginals":

> After doing this research, I suddenly realized that what we call vulnerable groups are simply people who have things to say that they do not express, and because they do not speak out, a lot of people think they do not exist or are very far away. People still don't believe that homosexuals exist in China. . . . Later I had another sudden realization: that I belonged to the greatest vulnerable group in history, the silent majority. These people keep silent for any number of reasons, some because they lack the ability or the opportunity to speak, others because they are hiding something, and still others because they feel, for whatever reason, a certain distaste for the world of speech.[79]

This shared sense of disenfranchisement defines the silent majority of all the ordinary people who have no say in the organization of Chinese society and remain politically invisible.[80] This elaboration marks a break with the Marxist class-based representation of society and the leading role of the working class in liberating the oppressed members of society. Wang's vision of a society in which everyone is a member of a disenfranchised or marginalized social group has become emblematic of the post-1989 era, marked by the rise of migrants workers, petitioners, expropriated urban residents, and laid-off workers. As Yang Guobin wrote in 2011, "Indeed, disempowerment is so much a part of the increasingly market-driven process that a new term, *ruoshi qunti* ('powerless social groups'), has become a key word in contemporary Chinese discourse."[81]

Finally, Wang defines a new role for intellectuals, underlining that it is only at the age of forty that he himself decided to finally "come out" of silence. The "public" dimension of Wang's activities is significant: in the final years of the pre-Internet era, he was able to "speak out" so effectively because commercial journals were in great need of popular columnists. For example, a former editor of *People's Literature* (*Renmin Wenxue* 人民文學) was hired by *Sanlian Shenghuo Zhoukan* 三聯生活週刊 (Sanlian life weekly) to use his connections to recruit famous columnists, among them Wang Xiaobo as well as the fiction writers Yu Hua 余華 and Su Tong 蘇童.[82] As Li Yinhe points out, Wang was able to publish so much because through his family history he was very familiar with the tacit red lines that could not be crossed but also because he kept his distance from politics in the conventional sense.[83] Many of his essays were provocative, but they looked at political issues from unexpected angles. Li Yinhe also insists that Wang's choice to leave the system and live by his writing had no economic motivation because he wanted to write "serious literature" (*chun wenxue* 純文學), not commercial literature: "He knew that serious writers are the poorest in the world."[84] Positioning oneself beyond the dichotomy of state and market is a characteristic of the *minjian* intellectuals of the time.

Although choosing public speech, Wang came out of silence only to describe his experience, not to enlighten society: whereas the critical intellectuals of the 1980s saw themselves as part of a vocal minority, speaking out by virtue of an elite sense of responsibility "for" those who couldn't do so, Wang Xiaobo speaks for himself. A friend to whom he gave a copy of his novella *The Golden Age* disliked it, as Wang recalls: "In his view, books should educate the people, and elevate their souls. . . . But among all the people of the world, the one I wish to elevate most is myself."[85] Taking issue with the "endless moralizing" of intellectuals, Wang affirms that there is no need to emancipate others through speech; he writes to educate himself in seeing the world from the point of view of members of the silent majority. Similarly, in the conclusion to her study, Zeng Jinyan quotes Foucault's notion of *parresia* (the ability to say anything) to argue that by "observing oneself and changing oneself, changing oneself and changing society can take place at the same time; rather than simply restricting oneself to taking the moral high ground and criticizing to change others."[86]

Unsurprisingly, there is some ambiguity about how to understand this position on a theoretical level. Li Yinhe argues that because Wang Xiaobo was trained in both sciences and humanities and spoke out on many different topics, he can be considered a member of the "last generation" of universal intellectuals.[87] On the contrary, in an influential article the PKU cultural studies scholar Dai Jinhua 戴錦華 notes that although Wang appears to be "a classic humanist intellectual, a free person, an all-around talent, a free writer, thinker, and creator, removed from the crowd, independent and unrestrained," at the same time "he undoubtedly rejected the role of holder, defender, and interpreter of truth and the right to establish absolute justice."[88] In this sense, he positions himself "among the people" rather than as an intellectual separate from them. Wendy Larson describes him as an intellectual indifferent to the state, neither its enemy nor its ally.[89]

"The Silent Majority"—summing up Wang's critique of Maoism and of enlightenment, his turn toward Foucault's preoccupation with the marginal, his highlighting of the intellectual's reflexive preoccupation with his or her own experience, and marking a deep break in the special relationship between intellectuals and the state—opens up a new spectrum of experiences and provides a new perspective for the present study. Wang's analysis breaks away from the Marxist view of intellectuals as "organic" to a class,[90] suggesting that intellectuals are one of the groups on the margins of society that, taken together, make up the silent majority. The critical position of intellectuals who base their legitimacy on marginality, somewhat new in the Chinese context, may also open avenues of inquiry beyond China.

METHODOLOGY

The loose networks of marginalized but arguably not insignificant grassroots or *minjian* intellectuals are the object of the present study. Compared to the 1980s and

1990s, it has now become increasingly difficult to provide a unified narrative of China's intellectual evolution due to the fragmentation and marketization of the public sphere, the internationalization of exchanges, and the development of the Internet and social media. Here the focus is on a series of interventions and their larger contexts, attempting to provide in-depth approaches to assess how the intellectual field has changed over the past two decades. The intellectuals and groups discussed in this book are defined by the public dimension of the discourse they produce on social and political issues, based on specific knowledge, which can be professionally or "independently" acquired. They are also defined in connection with a given public. It is theoretically possible to be an exiled or overseas intellectual and to engage (mainly) with the public sphere within China (for example, Xu Ben 徐賁); in practice, however, this is quite difficult for exiled dissidents (due to constraints in China) and not always easy for overseas academics or professionals (due to obligations in their country of residence). For this reason, this study looks mainly at intellectuals residing in China.

The chapters are focused not on individuals but on multidimensional networks and activities (journals devoted to memories of the Mao years; independent film; online communities). Each chapter begins with an important event and investigates significant texts by one or several authors that are relevant to the event, situating them within the social or virtual spaces ("communities of discourse") in which they are produced and circulated. Of course, there are also key individuals, many of whom who can move back and forth between categories—for instance, as academics, independent filmmakers, NGO activists, and bloggers, such as Ai Xiaoming. But the book is not a who's who of Chinese academic "stars." Academics in China (and indeed around the world) delight in classifying their colleagues into factions and subfactions; this project, by contrast, is not mainly about academics engaged in elite debates.

The first chapter provides an overview of how *minjian* intellectuals fit into the larger category of intellectuals on a theoretical level and in the historical context of twentieth-century China. The second chapter, situated in 1992, when Wang Xiaobo began to publish and left his work unit, focuses more precisely on Wang's essays, arguing that they redefined a new figure of the grassroots intellectual. The third chapter, taking its cue from the fortieth anniversary of the Anti-Rightist Movement (1957) in 1997, explores how an alternative memory of the Mao era was actively produced and debated by a group of grassroots witnesses and historians. The fourth chapter, kicking off with the first independent film festival held in

China that took place in Beijing in 2001, is devoted to independent film directors and the spaces they inhabit. The fifth chapter studies the rights lawyers, NGO workers, and other grassroots activists who took the stage in the wake of the Sun Zhigang affair of 2003. Finally, the sixth chapter looks at the new public culture that was produced by the metropolitan media and the Internet, sparked by blogger Han Han's intervention in the Carrefour boycott in April 2008 and Ai Weiwei's use of blogging to question the reasons for mass loss of life in the Sichuan earthquake in May of the same year.

These chapters rely on research on writers, filmmakers, historians and other academics, journalists, and political activists that I have carried out over the past decade, mainly in Beijing, but also in Chengdu, Guangzhou, Kunming, and Shanghai. Many of these figures, the texts they write, and the social spaces they populate have been studied separately elsewhere, in a more comprehensive manner, and often within a disciplinary framework (politics, literature, film studies, media studies). However, this study argues that they also need to be seen as a whole in order to gain their relevance. The frequent contact between different domains to exchange experiences, writings, or information is empirically documented. Hence, a transversal approach is needed.

This study differs from some previous endeavors in several ways. Its main preoccupation is not on academics or elite intellectuals in think tanks or government service, nor is it on individuals or important personalities, like many classic studies in intellectual history. On the contrary, it argues that speaking out publicly about social or political issues based on one's knowledge is no longer reserved to a few famous elite personalities; more and more scholars, professionals, journalists, and bloggers are willing and able to give interviews or to editorialize on issues related to their expertise. The focus is therefore on informal groups or networks of individuals, who don't always know each other but share a common identification. The argument is not so much about the class position of *minjian* intellectuals (some of them may indeed be seen as elite) or about the accumulation of (economic, social or symbolic) capital as it is about how they justify their claim to public speech. Therefore, this study looks at questions of social status and class through a focus on the texts produced by actors in various positions rather than empirically. This focus on public texts also underscores the continued importance of publics and public culture in contemporary China.

Although this study borrows from methodologies developed in sociology or political ethnography, its framework hews to the approach favored by contemporary history, which relies mainly on public texts, considered within a chronological perspective, to understand how recent political and social developments have unfolded. The original, published texts (essays, blogs, films, novels) are always considered within the social context of both their production and their circulation or reception. Unofficial social spheres (social media, NGOs, artist villages) play a decisive role in the circulation of such texts and the social meanings they produce. Echoing Jan-Werner Müller's call to consider contemporary European history as intellectual history,[91] this project tries to tease out the ideas and ideologies underpinning social transformations in contemporary China.

That China has seen an affirmation of the role of *minjian* intellectuals, although impeded by the increasing interference from the state in social activities since 2012, may appear as a kind of paradox to readers in Western societies, where intellectual debates are often dominated by traditional elites. Of course, structures of economic, social, and cultural inequality are quite different in Europe, the United States, and a developing country with a communist system, such as China. However, it is to be hoped that this apparent paradox in considering the role of intellectuals, particularly in connection with Foucault's critical reflections on Western societies, may open fruitful spaces for comparative debates.[92]

CHAPTER 1

Grassroots Intellectuals

Theoretical and Historical Perspectives

Some preliminary considerations are in order to clarify how historians and social scientists have conceptualized the category of intellectuals.[1] The object of the present study is situated at the intersection of two sets of discussions. On the one hand, there is an ongoing dichotomy between a humanities approach (intellectual history, literature, philosophy), focused on the classical ideal of the intellectual as moral critic, and a social science approach, which conceptualizes intellectuals as a social category. On the other hand, there is a large body of literature about the specificities of Chinese intellectuals, related to China's classical examination system and political institutionalization of knowledge and moral authority. By focusing on grassroots intellectuals, the present study aims to displace some of these lines, questioning both Chinese specificities and the elite nature of intellectual pursuits.

INTELLECTUALS: NORMATIVE IDEALS AND SOCIAL PRACTICES

Definitions of the intellectual vary widely.[2] They can usefully be divided between normative (moralist) and sociological (realist) definitions—that is, between definitions of intellectuals as critics (exercising a moral responsibility to serve universal values) and definitions of intellectuals as experts (people working more broadly with knowledge or "symbolic producers," as in Pierre Bourdieu's definition). This distinction is often accompanied by a methodological divide between a traditional history-of-ideas approach based on (politically critical) texts and a sociological-critical approach that highlights intellectuals' (generally dominant) position within class and social relations.

In an insightful study, Lloyd Kramer, an intellectual historian of Europe, argues for a definition that brings together both aspects, highlighting intellectuals' entwinement with the production of knowledge as well as their critical role in society. He contrasts Michel Foucault's expert and Jürgen Habermas's critic as the two faces of the Enlightenment, exemplified in the historical figures Jeremy Bentham and Heinrich Heine. Drawing on Habermas's *Structural Transformation of the Public Sphere* (1962), Kramer notes that intellectuals came into being during the Enlightenment as a "community of critical debaters whose work shaped a new sphere for politics as well as a new literary culture" and as "independent critical thinkers who evaluated art, literature, theatre, and political theory with rational judgment that defied the authority of kings and churchmen alike."[3] By contrast, in Kramer's reading of Foucault's work *Discipline and Punish* (1975), Enlightenment intellectuals play the role of producers of knowledge used to institute "new forms of social control and surveillance in asylums, prisons, clinics, schools and armies—all of which relied on new forms of knowledge in the emerging 'sciences of man.'" Kramer defines Foucault's view of the Enlightenment by the accessibility of social space to the surveillance of experts: "the Enlightenment that produced new definitions of madness, criminality, and knowledge also produced a new class of persons: the sovereign intellectual expert of modernity."[4] Although the new intellectuals as experts thus take up the role of sustaining power through surveillance, Kramer emphasizes that Foucault's own analysis remains an expression of the rational-critical role of the Enlightenment intellectual.[5]

Many twentieth-century contributions to a theory of intellectuals follow a similar divide: whereas philosophers and intellectual historians highlight the distinct nature of intellectual activity, social science approaches underscore intellectuals' role in the social hierarchy. Little attention has been paid to intellectuals situated outside the elite. Antonio Gramsci distinguishes between "traditional" intellectuals, who define themselves as disinterested defenders of universal rationality ("autonomous and independent of the dominant social group"), and "organic intellectuals," who speak for the interest of a (usually dominant) class. Under the veneer of universalist discourse, Gramsci understands all intellectuals as intrinsically organic: "The intellectuals are the dominant group's 'deputies' exercising the subaltern functions of social hegemony and political government."[6] These functions are organized on two levels: manufacturing "spontaneous consent" in society and sustaining the state apparatus of coercive power. Gramsci therefore believes that the working class should create organic intellectuals of its own, which opens a possibility for intellectuals to emerge from the grassroots, although they may not be autonomous.

Bourdieu in some ways continues the Gramscian vein in "demystifying" the universalist pretensions of intellectuals. In a short interview that sums up the main paradoxes in his conceptualization, Bourdieu argues that "artists and writers, and more generally intellectuals, are a dominated fraction of the dominant class. They are dominant in so far as they hold the power and privileges conferred by the possession of cultural capital . . . but writers and artists are dominated in their relations with those who hold political and economic power." This dominated status of art, literature, and academia (Bourdieu's three main categories of intellectual pursuits) is structural in that "fields of cultural production occupy a dominated position in the field of power." Hence, intellectuals' positions are ambiguous: "Despite their revolt against those they call the 'bourgeois,' they remain loyal to the bourgeois order." Bourdieu defines intellectuals as "cultural producers [who] hold a specific power, the properly symbolic power of showing things and making people believe in them." The intellectual can put this power in the service of the dominant class as an expert or in the service of the dominated as a "free, critical thinker, the intellectual who uses his or her specific capital, won by virtue of autonomy and guaranteed by the very autonomy of the field, to intervene in the field of politics, following the model of Zola or Sartre."[7] In the first case, the assertion of autonomy should be understood as a sign of distinction, a means in the pursuit of symbolic capital, whereas in the latter case the autonomy gained by the writer or the critical sociologist in his or her own field (Noam Chomsky as a linguist, Émile Zola as a writer, Bourdieu as a sociologist) can provide them with the means of contesting the "monopoly of the legitimate representation of the social world."[8] Bourdieu's theory therefore defines a spectrum of positions according to a varying degree of autonomy. Ideally (at one extreme of the spectrum of possibilities), as Bourdieu argues in a late text, the intellectual "can exist and survive as such if (and only if) he is invested with a specific authority, conferred by an autonomous intellectual world (that is independent from religious, political, economic power), whose specific laws he respects, and if (and only if) he engages this specific authority in political struggles. . . . [I]t is by increasing their autonomy . . . that intellectuals can increase the efficiency of a political action whose ends and means are grounded in the specific logic of fields of cultural production."[9] In this configuration, universal competence can be restored, at least at the most autonomous end of the spectrum: "an intellectual, to put it very simply, is a writer, an artist or an academic who, using the authority acquired in his or her own field, goes beyond his or her field and exercises a symbolic action of political nature."[10] Characteristically, for Bourdieu, it is social prestige rather than knowledge that grounds the intellectual's claim to public speech (a view that, in the perspective of intellectual history, may pay insufficient attention to what intellectuals actually say and write).

In the final analysis, Bourdieu remains entrenched in a binary schema: "But, and this is true also of the so-called 'organic intellectuals' of revolutionary movements, alliances founded on the homology of position (dominant-dominated = dominated) are always more uncertain, more fragile, than solidarities based on an identity of position and thereby, of condition and habitus."[11] Objective conditions will therefore prevail, and the social status of the intellectual will ultimately decisively shape (if not entirely determine) his or her political position. Like Gramsci, Bourdieu "unmasks" the ties of the intellectual to his or her position in the social hierarchy; unlike him, he does not seem to envisage a possibility for organic intellectuals to appear outside of the institutions of symbolic legitimation controlled by the bourgeoisie. In this sense, one could argue that Bourdieu remains convinced of the intellectual's elite status.

Foucault's earlier critique (formulated in 1976 in his essay "The Political Function of the Intellectual"), which Bourdieu partially but not entirely acknowledges, is in some ways more radical than Gramsci's. Foucault sees the working class (and its organic intellectuals) as simply the last incarnation of an illusory claim to universality: "For a long time, the so-called 'left-wing' intellectual has spoken out and has seen recognized his right to speak out as the master of truth and justice. One listened to him, or he wanted to be listened to, as the representative of universality. . . . [J]ust as the proletariat, by virtue of its historical position, is the carrier of universality (albeit an immediate carrier, hardly reflexive or conscious of itself), the intellectual, through his moral, theoretical and political choices, claims to be the carrier of this universality, but in its conscious and elaborated form."[12]

In a text written only a few years after *Discipline and Punish*, Foucault defines a new figure of the intellectual; his critique of the universal intellectual is in some ways more radical than Bourdieu's: autonomy in a specific field is not simply a stepping stone to prop up a universal discourse; rather, specific knowledge, with the constraints it implies, becomes the intellectual's contribution to social critique. In a significant break with previous characterizations of the prophetic, universal, or "total" intellectual, Foucault takes stock of the modern figure of the specific expert (as opposed to the Enlightenment intellectual), whose genesis is described in *Discipline and Punish*, but crucially endows it with a critical function. Since World War II, Foucault argues, intellectuals have taken to working in "specific points": public housing, hospitals, asylums, laboratories, universities, family or gender relations. Here, they are confronted with "specific, non-universal" problems, different from those of the proletariat or the masses but deriving from "real, material, quotidian struggles" that bring them closer to the "masses." Whereas the epitome of the (universal) intellectual was previously the writer (derived, in Foucault's view, from the gentry lawyer, the man of justice), now "transversal links appear between fields of knowledge, from one point of politicization to another: judges and psychiatrists, doctors and social workers, laboratory workers and sociologists" work together, and the university becomes a point of interchange or intersection.[13]

The specific intellectual as expert is always in danger of being marginalized, cut off from the masses; however, "it would be dangerous to disqualify his specific relationship with local knowledge, under the pretext that these are questions for specialists that do not interest the masses (which is doubly wrong: they are conscious of them and in any case implicated in them), or that they serve the interests of the state or capital (which is true, but shows the strategic position they occupy), or propagate a scientistic ideology."[14] It is the intellectual's critical understanding of the "production of truth" within his or her particular field of expertise that allows him or her to contribute to the "fight for truth" at the level of society.[15] As detailed later in this chapter, this paradigm shift—the decline of the writer as epitome of the universal intellectual, the rise of the specific critical intellectual, and the nodal position of academia, as well as the end of the working class's claim to universality—proves to be quite significant for Chinese society after 1989.

We may note that Bourdieu's and Foucault's approaches have a similarity in that both take into account the connection between the expert's use of specific knowledge in the service of power and the intellectual's emancipation from expert status to question relations of power. In Bourdieu's view, however, what the expert gains from his or her own field is authority and prestige that allow him or her to take universal political positions; in Foucault's view, it is the expert's knowledge that is crucial and leads him or her to specific rather than universal stances. It is in fact possible to combine the two approaches by measuring the degree of autonomy against the degree of universality, adapting a typology proposed by Gisèle Sapiro,[16] which produces a four-box table (see table 1.1). The category of specific intellectual highlights that specialization is not necessarily synonymous with heteronomy (cooptation by power): there are both dependent specialists and autonomous specialists. This historical evolution is particularly relevant to the empirical material from contemporary China discussed later.

Studies of intellectuals under coercive regimes deserve a mention, although the political framework does not require significant adjustments to the typology set out earlier. Intellectuals in authoritarian or totalitarian regimes have generally been discussed from a similar perspective, though in different terms, to the discussion of intellectuals in democratic societies.[17] If we stick to Bourdieu's spectrum of positions from the loyal expert to the autonomous critical thinker, in an authoritarian context the former are usually designated as "regime intellectuals," whereas the latter are lionized as "dissidents" who "live in truth" (Václav Havel) and hence as representatives of civil society against the state.[18]

Czeslaw Milosz famously noted in 1951: "To belong to the masses is the great longing of the 'alienated' intellectual. . . . It is a rich reward for the degradation he felt when he had to be part of the middle class."[19] In the context of post-Stalinist eastern Europe and in the wake of Milovan Djilas's critique of the bureaucratic "new class," György Konrád and Iván Szelényi defined intellectuals as the ruling class of late socialism, arguing that they constituted "a dominant class *in statu nascendi*" because of their strategic position as experts in directing the rational redistribution system in the planned economy. Based on a definition of intellectuals as "the monopolistic proprietors of knowledge, which society accepts as having cross-cultural validity and which it uses to orient its members," they retrace

TABLE 1.1 Intellectuals' Specialization Versus Autonomy

	dependent	**autonomous**
universal	court adviser	enlightenment intellectual
specialized	expert	specific intellectual

Source: Adapted from Gisèle Sapiro, "Modèles d'intervention politique des intellectuels," *Actes de la Recherche en Sciences Sociales*, no. 176–177 (2009): 14.

their evolution "from a sacerdotal personage into a secular expert" in modern societies, where they sell their ideologies on the open market. Highlighting the unprecedented role of expert knowledge under socialism, they identify intellectuals in post-Stalinist eastern Europe with the "rational-redistributive bureaucracy" of the central-planning apparatus and therefore see them as the prime exponents of the leading ideology of "rational redistribution" under late socialism: "the classical antagonism of capitalist and proletarian is replaced by a new one between an intellectual class being formed around the position of redistributors, and a working class deprived of any right to participate in redistribution."[20] This dominant position in technocratic commodity socialism—despite the stigmatization of intellectuals in most Marxist class analyses—may well characterize Chinese intellectuals in the 1980s.[21]

Nor are critical intellectuals in authoritarian contexts necessarily closer to the "grass roots." An interesting perspective is offered by Miklós Haraszti, who describes the "late socialist" culture in eastern Europe in the 1970s and 1980s as a "velvet prison" in which co-optation, self-censorship, and the material benefits offered by the state under "goulash communism" (similar, as others have pointed out, to postreform China) replace coercion as the main means of control of the cultural sphere. In this context, Haraszti argues, writers internalize their obligations: "Our responsibilities are the same as other members of the elite. We all have stock in the same company."[22] Geremie Barmé uses this framework as the theoretical starting point of his study of China's cultural scene in the 1990s, *In the Red*, which is discussed later in this chapter.[23] From Konrád's rational-redistributive bureaucracy to Havel's living in truth, via Haraszti's velvet prison, the entire spectrum of graduated autonomy can be reconstituted in a nondemocratic context.

Finally, it is important to mention two more recent contributions that engage critically with the idea of postmodernity. Zygmunt Bauman's now classical theorization of the postmodern intellectual draws a distinction between the intellectual as "legislator" in the context of the Enlightenment and modernity and as "interpreter" in the new environment of postmodernity. If we try to place Bauman's view within Kramer's dichotomy, we might say that Bauman unmasks the Habermasian Enlightenment intellectual (Heine) as a Foucauldian expert (Bentham) who seeks to administer society and order knowledge rather than to disseminate it. By contrast, the postmodern "interpreter" plays a role that facilitates communication between autonomous participants or communities rather than one that seeks to achieve the best social order, in a context in which relativity of systems of knowledge is accepted as a lasting feature of the world.[24] Consumers no longer turn to intellectuals for guidance but rely on the market. Continuing Foucault's critique of intellectuals' special relation with the proletariat, Bauman points out that the proletariat formerly played the role of the intellectuals' collective Pygmalion: "Workers gave the intellectuals the force they needed, but this force was to be formed and controlled by the power intellectuals, and only they, had."[25] To reverse Bourdieu's formulation, Bauman would probably view intellectuals as the "dominant part of the dominated class." This role of the proletariat as cultural hero leading humankind to the land of reason under the guidance of intellectuals has disappeared together with the intellectuals' role as legislators. Interestingly, although Bauman "unmasks" the Enlightenment intellectual as a producer of knowledge within the social hierarchy ("realist" approach), he reasserts an alternative, normative definition for "postmodern" intellectuals that can overcome the critique of the Enlightenment.

Edward Said's unique contribution to intellectual studies in the series of BBC lectures he gave a few years after the fall of the Berlin Wall takes a more critical view of postmodernity. Overall, Said reaffirms what Lloyd Kramer describes as the model of the Enlightenment intellectual in Habermasian terms, with a notable normative dimension, also influenced by Said's understanding of the position of intellectuals in socialist or authoritarian countries. However, Said in some ways incorporates Foucault's critique. Although acknowledging the binary of social position (the paid expert) and the moral pursuit of truth, Said highlights eccentricity in his description of the intellectual "as exile and marginal, as amateur, and as the author of a language that tries to speak truth to power," whose method is "scouring alternative sources, exhuming buried documents, reviving forgotten (or abandoned) histories."[26] Whereas Bourdieu might identify with Said's "struggle on behalf of underrepresented and disadvantaged groups,"[27] this "eccentric" method bears the imprint of Foucault's archaeology of knowledge and interest in marginality. Questioning established categories such as the nation-state, Said identifies exile as a paradigm for an ironic, skeptical, playful, but not cynical attitude to society.[28] Similarly, it is possible to be an exile within one's specialization, to be a "specific" but not a "professional" intellectual, an amateur who makes connections across disciplines and barriers. The categories "eccentric amateur" and "exile" suggest the influence of Foucauldian critique, although Said distances himself from postmodernism as a theory. This self-understanding—including the rejection of postmodernism as such—strongly resonates with some of the more critical self-definitions of the intellectual in post-1989 China, such as those formulated by Wang Xiaobo and the exile Gao Xingjian.

If we go back to Kramer's dichotomy, the theories summed up earlier discuss the tension between the normative ideals and social practices of intellectuals. The main argument developed here concerns a paradigm shift that closely resembles what Foucault describes as the rise of the specific intellectual. In formulating this argument, the present study attempts to examine both cultural and intellectual productions (and the ideas they construct) and the social functions and hierarchies these productions may serve. Intellectual discourses will therefore be situated both within a social hierarchy of intellectual productions and within a—somewhat contentious—notion of an emerging public sphere in China. On the one hand, the public sphere functions as a framework to deploy the regulatory ideal of the intellectual; on the other, the elite/subaltern binary highlights the hierarchy associated with intellectual practices. The changing role of the intellectual cannot be separated from the appearance of new spaces, whether physical or virtual, through which discourses of knowledge are disseminated or from the momentous changes in social hierarchy brought about by the Reform and Opening policies implemented in China beginning in the late 1970s. Finally, it is suggested that the fading of the universal writer-intellectual, who was still ubiquitous in the 1980s, corresponds with a deeper equalization (or "democratization" in the Tocquevillian sense) of Chinese society (the appearance of *minjian* intellectuals), which conversely questions assumptions about the egalitarian nature of society under Mao.

OBSESSED WITH THE STATE: A HISTORICAL OVERVIEW

Intellectuals played a defining role throughout twentieth-century China, and historical studies provide useful empirical qualifications of the typologies discussed in the previous section. They are usually successively characterized as "scholar officials," "establishment intellectuals" (mainly in the Mao era and sometimes contrasted with nonestablishment or "disestablished" intellectuals, respectively, in the 1980s and 1990s), and most recently "public intellectuals."[29]

Before the Xinhai Revolution of 1911, traditional literati occupied a central position in Chinese society. The figure of the *shi dafu* 士大夫, or scholar-official, selected through the imperial examination system until its demise in 1905, survives up to today as an ubiquitous cultural stereotype. Educated members of society, defined in the broadest sense as graduates of at least the first level (out of three) of imperial exams—as opposed to "commoners" (*shumin* 庶民)—were expected to provide support and (ideally) moral guidance to the state, acting as a political and social conscience for a harmonious moral community.[30] Several classical formulations of the literati's role have been handed down to today and were repeatedly mobilized throughout the twentieth century:

"To be the first in the world to assume its worries, the last to enjoy its pleasures" (*Xian tianxia zhi you er you, hou tianxia zhi le er le* 先天下之憂而憂，後天下之樂而樂).
"To take responsibility for all under heaven" (*Yi tianxia wei ji ren*).
"Writing serves to transmit the Way" (*Wen yi zai dao* 文以載道).[31]

These formulations highlight the moral role of the literati and the essentially moral nature of their writings or interventions in the public sphere. Perry Link quotes the first two epigrams to capture the strong feeling of attachment to the state even among critical intellectuals on the eve of the Tiananmen democracy movement.[32] In his history of modern Chinese literature first published in English, C. T. Hsia refers to an "obsession with China" throughout the twentieth century. The expression he uses in the subsequent Chinese versions of his text may more precisely be translated as "feeling concern for the times and the country [*gan shi you guo* 感時憂國]."[33] There are many variations of the formulation, including the "worrying conscience" (*youhuan yishi* 憂患意識) discussed by Gloria Davies or the popular saying "worrying about [one's] country and [one's] people" (*you guo you min* 憂國憂民). They all raise the question of whether these intellectuals' obsession is uniquely Chinese or whether it can be more generally rephrased as concerning their relation to the state.

Andrew Nathan has pointed out that the identification of the people's interests with those of the state has dominated the Chinese vision of democracy articulated by elite intellectuals since Liang Qichao 梁啟超.[34] Although the New Culture Movement, from its inception in 1915, when the journal *Qingnian Zazhi* 青年雜誌 / *La Jeunesse* was established, to the demonstrations on May 4, 1919, claimed a full-scale rejection and critique of Confucianism, historians have pointed out the strong continuities between the May Fourth intellectuals and the late-Qing literati: both generations shared a moral commitment to the higher good of the state (although the all-under-heaven state in the Confucian tradition began to be redefined in those years as a nation-state among other nation-states) and the firm belief that elite intellectuals should take moral and political leadership. Benjamin Schwartz concludes that the "20th century intelligentsia is to a considerable extent the spiritual as well as the biological heir of the scholar official class."[35] By contrast, Lu Xun 魯迅 was almost unique in insisting that intellectuals and writers were in an intrinsically conflictual position with respect to the state, even a revolutionary state.[36]

There is also a grassroots tradition running from the late Qing to May Fourth times. Reflecting on elite-led democratization attempts throughout the twentieth century, He Baogang 何包鋼 notes: "The populist idea of democracy developed in the May Fourth Movement held a belief in the moral worth of the ordinary, uneducated people. Nevertheless, few intellectuals articulated populist policies. Under the influence of the Confucian notion of representation, populism finally led [back] to elitism. The populist democracy became a workers' and peasants' dictatorship in theory and a dictatorship by a few intellectuals-cadres in practice."[37] This historical summary pinpoints the resilience of elite distrust of mass democracy and traces a historical continuity between Confucian literati, May Fourth elite-led modernization, and the latter's metamorphosis into top-down policies led by cadres under the Communist regime.

The modern word for "intellectual," *zhishifenzi*, appeared among literary and academic circles in the 1910s and 1920s to refer to people who had received some form of advanced education.[38] Under Mao, it was redefined to refer to anyone who did not engage in manual work and was institutionalized as a political-ideological tool to stigmatize individuals or groups.[39] Although Mao's ideal of a classless society served as a justification for the sometimes violent persecution of "intellectuals," at the same time the state actively co-opted technocrats in the 1950s.[40] Timothy Cheek, in his study of Deng Tuo 鄧拓, refers to the new class of "establishment intellectuals" as "Leninist scholar-officials" in the tradition of the *shi dafu*.[41] These "'scholar-cadres' uphold the status quo and go along with official policy even though they may privately disagree with certain features of it."[42] Yang Kuisong 楊奎松 has recently made a similar argument about Wang Yunsheng 王芸生 (1901–1980), the editor of the liberal newspaper *Ta Kung Pao* 大公報 (L'Impartial), who dramatically "converted" to party orthodoxy in 1949.[43] More generally, rather than a classless society, Mao re-created an intensely stratified social structure based on access to certain types of privilege, which were used to co-opt intellectuals.[44] Many of these intellectuals remained loyal to the PRC state even when they were persecuted, and most were recruited back into the bureaucracy after 1978.[45] Michel Bonnin and Yves Chevrier note that after 1949 many intellectuals who rallied to the Chinese Communist Party (CCP), although they were not provided with the same position of privilege as Confucian literati, were willing "to submit to the transformation and criticism imposed by the Party, provided they could reform and criticize the state from within. . . . As a result, modern Chinese intellectuals since the turn of the [twentieth] century have been drawn by the attraction of the state, and tended to identify political action with action within the state, thereby reducing the margin for political opposition to individual withdrawal from politics or to heroic dissent with no hope of finding support in society at large."[46] In this process, grassroots traditions were marginalized and largely forgotten until the likes of Qian Liqun and Zhu Xueqin turned to excavating them.

After 1978, the term *zhishifenzi* again began to refer more narrowly and sociologically to college graduates and normatively to people engaged in intellectual or cultural pursuits.[47] Deng Xiaoping 鄧小平 officially reinstated intellectuals as part of the working class.[48] New public spaces appeared in the 1980s with the reconstruction of the social sciences in academia[49] and the development of government-sponsored think tanks, liberal publishers, and salons, thus providing new opportunities for a group with a name that was unthinkable under Mao, "nonestablishment (*tizhi wai*) intellectuals."[50] As Bonnin and Chevrier note, in the 1980s "the intellectual with an autonomous base in a more autonomous society emerged from the prevalent pattern of technocratic intellectuals operating within the state framework."[51] Although Bonnin and Chevrier's study is structured around the central notion of increasing autonomy, this trend, in their view, relied on two (potentially contradictory) evolutions: increased professionalization of intellectuals in the context of economic reforms and privatization, creating new institutional spaces for civil society (research centers attached to enterprises such as Capital Steelworks or the *World Economic Herald* (*Shijie Jingji Daobao* 世界經濟導報) published under the Shanghai Academy of Social Sciences), and the continued importance of patronage networks since the 1970s, in which intellectuals could reactivate their traditional role of "advise and dissent."[52] Discussing the Study Group on Problems of Chinese Rural Development, John Burns similarly notes a "continuum of autonomy" among "the state's intellectual advisers."[53] In this context, increased specialization went together with greater autonomy but was counteracted by the prevailing reliance on patron–client networks embedded in the state.

Even intellectual critics, dissidents (*yiyi fenzi* 異議分子), and activists in the democracy movement of 1989 still shared many of the traditional (elite) characteristics of Chinese intellectuals. As He Baogang notes, "The intellectuals and students at Tiananmen, by remonstrating with the ruler at the risk of their own lives and careers, embodied the Confucian ideal of intellectuals and the Confucian sense of responsibility to save the nation and make their society more humane and their leaders more accountable."[54] Craig Calhoun points out the limitations inherent in this stance: "But until deeper roots are laid, Chinese protests are apt to continue to echo the old Confucian idea of the people (or the intellectuals) remonstrating with the ruler. They will not be manifestations of alternative bases for government so much as attempts by the powerless to remind those in power of their true responsibilities."[55] Despite intellectuals' role as a driving force for democracy since the early twentieth century, the intellectual-led democratization model continued to rely on an elitist framework: "The question itself [of how intellectuals can return to the center of society after 1989] reflects the Confucian legacy that there ought to be a central position reserved for intellectuals. It overlooks the plurality of democratic society where intellectuals are only one of the political voices and forces."[56] The failed democracy movement of 1989, driven by "nonestablishment" intellectuals who were really still part of the establishment, can be seen as yet another example of the weight of Confucian tradition on contemporary political life. Timothy Cheek argues that it was only after being forcibly exiled from their symbolic "priesthood" as a result of the movement that intellectuals began to "professionalize."[57]

In the 1990s, intellectuals were confronted with large-scale commercialization and marketization, which provided new spaces of expression and which both professionalized and at the same time marginalized intellectuals with respect to mainstream society. Joseph Fewsmith notes: "As the 1980s gave way to the 1990s, however, intellectuals found their income shrinking relative to other groups and that their ideas and ethos were no longer esteemed. One might argue, as Yü Ying-shi[h] 余英時 has, that intellectuals have been increasingly marginalized throughout the twentieth century, yet intellectuals have been slow to give up the traditional notion that they are the bearers of the highest cultural values of society. Nonetheless, the 1990s presented very strong evidence that intellectuals as a group were not valued by Chinese society."[58]

In a speech originally delivered in 1988 at the Chinese University of Hong Kong and later reworked, the Princeton historian Yü Ying-shih blamed the culture of radicalism embraced by Chinese intellectuals throughout the twentieth century for the repeated tragic outcomes of all democracy movements.[59] Echoing his concerns, the PKU professor Chen Pingyuan 陳平原 argued for the importance of academic norms (*xueshu guifan* 學術規範) rather than "the moral heroism" of Lu Xun's Gate of Darkness, preferring the term "scholar" (*xuezhe* 學者) to "intellectual" (*zhishifenzi*).[60] In *Xueren* 學人 (The scholar), the new journal Chen set up in 1991, he advocated a more modest but more rigorous form of scholarship that would steer clear of overly broad theories and ideologies. This form of self-reflection led to a relative retreat of some academics from public life, even as academia began to internationalize and professionalize. Academics refrained from directly criticizing the regime's principles, and the state no longer carried out ideological campaigns in academia, as it did in the 1980.[61]

Others, by contrast, threw in their lot with Deng Xiaoping's market reforms, embracing the lowbrow pop culture brought about by marketization as the decisive force that could liberalize China.[62] Zha Jianying 查建英 singles out Wang Shuo's fiction and the television series Wang coauthored in the early 1990s (such as *Yearning* [*Kewang* 渴望]), Jia Pingwa's 賈平凹 novel *Fallen Capital* (*Feidu* 廢都, 1993), and Chan Koonchung's 陳冠中 early ventures into the mainland market (under media tycoon Yu Pun Hoi 于品海) as examples of the new fascination with culture as a market product.[63] Many elite sympathizers of the democracy movement "dived into the sea" (*xiahai* 下海—that is, left state service for the private sector), in some cases with the explicit goal of providing private funding and backing for more pluralism, sometimes referred to as "nurturing politics through business" (*yi shang yang zheng* 以商養政).[64] This split triggered the so-called debate on the "humanist spirit" (*renwen jingshen* 人文精神) in the early 1990s between advocates of a more academic humanism, preoccupied with "ultimate concerns" (*zhongji guanhuai* 終極關懷), on the one hand, and proponents of embracing consumer culture to further liberalize society as well as advocates of "post" theories, on the other.[65]

Xu Jilin, a participant in as well as an observer of these debates, characterized the 1990s by three concurrent developments: a turn away from "thought" and toward "scholarship," a turn toward the market as the best defense against ideology, and a turn toward consumer culture and postmodernism.[66] Xu equates these turns, which he considers unwelcome, with the rise of the notion of the "specific intellectual" and argues for the need for intellectuals to proceed from specific to universal, advocating a new "publicness." In his view, the "universal" or "enlightenment intellectual" of the 1980s split into two distinct categories: the "experts" who worked for the government and the "media intellectuals" whose intellectual position became increasingly influenced by market demand.[67] In this sense, whether they chose business or academic professionalization, intellectuals renounced both their autonomy and their symbolic central position in society. Xu has argued for a "third way"[68] in which intellectuals break out of political expertise and media marketization to play a new role as "interpreters" between different communities and in so doing create a new public.[69]

Wang Chaohua 王超華 observes two similar trends in the 1990s: the critique of radicalism and the turn to academia in the immediate aftermath of 1989 as well as Deng's push for marketization and the ensuing debate about the humanist spirit. However, she also points to a third moment, when the debates on state capacity and "democracy in a large country" in the second half of the 1990s paved the way for the formation of a group self-identified as the New Left, in tension with another group that defended liberalism.[70] After the repression of the democracy movement in 1989, the consensus between intraparty reformers and intellectuals that existed throughout the 1980s broke down, and economic reforms accelerated in the aftermath of Deng Xiaoping's "Southern Inspection" in 1992, while political reforms were put on a slow track. In the ongoing debates, two camps emerged on the academic scene.[71] The discussion, in fact, once again concerned the nature of reforms, continuing the early debate dismissed by Deng about whether reforms should be "surnamed C or S" (*xing zi* 姓資 or *xing she* 姓社)—that is, capitalism or socialism.[72] On the one hand, a group of academics, journalists, and technocrats described as "liberals" argued that in a situation of political stalemate, market capitalism and economic reforms would ultimately democratize society.[73] On the other hand, a group of critics gradually congealed, contesting the "fetishism" of transition theory and asserting the plurality of historical paths to modernization. Some (e.g., Wang Hui 汪暉) argued that economic liberalization in fact impeded democracy because of capitalism's intrinsic link with authoritarian politics.[74] Others (e.g., Cui Zhiyuan 崔之元 and Gan Yang), expressing a more fundamental distrust of representative democracy, advocated reexamining the intellectual resources of the Mao era for critical tools to fight capitalism.[75] Although some (e.g., Wang Hui) were initially skeptical of the Chinese government and its embrace of globalization, others (e.g., Wang Shaoguang

王紹光 and Hu Angang 胡鞍鋼) were directly engaged in elite power struggles to reinforce and recentralize "state capacity" (Wang Shaoguang and Hu Angang were instrumental in the fiscal reforms Zhu Rongji 朱鎔基 implemented from 1995 and then as premier from 1998). As time went by, most of them increasingly sided with the Chinese state against globalization and westernization, often striking a nationalistic tone. Because the New Left was increasingly absorbed by the state, it encountered growing difficulties in sticking to a coherent socially critical agenda while endorsing the institutions of an authoritarian political system. Although prompt to "defend" the masses against capitalism or Western pop culture, New Left intellectuals rarely spoke out in public when the state persecuted "vulnerable groups" such as petitioners, victims of evictions or state violence, migrant workers, and sex workers.

On the most ideational level, whereas liberals emphasized democratic institutions and their ability to protect individuals from state encroachment, the New Left understood democracy primarily to mean social equality. However, on another level these philosophical differences often paled in comparison with short-term political agendas, a classic phenomenon in intellectuals' quest for status and influence. It can indeed be argued that some liberals lacked a critical appraisal of the realities of market capitalism and its compatibility with, if not propensity for, authoritarian politics. However, other liberals readily endorsed the critical concept of "crony capitalism" (*quangui zibenzhuyi* 權貴資本主義) put forward by the economist Wu Jinglian around 2001[76] or called for the establishment of a welfare state on the European model (e.g., Qin Hui[77]). In this sense, it could be argued that capitalism only plays the role of a "red herring" in the "liberal versus New Left" debate.[78] Conversely, many left-wing critics have tended to use egalitarian definitions of democracy only as a foil to avoid engaging in a critical reflection on Maoism and to legitimize the role of an unelected party in governing China today, which suggests that the true heart of the debate is not the current economic system but rather how to evaluate the Mao era, a question that is discussed more fully in chapter 2.

Under Jiang Zemin, left-wing thinkers targeted the alliance between market liberals and neoauthoritarians (Zhu Rongji and Xiao Gongqin 蕭功秦), but under Hu Jintao 胡錦濤 and his "harmonious society" slogan, the New Left increasingly took on the role of intellectual cheerleader for the regime, endorsing the role of the state and the state-promoted nationalist discourse that emerged after the Belgrade bombing of 1998.[79] A group of "neostatists" or "sovereignists" brought the

New Left increasingly closer to the old Left and to the state.[80] With Hu's increasing emphasis on traditional concepts borrowed from Confucianism, a group of neo-Confucian thinkers also gained influence, although their political position remains ambiguous. Therefore, some observers argue for a tripartition of the intellectual sphere among liberals, the Left, and Confucians. However, the latter are in fact divided between a few liberals and culturally conservative proponents of a strong state, who remain firmly committed to an elitist role for intellectuals as "legislators" modeled on traditional Confucian patterns.[81]

Despite the theoretical abstraction deployed on both sides, many disputes ultimately boiled down to whether participants supported the party or not. Academic intellectuals further remained plagued by elitism and factionalism, compounded by verbal violence inherited from earlier times, which rarely proved conducive to productive discussion of disagreements. On the whole, many of the debates were overly theoretical and skewed as both sides often caricatured their opponents, and they became more and more sterile as time went on.

APPROACHES TO CONTEMPORARY INTELLECTUALS: LITERATI TRADITION, SOCIAL NETWORKS, GLOBAL POSTMODERNITY

Intellectuals in China today are intensely scrutinized, and it can be difficult to classify the many existing studies across neat disciplinary lines. It is possible, however, to distinguish between several approaches grounded in somewhat different disciplinary perspectives, as is attempted in the cursory review of the existing literature in this section.

Intellectuals and the State: "Advise and Dissent"

A number of studies, mainly by intellectual historians and sinologists, focus on Chinese intellectuals' place in the political system and in particular on their "autonomy" from the state as expressed in their writings. These studies draw on the role of the traditional literati, whose often intimate relationship with the Confucian state was situated along a continuum of advice, remonstrance, and withdrawal.[82] In this perspective, a contrast is often pinpointed between intellectuals' loyalty to the state and their role as moral critic. Zhidong Hao formulates this tension as the conflict between morality (*dao* 道) and power (*shi* 勢), which induces a form of schizophrenia among modern Chinese intellectuals.[83] Merle Goldman's book *China's Intellectuals: Advise and Dissent* (1981) discusses the reappearance of critical intellectuals outside the orbit of the state in the 1970s.[84] In the introduction to their collection *China's Intellectuals and the State: In Search of a New Relationship* (1987), Goldman and Timothy Cheek consider that the autonomy of intellectuals, strongly affirmed during the "May Fourth enlightenment," was subsequently curtailed: "Although intellectuals in modern times have switched from serving their culture to serving their nation, their service to the nation has severely limited their intellectual and moral autonomy."[85] This assessment echoes Li Zehou's 李澤厚 famous notion that throughout the twentieth century "enlightenment" (*qimeng* 啓蒙) has been repeatedly subordinated to the requirements of "saving the nation" (*jiuwang* 救亡), a notion that informs much of the scholarship published on the subject in mainland China.[86]

One domestically influential author writing from this perspective and from a liberal standpoint is Zi Zhongyun 資中筠 (b. 1930), a former diplomat and head of the Institute of American Studies at the Chinese Academy of Social Sciences (CASS) in the 1980s, who began publishing widely debated essays in the 2000s. She argues that intellectuals can be defined by a varying combination of three characteristics of traditional literati (*shi*) that have been handed down to the present: loyalty to the state, personal integrity, and the culture of "praising the emperor [*song sheng wenhua* 頌聖文化]," in which the sovereign becomes confused with the state and the nation. Taking up the dialectics of enlightenment and national salvation, she retraces how reforms have been repeatedly undermined by professed patriotism. She describes the return of a culture of sycophancy with the rise of state power in the 1990s and concludes by calling on intellectuals to reform themselves: to end their dependency on the state, to become more autonomous, and "[to] fac[e] the public."[87]

Goldman and Cheek divide contemporary intellectuals in China into three roles: ideological spokesperson, professional elite (in particular after the rehabilitation of the professions and social sciences after 1978), and moral critic in the traditional vein (using the respective examples of Tian Han 田漢, Wang Meng 王蒙, and Liu Binyan). In a more recent contribution titled "The End of Intellectuals," Timothy Cheek rephrases the roles of intellectuals throughout the PRC as "service, subversion, and selling."[88] He notes intellectuals' disestablishment from the party-state and increasing professionalization of intellectuals as the most significant contemporary developments, but he does not believe they have substantially transformed the traditional role of intellectuals. In his view, they continue both to seek influence within the system and to cultivate their moral stature: "The august and terrible social place of the intellectual under Mao—the despised political class and privileged political advisor—may have ended, but not the effort of China's educated citizens to achieve the moral ends of an intellectual." Intellectuals still remain defined by their relation to the state, even (especially) when they function as its moral critic. However, deploring their loss of influence, Cheek notes the fragmentation or "disaggregation of intellectuals" which he explains as the growing difficulty to simultaneously satisfy the requirements of the party, the professions, and the commercial public: "the intellectual field, like the public arena, in China has exploded."[89]

A series of studies that deal with the contemporary scene of elite intellectual debates, more or less closely connected to factions within the state, adopt a taxonomic approach. For example, He Li's 李和 book-length study *Political Thought and China's Transformation* (2015) envisages "intellectual discourse" in its relation to political power, grouping contemporary intellectuals into five main families of thinkers (liberal, neoauthoritarian, New Left, social democratic, neo-Confucian) and examining three major debates in which their ideas are illustrated (democracy, economic reforms, sources of legitimacy).[90] Zhang Boshu 張博樹 similarly proposes nine main groups (liberals, authoritarians, the New Left, the Mao Left, constitutional socialists, innerparty democrats, followers of Confucian rule, followers of New Democracy, neostatists).[91] In this perspective, the different groups are defined mainly by the political views they work to advance among the elite.

Social Position: Bureaucratic Elite

Sociological approaches, relying on nonnormative definitions (i.e., not based on a regulatory ideal of morality), consider intellectuals primarily as members of a social and bureaucratic elite, regardless of how "autonomous" their ideas may be from the state. Here, autonomy is not viewed as a key variable but rather as one tool among others wielded by individuals to seek status. Perry Link has provided the most systematic and enlightening study of the "socialist Chinese literary system" as a bureaucracy and co-optation network, inspired by the Soviet model and underpinned by an assumption of the relevance of literature widely shared in Chinese society. Link uses Andrew Walder's idea of "organized dependency" to describe how the system, avoiding direct coercion, achieves a high degree of self-censorship thanks to the advantages offered to writers and other artists by their work units.[92] Although Link has written that the system as such ended in the 1990s with the partial dismantling of work units, in more recent publications he continues to refer more generally to writers "working in the system," highlighting its resilience and adaptability.[93]

A volume edited by Edward X. Gu and Merle Goldman draws on Bourdieu's categories to assess how intellectuals use cultural and symbolic capital to maximize their influence and highlights the importance of patron–client networks in the mutual reinforcement of political and cultural authority: critical intellectuals often rely on establishment intellectuals for crucial support, while providing them with symbolic capital in return.[94] Despite the growing pluralization of ideas, marketization of the cultural field, and professionalization of society in the 1990s, Gu emphasizes the continuities with the 1980s: the development of nonofficial (*minban* 民辦) research institutes, consulting firms, and editorial boards (the term *shehui tuanti* 社會團體, "social organization," appeared in official documents in 1988) still relied strongly on social networks for funding and authorization, in particular on building patron–client ties with establishment intellectuals, as it had in the 1980s. In this sense, the growth of a more pluralized social sphere, based on ties with officials from different factions and situated within the orbit of the state, was not interrupted by the crackdown in 1989: in Gu's view, the regulations issued in October 1989 to restrict social organizations and revised in 1998 mainly reinforced what he calls the "state-corporatist framework."[95]

Similarly, in a study that takes a broad definition of intellectuals as "knowledge workers," Zhidong Hao emphasizes that even in the diversifying society of the 1990s intellectuals remained "organic" to the ruling class, espousing its evolution. He acknowledges that after 1989, "rather than arguing ineffectually for a democratic movement, most intellectuals had turned to projects that were more doable and less ideological," and he notes the appearance of new critical spaces: semi-independent intellectual journals and publications and think-tanks (e.g., Unirule, also known by its Chinese name Tianzesuo 天則所, founded in 1993, which separated into a nonprofit and a consulting firm in 1999).[96] However, they still relied on patron–client relations to survive, and in the absence of a significant measure of professional autonomy, the bulk of Chinese intellectuals Hao interviewed in the 1990s had been, in his view, "bourgeoisified and professionalized," pursuing lucrative side careers and forsaking the humanist spirit and the sense of "scholarship as the loftiest ideal of an individual."[97] Intellectuals followed the general trend among social elites, who remained attached to the state while seeking benefits from the market. Although Hao believes—perhaps in an echo of Konrád and Szelényi's thesis—that conditions may be ripe for intellectuals to form their own class, such a class formation is prevented by the state's ban on independent political organizations.

Marketization can reinforce patron–client and elite networks in unexpected ways. In his study *In the Red* (1999), Geremie Barmé investigates the commercialization and cynicism of the world of post-Tiananmen intellectuals, borrowing Miklós Haraszti's notion of the "velvet prison" to outline how the state developed flexible strategies for co-opting artists and writers who were rejected by the market and allowed a category of "tolerated" art and writing to appear between the categories "supported" art and "forbidden" art. "Tolerated" critical art can have many purposes, including a propaganda function directed at the outside and an internal safety-valve function, which allows the state to better monitor the activities of a small group of critical individuals. Haraszti had already highlighted the function of dissidents within the state apparatus of culture:

> Even in their tolerated, threatened ghetto, the dissidents serve a purpose: they are a cautionary tale. . . . The occasional stigmatizing of dissidents guarantees a sense of security to state artists by circumscribing the permissible. . . . in their isolation they have become predictable, and their numbers can be planned for systematically. . . . Just as in ancient, long-enduring empires, renegade mandarins might establish Taoist monasteries, similarly, the modern socialist state regards its die-hard dissidents as members of a monstrous, weird, misanthropic sect, disenchanted with educating the people . . . but nonetheless essentially innocent and, indeed, not without its uses.[98]

Accordingly, Barmé notes that "maverick artists" are "at their most dangerous and antisocial when they show themselves willing to sacrifice the privileges of the assimilated in order to retain their independence"; however, even these individuals can be dealt with "when the state decides to breed or tolerate a small number of Maverick Artists for propaganda purposes."[99] Wang Shuo's "hooligan" (*liumang* 流氓 or *pizi* 痞子) literature of the early 1990s, valorizing an urban brotherhood of sarcastic, cynical "smart-asses," represented both the appearance of a new alternative culture and the epitome of intellectual interventions that coexisted peacefully with party censors and proved lucrative for their authors.

The co-optation of critical intellectuals into bureaucratic networks through material advantages was therefore not impaired by the crackdown on the democracy movement; it only benefited from further marketization in the 1990s. In academia, the state provided new opportunities under Jiang Zemin by increasing and streamlining research funding for projects chosen according to state priorities,[100] all under the broader slogan "Reviving the nation through science and education" (*kejiao xingguo* 科教興國) proposed by Jiang.[101] In this sense, analysis of socioeconomic networks and patron–client connections continues to prove useful in understanding the deeper connections between intellectuals and elite interests.

Postmodernism, "Postsocialism," "Lowbrow" Culture

Finally, a series of recent contributions, originating mainly in the field of cultural studies, has asked whether China's intellectual scene today should be understood as part of global "postmodernism," often in conjunction with the term "postsocialism," which is understood as referring both to the undermining of socialist doctrine by capitalist practice after 1992 in China and to an equivalent of "postmodernism" in a society where modernity was essentially socialist. For example, Jason McGrath views China's "postsocialist" marketization of culture as a "global condition" resulting from the collapse of the Soviet Union and the apparent worldwide triumph of capitalism. China thus takes its place at the center of a global capitalist modernity that has lost its reference points in both traditional and revolutionary culture.[102] The notion of "postmodernism" was first discussed in China in the 1980s in connection with Fredric Jameson's lectures given in 1985 and published in 1986.[103] In the aftermath of the debate on humanist spirit, postmodernism was extolled as the theoretical legitimization of the new consumer culture by scholars such as Chen Xiaoming 陳曉明 and Zhang Yiwu 張頤武 and duly rebutted by Henry Zhao 趙毅衡 and Xu Ben.[104] Postmodernism as a cultural and intellectual agenda can be characterized by three main traits: the rejection of the ideal of autonomy of art and thought, their critical stance, in favor of consumption and enjoyment; the rejection of the division between elite and popular culture and the intention to legitimize popular culture rather than to democratize high culture; and the rejection of historical evolution in favor of eclectic borrowing.[105] It should be noted that "postmodernism" was a key term in the Soviet and post-Soviet context, referring to critiques of the transparency of language and the existence of an "absolute truth," intertwined with critiques of the regime that emerged in the underground culture of the 1970s.[106] In China, on the contrary, it has tended to be used to buttress state discourse and to critique "autonomy," a tendency Gloria Davies describes as a "positivist" use of postmodernism.[107]

Zhang Xudong 張旭東 and others have argued for a paradigm shift in the cultural sphere: in their view, the "postmodern" or "postsocialist" turn after 1989 can be observed in the critique of elites and the embrace of a new kind of "popular" (*tongsu* 通俗) or "lowbrow" (*disu* 低俗) culture. A similar argument was made early on by Jing Wang 王瑾, suggesting that the crushing of the student movement put an end to the rule of the intellectual elite: "[It is difficult to say] which historical course would better empower the masses politically, culturally and materially: the victory of the enlightenment intellectuals, were the students to succeed in their revolt, and hence the continual monopoly of an elitist cultural agenda, or Deng Xiaoping's political survival, the ensuing economic boom, and the perpetuation of Chinese socialism (no matter how ideologically corrupt it turns out to be) as a challenge and alternative to Western liberalism?"[108] Although the failure of the Tiananmen movement may indeed have undermined the special position of the intellectual elite, it remains uncertain to what extent China has articulated a progressive alternative to Western liberalism.

Zhang Xudong points to several important trends in the post-1989 context, among intellectuals and within society. First, intellectuals were confronted with the collapse of some fundamental assumptions: their role as moral conscience for the people, their inseparable connection with the bureaucratic state, and the broad consensus on achieving "modernity" as a universal set of institutions and values. The second development was the rise of a mass consumer culture, which he views as "a democratizing, liberating development, conducive to the building of a 'popular memory' free from elitist restraints and the division between 'high' and 'low' cultures."[109] He views consumerism (a catalyst of "postmodern democracy") as one of three important trends in the 1990s, together with neoliberalism (which stimulated the New Left) and globalization (which provoked nationalism).[110] Wang Shuo's embrace of the vulgar and his professed anti-intellectualism was thus famously endorsed by the former minister of culture Wang Meng (hence, the reference to these two figures as the "two Wangs") in the debate on humanist spirit in 1993, marking the alliance between intraparty liberalism and market-driven consumer culture against a similarly unlikely combination of "humanists" (Shanghai academic Wang Xiaoming 王曉明) and "moralists" (the "two Zhangs," novelists Zhang Chengzhi 張承志 and Zhang Wei 張煒). Wang Shuo thus became the epitome of the postmodern intellectual who both celebrates lowbrow culture and makes it into a source of profit.[111]

Although there is certainly a group of intellectuals in China espousing the theoretical positions of postmodernism, to what extent postmodernism as a theory can shed new light on the status of intellectuals there in general remains an open question. Modernity as a coherent "narrative" has indeed been questioned. But is it the case that the blurring of elite and lowbrow culture has truly democratized the status of the intellectual and severed intellectuals from their dependence on the state and elite modernization or that it has empowered the grass roots?

Gloria Davies argues that China's self-defined postmodern intellectuals are in fact simply a new incarnation of the traditional elite intellectuals. Her study *Worrying About China: The Language of Chinese Critical Inquiry* (2007) provides the most comprehensive assessment of the critiques of modernity and the "linguistic turn" that have appeared under the heading of "postmodernism" in China. Davies critically highlights continuities between contemporary intellectuals who describe themselves as "postmodern" and the traditional role of the literati as moral advisers to the nation, a role encapsulated in the notion of "worrying," or *youhuan*, which in her view carries a strong patriotic dimension.[112] Similar conclusions had previously been formulated not only by liberals such as Henry Zhao[113] but also by "critical" intellectuals such as Wang Hui, who wrote in 1997: "What is particularly amusing is that Chinese postmodernists turn the postmodernist critique of Eurocentrism on its head to argue for Chineseness and to search for prospects for China repositioning itself at the center of the world."[114]

Davies notes three main trends germane to postmodernism: the critique of modernity, the affirmation of academic inquiry or scholarship (*xueshu* 學術), and the linguistic turn; however, each of these developments leads back to a traditional understanding of the intellectual. First, the critique of enlightenment becomes a selective tool for Chinese intellectuals to "deconstruct" capitalism and "Western rationality," reaffirming the authenticity of Chineseness and sometimes going so far as to redefine Chinese tradition as proto-socialist. Postmodernist and postcolonial theory thus become tools affirming the uniqueness of Chinese culture within globalization.[115] Second, the affirmation of "scholarship" (*xue-shu*) against the figure of the enlightenment intellectual and the preference for "thought" (*sixiang* 思想) over academic inquiry in the 1980s still relies, in Davies's view, on a normative evaluation of intellectual "progress" or "improvement." One wonders whether *xueshu* might not also lead to a more "specific" definition of the intellectual that echoes Foucault's perspective,[116] though Davies does concede that *xueshu* is strategically useful to place intellectual activities out of reach of a third type of intellectual pursuit, "theory" (*lilun* 理論), which remains the privileged domain of the party. Finally, she notes that despite the asserted "linguistic turn" in Chinese thought, linguistic certitude and the confidence in the transparency of reality remain strong, underpinned by the traditional affirmation of moral self-cultivation (*xiushen* 修身), May Fourth scientism, as well as Mao-era "ideol-anguage." In her view, this "linguistic certitude" and the resilience of a moral concern to "perfect China" set Chinese intellectuals apart from Jacques Derrida and Western "postmodernists" and tend to reaffirm the traditional literati role of "advice, remonstrance, withdrawal." More generally, Davies believes that Chinese intellectuals' attempts to challenge orthodoxy have failed to challenge its underlying assumptions: Chinese exceptionalism; positivistic Hegelianism and the postulated transparency of language; moral patriotism and an instrumentalist attitude to theory, what she sums up as a "preference for the certainty of arbitration as opposed to the contingency of interpretation."[117]

Davies's critique of recent intellectual trends is thought provoking, highlighting how traditional models survive precisely under the robe of Western theory. Nonetheless, she does not quite avoid the pitfalls of normativity that the thinkers she analyzes are, in her view, guilty of. In her argument, deconstructionism, as expressed in the theories of Slavoj Žižek and Derrida, sometimes appears once again as a normative ideal for any "true" intellectual, which Chinese thinkers "fail" to measure up to. This approach may pay insufficient attention to other intellectual traditions that continue to exist throughout the world and that are no less worthy of attention than postmodernism and may have devoted followers in China. However, Davies is particularly persuasive when she holds up self-professed "postmodernists" to their own ideals and argues that their embrace of "popular culture" and "consumerism" is often simply a foil for their endorsement of popular nationalism and political conformity.

The three approaches presented in this section—intellectual history, social science, cultural studies—do not contradict or exclude each other; they are three different angles that the present study draws on while at the same time attempting to propose a new perspective. The traditional "advise and dissent" model defines an intellectual dialectics of responsibility for and service to the state and loyalty to ethical ideas that is part of any definition of the intellectual in China. At the same time, it is important to remember that Chinese intellectuals are deeply entwined with bureaucratic elites and that—as in many other societies—their interests are generally aligned with those of the ruling class. Although postmodernism may seem to capture the loss of elite status that intellectuals have experienced in the post-1989 era as a result of the growing marketization of culture and society, Davies highlights that it is often a postmodernism "with Chinese characteristics," one that may hide the endless return of the traditional literati under the robe of the postmodern (or nationalist) cynic. Elite academics may like to embrace low-brow culture, but they remain part of the elite. Overall, it seems clear that the old figure of the elite literati dies hard. Yet in all three perspectives the grass roots are conspicuously absent.

By contrast, the present study focuses on a different set of thinkers than the ones captured by most of the previous work on intellectuals. These thinkers are not liberated from the double-bind of responsibility to the nation and to their ethical convictions, but they devote less time to abstract political theories and moralizing and call attention to the grave consequences of intellectuals' unshakeable loyalty to the state. They are not disconnected from the social and political elites, and many maintain links with universities or professions, but they are also much more strongly linked to nonelite groups than were the intellectuals studied in previous decades. Are they postmodern? Wang Xiaobo, whom Gloria Davies does not mention, referred to postmodernism and Foucault as early as the 1990s but in a very different manner from how today's cultural relativists invoke him. Wang is more indebted to the Foucault of the essay "What Is Enlightenment?" As a critical universalist, he rejects the claims to moral superiority made by traditional Chinese intellectuals and explicitly criticizes postmodernism. Among the new cohorts of NGO workers, grassroots activists, and independent writers and journalists, we may discern not so much postmodern cynicism as a critical attitude toward elite narratives and postures.

CHAPTER 2

Wang Xiaobo and the Silent Majority

Redefining the Role of Intellectuals After Tiananmen

In March 1992, Wang Xiaobo published the novella *The Golden Age* in Hong Kong: it was reprinted in Taiwan in August and awarded a prize by the Taiwan newspaper *United Daily News* (*Lianhebao* 聯合報) in September 1992.[1] Wang Xiaobo subsequently decided to resign from his position as a teacher of professional English in the Accounting Department of People's University. In the following five years, he rose to meteoric fame in China (and to an extent in Taiwan, where he won several prizes) and began frenetically publishing novels and short stories, some of them that he had accumulated in his desk drawers, others freshly composed.[2]

Wang's establishment as the most prominent "freelance writer" (*ziyou zhuan'gaoren*) in China for many decades represented a landmark for the emergence of grassroots intellectuals. Ai Xiaoming, later a famous feminist scholar, was at this time studying for a Ph.D. in literature at Beijing Normal University and was asked by a professor to help proofread a manuscript by Wang for publication. Ai became Wang Xiaobo's most dedicated reader and interpreter and continued to exchange frequent letters with him after graduating and taking up her first teaching position at Guangzhou's Sun Yat-sen University in 1994.[3] When Wang Xiaobo unexpectedly died of a heart attack on April 11, 1997, at the age of forty-four and just a few months after Deng Xiaoping, his sudden death further made him into an icon for the post-Tiananmen era: a streetwise provocateur who mocked all forms of authoritarianism, both Maoist and Confucian, and tried to speak up for what he termed the subordinate or "vulnerable groups" (*ruoshi qunti*) that made up the "silent majority" of society.

Wang Xiaobo was not only the first freelance writer since 1949 but also a free thinker who, drawing on the form of the Chinese essay (*zawen* 雜文), used details from daily life and from his readings to reflect on politics and history, formulating a profoundly iconoclastic critique of the position of Chinese intellectuals. Censorship often made it difficult to publish his fiction,[4] so Wang began writing essays, which became hugely popular among the disillusioned young readers of the 1990s and provided him with a steady source of income. The rules on profitability imposed on state press organs after 1992 created windows of opportunity for publications that, although still under state ownership, could use the market and the expectations of the urban readership to publish edgier content, such as the publications by the Southern Media Group, in particular the *Southern Weekly* (*Nanfang Zhoumo* 南方週末, literally "Southern Weekend").[5] Several newsmagazines were established, including *Sanlian Shenghuo Zhoukan*, set up by the highbrow publishing press Sanlian). Intellectual journals also appeared or resurfaced, such as *Tianya* 天涯 (Horizon; based in Hainan under the editorship of the writers Han Shaogong 韓少功 and Jiang Zidan 蔣子丹) and *Dushu* (then edited by Shen Changwen 沈昌文 but later taken over by Wang Hui and the sociologist Huang Ping 黃平), both with a socially critical edge; *Strategy and Management* (*Zhanlüe yu Guanli* 戰略與管理), backed by retired People's Liberation Army general Xiao Ke 蕭克), which served as a forum for proponents of neoauthoritarianism; *Res Publica* (*Gonggong luncong* 公共論叢, edited by Liu Junning 劉軍寧), a liberal venue; and *Orient*, which explored new social topics. Wang Xiaobo's preferred outlets were *Dushu* and *Orient*; he also frequently published in the more mainstream, large-circulation weeklies *Southern Weekly* and *Sanlian Shenghuo Zhoukan* as well as in the *China Youth Daily* (*Zhongguo Qingnianbao* 中國青年報) and some others. These venues, thanks to the new system's commercial incentives, were able to publish Wang's often provocative articles; in turn, Wang's writing provided them with a new readership, which could be described as a "counterpublic" that identified with a set of concepts and values different from mainstream discourse.

Wang's critique and redefinition of the status of intellectuals encompass three aspects. First, he targets the perennial role of Chinese intellectuals as self-appointed guardians of morality who "take responsibility" for the nation and the world, in this way connecting Foucault's view of language as a tool of power with a critique of authoritarian neotraditionalism. On the contrary, he argues that intellectuals must abandon moralizing and embrace value neutrality à la Max Weber, leaving aside ideology and dogma (focusing on problems rather than isms, or on *wenti* rather than *zhuyi* in Hu Shi's 胡適 famous formulation) and relying only on knowledge (in particular empirical knowledge). Knowledge need not be instrumentalized in the service of power but can procure its own form of pleasure. Second, Wang blames intellectuals for their endorsement of utopias, in particular the Maoist utopia. This point leads Wang to a critique of enlightenment and modernity in contrast with the writings of the 1980s, in which Maoism was criticized as a return to feudalism. Finally, his argument for axiological neutrality leads Wang Xiaobo to rethink the entire social structure in terms of "vulnerable groups" rather than in terms of classes or social strata, thus undermining the Marxist view of society. This method has of course been famously continued by scholars such as Wang's wife Li Yinhe in her studies on gender and sexuality and Yu Jianrong in his studies on petitioners.

CHINESE INTELLECTUALS, MORALITY, AND SERVING THE STATE

Wang Xiaobo's essays offer a full-fledged critique of Chinese intellectuals' symbiotic relationship with the state and hegemonic use of discourse to establish their own status in society. This role, defined in the Confucian context, had not changed much in the twentieth century: whether intellectuals are advocating enlightenment or class revolution, they have continued to aspire to the moral high ground and have criticized groups in society that do not conform to their moral and ideological framework. As noted in the introduction, in his essay "The Silent Majority" Wang establishes a parallel between the (similarly formed) characters for the terms *shuo*, "speech," and *shui*, "tax": "Educated Chinese people have a very strong sense of responsibility to society: they must pay their taxes, be a good taxpayer—this is the unpleasant way to say it. The nicer-sounding way is 'taking the world under the heavens as your responsibility.'"[6] Taking a public stance, whether specifically in the Communist context (*biaotai*) or more generally, is like paying tribute to the necessity of entering the world of power struggles and at the same time confirming the intellectuals' privileged connection to the state. The traditional notion of "taking the world under heaven as their responsibility" (*yi tianxia wei ji ren*)[7] is described as part and parcel of the oppressive power structure of the world of speaking out. Of course, such an attitude should not be seen as uniquely Chinese. Wang's critique of traditional Chinese intellectuals is not unlike Gramsci's definition of intellectuals as producers of hegemonic ideology in the service of the state.

Monopolizing Morality

Wang Xiaobo's main critique of Chinese intellectuals is directed at their unchanging propensity to occupy the moral high ground and to construct their authority in moral terms. He takes to task the classic comment "think no evil" (*si wu xie* 思無邪) made by Confucius with reference to the *Book of Songs* (*Shijing* 詩經): "The people who make this kind of suggestion are themselves without evil or without selfishness; of course they do not know what evil is; therefore this recommendation simply means: I don't want others to have what I don't have."[8] Effectively portraying this comment as the epitome of Confucian hypocrisy, Wang Xiaobo goes on to observe that intellectuals under Mao continue to establish their authority by denouncing individuals for their moral shortcomings. In "Word Fights and Morals," he discusses ad hominem attacks on his father during academic conferences in the 1950s and describes the Anti-Rightist Movement as mainly preoccupied with investigating women rightists' "morals." He sees a continuation of this tendency in attacks against Jia Pingwa (in the debate on humanist spirit) for his "morality" rather than for the quality of his writing.[9]

Chinese intellectuals always tend to focus too much on people and not enough on ideas: "In our country, when intellectuals discuss social problems, what they always repeat is that people are too ignorant. . . . I do not believe this is a criticism of society, it is rather personal criticism."[10] Intellectuals should abandon this moral high ground:

> Some say that they should "worry before all others and rejoice after all others under heaven" (Are they pessimists?); some say they should "take responsibility for the world under heaven" (Are they internationalists?). I think this is not the most classic formulation. That would be that they believe in their own superior morality (a scholar is versed in all trades [*shi you bai hang* 士有百行]), their dominating position (the most important of the four estates [*si min zhi shou* 四民之首]), and their qualification to educate others (educate the people [*jiao hua yu min* 教化於民]). This is how we see ourselves. The problem is how others see us. What I hear is really pitiful: we have spent so many years "taking off our pants and cutting our tails" [*tuo kuzi ge weiba* 脫褲子割尾巴], and we have just made it into the ranks of the working class, a classic case of "an ambition higher than the heavens, but a life thinner than a sheet of paper!" Since this is the case, I recommend forgetting completely

> about the scholar-official [*shi* 士] tradition because otherwise we will just be dreaming with our eyes open. When we talk about social problems, we should use "hard reasoning": either we know what is being discussed and others don't, or we can clarify a complex problem that others can't; that is, we should display the abilities of intellectuals according to modern criteria. Although this may lack Chinese characteristics, that may not necessarily be a bad thing.[11]

Going back to Fan Zhongyan's 范仲淹 original formulation of the role of intellectuals, Wang Xiaobo offers a comprehensive indictment of the exalted self-image of Chinese intellectuals, including under Mao, as morally superior and uniquely qualified to lead the nation. After obediently "cutting the tail" of their bourgeois habits during the rectification of the early 1950s (as illustrated memorably in Yang Jiang's novel *Shower*[12]), intellectuals were frustrated in their expectation to take on the leading role once again. But if intellectuals are defined as people who "criticize society" (a definition Wang says he read in the *New York Times*), then China has no intellectuals, only people who criticize individuals for their moral shortcomings. Wang concludes by proposing a clean break with this whole tradition; rather than morality, he insists on using two criteria for judging meaningful contributions to the intellectual discussion, empirical knowledge and strength of deduction, calling them "hard truths" (*ying daoli* 硬道理) in an ironic reference to an aphorism by Deng Xiaoping, who believed that "development" was the only "hard truth." Wang thus coined his idea of the intellectual as a "clarifier" well before Bauman's "interpreter" became fashionable in China.

Wang Xiaobo developed his critique of Confucianism in a series of essays published in widely circulated journals. In "The Misfortune of Intellectuals," he reflects on the similarity between "beliefs" (*xinyang* 信仰) and "ideology" (*yishixingtai* 意識形態), taking issue with those who criticize science for having forfeited ethical values and created the means to destroy the world. In his view, although beliefs are not necessarily dangerous per se, they can easily become "a stick with which to beat other people."[13] Reflecting on the beliefs of Japanese kamikaze pilots in World War II and of the Red Guards in the Cultural Revolution, he advocates a more skeptical attitude based on reason and the refutation of all forms of ideology. In intellectuals' propensity to embrace ideology, Wang sees a Confucian inheritance: "Chinese humanist intellectuals have a sense of mission to 'take responsibility for the world under the heavens,' thinking they must produce something for ordinary people to believe in. Strangely, they not only want to be priests or theologians but also gods (in Chinese we say 'sages' [*shengren* 聖人]). Unfortunately, what ordinary people should believe in and to what degree cannot simply be decreed, which makes them [intellectuals] feel very regretful."[14]

Therefore, Wang observes, it is not surprising to see intellectuals use filial piety, "national studies" (*guoxue* 國學), or class struggle to lecture others: "My view of national studies is that this thing is indeed frightening, especially the "national" part.... you cannot deny that it has the potential to become a stick. Just like, in those years, intellectual hooligans like Yao Wenyuan 姚文元 used class struggle as a stick, with which they killed or injured countless people."[15] For these reasons, Wang believes that beliefs and values should be left to form naturally rather than be promoted by intellectuals, who should focus on reason. In "My View of National Studies," he compares reciting Confucian classics to reciting the Little Red Book during the Cultural Revolution: "As good as the four books and five classics may be, they cannot be read for thousands of years, just like chewing gum that, as good as it may be, cannot be chewed by a second person."[16] Criticizing the "cultural fever" of the 1980s in *Southern Weekly*, Wang pokes fun at the Confucian scholars who, after thinking that Maoism and class struggle would save the world during the Cultural Revolution, have now seamlessly embraced the notion that Chinese culture will save the world.[17]

In their embrace of Mao's ideology, intellectuals not only displayed their eagerness to side with power but also construed the hardships they were made to undergo as a form of self-sacrifice and moral elevation, echoing another Confucian theme ("propriety outweighs benefit; righteousness outweighs survival [*li gaoyu li, yi gaoyu sheng* 禮高於利，義高於生]"). By contrast, Wang Xiaobo advocates the search for happiness and self-interest, which he connects with John Locke and Bertrand Russell, writing that he does not fear being branded a "national nihilist [*minzu xuwu zhuyi* 民族虛無主義]."[18] Although some members of his generation recall their rustication with nostalgia, prizing their own difficulties (*chiku* 吃苦, "enduring bitterness"), Wang argues that these sacrifices were generally terrible and worthless, submitting the example of an educated youth who jumped into a river to save an electric pole and drowned, only to be celebrated as a revolutionary martyr: "This sparked a small discomfort: Could the life of one of us educated youths compare in value to a wooden pole? As a result, the people who felt uncomfortable were severely criticized.... Even a straw of rice plant belonging to the nation deserved to be rescued if it fell into water....

Calculating how much your life is worth, this kind of thinking is intrinsically lacking in elevation."[19]

Opposing this cult of suffering and self-sacrifice, Wang Xiaobo turns to Sigmund Freud's definition of masochism, in which Freud suggests that when living in terrible pain, some people end up falling in love with it and deriving pleasure from it. Wang argues that in order to have value, suffering needs some form of compensation: "I personally believe that what I suffered in the 1970s [*chi de ku* 吃的苦], the sacrifices I made, are without value; therefore they cannot be called sublime [*chonggao* 崇高]. I say this not because I want to underestimate myself but in order to have a lucid judgment on the present and the future. . . . Viewing a worthless sacrifice as sublime means you have accepted an erroneous premise."[20] Wang connects this worldview with the elitist bias of Chinese intellectuals, who have no firsthand experience of what ordinary people have to endure. Referring to how a group of rusticated youths in Yunnan were subjected to a "meal of remembering past suffering" (*yiku fan* 憶苦飯) by their team leader in the Communist tradition of "remembering past bitterness and enjoying present sweetness" (*yiku sitian* 憶苦思甜) that was widely performed in the early 1950s, Wang Xiaobo wonders whether it is really worth being sick all night and lining up to use the ditch simply to "experience" suffering.[21]

As a consequence, Wang avers, victims of the Cultural Revolution should not have a special status by virtue of a moral superiority derived from suffering. As a member of the "three old cohorts" (*lao san jie* 老三屆) who were sent to the countryside, Wang Xiaobo originally felt guilty that his parents did not receive an education. Some people argued later that if you did not suffer in the Cultural Revolution, you could not become a writer. Wang rebuts both of these arguments: "Any theory of the superiority of the *lao san jie* lacks detachment. Of course, I also oppose any theory demonizing the *lao san jie*. . . . On the issue of being a *lao san jie*, I am indeed very detached: Didn't I waste ten years of studies?" He concludes by referring to studies of groups discriminated against and argues that all people should be considered equally: "Mr. Russell has argued that a truly ethical principle should consider all people equally. I believe this means that when talking about others, you should first consider them as normal people before you begin discussing their moral virtues or shortcomings."[22] Victims of rustication or other forms of violence in the Cultural Revolution should not, in Wang's view, use their experience to take a position of moral superiority.

KNOWLEDGE AND PLEASURE

Taking issue with an article also published in *Orient*, in which Wang Lixiong 王力雄 criticizes intellectuals for their "moral decay" (part of the debate on "humanist spirit"), Wang Xiaobo replies that an intellectual's duty is only toward science and that science holds nothing sacred. Intellectuals have no need to feel shame ("it is always better to live without shame").[23] On the contrary, they should free themselves from all fetters in seeking knowledge. Wang Xiaobo argues that his critique of Wang Shuo is not a moral one: he believes Wang Shuo does not lack shame but rather experience of the wider world. In his view, Chinese writers in general need to read more, learn more, understand more about the world in order to have more interesting things to say, an ideal that can be seen as an echo of a cosmopolitan *humanitas*.[24]

Wang Xiaobo intermittently studied computing and was among the very first academics in China to use email in the mid-1990s. He refers to the challenges of writing software (mentioning Bill Gates) as one of the "concrete problems" that you learn to solve by blundering and "doing exercises." By contrast, some "experts on everything [*xuewenjia* 學問家] . . . suddenly understand a great truth," are so persuaded by their intelligence that they feel they don't need to provide proof, and declare that people who don't agree with them are "birds and beasts [*qin shou zhi lei* 禽獸之類]."[25] Although there are very many famous *xuewenjia* in China, Wang Xiaobo once again states his preference for "common experience [*gongtong tiyan* 共同體驗]," which grounds his definition of the intellectual in concrete problems and empirical, value-neutral knowledge, not in the great truths of the "universal intellectuals" of the 1980s or in the arguments of authority developed by Confucians (he regularly takes Mencius [380–289 B.C.E.] to task for calling his opponents abusive names). This critique lays the ground for a more bottom-up production of knowledge that will serve as the base for the grassroots intellectuals' public interventions.

For Wang Xiaobo, knowledge is a universal type of reasoning that is valid because it can be reproduced by everyone and requires no position of authority to find acceptance; it is democratic in its method, as opposed to the "philosopher king's" conclusions: "As for myself, I have always hoped that the principles of existence, the foundations of ethics, could be self-explanatory ideas. And if there are unclear aspects, I welcome the valuable views of scholars, provided that, like scientists of earlier generations, they persuade others using reason [*yi li fu ren* 以理服人] or that, like Socrates, they engage in an equal dialogue with us."[26] Contrary to the Confucian ideal of "knowing the commandments of heaven" and to the "spiritual atomic bomb" of Mao Zedong thought, knowledge (*zhihui* 智慧), in Wang's view, is best described in a quotation from Socrates: "The people who know that their knowledge is worth nothing are the wisest."[27] It should not be used as a tool of power or coercion.

Again referring to Russell, Wang writes in "The Beauty of Science":

> As Mr. Russell said, since modern times, science has established the authority of reason—this type of authority is different from past forms. The justification of science is different from "the Master says" or from "Red letterhead documents." When scientists publish results, they do not ask to be believed on the grounds of their own status. . . . Science is completely different from other human pursuits in that it is egalitarian. There is a reason why real science did not take root in China. This is because China's tradition lacks equality: since the days of attacking Confucius and Mencius up to now, it is always about deference and hierarchy. When you are told that steel can be tempered in a coal stove, do you dare ask for evidential proof? You don't. Even when you have tempered cow shit you close your eyes and praise the fine steel. In this framework, there can be no science.[28]

Scientific knowledge is the opposite of both Confucian learning ("the Master says") and ideology (the "Red letterhead"), and its most important characteristic in Wang's eyes is its democratic quality, which empowers anyone to speak out on the basis of his or her results.

Comparing the spontaneous appearance of science with that of the Internet and the market economy, Wang also warns against making science into a cult: "For Chinese people, science came from the outside; therefore, our understanding of it is skewed: first we feared it as a wild force of nature; then we understood it as a form of magic; finally we worshipped it like a religion. These understandings are all wrong: science is a form of continuous learning."[29] This is a critique both of the May Fourth Movement and of the cult of science of the 1980s, which transformed science into a dogma and a cudgel to criticize other discourses. What Wang Xiaobo takes away from science is mainly its empirical, skeptical disposition, which he transposes to the social sciences.

In the preface written for his collection *The Pleasure of Thinking*, Wang quotes Russell's distinction between science (relying on evidence) and ethics (which cannot be decided by science), noting that Russell cannot scientifically prove that it is wrong to beat people but frames his preference not to beat people as a plea to others. "Many of my views expressed in this book are similar—they have no scientific evidence, nor are they supported by dogma. They are nothing but pleas made by the author. My only request to the readers is that they will not ignore my sincerity."[30] In the heavily prescriptive post-Mao intellectual context, this was a very new and "modest" way of framing moral injunctions.

Wang takes up this theme again in the preface to his collection *My Spiritual Home*, in which he argues that remaining silent is also a way to avoid passing judgment on others too quickly. He quotes George Bernard Shaw's play *Major Barbara* (1907), in which the idle young man Stephen brags to his father that he can tell right from wrong. Wang vows never to become someone like Stephen, whose only ability is to make moral judgments: "For this reason, I became a member of the silent majority. People I saw in my youth only understood some crude (not to say absurd) principles, but thinking they knew everything, recklessly passed judgment on the world, inflicting great harm as a result."[31] Wang's own ambitions, by contrast, are to "fight ignorance" as well as "within the field of social theory to fight boredom and meaninglessness [*wuqu* 無趣]—that is to say, holier-than-thou solemnity." Wang concludes: "The demands I make on myself are quite low: as I live in this world, I simply want to understand some ideas, experience some interesting [*youqu* 有趣] events. If I could fulfill this wish, my life would be a success. In order to do so, I also have to discuss right and wrong; otherwise, one can't understand ideas or experience interesting events. I started too late and may not achieve anything, but at least I want to declare my position; that's why this book exists—for myself and to represent the silent majority."[32] Therefore, although ignorance must be fought with knowledge, in the field of social theory it is essential to avoid making knowledge into a boring, "solemn" form of moralizing.

Knowledge is a form of pleasure, as the title essay of the collection *The Pleasure of Thinking* suggests. Deploring that his father never experienced the pleasure of knowledge because he lived in constant terror that his findings might be criticized for political reasons, Wang argues that the brain is the "organ with which we perceive the greatest pleasure."[33] He critiques the Chinese tradition in which, in his view, knowledge is always utilitarian or instrumental: "Zhu Xi recognized that his view to obtaining knowledge through the 'investigation of things' was motivated by his wish to order the home, rule the country, pacify the world [*qi jia zhi guo ping tianxia* 齊家治國平天下]," whereas scientific knowledge is without ulterior motive, is based on proof, and has intrinsic value.[34] Rejecting this utilitarian approach to knowledge, Wang writes: "I prefer the donkey's approach: knowledge itself is good. One day we all will die, but others will pursue the road to seeking knowledge. I will not see what happens after my death. But thinking about this fact while I am alive makes me very happy."[35]

CRITIQUE OF UTOPIAS AND ENLIGHTENMENT

The Power of Speech

In what became his most famous essay, "The Silent Majority," Wang Xiaobo lays out the necessity of keeping silent under certain circumstances. This choice is linked to Wang's understanding of the specifically linguistic dimension of oppression. In response to an article by the Taiwanese intellectual Lung Ying-tai 龍應台 (later minister of culture) asking why Chinese people don't speak out more, Wang suggests that the realm of speech is dominated by propaganda and ideology: "When the 'Cultural Revolution' began, I was fourteen and in the first year of junior high school. One day, a frightening change occurred: some of my classmates suddenly became members of the five red categories, and the others became members of the five black categories."[36] In the linguistic remolding of reality, Wang finds a confirmation of Foucault's notion that language is power and that using categories of language is a way of imposing or even creating domination. In this context, using language unavoidably makes the writer into one of Stalin's "engineers of the souls." Speaking out in public means entering the world of *yang* 陽, the world of power relations, politics, oppression, and lies, like the propaganda slogans praising the unequalled happiness of the Chinese people during the Great Leap Forward. "Compared with any form of discourse, famine is always a greater form of truth." Conversely, to oppose this world, it is always possible to choose silence: "we can always make a choice between two types of culture: silence and language."[37] The CCP has since its early days perfected the art of linguistic domination with such notions as "declaring a stance" (*biaotai*), "self-criticism" (*jiantao* 檢討), and, more recently, "the right to speak" (*huayuquan* 話語權), which is both forcefully claimed by the government for the Chinese people and forcefully denied to anyone who is not a "member" of the Chinese people.

By contrast with the madness and hysteria of the Cultural Revolution, silence offers a refuge for a different set of values associated with humanity and reciprocal respect. On one occasion, Wang writes, after a fight broke out in the lavatories of a dorm and two of his young comrades bit each other's ears, the missing pieces of ear were later found spit out onto the floor: Wang concludes optimistically that there was no cannibalism, and human nature prevailed. On another occasion, the author himself was carried to a hospital by one of his companions over a dangerous river fording. He concludes: "Because of these acts, I do not think we were bad people; we do not necessarily believe in 'youth without regrets' or think we should have stayed in the villages and not come back; nor do I think we should follow some of the hints encouraging us to commit collective suicide, to open up some positions for the young people of today. However, for the aspects of our morality that can be saved, we should be thankful for the education of silence."[38] Silence and the private world of *yin* 陰 thus serve not only as a refuge for humanism but also as a bulwark against violence and against the lies of rosy propaganda. Therefore, although Wang of course refuses the catchphrase "youth without regrets" (*qingchun wuhui* 青春無悔) that was put forward by the Cultural Revolution nostalgics, he symmetrically avoids portraying the educated youth as victims.[39]

An atypical member of the educated youth generation, Wang returned to Beijing quite early (in 1972 at age twenty), and after six more years as a factory worker he enrolled in university in 1978 at the "almost normal" age of twenty-six. Like many others who shared his experience, he rapidly began writing about his life on a military farm in Yunnan, his appraisal of the ideology-driven totalitarian Maoist state, and his understanding of intellectuals' roles in the post-Mao context of the 1980s. However, unlike almost all of his contemporaries, he did not publish a single piece of writing during the decade of "cultural fever" that culminated in the student movement (his first collection of fiction appeared in September 1989). From 1984 to 1988, Wang accompanied his wife, Li Yinhe, who was enrolled in a Ph.D. program in sociology at the University of Pittsburgh, and while there he studied for an MA in the East Asian Studies Program under historian Hsu Cho-yun 許倬雲. This may be when he first heard about Foucault's *History of Sexuality* (1976–1984), which left a lasting impression on him.[40] His understanding of society and its relation to the state bears the imprint of Foucault's theory of power: Wang viewed social phenomena as power relationships, in which the disciplinary techniques developed by states are counteracted by bodily resistance. After teaching sociology at PKU and then English at People's University, he finally published in the summer of 1992 the short story he had been working on for almost twenty years, *The Golden Age*.

In this sense, his silence contrasts with the chorus of the "scar" writers, who, once they were able to return to the cities in the 1980s, spoke out to denounce their sufferings and oppression during the Cultural Revolution, making themselves into loyal and unfairly targeted victims.[41] Wang Xiaobo's Cultural Revolution fiction, by contrast, took more than a decade to reach fruition, and when *The Golden Age* did appear, it took a radically ironic stance toward the whole Cultural Revolution theme, descralizing and trivializing the experience of the sent-down youth by pointing out its meaningless absurdity and playing down the hardships of rural life.

Wang was at pains to provide a level-headed account of his own biography:

> Like most people my age, I've had all sort of encounters. For a while, I was a member of the five black categories (now these words refer to black sesame, black rice, etc.); then it was discovered that I needed to be reeducated, and I was sent to roll in the mud under the immense sky for a while, to forge my red heart. Later yet, I came back to the city; I became part of the working class; we were supposed to lead everything, but I never found out who we were leading. Later again, through immense efforts, I tested into university and suddenly realized with emotion: now I'm a stinking ninth—a lot more changes happened later, but I won't list them one by one. Overall, throughout life, you often get caught up in some "labels" [*shuofa* 說法]. Some of them are incorrect; they fall onto your head, and you take them to be true; then after a while even figuring out how to understand yourself becomes a problem.[42]

This dispassionate autobiographical account of the Mao years—including the ironic mention of Mao's label for intellectuals as the "stinking ninth" category of society—highlights both the prosaic and deeply unromantic experience of the Cultural Revolution as well as the contrast between the "labels" of ideology and the actual experience of absurdity. Rather than always complaining, says Wang, intellectuals should at least admit they were tricked by the world of speech: "it is unfortunate that many people of my generation have missed out on the only form of wisdom we picked up in those years—knowing when we had been tricked."[43]

When explaining why he remained "silent" for so long, Wang Xiaobo inevitably recalls his family history. Around the time of his birth, in 1952, his father—a famous logician who had joined the Communist base in Yan'an, taught at People's University after 1949, and now worked in the Ministry of Education—became a target of the "Three Antis" Movement and was labeled an "alien class element" (*jieji yiji fenzi* 階級異己分子): although he continued his academic work and was even received with a group of scholars by Mao in 1957, his party rank was not reinstated until 1979. Wang's given name "Xiaobo" (Small Wave) refers to his parents' hope that the persecution would be short-lived.[44] In "Why I Decided to Write," he points out that his father was so worried about political pressure that he persuaded all five of his children to study science—the more esoteric and specialized the topic, the better. Wang Xiaobo humorously remarks that it's easy to understand why his father felt this way, if one recalls the fates of literary scholars such as Wang Shiwei 王實味 (who died under duress in Yan'an), Hu Feng 胡風 (who was sent to a labor camp for several decades), and Lao She 老舍 (who died, probably through suicide, after being persecuted in the Cultural Revolution). This is why although Wang Xiaobo wrote some satirical stories as a rusticated youth, he chose to burn them and "repressed the dangerous tendency" of writing.[45]

Enlightenment Reason and Irrationality

Wang Xiaobo connects his dystopian memories of the Cultural Revolution with enlightenment and utopian thinking in "The Pleasure of Thinking," one of his most popular essays originally published in *Dushu*, which later gave its title to a collection of Wang's essays: "Sir Thomas More devised a detailed and complete plan of his utopia but, just like Russell, I would certainly not agree to live in it."[46] In another essay, he adds: "In a utopia, any kind of happiness has strict rules, for example 'take pleasure in suffering,' 'take pride in suffering,' or 'prefer socialist weeds to capitalist sprouts.' In a utopia, it is very hard to find anyone who is unhappy."[47] Finally, utopia is a form of social engineering: "Utopia is a mistake made by previous generations. No matter what type it is, utopia is always a view of human society that originates in one person's mind, including a virtual political system, ideology, way of life, rather than a naturally developed one."[48] Although Wang explicitly refuses to define himself as a "liberal" (*ziyoupai* 自由派), he agrees with the liberal critique that connects China's coercive environment with previous philosophies of utopia: "generation after generation of young people have read Plato's *Republic* [translated into Chinese as *Lixiangguo* 理想國, "The Ideal Country"], which kindled a burning fire in their hearts and made them want to become Lycurgus or a philosopher-king."[49]

Connecting More's *Utopia* with Plato's *Republic*, as Russell did, Wang describes Mao as a philosopher-king: "Philosopher-kings are preoccupied with the future of humankind; however, one person is less than one billionth of humankind, which is in fact almost nothing. . . . All in all, philosopher-kings despise humankind. . . . Their proponents say that only people who despise humankind can bring it great benefits. I would say that only such people can bring humankind great disasters."[50] Mao's indifference to empirical realities is in this way connected with a deformed enlightenment project based on pure ideas. Criticizing Friedrich Nietzsche's views on women, Wang notes: "Philosophical reasoning is quite unique; some conclusions are impossible to accept because they are based neither on evidence nor on deduction. The only proof is the philosopher-king himself."[51]

In its attempt to emancipate humanity, the Cultural Revolution ultimately resorted to a coerced form of enlightenment: "When I was sent down to the country as an educated youth, I absolutely wanted to liberate the entire human race; I never thought in the least of myself. At the same time I must admit that I was very ignorant. . . . [W]anting to educate others with your own ignorance is the greatest sin that good-hearted people can commit."[52] Contrary to the "scar" writers and rehabilitated intellectuals of the 1980s, who described the Cultural Revolution as a return to "feudalism," Wang argued that the Maoist project was rooted in a misguided view of the Enlightenment (based on coercion in the name of a monistically defined truth), which justified ideological indoctrination by the emancipation of humanity. Yet emancipation is possible only through knowledge, not through ideology grounded in "ignorance." As Wang notes in another essay, according to Russell, anything can be deduced from a false premise: the countless strange things Wang encountered during his rustication "were the result of a false premise, which I can now pinpoint: being an educated youth because I indeed qualified as young (age sixteen) but not as educated."[53] Wang's former editor, Li Jing 李靜, captures this point when she notes that, contrary to his contemporaries, Wang preferred to use the word *zhihui* (knowledge, wisdom) rather than *qimeng* (enlightenment).[54]

At its heart, the Maoist experience encapsulates the irrational dimension of politics and, indeed, of power relations in general, which Wang views through a Foucauldian lens. He describes Maoism as an experiment in humiliation: "Some masochists like to call themselves an insect, and their partner the sun—Chinese people don't say an insect but rather a screw [*luosiding* 螺絲釘] or a brick. As to the sun, that would be too plain: they must add 'the reddest red sun in my heart.'"[55] This comparison of political domination (the "red sun" was of course the standard way of referring to Mao in the Cultural Revolution) to sadomasochism provided the central metaphor for Wang's most popular (and shocking) fictional work, *The Golden Age*. Although some may criticize this view of Maoism as simplistic (Foucault, too, was regularly taken to task for his blanket critique of the mechanisms of power under democratic and nondemocratic systems), its shock value as well as its desacralization of Maoist violence were crucial in breaking away from misplaced nostalgia for the Cultural Revolution. More generally, Wang Xiaobo viewed politics, in particular totalitarian politics, as irrational.[56] In an essay on the "poisonous propaganda of narrow nationalism," he compares Adolf Hitler's charisma with the power of the literary figure of the Russian madman and with Yao Wenyuan's eerie smile.[57] In another essay, he ironically describes medical operations by novices in the countryside during the Cultural Revolution, who had to apply Mao's maxim and "learn war by fighting": he compares the "intestinal battle" during which over a period of several hours an amateur surgeon searched for his friend's appendix while taking care to avoid "leftist or rightist deviations" to a lengthy washing of pig's intestines by the butcher.[58]

Wang also includes the New Left thinkers among the masochists in a satirical column written for the widely read *Southern Weekly*. Just as the Tang dynasty fantastic tales known as *chuanqi* 傳奇 reveal all sorts of bizarre enjoyments, such as bathing in excrement, nowadays, Wang writes, scholars with American Ph.D.s and green cards express nostalgia for the days when intellectuals lived in cowsheds:

> As for those overseas scholars, I would guess they haven't really fallen in love with the Cultural Revolution, but rather with the special atmosphere at that time. They don't want to re-create that atmosphere in the United States because that is where they have decided to make their lives [*anshen liming* 安身立命]. They just want to throw China into turmoil so that they can come and experience it during their summer vacation, before returning to the United States, to teach in U.S. schools and earn U.S. dollars. This is not a bad idea in

> itself, but we must object: we do not share their fetish for extreme experiences, so don't come and torment us.[59]

Nor did Wang Xiaobo condone the affinities between the New Left and nationalism. As he wrote a few weeks before his death, alluding to the nationalistic best seller *China Can Say No* (1996): "A foreigner recently said to me: I hear you Chinese people are all saying no?. . . I very firmly replied: '. . . The Chinese people you know are saying no. I know no such people. . . . I know many wise people, but they all are keeping silent.'"[60]

In the midst of the turbulent debates of the 1990s, different sides sometimes claimed Wang Xiaobo as one of their own, either as a liberal empiricist in the tradition of Russell or as a Foucauldian critic of enlightenment. Xu Jilin argued that Wang had chosen the path of English empiricism against the Hegelian tradition of idealist rationalism.[61] By contrast, Dai Jinhua read Wang's work as a subversive deconstruction of the allegory form that traps the reader in a "maze of conflicting interpretations."[62] To an extent, Wang remains unclassifiable. In an essay on the "humanist spirit" debate of the early 1990s, he ironically points out how the reference to "culture" came to represent a kind of moral cleansing from the evils of consumption and desire and thus pokes fun at the "humanists."[63] Dai Jinhua underscores that Wang is always situated at a nodal point: he both appeals to the masses and turns his back on the masses; works with media both inside and outside the system; and combines the "stinging satire of the 'debate on humanist spirit,' 'cultural fever,' 'national studies fever' with a true affection for the spirit of humanism, the project of humanity, and writing in his mother tongue." In her view, this balancing act situates him "between the nineteenth and the twentieth century, or between modernity and postmodernity."[64] Indeed, Wang Xiaobo pokes fun at postmodernism as just another fashionable "knack" (*jueqiao* 訣竅) that—no more than chicken blood or ultrasounds—can make people intelligent.[65] Whereas elite academics often tried to "theorize" social issues, Wang Xiaobo and the "grassroots intellectuals" who appeared in his wake took a more detached, eclectic approach to social questions.

In fact, Wang Xiaobo never engaged in abstract theorizing. As Li Yinhe wrote, "Some people say that a society like ours can produce only theoreticians, authoritative interpreters of theory, and specialists of ideology, no thinkers; but in my mind Xiaobo was an exception; he was a free thinker [*ziyou sixiangjia* 自由思想家]."[66] His thinking was removed from an ideological mindset: "There is a typology that distinguishes between ideology, anti-ideology [*fanmian yishixingtai* 反面意識形態], and nonideology [*fei yishixingtai* 非意識形態]; I believe Wang Xiaobo was nonideological, not anti-ideological. The issues he cared about went beyond the scope of ideological disputes."[67] Tsinghua economic historian Qin Hui shared this view, noting that beneath Wang Xiaobo's unconventional and unaffected writing style, it was impossible not to discern a deep concern with society: "But if 'thinker' refers to builders of one of those imposing theoretical systems, then indeed Xiaobo was not that kind of person."[68]

Nonetheless, faced with the irrationality of politics, Wang Xiabo believed in the lasting power of reason. Although Maoist politics, with its tales of forging steel from bricks or growing three hundred thousand *jin* of grain per *mu*, might suggest that it is "April Fool's day every day" in China, the important thing is to remain rational: "Rationality is like virginity: once you lose it, it cannot be regained." After Lin Biao's death in 1971, Wang Xiaobo was told by his army commissioner that they must "protect Mao and the red rivers and mountains." His inability to obey proves that he was not trapped in the "kaleidoscope" of ideology.[69]

"COMING OUT" OF SILENCE AND TAKING THE POSITION OF THE POWERLESS

Vulnerable Groups

As noted earlier, some of Wang Xiaobo's ideas are inspired by his reading of Foucault, in particular his recurrent analysis of power as the fundamental phenomenon in human interactions, of which political power is only one variant. Although the description of Maoism as a form of sadomasochistic performance is certainly conceived in a humorous spirit, it highlights what Wang Xiaobo sees as a defining trait of Chinese society: the fact that everyone belongs to what he calls a "vulnerable" or "subordinate group" (*ruoshi qunti*).

> A few years ago I took part in some sociological research and so came into contact with some "vulnerable groups," the most unique of which were homosexuals. After carrying out this research, I suddenly realized that all "vulnerable groups" are made up of people who do not speak out about certain

> things. . . . And then I also suddenly realized that I was part of the largest of these "weak groups," and one that has always existed: the silent majority. The reasons why these people choose to keep silent are varied and many: some don't have the ability or the opportunity, to speak out; others have some private feelings they prefer not to speak about; others yet, for all sorts of reasons, dislike the whole world of speaking. I belong to the latter category. But as someone of this kind, I still have a duty to talk about what I have seen and what I have heard.[70]

The world of *yin*, the world of the "powerless," although it survives in the shadows, is therefore not only the place where the values of humanity are preserved in difficult times but can also be estimated to make up a large part of Chinese society. Wang's manifesto, which completely upends the mainstream class-based view of society, triggered a wide interest among Chinese intellectuals for marginal groups and the subaltern.

The notion of *ruoshi qunti* first appeared in the 1980s in the field of biology. It is very likely that Wang Xiaobo was the first to widely use it in the field of the social sciences.[71] Li Yinhe believes that the term was a translation of Gayatri Spivak's term "subaltern."[72] However, it is also possible that Wang Xiaobo was influenced by certain Marxist texts, in particular Gramsci's notion of the "subordinate."[73] Furthermore, although they are not synonymous, *ruoshi* also resonates with Václav Havel's notion of the "powerless," presented in his famous essay "The Power of the Powerless" (1978).[74] In any hypothesis, the term *ruoshi qunti* marks a decisive shift from orthodox representations of society in China.

Under the Mao era, sociology was banned, and social classes were viewed exclusively through officially approved theories. In 1949, the PRC was to be led by four classes, with the working class in the lead. Starting in 1950, each citizen was assigned two class descriptors that appeared on his or her household registration (*hukou* 戶口), based on a detailed schedule containing sixty-two labels. Class origin (*jieji chengfen* 階級成分) was determined by a person's activities in the period 1946–1949, whereas class background (*jiating chushen* 家庭出身) reflected the father's activities at the time of the person's birth and rapidly became the key indicator. After 1957, when private property was officially abolished, the main class contradiction was understood to have been resolved, although the four negative groups singled out beginning in 1949 (landlords, rich peasants, counterrevolutionaries, and bad elements) persisted as the "five black categories," with the addition of rightists.[75] In the 1960s, Mao developed further theories of class struggle against the "bourgeoisie" inside the party; however, it can been argued that between 1957 and 1976 "class" was essentially a political term, sidelining socioeconomic conditions.[76] The "Resolution on Certain Questions in the History of Our Party Since the Founding of the People's Republic of China" adopted in 1981, breaking with the Cultural Revolution practice, reaffirmed that "class struggle no longer constitutes the principal contradiction after the exploiters have been eliminated as classes."[77]

After 1978, sociology was gradually revived in academic departments, and eventually, as party doctrine evolved, scholars such as Lu Xueyi 陸學藝 developed an analysis based on "strata" (*jieceng* 階層), which usefully side-stepped the sensitive notion of class.[78] Under Deng, although the crucial distinction between rural and urban household registration (implemented in 1957–1958) was maintained, the dilution of class labels entailed a redefinition of "peasants" as either rural capitalists or "vulnerable groups."[79] The new dichotomy that appeared under the impetus of Wang Xiaobo's and others' writing distinguished between "vested interests" (*jide liyi* 既得利益) and "vulnerable groups" (*ruoshi qunti*), suggesting a social tension between the party, with its networks of officials and entrepreneurs (under "crony" [*quangui*] or "nepotistic" [*qundai* 裙帶] capitalism), and "marginalized" members of society. The latter included anyone whose official status was somehow precarious: migrant workers without an urban residence permit, petitioners from the countryside, former victims of ideological discrimination under Mao, people without a proper work unit (especially sex workers or others who operated at the borders of legality), unmarried adults, and especially homosexuals (then still illegal and potentially vulnerable to prosecution). The subversive potential of Wang Xiaobo's new category of analysis is well illustrated in Lin Chun's 林春 discussion published in *Dushu* after Wang's death. Her essay contests his notion of the "silent majority," arguing that critical intellectuals can represent only an "awakened minority," while the dominated classes are always subject to the cultural hegemony of the elite, which in her view explains their positive attitude toward the revolution and the party.[80]

Wang Xiaobo's skepticism about the class-based analysis of society stems directly from his experience of the Cultural Revolution:

> Up to now I am not clear about who counts as an intellectual and who does not. When I was rusticated, the military delegate said I was a "petit-bourgeois intellectual." That year I was only seventeen; I had attended six years of primary school and had but a crude grasp of writing, so I felt somewhat ashamed

> of the word "intellectual." Come to think of it, I also felt ashamed of the words "petit-bourgeois": we were a family of state employees; we did not sell cigarettes from a stand in front of our door, so how could we be petit-bourgeois? As an individual, I ought to belong to a class, and I was not opposed to belonging to one, but up to now I cannot figure out what class "educated youth" belonged to. If you really had to be included in one, I thought the most suitable might be hooligan-proletariat.[81]

As discussed earlier, class labels were mainly tools for political violence rather than the reflection of a social reality; furthermore, intellectuals were stigmatized as a dominating class even as they were marginalized and exploited. This lived experience of the absurdity of Marxist class analysis contains the seed of Wang's understanding of society as a mosaic of marginalized weak groups.

Wang's approach was echoed in March 2000 when the journalist He Qinglian 何清漣 published her famous article "General Analysis of the Changes in Current Chinese Society," which swiftly came under pressure from the government.[82] In it, she divided Chinese society into the following categories: a small elite, largely embedded in the old planned economy and political circles; an insufficiently developed middle class (*zhongjian jieceng* 中間階層) of managers, technical workers, and foreign-enterprise employees; an exploited working class; and a vast marginalized population (*bianyuanhua qunti* 邊緣化群體). This categorization seems to echo Wang Xiaobo's vision of society: "It is estimated," He Qinglian stated, "that 'off-post' unemployed and pauperized rural population together make up some 100 million people, about 14% of the total available workforce. In other words, about 80% of the Chinese people live either at the bottom or on the margins of society."[83] This article eventually led to He Qinglian's departure from China, clearly illustrating the challenge this reconceptualization of the sociopolitical structure of China's population posed to China's intellectual circles.

Value Neutrality

Designating groups such as petitioners, homosexuals, and sex workers as "vulnerable groups" rather than using the political terms that had currency under the Mao era, such as "hooligans" (*liumang* 流氓), already evinces in the Chinese context the nonnormative nature of Wang Xiaobo's approach. He further explored his ethical position as a scholar and commentator in an article entitled "Moral

Conservatism and Other Things." Inaugurating a new "social ethics" column in *Orient*, Wang Xiaobo insisted on the axiological neutrality that social science must bring to intellectual debates. Recalling a conference in which a colleague wore a T-shirt inscribed with the sentence "OK, let's pee," Wang distinguishes between people who think that encouragement is always good, whatever the goal, and people who prefer to think about the goal rather than encourage others to do things. Therefore, he underlines that although he has agreed to write a "social ethics" column, with the recommendation to "raise the level of social morals," he is not interested in encouraging people to do things they do not want to do. "OK let's pee" is not an appropriate slogan for a gathering of adults—it is widely accepted that after a certain age everyone can decide for himself or herself when it is time to pee. Therefore, Wang Xiaobo announces that he will devote his column only to the elaboration of moral standards, not on how to enforce them: "Ethics and morals are just the same as all other areas of research, you first need to understand the related facts before you draw any conclusions," and moral conservatism is the same thing as disregarding the content of the facts you are judging.[84] For this reason, in Wang Xiaobo's view there is no real difference between placing faith in a moral or religious canon and placing faith in a little red book: in both cases you are devoted to encouraging other people to pee. This shift toward axiological neutrality and the distrust of the educational role of the intellectual it implies again mark a break with the understanding of enlightenment that dominated in the 1980s.

In "To Have and Have Not," Wang Xiaobo further discusses the problem of normativity in relation with Li Yinhe's sociological research and wonders how a sociologist deals with a community where the norm (he uses the English word) is harmful: "I believe that every farm head will believe that the *norm* on his farm is the best for the pigs—pigs don't have to do anything but eat and fatten themselves up. Of course, this kind of excellent *norms* also implies that the pigs must end their lives at the slaughterhouse. . . . But something tells me some of the pigs may find that their life has very little meaning."[85] This disjunction between the obviously subjective evaluation of the norm and the need to dissociate a descriptive investigation from a normative judgment confirms Wang Xiaobo's belief in the need to separate knowledge and ethics.

In another famous essay, Wang Xiaobo makes the case for casting aside all manner of social norms, ironically enshrining as a model an indomitable pig that he encountered in Yunnan. Wang notes that pigs and cows usually live well without humans but that humans are eager to give pigs and cows' lives "meaning": either putting them to work or making them into meat. Just as some of the educated youth resisted Maoist coercion and absurdity by withdrawing from society and "going native" (a possible reading of *The Golden Age*[86]), this pig resists being enrolled in a social function, refuses to let himself be castrated, and continues pursuing pretty sows: "All the educated youth who fed the pigs loved him, loved his unconventional and independent [*teli duxing* 特立獨行] style, and described his life as unrestrained [*xiaosa* 瀟灑, one of Wang's favorite words]." On one occasion, the pig imitates the factory siren, prompting all the workers to leave their position one and a half hours early. When the team leader tries to catch and kill the pig, it escapes and lives a half-wild life in the sugarcane fields. Wang concludes: "I am now forty years old, and, apart from this pig, I have never seen anyone so indifferent to an organized life.... Because of this, I still fondly remember this unconventional and independent pig."[87] The resistance against absurd orders given by authoritarian organizations is closely connected to an intellectual attitude that resists naturalizing social norms.

In a series of short pieces commenting on his wife's research, Wang emphasizes the role of social science in constructing new forms of knowledge by gaining a deeper understanding of its object than ordinary discourse usually displays, by maintaining value neutrality, and by leaving judgments to the reader: "The author's goal is to reveal reliable results of his investigation to society, and to hand over the power of judgment to the reader."[88] The production of knowledge itself is separated from the moral judgment, which is left to the reader. Wang further takes to task those critics who accuse Li of advocating homosexuality: "The culture we discuss belongs to the realm of what exists. Evidential science investigates only what exists.... If we researched only objects we could advocate, I'm afraid most of our research would be empty, and we wouldn't know anything about the majority of things happening before our eyes."[89]

In the texts devoted to his and Li's groundbreaking study of male homosexuals, *Their World*, Wang repeatedly argues that homosexuality (in the early 1990s still under the threat of illegality[90]) should not be viewed as a moral issue but as a natural form of sexual activity: "people differ from one other, they have different genders, different intelligence, and differences between homosexuals and heterosexuals; these are all natural phenomena. Calling natural phenomena repulsive is not a serious attitude."[91] Therefore, "things that are unavoidable and that do not harm third parties cannot be called immoral."[92]

In the preface to *Their World*, Wang and Li further place their work under the authority of Fei Xiaotong 費孝通, the founding father of Chinese sociology, who supervised Li's postdoc at PKU, in trying to examine all aspects of society while steering clear of ideologies: "There are two opposite attitudes: one says that science pursues truth and that truth can be sought in facts; the other that truth is derived from a religious doctrine and that science pursues further praise for that doctrine."[93] Finally, research on marginal groups requires working outside the orbit of the state, on the ground level (*bentu* 本土, a term Wang borrows from Fei Xiaotong[94]) rather than on the "official" (*guanfang*) level, to carry out interviews without the representative of the neighborhood committee or other officials.[95] This situates Wang and Li's project within a *minjian* tradition connected to Fei Xiaotong.

This approach also ensures that criticizing the inequalities and violence arising from the marketization of the Chinese economy is not misconstrued as nostalgia for the Maoist form of egalitarianism. Focusing on another "marginal" group, Wang Xiaobo devoted a series of essays to migrant workers, who emerged as one of the new social groups of the 1990s: known originally as "rural migrant workers" (*nongmingong* 農民工), they represented a disenfranchised population deprived of citizen rights (they administratively were not permitted to settle in cities because of their rural residence permits) but were instrumental in building China's economic miracle. But rather than considering this group in a neo-Marxist class perspective, Wang writes about the question of dignity (*zunyan* 尊嚴, a word he uses in both English and Chinese), a notion he may have absorbed from Charles Taylor.[96] He describes how migrant workers return to their homes over the New Year's rush (*Chun yun* 春運), with hundreds of people squeezed into train carriages and tens of people squeezed into toilets. "When this topic is discussed, people say the railways need to be further developed, that railway workers have a hard job, talk about safety issues, but no one mentions that when people are squeezed together in this way they lose their personal dignity—as if this didn't matter."[97] He further develops this idea by pointing out that people who are denied dignity do not treat others with dignity. Street-food stalls run by migrant workers are dirty because migrants themselves are not treated with dignity; this situation is addressed by certain NGOs that offer migrant workers clean, simple living quarters.[98] Similarly, Wang's neighbors in his work-unit housing keep the insides of their homes clean but feel no responsibility for the shared parts of the building: "I always think that when the majority of people will receive attention, their behavior will improve."[99] To address the inequalities and disenfranchisement in Chinese society, it is not sufficient simply to denounce the market economy; the deeper reasons why society has become fractured in this way are to be found in the lack of citizen status and individual respect inherited from the Mao era.

In another text, Wang ironically contrasts the Confucian ideal of the gentleman (*junzi* 君子) with the "gentleman" in English (glossed in Chinese as *shenshi* 紳士), arguing that Confucian literati lack the idea of personal dignity: "China's *junzi* 'maintain their own integrity' [*du shan qi shen* 獨善其身]; in this sense they lack dignity. Dignity belongs to the individual, it is an incompressible space that must be defended on one's own—defending it means daring to argue, daring to sue in court, daring to use your hands. I think it's still preferable that people have some dignity; if individuals don't even have a minimum of space for themselves, they can't do anything for others, let alone be a model."[100] Wang's reasoning illustrates a whole new way of looking at the role of intellectuals. He suggests that intellectuals, rather than cultivating virtue (to be a model, like traditional literati), should, using the pen or the courtroom, join the fight of those groups who are deprived of personal dignity. Rather than just writing slogans on toilet walls (such as the slogan "Liberate Salvador" that he saw in a Brussels airport toilet when traveling in Europe[101]), they should defend the personal dignity of concrete people who are denied recognition by society. In his New Year essay for 1996, Wang recognized the progress made by society in recent years and did not regret returning from overseas, but he formulated a wish for "more rationality, more justice, and tolerance in society."[102]

NEW *MINJIAN* LITERATURE

Despite their popularity and significance, it is a well-known fact that Wang Xiaobo did not like his own essays, which he considered less important and less "serious" than his fiction. Describing the role of essay writer as that of a "watchdog" (in English), Li Yinhe recalls that when certain social problems appeared, "he felt that he had to sometimes come out and say something; this was his incentive for writing, but his real pursuit, what he thought was most important, was still his fiction."[103] Despite his reservations, she encouraged him to write newspaper essays as a means of reaching a broader readership. Nonetheless, as

Ai Xiaoming points out, the contrast between essays and fiction should not be overstated: "He made fiction into a way of thinking. In his fiction, his imagination, his thoughts, his deductions were much more complex and much deeper than in his later essays."[104] In this sense, his novels and essays are part of the same intellectual project. The critic Yi Hui 易暉 argues that Wang Xiaobo's novels are always in some way about the cultural dilemmas of Chinese intellectuals.[105] Similarly, the literary scholar Sun Yu points out that redefining the role of the intellectual as a liberator of knowledge allowed Wang Xiaobo to make fiction into a kind of cognitive game, in which he could use absurdity to counter absurdity.[106]

In "The Silent Majority," Wang Xiaobo asserts a specific role for literature as a "foothold to attack the circle of language, to attack the entire world of *yang*."[107] Literature differs from ideology and the world of *yang* in that it does not have all the answers; it is purely individual, and it touches others not through constraint but through pleasure. As Wang's editor Li Jing, who later became an author in her own right, wrote in 2008, "Wang Xiaobo used essays to express his 'beliefs' and fiction to sustain his 'doubts.'"[108] Wang concludes his essay with a provocation against the views of literature propounded both by officials and by many writers of the 1980s: "According to him [a friend Wang Xiaobo had given his first book to], writing must allow you to educate the people, to elevate their soul. These are truly golden words. But among the inhabitants of this world, the one I would most like to elevate is myself. This is a very base, very egoistic conception, but it is a very frank one."[109] Literature, just like knowledge, has only one finality: procuring pleasure, both to the writer and the reader. It is this ultimately antiauthoritarian, individualistic conception that guards literature against misuse by propaganda or ideology and places it outside the "meshes of power" defining social and political relationships.

In "The Art of Fiction," Wang sketches out the difference between his essays and his fiction. Connecting his essays with the tradition of the modern *zawen* (which can be traced back to Lu Xun), Wang modestly downplays their significance: "Essays [*zawen*] are simply a way of talking sense [*jiang li* 講理]. . . . Therefore, although I am good at talking sense, I don't think this is a quality, but rather a congenital fault that I must overcome. Of course, as a human being, I must take responsibility for morality and justice [*dao yi* 道義]; when I can't suppress it, I must speak; this is my motivation for writing essays. So I can overcome my propensity for essays only partially, not entirely." By contrast, fiction should be liberated from this kind of burden: "Taking responsibility for justice and morality is not a criterion for art, especially not for the art of fiction."[110]

Wang Xiaobo returns to this dichotomy in "Art and Caring for Vulnerable Groups." Although speaking out for vulnerable groups is important in essays, he argues, the specific role of art is to offend strong groups, not to care for vulnerable groups:

> Every society has vulnerable groups—for example, children, cognitively impaired people (actually children are not vulnerable, but their parents think they are). . . . In civilized countries, they are protected by welfare systems. However, I have always believed that science and art do not belong to welfare; their main subject should not be to care for vulnerable groups. . . . I not only believe that art and science's true path is not to care for vulnerable groups, but that it is to offend strong groups and make them feel offended.[111]

He specifically sets his novella *The Golden Age* apart from the main trend of Cultural Revolution literature:

> This book discusses sex in many places. This kind of writing not only tends to attract negative criticism, but in itself it incurs the suspicion of vulgarity. Even I don't know why, that's just how I wrote it. . . . As everyone knows, in the 1960s and 1970s, China was in the midst of a sexless era. It is only in a sexless era that sex can become a central topic of life. . . . However, in my story . . . the real theme is a reflection about people's living conditions. The main logic is: there are so many obstacles in our life, it's really fucking interesting. This type of logic is called black humor. I think black humor is my temperament; I was born with it. The characters in my fiction always laugh; they never cry. I find it more interesting this way. . . . Of course, some authors believe crying is more moving.[112]

Most educated youth literature consists of tearful melodrama, in which the former rusticated youth collectively feel sorry for themselves, but Wang Xiaobo eschews gratuitous emotion for a style of irony designed to provoke introspection.

Wang Xiaobo established a new type of position for a *minjian* writer: freelance, unofficial, and unfettered by traditional elite moral discourse. Although his impact on contemporary literature has been limited, his work did give rise to a distinctive strain of *minjian* writing. Chen Xiaoming argues that Wang Xiaobo's fiction also represented a decisive turning point because he "shattered the mystery enshrouding the literary institution and demonstrated the multifaceted feasibility of writing outside the system."[113] The most prominent collective expression of this strand was the "Rupture" (Duanlie 斷裂) questionnaire of 1998, organized by Zhu Wen 朱文, who was quite closely associated with Wang Xiaobo, one year after Wang's death. Published in *Beijing Literature* (*Beijing Wenxue* 北京文學) as a set of provocative questions sent by Zhu and the poet Han Dong 韓東 to fifty-five writers (including Han), along with their responses, "Rupture" generally ridicules all forms of literary authority: older writers, literary critics, foreign sinologists ("primary student-level criticism," according to Yu Jian 于堅), contemporary models (Chen Yinke 陳寅恪, Gu Zhun 顧準, Wang Xiaobo), foreign theorists (Foucault, Barthes, Heidegger), Lu Xun, the Writers' Association (a "rotting corpse," according to Zhu Wen), leading journals *Dushu* and *Shouhuo* 收穫 (Harvest), and literary prizes.[114] The responses were generally dismissive and laconic, although in the case of Wang Xiaobo, several writers pointed out that they did not "worship him as an idol" (the wording of the question) but nonetheless respected him as a writer.[115] In an appendix to the questionnaire, Han Dong points out the significance of Wang Xiaobo (while at the same contesting his appropriation by the mainstream as an "idol"), retracing the *minjian* tradition in contemporary literature:

> A point of reference for our practice of writing can be found in the *minjian* stance [*minjian lichang* 民間立場] of the early *Today* and *Tamen* 他們 [the poetry journal founded by Han], in the real Wang Xiaobo, the unknown Hu Kuan 胡寬, Yu Xiaowei 于小偉, the unfortunate Shi Zhi 食指, and the genius Ma Yuan 馬原, certainly not in Wang Meng, Liu Xinwu 劉心武, Jia Pingwa, Han Shaogong, Zhang Wei, Mo Yan 莫言, Wang Shuo, Liu Zhenyun 劉震雲, Yu Hua, Shu Ting 舒婷, and the so-called scar literature, root-seeking literature, and avant-garde literature. . . . For example, Wang Xiaobo, who passed away recently, was a contemporary of many of these writers, but their writing couldn't be more different. Wang Xiaobo was not accepted by the literary establishment during his lifetime but was brandished as a spiritual idol by the mediocre after his death: the shamelessness and absurdity of the established order is simply startling! Wang Xiaobo's achievements prove the correctness

> of a different type of writing. Although this type of writing was isolated and without support, it cannot be overlooked.[116]

This *minjian* tradition, which Han traces back to the unofficial journals of the late Mao era, found a particularly significant expression in Wang Xiaobo's writing, which Han contrasts with the literary establishment (and its attempt to co-opt Wang Xiaobo after his death). Han then goes on to provide a fully contrasted discussion of these two types of writing: one that is "adaptive, that changes according to its interactions with the established order," represented not only by the official Writers' Association but also by a whole "authority system that tries to control and monopolize literary pursuits and aesthetic tastes," and another that "is always in the extreme minority, on the margins, nonmainstream, *minjian*, rejected, and overlooked."[117]

This dichotomy in some ways reconfigured the literary field. Zhu Wen's short stories and Han Dong's poetry were the most prominent products of this group, but the group also included women writers such as Mian Mian 棉棉, Wei Hui 衛慧, and Lin Bai 林白; poets with strong local styles, such as Yu Jian in Kunming and Zhai Yongming 翟永明 in Chengdu; and the Liaoning editor and fiction writer Diao Dou 刁斗. Their challenge was not only to the literary establishment but also to dissident writers who were loyal to the traditional ideal of the intellectual. Ma Jian 馬建 for example famously took issue with Zhu Wen's glib statement that he was asleep in bed on June 4, 1989, which Ma described as a "carefree denial of the meaningful role of an artist in society."[118] Zhu Wen, after publishing several collections of fiction, turned to making feature films, which remains his primary activity today.

Yu Jian and Han Dong became the standard-bearers for *minjian* poetry, which challenged not only official poets but also what they described as the "neoliterati" style of Bei Dao 北島 and other "intellectual poets." Yu Jian had first become famous in the 1980s with poems devoted to daily life in Kunming among a group of like-minded friends and memories of the Cultural Revolution that, although related to politics, were concrete and firmly grounded in everyday life and language. He established a theoretical system based on the superiority of local language over national language, the rejection of metaphor as a poetic device, and the superiority of oral speech over the written word. Yu Jian and Ding Dang 丁當 were cofounders of Han Dong's Nanjing *minjian* poetry journal *Tamen* in 1984.[119] Han and Yu were seen as emblematic of a *minjian* school in Chinese poetry: Maghiel van Crevel uses the dichotomy of earthly and elevated or heavenly aesthetics to summarize the series of contrasts that defined their writing. *Minjian* poets advocated using colloquial and demotic language over standard language; skeptic humor as opposed to formulaic or propaganda discourse; marginality and the rejection of any social role as opposed to the traditional guiding role of literature and utopianism, which they understood as encapsulated in the poetic device of metaphor; authenticity and quotidianism as opposed to "intellectual" or elite subjects; and the use of blanks and nonstandard syntax to oppose the foreign-tinted punctuation of modern Chinese syntax.[120]

After 1989, Yu Jian wrote his first long poem, "File 0," which, although not directly connected to the democracy movement, could be seen as a product of the stifling atmosphere after the repression. The poem was first published in the journal *Grand Master* (*Dajia* 大家) in 1994. In the 1990s, beginning with his famous poem "Naming of a Crow" (1991), Yu Jian began producing a large body of critical writing on poetry, including essays such as "Rejecting Metaphor" (1991), "Backing Away from Metaphor: Poetry as Method" (1997), "The Hard and Soft Tongue of Poetry: About Two Types of Linguistic Directionality in Contemporary Poetry" (1998), and "Poetry Expresses the Body" (2001). Shortly after the "Rupture" questionnaire, a major polemic broke out between "intellectual" and "*minjian*" poetry and writing in general, partly played out in the same journal that published the questionnaire, *Beijing Literature*. Yu took a central role in denouncing "intellectual poetry" and advocating a return to *minjian*, particularly in his essay "The Light of Poetry: Cutting Through the Chinese Language" (1999). Maghiel Van Crevel discusses how Yu Jian polemically constructs *minjian* in opposition to both "official" and "elite," thus rhetorically lumping together the "elite" and "avant-garde" Republican or Misty poets (what van Crevel terms their "self-aggrandizing tragic heroism") with the "official" poetry of the Mao years.[121] In an essay titled "On *Minjian*," Han Dong further opposes the "three Big Beasts"—the system, the market, and the West—and advocates an authentic, quotidian, indigenous form of writing.[122] The polemics eventually subsided, and a decade later Yu Jian reconciled with Bei Dao and published several works in *Today*. He also increasingly translated his interest in vernacular forms and montage technique into documentary film, as discussed further in chapter 4. In summary, the Rupture Movement marked an important affirmation of *minjian* literature, but it was ultimately short-lived as literature moved farther into the mainstream of commercial culture in the 1990s, and the critical position on the margins was increasingly taken up by documentary filmmakers, amateur historians, and legal activists.[123]

The three main themes explored in this chapter implicitly define Wang Xiaobo's theory and practice as a *minjian* intellectual: the critique of traditional discourses of moral superiority, the critique of political utopias and top-down discourses of enlightenment, and the advocacy of value neutrality and a grassroots position. Nonetheless, although Wang challenges the framework of "responsibility for all under heavens," he does leave open the possibility that intellectuals can "come out of silence" and speak out about their own experience and that of others from a position of being themselves on the margins of society. Wang mentions a "duty" (*yiwu* 義務) to "talk about" what he has seen and heard, be it in Yunnan with the peasants and educated youth or during his sociological investigations. This duty implies a perspective of axiological neutrality rather than the perspective of society's central values. Although the "duty" to speak out is reminiscent of the position of enlightenment intellectuals in the 1980s, this duty, as Wang sees it, is an individual form of responsibility to oneself that seeks to escape the relationships of moral or intellectual superiority that can arise from the sense of social responsibility. There is a need to speak out in a way that uses language differently from the voices that monopolize the "world of speech." Coming out of the world of silence and into the dangers of the world of power and language has a sort of exemplary value in demonstrating the antiauthoritarian force of speaking out. In Wang Xiaobo's view, it is only by virtue of occupying a marginal, nonrepresentative position in society that a writer or an intellectual can possibly enter the world of public speech and politics and thus break with a long tradition of intellectuals as loyal critics and principal interlocutors of the state.

In the list of "public intellectuals" published by *Southern People Weekly* in 2004, Wang Xiaobo was among six names on an "honor list" of those who were no longer alive but still influential.[124] His stance, espousing the viewpoint of the vulnerable and the marginal, has continued to develop among the post-Tiananmen generation. Documentary filmmakers, using inexpensive equipment intended for amateurs, have filmed socially excluded groups, such as migrant workers, sex workers, victims of political campaigns or of the famine. The arguably most prominent filmmaker from this group, Jia Zhangke, often mentions Wang Xiaobo as the writer who inspired him to consider the value of the individual and the necessity to turn away from collective narratives.[125] Writers such as Yan Lianke 閻連科 and Liao Yiwu have turned to the most vulnerable or illness-stricken members of society and adopted their perspective.[126] Sociologists such as Li Yinhe and Guo Yuhua have turned to studying specific social questions in the nonaxiological manner Wang advocated. Local activists have focused on environmental issues, heritage destruction, and housing evictions rather than on institutional change—all issues that Wang Xiaobo discusses in his essays.

Nor has the state stood by as these developments have taken place. After the list was published in *Southern People Weekly* in 2004, the notion of "public intellectual" was attacked and impugned in the *People's Daily*. The party organ not only pointed out that claims to the autonomy of intellectuals were misleading ("intellectuals represent the working class") but also particularly singled out their ambition to be "spokespeople for the silent majority."[127] Given Wang Xiaobo's prominent place on the list, the explicit mention of the "silent majority" may well have been an allusion to his understanding of intellectuals' role. In 2012, when the state began cracking down on liberal activists, an editorial in the overseas edition of *People's Daily* designated "vulnerable groups" (*ruoshi qunti*) as one of five dangerous groups (ironically dubbed by critics as the "five new black categories") who, together with rights lawyers, followers of underground religions, dissidents, and Internet leaders, represented tools for hostile foreign forces "using bottom-up methods to penetrate China's social foundations and create conditions for 'change.'"[128] The term subsequently became sensitive and has all but faded from the official sphere, as political control was reasserted over the media.

CHAPTER 3

Minjian *Historians of the Mao Era*

Commemorating, Documenting, Debating

The fortieth anniversary of the Anti-Rightist Movement in May 1997 came just a few months after Deng Xiaoping's death, which lifted a significant obstacle to the recognition of the "rightist" victims because Deng, as head of the CCP Secretariat, had been the main organizational force executing Mao's orders in 1957. The Fifteenth Congress in the fall of 1997 repeatedly mentioned "political reforms," signaling liberalization. This political constellation set the stage for a reappraisal of the events of 1957, which had not been officially condemned by the party in the same way the Cultural Revolution was in the early 1980s. A series of party documents published in 1978 had established a framework for dealing with people "labeled" (but never convicted) as rightists (*huacheng youpai* 劃成右派): in them, the party had reaffirmed the necessity of the Anti-Rightist campaign, while at the same time recognizing that more than 99 percent of actual designations of rightists were unwarranted.[1] It did not apologize or offer compensation for the years of wages and pensions it had withheld but advised each work unit to take responsibility for finding a new position for the returnees and making up for unpaid wages or pensions. Throughout the 1980s and most of the 1990s, the foundational period of the PRC (1949–1966) continued to be eulogized as a golden age of idealism, in which the party had enjoyed broad support among intellectuals and the population at large. For these reasons, commemorating the Anti-Rightist Movement by definition entailed a more radical challenge to the party's authority and historical legitimacy than the Cultural Revolution, which had been officially criticized. Such a commemoration proved almost impossible during the 1980s, despite an attempt by Liu Binyan and Fang Lizhi to mark the thirtieth anniversary in 1987.

By contrast, shortly after the fortieth anniversary, a set of three books was published in early 1998, collecting historical documents, testimony, and calls for rehabilitation from the former rightists at PKU.[2] Zhu Rongji, a former rightist, became premier in March. On May 4, 1998, Jiang Zemin gave a speech for PKU's one hundredth anniversary that was understood as endorsing liberal ideas. The speech was followed by a small wave of memoirs and studies by well-known intellectuals, such as Hu Ping 胡平, Zhu Zheng 朱正, Dai Huang 戴煌, and others,[3] and by Zhang Yihe's 章詒和 best-selling family memoir *The Last Aristocrats*, which deals with the persecution of political elites connected to Zhang's father and "number one rightist" Zhang Bojun 章伯鈞.[4] The first wave of publications tended to be personal or family memoirs, such as Dai Huang's autobiography *Nine Deaths, One Life*, which was a great success until it was banned in 2007.[5] Dai Huang had been labeled a rightist for a speech opposing the "deification of Mao" in 1957 and spent twenty-two years in a labor camp; although his rightist label was removed, he never received the twenty-two years' worth of withheld salary. His daughter, Dai Weiwei 戴為偉, subsequently became involved in editing the journal *Remembrance* (*Jiyi* 記憶), illustrating how descendants of rightists often carry on their parents' work.[6] However, the influence of memoirs should not be exaggerated. Dai Huang's book was exceptionally engaging, but many other memoirs were long and rambling, printed by obscure publishers or self-printed. More profoundly, their subjective nature limited the scope of their arguments and thus made them less dangerous to the authorities.

A more systematic engagement with the episode followed. Peking University literature professor Qian Liqun, who had experienced the movement as a freshman in the university's Chinese Literature Department in 1957, published a commemorative text on the Anti-Rightist Movement shortly after the PKU centennial in 1998 under the title "An Intellectual Heritage That Should Not Be Erased—Re-reading *A Collection of PKU Rightists' Reactionary Theories* and *A Collection of Rightist Theories from Inside and Outside the University*." In this essay, he symbolically re-read the "negative teaching materials" in which texts from the student journals of 1957 have been "miraculously" preserved.[7] He also called on former rightists to remember and speak out, and this call was answered by a tidal wave of mail, often accompanied by published memoirs, which began piling up in his study.[8] Around 2003, he began compiling a collection of studies on important literary testimonials of the movement, which was published under the title *Refusing to Forget: Notes for "1957 Studies."* It includes chapters on the three student journals published at PKU in 1957; on the "rightists" Lin Xiling 林希翎 (1935–2009), Liu Qidi 劉奇弟 (1934–1963), Tan Tianrong 譚天榮 (b. 1935), and Yao Renjie 姚人傑 (b. 1924); on two memoirs by He Fengming 和鳳鳴 (b. 1932) and Zhang Xianchi 張先痴 (b. 1934); and on three iconic victims of the movement: Lin Zhao 林昭 (1932–1968), Gu Zhun (1915–1974), and Zhang Zhongxiao 張中曉 (1930–1966, who was arrested during the anti–Hu Feng purge and died in prison). In the brief preface, Qian underlines that all of these individuals are "ordinary people" (*putong ren* 普通人):

> In the following prefaces and book reviews, I have tried always to focus my gaze on the people in the movement, in particular ordinary people, their fate, their psychology, which is overlooked by most of our historical research: as I have written previously, "On our historical horizon, we often only see events, no people, or else there are great people, but no ordinary people, there is collective politics, but no realm of the individual mind." Therefore, the work I do is to supplement what is omitted in official histories, which necessarily has its meaning and value.[9]

This assertion marks a turn away from the elite history of the Anti-Rightist Movement and toward *minjian* history, focusing on how the movement affected many low-level clerks and administrative cadres. In a public lecture that became a manifesto included in *Refusing to Forget*, Qian formed the project of "1957 studies," with the aims of rehabilitating the *minjian* thinkers of the Mao era, such as Tan Tianrong and Gu Zhun, and using academic research to resist forgetting. His object was not simply 1957 as an event; rather, he argued, "critical thinking should extend to deeper sources in the entire span of Chinese history."[10]

FROM ELITE TO SUBALTERN: *MINJIAN* HISTORIANS, OBJECTS, AND METHODS

The activities around the fortieth anniversary of the Anti-Rightist Movement marked the starting point of a series of unprecedented grassroots initiatives around China to investigate the movement: gathering documents in flea markets or through other unofficial channels, interviewing survivors or witnesses,[11] and sometimes making documentary films about them, which were screened in festivals, bookshops, and universities.[12] The history pages of *Southern Weekly*, edited by the poet Ma Li 馬莉, and other media such as *Beijing Youth Daily* (*Beijing Qingnianbao* 北京青年報) also became spaces willing to publish research uncovering problematic episodes of early PRC history, as the newfound enthusiasm led to probing a broader chronological range of events.[13]

The debate on the twenty-seven years of Mao's rule (1949–1976) had been one of the structuring discussions of China's intellectual sphere since the 1980s. The "scar literature" movement, eulogizing intellectuals as victims but largely eschewing the structural mechanisms of the Maoist state, began even before the Third Plenum of the Eleventh Central Committee in December 1978, later inspiring works such as Zhang Xianliang's 張賢亮 novels and films by Fifth Generation directors, such as Tian Zhuangzhuang's 田壯壯 *Blue Kite* (*Lan Fengzheng* 藍風箏, 1993). When their discipline was officially reinstated in the early 1980s, sociologists undertook oral history research on the early PRC to redefine the categories of Chinese society. Nonetheless, the prevailing consensus about the Mao era among writers and intellectuals in the 1980s was largely compatible with the "Resolution on Certain Questions in the History of Our Party Since the Founding of the People's Republic of China" that was passed both to condemn the Cultural Revolution and to circumscribe criticism of it:[14] focusing on the "errors" of the Cultural Revolution, novels, essays, and scholarly works subsequently bypassed any systemic critique of the regime. Intellectuals remained in an elitist posture of "loyal victims" of unjust state persecution, eager to take back their rightful role as loyal advisers to the state. For this reason, challenging the mainstream narrative was closely connected to renouncing their elite posture and rethinking how the social engineering often theorized and supported by intellectuals under Mao affected ordinary people.

The victim narrative was occasionally questioned: first by the writer Ba Jin, who had lost his wife to an untreated illness in the Cultural Revolution and had recently visited the Auschwitz memorial. In an essay published in the Hong Kong daily *Ta Kung Pao* on April 1, 1986, Ba called for the establishment of a museum of the Cultural Revolution devoted to "remembering our responsibility" and where both "victims and perpetrators [could] scrutinize themselves in a mirror."[15] This call was taken up first by the established literary scholar Liu Zaifu 劉再復, who in an essay published in *People's Daily* on September 8, 1986, called for *chanhui* 懺悔, a term that refers to both "confession" and "repentance." He detailed the need for repentance by referring to two specific forms of collective guilt: guilt for the backwardness of the Chinese nation and "survivor's guilt" in view of "sacrificed comrades" such as Lao She. He points out that such repentance must go deeper than a simple conformity with external norms, as often understood in Confucian culture.[16] His call was echoed by a young firebrand critic, Liu Xiaobo 劉曉波, who made a name for himself by attacking the established writers of "scar literature" in an article published in *Shenzhen Youth Daily* (*Shenzhen Qingnianbao* 深圳青年報) on October 3, 1986. In it, he accused Wang Meng and Zhang Xianliang of fostering nostalgia for the original "purity" of socialism during the "seventeen years" before the Cultural Revolution (1949–1966) and of praising the reeducation process for bringing intellectuals closer to the "people."[17]

The question of how to deal with the Mao era thus became a central one for intellectuals attempting to redefine their social status and role in the 1990s. In the historical field, early critical interventions concentrated on the Cultural Revolution. Yan Jiaqi 嚴家其 and Gao Gao's 高皋 history of the "turbulent decade" was written in the early 1980s and first published in Hong Kong in 1986 by *Ta Kung Pao* (first in serial form and then in book form by the paper's in-house press), breaking with the official narrative as enshrined in the 1981 Resolution.[18] The independent director Wu Wenguang 吳文光, at the time still working for Beijing television, completed *1966—My Time in the Red Guards* (*1966 Wo de hongweibing shidai* 我的紅衛兵時代) in 1992, in which he interviewed several high-profile former Red Guards, including the philosophy scholar Xu Youyu 徐友漁, who had worked with Wu.[19] Early challenges to the official narrative in the field of fiction came from Wang Shuo's short story "Animals Are Wild" (1991),[20] later made into a film by Jiang Wen under the title *In the Heat of the Sun* (*Yangguang canlan de rizi* 陽光燦爛的日子, 1994), and of course from Wang Xiaobo's novella *The Golden Age* (1992), which pokes fun at the educated youth who were rusticated during the Cultural Revolution, suggesting that intellectuals were consenting victims of Maoist humiliations.[21] In 1994, Zhi Liang's 智量 novel *A Starving Mountain Village*, the first large-scale work to discuss the famine during the Great Leap Forward, became a best seller, with two hundred thousand copies sold in a few years.[22]

Subsequently, from the late 1990s, a series of discursive productions and publications appeared that challenged the status of intellectuals under Mao in a much more systematic and radical way. Wang Xiaobo foreshadowed this evolution when in "The Silent Majority" he wrote about a loudspeaker blaring propaganda during the Great Leap Forward: "From that speech, I also learned that a *mu* of land can produce three hundred thousand *jin* of grain; then we nearly starved to death. In short, ever since I was young, I haven't had much faith in the spoken word, and the more vehement the voice, the more fervently it is pitched, the more I doubt. This habit of doubt had its origins in my starving belly. Compared with any speech, starvation holds the greater truth."[23] Wang's essay suggests a more radical conclusion: speech, as mendaciously produced by intellectuals, was the regime's main vehicle of propaganda and a deadly weapon in the context of the famine. Intellectuals were willing collaborators in Mao's policies. Wang's decision to "come out of silence" was therefore possible only on the condition that intellectuals make a clear break with this practice.

This chapter attempts to show how amateur or unofficial historians working outside the system, sometimes in collaboration with groups of grassroots victims or witnesses of the Mao era, gradually articulated a more profoundly critical and self-critical discourse on the Maoist state.[24] Previous scholarship on memory has focused on the importance of memory within party discourses, on how cultural elites used "hidden transcripts" to criticize the Mao era, and on how positive memories of Maoism were appropriated by laid-off workers and other dissatisfied groups in the 1990s.[25] By contrast, the new critical discourse that developed after 1997 was, first, more systematic in that it did not exclusively focus on the Cultural Revolution as an "accident" in the development of the socialist state (or as an "error," as the Resolution on party history puts it) but attempted to address the entire historical span of the Mao era (1949–1976), extending to the continuities between Mao's politics and the post-Mao regime. Second, this new discourse questioned the accepted wisdom that Mao's policies mainly targeted the pre-1949 elite while benefiting the "lower classes" and attempted to rethink the categories "elite" and "subaltern." The memory of the famine was for a long time hidden because most of its victims were poor, rural people who had no access to the realm of public discussion and who had been successfully trained to frame their grievances in the vocabulary of the party (although active repression by the state certainly also played a role in their silence).[26] Foregrounding the famine changed the perspective on class in Mao's China. Third, due to the role of intellectuals in abetting the state's social engineering, a discourse of "confession and repentance" (*chanhui*) developed among former Red Guards and others who had been associated with violence. Even as the state tried to push commemorations back into the private realm, a series of public apologies gave the discourse of "confession and repentance" an opportunity for wider dissemination.

Unofficial historians can be viewed as *minjian* intellectuals because they work (at least in part) outside the system, relying on their specific knowledge rather than on official channels or commercial incentives (many of them disseminate their journals via email and rely on retirement pensions as their only income) to collect and publicize material that challenges the official historical narrative. Their work can be described as *minjian* in more than one sense, once again reflecting the polysemy of the notion. First, many of the investigators were not trained historians or, if they were, were not specialized in contemporary history, which is still largely absent from academic history departments in China (*minjian* as freelance). Even the more academic among them often began working outside academia. Second, their object of investigation shifted from elite politics to everyday history and memory (*minjian* as grassroots). Third, their methodology turned to approaches that were often not recognized by academic historians, such as oral history, rather than relying on (unavailable) official documents (*minjian* as unofficial). More generally, their collective efforts represent a concerted attempt to rewrite the historical narrative of the PRC in a way that gives more prominence to marginal groups rather than to the dominating classes (a history written by the losers).

The fortieth anniversary of the Anti-Rightist Movement in 1997 arguably marked a turning point in the development of *minjian* discourses on the Mao era, no doubt because the Anti-Rightist Movement was particularly associated with the early persecutions of intellectuals. This anniversary was followed by renewed interest in the Great Famine of 1959–1961 and its ordinary victims. Finally, *minjian* intellectuals returned to the Cultural Revolution in a new set of public forums in the late 2000s with the development of unofficial journals. In each of these three stages, which are examined in this chapter, the focus is on a specific type of practice: commemoration of the Anti-Rightist Movement (because its victims have been denied recognition), documentation of the famine (because its victims have been erased from history), and debate on the Cultural Revolution (because there are different, competing narratives of it).

COMMEMORATING GRASSROOTS RIGHTISTS

Before its rediscovery in the late 1990s, the Anti-Rightist Movement was seen largely as an elite ideological purge, targeting a relatively small number of prominent nonparty politicians and cultural elites. Although it was officially recognized that half a million people had been "labeled" rightists, little attention was paid to how ordinary citizens might have been implicated and systematically persecuted. As Rubie Watson has pointed out, public commemorations are one of the classic tools through which victims or witnesses try to open a legitimate social space for discussing controversial historical events, whereas the state usually tries to confine their memory to the private realm.[27] Commemorations can be all the more effective when the event involves identifiable victims of state violence because a private ceremony organized by their companions or family members can develop into a larger public event. Although Zhang Yihe's book about the three "top rightists" in Beijing played an important role in rekindling interest in the Anti-Rightist Movement, it is noteworthy that many of its victims were not to be found among the elite. Three examples of commemorations of "grassroots" victims of the Anti-Rightist Movement stand out: Lin Zhao, who, although she was executed during the Cultural Revolution, was persecuted earlier as a rightist along with other students at PKU; the members of the group that published the journal *Spark* (*Xinghuo* 星火) in Lanzhou, an even more grassroots organization made up of local graduates from Gansu, several of whom were executed; and the several thousand rightists who died of starvation in Jiabiangou, a Reeducation Through Labor Camp also in Gansu, many of whom were petty employees without any political activities. These examples highlight the connection between commemoration and victimhood, which served as an impetus to rethink a set of historical events.

Lin Zhao and Peking University Students

Lin Zhao (Peng Lingzhao 彭令昭, 1932–1968), a famous PKU rightist who was arrested in October 1960 in connection with the *Spark* affair and eventually executed in 1968, was one of the voices who was rediscovered by a new generation of *minjian* intellectuals in the early 2000s and who became the object of growing discussions and commemoration. A star student and early party member from Suzhou who was admitted to PKU's Chinese Department, she was involved in producing student wall posters (she supported Zhang Yuanxun's 張元勛 poster "It is time"), the underground journal *Honglou* 紅樓 (Red building) at PKU, as well as the journal *Spark*. Her case highlights that the Anti-Rightist Movement was not just a factional struggle within the party but also a student movement at

PKU, calling for free speech and invoking the May Fourth tradition. During Lin Zhao's years in prison, she continued to write politically critical texts with any tools she could find, including using her own blood to write on sheets or clothes.

Lin Zhao's sister Peng Lingfan 彭令范 wrote her first long article on her sister's case in 1998, just after the fortieth anniversary of the Anti-Rightist Movement.[28] As Jie Li 李潔 notes, Lin Zhao's case first became widely known when she was rehabilitated by a Shanghai court in 1980 thanks to an article in an academic journal that described her sentencing and execution (her family was famously rumored to have been forced to pay fifty cents for the bullet that killed her). Her personal dossier containing the "letters written in blood" was briefly available at this time, which allowed her writings to become public, although her file was subsequently sealed again.[29] However, not much further public discussion took place until the film *Looking for Lin Zhao's Soul* (*Xunzhao Lin Zhao de linghun* 尋找林昭的靈魂) was made by Hu Jie 胡傑. The director, a graduate of the People's Liberation Army Arts College, where he had specialized in oil painting, resigned his job at Xinhua in 1999 in connection with his decision to investigate Lin Zhao's story and devoted the following years to interviewing her friends and family and gathering documents on her case. *Looking for Lin Zhao's Soul*, finished in 2004, could not be broadcast or distributed through normal channels, but Hu Jie traveled with the film all over China, organizing screenings, distributing free copies, and taking part in discussions with audiences.[30] The film became well known among intellectuals and made a name for Hu Jie, who continued to work on similar topics, devoting another controversial film, *Although I Am Gone* (*Wo sui siqu* 我雖死去, 2006) to Bian Zhongyun 卞仲耘, a girls' school headmistress who became one of the first victims of Red Guard violence in August 1966, and then returning to the Anti-Rightist Movement with the film *Spark* (*Xinghuo* 星火, 2013).

On the fortieth anniversary of Lin Zhao's death in 2008, a commemorative article appeared in *Southern Weekly*.[31] Lin Zhao's remains had been transferred to the family grave outside Suzhou in 2004. After Hu Jie's film had made her somewhat famous, commemorations began at the site, which reached a peak in 2013 on the forty-fifth anniversary of her execution.[32] Her sister published several interventions in wide-circulation media, in particular the liberal *Southern Weekly*, including a rebuttal of claims that Lin's tomb had been moved away from Suzhou or that she (Peng Lingfan) had died and a justification of her donation of a copy of Lin Zhao's dossier to the Hoover Institution Archives.[33]

Lin's case gained prominence on various media. In 2015, Ai Xiaoming published the first of three long essays on Lin Zhao's posthumous manuscripts in *Oriental History Review* (*Dongfang Lishi Pinglun* 東方歷史評論, a semi-independent journal founded by the columnist, critic, and cultural entrepreneur Xu Zhiyuan 許知遠 in 2013), focusing on the "Letter to the Editorial Department of *People's Daily*" and the more recently rediscovered manuscript of a novel written in dialogue form, "Chatter of Soulmates" ("Ling'ou xuyu" 靈耦絮語), in which Lin Zhao expressed a deep hatred of Mao and an intense love for Shanghai mayor Ke Qingshi 柯慶施. Ai draws a literary parallel between this text and Lu Xun's "Madman's Diary," paying particular attention to the fact that Lin Zhao's critique is not only a rational one but also an emotional one:

> Regarding the sources of Lin Zhao's ideas of resistance, Qian Liqun, Fu Guoyong 傅國湧, and other researchers as well as documentary director Hu Jie have all underscored her views of human rights, her liberal democratic value system, and her Christian faith. I would like to add a further point that deserves attention: In her 140,000-character letter, she stresses that her basic position and uncompromising attitude is to "prefer the resolute and ardent quality of the young generation." She continues: "All the acts of struggle carried out by young rebels are rooted in feeling, in emotion, not in rationality. I only occasionally use reason to examine, analyze and understand my emotive decisions. But it can absolutely not replace emotion.[34]

Analyzing emotion as a women's discourse, Ai Xiaoming reads this account as an implicit subversion of the patriarchal system under Mao, very much in the vein of her analysis of the Wang Xiaobo texts she had contributed to making popular two decades earlier. Ai's essay further contributed to commemorating and bringing to the forefront a subaltern, feminine voice of the Anti-Rightist Movement.

Spark

In 2010, Tan Chanxue 譚蟬雪, a former member of a small group of university graduates from Lanzhou who had been sent down to the countryside as rightists after 1957, published her memoirs in Hong Kong. They included the full text of the two original issues of the journal *Spark* that the group had published in the first months of 1960 when the famine had reached a peak, formulating perhaps the most radical critique of the regime that had been published after 1949.[35] *Spark* has acquired an almost mythical status as one of the only underground publications of the early PRC that directly criticized Mao's policy, compared CCP rule to fascism, and in particular drew attention to the famine. The entire group was arrested shortly thereafter, including eventually the contributor Lin Zhao, and several members were executed. In the foreword to her book, Tan discusses how she came to compile her memoirs and why they were so long delayed. In describing her position, she highlights two aspects: her nonelite status and her wish to satisfy professional standards of historical research. In the first paragraph, she describes the book as "a voice crying out from the bottom of society [*yisheng laizi shehui diceng de nahan* 一聲來自社會底層的吶喊]": "This is an historical episode that has been locked in dust for half a century, a group of young people struggling on the road to democracy and freedom, an unjust verdict paid for with youths and lives, a voice crying out from the bottom of society."[36] The book commemorates her dead comrades while situating the author on a different level from the intellectual elites involved in the Anti-Rightist Movement in PKU or among the United Front parties.

Tan Chanxue also underscores that the delay in publishing the book was not due to her lack of motivation but rather to the difficulty in obtaining reliable historical material. Of course, she is referring first and foremost to obtaining the two issues of the journal *Spark*. After having knocked on many doors, she finally received help from a few (unnamed) people at Lanzhou University, from which most of the contributors to *Spark* had graduated, who were either moved by her efforts or, in the context of the new century, had begun to feel that the events of 1960 reflected favorably on their alma mater. It was only after having secured a surviving copy of the two issues of the journal that Tan felt authorized to envisage a publication. She was acutely aware of the responsibility to provide reliable historical material on a suppressed episode: "The words and acts of those years are not individual fantasies, nor were they coincidences, but the necessary consequences of history. For those who have died in this way, let us hope that the settling of their remains can contribute to the development of history!"[37] Even though she writes as an amateur historian—and probably for this reason—she asserts her commitment to historical accuracy.

In his preface to Tan's book, "The Heart Is Quivering, the Blood Is Hot, the Soul Is Pure" (a quote from *Spark* group member Xiang Chengjian 向承鑒), Qian

Liqun further elaborates on the reversal of class standpoints associated with the *Spark* group, underlining the astonishing collaboration between the PKU student Lin Zhao and a group of grassroots students from faraway Lanzhou University, led by Tan, Zhang Chunyuan 張春元, and Xiang Chengjian. Quoting Lin Zhao's own words about their "deep commonalities [*shenke gongxing* 深刻共性]," Qian notes:

> It is very significant that Zhang, Tan, and Xiang elaborated their class consciousness in villages at the very lowest level of Chinese society. Furthermore, they went to the villages, not like the student participants in the Folk Literature Movement after May Fourth (or today's volunteers) who took the reform of village life as their responsibility and therefore could hardly avoid taking an attitude of superiority, but rather as criminals who were sent to villages to undergo coerced reeducation and whose actual position was even below the peasants. Therefore, they directly experienced all the hardships of the peasants, starkly confronted the reality of the villages, had more opportunities to observe the psychological experience of the peasants. To some degree, the problems, the destiny faced by the peasants, had already been internalized as their own problems and destiny. At the same time, they were "educated youth" who had attended university, and hence were able to more rationally reflect on the problems of peasants and villages.[38]

Qian's analysis highlights that the *Spark* group was made up of critical minds in the *minjian* intellectual tradition; their rediscovery and significance today are closely related to their status and to the vantage point from which they experienced the Maoist period and political experiment. Born in villages but university educated, they could see the world from the bottom, combining a May Fourth sense of mission with faith in the CCP's rural roots, and were deeply shocked by the disasters of the CCP's rural policy.

As children of peasants, the *Spark* writers analyzed the People's Communes and the subsequent pauperization of the countryside as a betrayal of the revolution, adopting the name of a journal Lenin published in 1905. Qian points out that in the first issue of *Spark* they published the oral testimony of a peasant under the title "A Day in the Village," thus allowing peasants to "speak for themselves." The village proletariat created by Mao was deprived of rights and freedoms and was submitted to intense psychological control, as Zhang

Chunyuan argued in his essay "Peasants, Serfs, and Slaves," which made the case for viewing the peasants as slaves of the People's Communes. Du Yinghua 杜映華, the county secretary of nearby Wushan (Gansu) who supported the group (he reportedly asked: "The revolution was victorious, and what did we bring the peasants? Starvation! And death!"), was arrested in the Anti-Rightist turn after the Lushan conference of 1959 and eventually executed.[39] The *Spark* writers at the height of the famine in 1960 attempted to make sense of the terrible discrepancy they experienced between discourse and reality by using Marxist concepts, in particular inspired by the Yugoslav critics of state socialism, which they rejected in favor of "democratic socialism." They formulated a comprehensive and theoretically grounded critique of the entire party-state system that did not simply point out its errors or excesses. The existence of such a critique to some extent undermined from the start the discourse that developed in the 1980s and blamed only the "excesses" of the Cultural Revolution. The journal *Spark* also published two long poems by Lin Zhao, "Prometheus" (which had already circulated among her friends) in the first issue; "The Seagull—Freedom or Death" (which was unpublished at the time) in the second issue, which met with a broad echo in the 2000s.[40] The careful documentation of the publications of the *Spark* group, coming from grassroots witnesses and participants in the movement, contributed to a re-reading of the Anti-Rightist Movement from a nonelite perspective. In this case, the perspective of *minjian* history, starting out from a personal commemoration, involved unearthing unofficial historical sources (copies of the journal) and ultimately challenging the dominant understanding of the Anti-Rightist Movement as an elite factional struggle. The connection between the grassroots intellectuals within the *Spark* group and the rural victims of the Great Famine, as documented in the journal, serves as a model to rethink the responsibility of intellectuals as *minjian* historians today.

Jiabiangou: Textual and Visual Investigators

Another immediately recognizable symbol of the Anti-Rightist Movement that began to be commemorated in the early 2000s was the Reeducation Through Labor (*laojiao* 勞教) camp at Jiabiangou (Gansu), which has now achieved a symbol status somewhat comparable to that of the Kolyma camp in the Soviet Union. The camp, which had been set up in 1954, was converted to a *laojiao* facility in 1958 to meet the demands of the Anti-Rightist Movement. Like all prison camps in China, it was conceived to be self-sufficient by producing its own food and clothing for inmates. However, Jiabiangou was situated in the middle of the Gobi Desert on the borders of Gansu, Inner Mongolia, and Xinjiang, and it was therefore impossible, even in the best of times, to produce enough to sustain even the basic needs of the several thousand rightists sent down in 1958 and 1959. With the onset of the Great Famine in 1959, the camp stopped receiving food for prisoners from outside and around 2,000 or 2,500 of the 3,000 inmates (or 3,136, according to survivor Si Jicai 司繼才 in Ai Xiaoming's film) died of starvation and were loosely buried in the shallow desert sand.

The first public mentions of Jiabiangou typically appeared in the form of a personal memoir: in 2001, He Fengming, whose husband, Wang Jingchao 王景超, died in Jiabiangou and who was herself labeled a rightist and sent to another labor camp nearby, published *Experience: My 1957*.[41] He Fengming had been active in trying to connect Jiabiangou survivors and coordinate claims for compensation since her return to Lanzhou in the early 1980s. Her book was discussed by Qian Liqun in his study of the Anti-Rightist Movement and gave rise to a first series of calls for a commemorative monument.[42]

However, to enter the sphere of public discussion, the Jiabiangou issue needed to be framed more broadly than in a personal memoir. The first person to take a systematic interest in Jiabiangou was another typical *minjian* intellectual. Yang Xianhui 楊顯惠 was a little too young to have been a rightist: born in 1946 in Lanzhou, he was only eleven when the Anti-Rightist Movement took place, though he remembers his schoolteacher suddenly disappearing (he later found out that his teacher died in Jiabiangou). In 1965, he joined the Gansu Production and Construction Corps as a volunteer educated youth and worked on a farm, during which time he came into contact with former rightists who had survived hard labor in nearby Jiabiangou: "We rusticated youths already considered ourselves to be at the bottom of society, but these rightists were even below us; the hardships they endured were even deeper and heavier. If you can say that at the time we were on the seventeenth level of hell, then they were on the eighteenth level."[43]

In the late 1990s, remembering his conversations with the survivors and the experience of occasionally finding human bones in the desert, Yang Xianhui (who had by this time moved to Tianjin) formed the project of writing a book about Jiabiangou and began to interview people he knew in Gansu: "It was all a personal initiative; I had no support. Since this was a 'forbidden area,' if the local government found out, they might well have kicked me out. There was no chance at all of getting near the archives. The people I interviewed were all contacted through unofficial [*minjian*] channels and friends, from one to another. For *Chronicles of Jiabiangou* [*Jiabiangou jishi*], I interviewed more than one hundred people, of which about sixty or seventy were survivors, the others were relatives."[44]

Most of the rightists sent to Jiabiangou were from various work units in Lanzhou and the surrounding area; few of them would have considered themselves elite intellectuals and certainly not members of an organized movement to harm the party. They were "intellectuals," but only in the Maoist sense: people who did not work with their hands (workers or peasants); many of them simply carried out menial administrative tasks in the bureaucracy. The emphasis in commemorating the victims of Jiabiangou was therefore on reversing the impression that rightists were elite intellectuals who had to be sacrificed to build a more equal society.

For this reason, Yang Xianhui's focus is on the techniques of dehumanization applied in Jiabiangou to ordinary people from all walks of life and the generalized moral collapse that these techniques entailed in China's society at large, rather than on the persecution of a small elite.[45] His lightly fictionalized interviews were serialized by the journal *Shanghai Literature* (*Shanghai Wenxue* 上海文學) beginning in 2000 and then published in book form, which went through three prints of respectively ten thousand, twenty thousand, and sixty thousand copies, although permission to reprint was withheld between 2005 and 2008, and the book, as well as two of Yang's other works, was reportedly removed from bookstores and electronic databases in July 2017.[46]

The director Wang Bing 王兵 read Yang Xianhui's book, took an intense interest in it, purchased the film rights, and set out to interview the same set of survivors with the idea of making a Chinese version of Claude Lanzmann's documentary *Shoah* (1985), a comprehensive montage of interviews of survivors and perpetrators of the Anti-Rightist Movement.[47] One of these interviews became a stand-alone documentary, *He Fengming* (和鳳鳴, 2007), but the larger project was not completed until 2018 under the title *Dead Souls* (*Si linghun* 死靈魂). Wang Bing then decided to make a feature film, *The Ditch* (*Jiabiangou* 夾邊溝, 2010), in which several story lines from Yang Xianhui's narratives are woven together to produce a single dramatized account.[48] Although Wang Bing's films may be better known outside China than among the mainstream Chinese audience, the arthouse awards he has won overseas have attuned certain publics to his work, and he enjoys a small but loyal following in China. Most importantly, the name "Jiabiangou" began to appear in the mainstream press in China: in December 2010, which marked the fiftieth anniversary of the closing of the camp, *Southern Metropolis Weekly* (*Nandu Zhoukan* 南都週刊) published a special issue with the cover title "The Rightist Labor Camp: 50 Years," with a photo of the rightist Liu Guangji 劉光基. The editorial references Yang Xianhui and comments that "this historical episode should not be forgotten." Several articles by a special reporter sent to Gansu discuss the cases of Chen Zonghai 陳宗海, Yu Zhaoyuan 俞兆遠, and Lin Xiling.[49]

Finally, in 2014–2015 Ai Xiaoming devoted almost two years to interviewing the same set of survivors and families of Jiabiangou survivors as well as survivors of other camps in the area, guards and children of guards, and a few former officials, producing a five-episode, 375-minute documentary titled *Jiabiangou Elegy* (*Jiabiangou jishi* 夾邊溝祭事, a homonym of the title of Yang Xianhui's book). Impressive in its vast scope and in situ interviews, the film echoes the themes of previous works devoted to Jiabiangou: the arbitrary attribution of rightist labels ("like lottery tickets," says one survivor); the humiliation and loss of sense of humanity, which results in self-humiliating or ethically questionable acts; and the many instances of cadre abuse and privilege. Asked about their failure to help the inmates, the guards and officials or their descendants recall that no one dared to protest because of the cadres' political control. Only the poorest peasants in the surrounding villages were sometimes willing to help escaped rightists find food or shelter. The long shots of the desert environment strikingly illustrate the inmates' feeling that although Jiabiangou had no walls or fences, it was impossible to escape because there was nowhere to go in such harsh surroundings and in a country entirely controlled by the grid of the registration and work-unit system.

An interesting, previously undocumented episode unearthed by Ai deals with the government's reaction to the reports of mass famine in the camp: the CCP's Northwest Bureau dispatched a senior female official, Minister of Supervision Qian Ying 錢瑛 (1903–1973, known as "Female Judge Bao"), to the camp in October 1960. One of the inmates, Guan Jinwen 關錦文, turned out to be Qian's Long March comrade and immediately took her to see the hundreds of halfway buried corpses. The camp director, not recognizing the official, began striking one of her bodyguards, before falling to his knees and apologizing. Qian subsequently made the decision to free everyone.

The most important aspect of the film, as suggested by the Chinese title, is its engagement with the question of commemorating Jiabiangou. The opening scene is set during Qingming, the Tomb-Sweeping Festival, in 2014, when a group of survivors tries to reach the labor camp to commemorate their dead friends and relatives. The closing scene takes place exactly the same day one year later, when the survivors are again blocked by local police. An informal association of survivors continues to request a public apology, the payment of withheld salaries (adjusted for inflation), and the establishment of a memorial. Some of them have obtained the removal of the rightist label from their personal files, sometimes with compensation or burial fees. But the local government destroyed the stone memorial set up on the site after money was raised through a subscription. As one of the interviewees asks, "Why is burying bones antiparty? Is it so glorious for the party to have bones scattered everywhere?" Ai's film was made in harrowing conditions, and it was no small feat to have completed it at all. Although it obviously cannot be shown publicly in China, the DVD enjoyed a well-publicized launch in Hong Kong in 2016. Ai previously declared that she works for the future: "Recording history is more important than participating in film festivals or considering foreign audiences. . . . [T]he films will be an important source of memory for future civil society."[50] In any case, the issues *Jiabiangou Elegy* raises continue to fuel public discussion, including in the Chinese media. Articles written about it are tweeted, retweeted, erased, and retweeted again.

Jiabiangou remains the most well-known camp, but other labor camps have begun to be discussed in the public sphere. After a memoir was written by the survivor Zhang Xianchi (also mentioned in Qian Liqun's book), several independent documentary films were made about the labor camp in Dabao, Sichuan: Hu Jie's *Book of Gelagu* (*Gelagu zhi shu*, 2013), Xie Yihui's 謝貽卉 *Juvenile Laborers Confined in Dabao* (*Dabao, xiao laojiao* 大堡小勞教, 2013), and Qiu Jiongjiong's 邱炯炯 *Mr. Zhang Believes* (*Chi* 癡, 2015).[51] A full report eventually appeared in the mainstream press, mentioning how former inmates of the camp gather for regular commemorative meetings in both Chengdu and Chongqing.[52]

Over the past twenty years, commemorations of rediscovered victims such as Lin Zhao have served to attract public attention to the Anti-Rightist Movement. This has suggested to the many "ordinary" victims of deportation to labor camps and their descendants that it is possible to publicly commemorate the events of 1957. *Minjian* historians have documented the movement's impact on grassroots employees in administrations or state units. In this way, discussions of the Anti-Rightist Movement and the Reeducation Through Labor Camps associated with it have achieved a previously unthinkable degree of publicness even as they become dissociated from a purely elite form of memory.

DOCUMENTING: ACADEMIC AND AMATEUR HISTORIANS OF THE FAMINE

A second model for unofficial historical activities was the impetus to document forgotten or repressed events in a context in which official archival documents could prove difficult to obtain. Efforts to compile such documentation span a wide spectrum, from groups operating within and on the borders of academia and collecting archives in a classic manner to journalists relying on obscure but published sources and all the way to unofficial groups proceeding mainly through oral history.

One of the first *minjian* historians to pioneer documentation of early PRC history through parallel channels at the boundaries of China's academic system in the early 1990s was Shen Zhihua 沈志華. Coming from a cadre family, Shen was sent down during the Cultural Revolution and almost could not get into a university. When taking the graduate exam to enter the CASS Institute of History, he sought out the president of CASS, the famous hard-liner Deng Liqun 鄧力群, at his home to persuade him. He was admitted, but shortly before defending his dissertation he was arrested for providing confidential documents to a foreign researcher and was imprisoned for two years. Upon his release in 1985, his bridges to academia burned, he headed south to Shenzhen and later to Guangzhou and made a fortune in the gold trade, which allowed him to return to research with fewer constraints. In the early 1990s, he took advantage of the opening of the Soviet archives to put together a research project in cooperation with CASS that lasted from 1996 to 2002: he provided all the funding (more than one million yuan), and CASS provided the paperwork. This agreement was essential because, lacking a work unit, Shen could not even obtain a passport. Hiring Russian historians in Moscow for easier access to the archive, they brought back a great number of archival documents, which Shen made available to other historians in China.[53] After teaching as an adjunct at PKU for several years, Shen was eventually hired at East China Normal University, where he established the Center for Cold War International History Studies with several other critical historians, such as Yang Kuisong. Cao Shuji 曹樹基 at Shanghai Jiaotong University was another like-minded researcher who pioneered work on the famine.[54] For these maverick academics, using documents gathered outside the official framework became a way to assert an identity as *minjian* historians.

Both Shen and Yang have published a series of revisionist works questioning established versions of sensitive episodes in PRC history. They also use the media to publicize their findings.[55] On the sixtieth anniversary of the Korean War Armistice in 2013, Shen gave a number of public lectures based on his research on the outbreak of the Korean War and Mao's decision to send troops across the Yalu River in October 1950.[56] When Wang Hui published an essay in December 2013 arguing that the Korean War was an extension of Mao's "People's War" for justice and revolution, provoked by the surprise attack of U.S. and United Nations forces,[57] Yang Kuisong wrote a long rebuttal. Finding many historical errors in Wang's essay, Yang concentrated his own argument on his professional standards as a historian and described Wang's essay as "history led by theory [*yi lun dai shi* 以論帶史]." He was particularly critical of Wang's equation of the "People's War" with the idea of an ideological war, pointing out that the "People's War" strategy originally referred to the CCP's return to a more moderate United Front strategy and a break with the ideological extremism of the Jiangxi Soviet. He concluded: "Today, any scholar who wants to develop his political debating skills and wants to take history as evidence, should please start by carefully reading some history books; concerning CCP history, the most basic requirement is to understand the essays in *Mao's Selected Works*."[58] His key arguments were therefore about professional standards and emphasizing empirical evidence over "big" theories. Yang further underscored this point in an essay published shortly thereafter in which he criticized Wang Hui's notion of "depoliticization" as predicated on the theoretical framework of class struggle. In contrast with his first essay, Yang explicitly pointed out that in this essay he was offering a personal opinion, not writing from a "professional standpoint."[59] In this debate, for Yang Kuisong, professional ethics required a clear separation between clarifying historical events and making a political argument.

Another example of unofficial work from inside academia is the Nanjing historian Gao Hua 高華 (1954–2011), whose seven-hundred-page study of the Rectification Movement in Yan'an, *How the Red Sun Rose*, became a best seller. Going back even before the idealized 1950s, it sets out to describe the CCP's "totalitarian roots," which prepared the ground for the Anti-Rightist Movement and other political campaigns. As David Chang points out in a review of the book, Gao Hua effectively combines systematic use of a broad spectrum of published sources with an analysis borrowing concepts from traditional Chinese historiography, making his book extremely readable to the Chinese public. This book's huge print run, far beyond the scope of academic works of history published by a university press and indeed far beyond the readership of Hong Kong, suggests that parallel channels of distribution into the mainland were active.[60] In public speeches, Gao Hua emphasized that rectification movements on the model of the Yan'an Rectification Movement became a structural element of the party's political strategy, questioning the exceptionality of the Cultural Revolution.[61]

Until the early 2000s, the deadly famine of 1959–1961, though acknowledged in official history, was widely attributed to the "Three Years of Natural Disasters" as well as to "diplomatic" factors: the need for the PRC to reimburse debts to the Soviet Union in the context of rising tensions. As Susanne Weigelin-Schwiedrzik has pointed out, the fact that an overwhelming majority of the tens of millions of victims were poor peasants in remote villages, isolated by rigid administrative controls as well as by their lack of access to any public forum, certainly contributed to a lack of challenges to this view among intellectuals.[62] In the early 2000s, interest in the famine steadily increased, due especially to the tireless energy of Yang Jisheng (b. 1940), another *minjian* intellectual. As a former Xinhua journalist since 1964, Yang was an official; however, retirement in 1996 freed him from previous restrictions, and his former status gave him access to precious documents and archives. Although his father died of hunger in the famine, he had continued to believe the official narrative unquestioningly until after 1989. Now, as a member of the editorial board of *Yanhuang Chunqiu* 炎黃春秋 (Annals of the Yellow Emperor or Through the ages), he wrote and edited a steady flow of articles questioning the official account, while carrying out his own unofficial research, gathering party reports prepared by subaltern cadres, internal documents, unpublished memoirs, and oral testimony, and eventually publishing the monumental study *Tombstone* in Hong Kong in 2008, which achieved unprecedented circulation within China.[63]

Other initiatives followed. The rediscovery of the journal *Spark* around 2008 brought to light the writings of the earliest critics of the Great Leap policies. Yan Lianke's novel *The Four Books* (2010) probed the responsibility of intellectuals in sustaining the system that allowed the famine to take place.[64] Yu Hua published an essay in the *New York Times* in 2014 calling on the CCP to apologize.[65] The Folk

Memory Project, initiated in 2010 by Wu Wenguang and a group of young documentary film directors, carried out a great range of oral history interviews with rural witnesses of the famine. The Tsinghua University sociologist Guo Yuhua's decade-long research on a northern Shaanxi village during collectivization, although not focused directly on the famine, brought important theoretical notions into the discussion. All these texts had a significant impact on the Internet and trickled down through the commercial media, shifting mainstream discourse on the famine over the course of a decade.

Tombstone

The greatest impact on the mainstream understanding of the famine was undoubtedly achieved by *Tombstone*,[66] the result of a decade of archival and oral history research. The unofficial or "amateur" nature, in the noblest sense, of Yang Jisheng's enterprise is immediately apparent and even claimed by the author in an interview:

> Traditional historians face restrictions. First of all, they censor themselves. Their thoughts limit them. They don't even dare to write the facts, don't dare to speak up about it, don't dare to touch it. And even if they wrote it, they can't publish it. And if they publish, they will face censure. So mainstream scholars face those restrictions. But there are many unofficial historians like me. Many people are writing their own memoirs about being labeled "rightists" or "counter-revolutionaries." There is an author in Anhui province who has described how his family starved to death. There are many authors who have written about how their families starved.[67]

The position of the author as "unofficial" (*minjian*) is reflected in Yang's lack of concern with methodology. The book is organized as a massive compilation of evidence rather than as a historical narrative and alternates between thematic and geographical studies, with not a few repetitions between them. The introduction clearly situates the book as an intervention in the public sphere rather than as a disinterested work of historiography: "The basic reason why tens of millions of people in China starved to death was totalitarianism."[68]

Yang argues that under Mao dehumanization and violence made each member of the system into a two-faced Janus: "Regardless of what kind of person went into the totalitarian system, all came out as conjoined twins facing in opposite directions: either despot or slave, depending on their position respective to those above or below them." Contrary to egalitarian ideals, the nature of the totalitarian system is strongly hierarchical: unthinkingly obeying leaders and violently bullying subordinates are its rules. Therefore, all members of society are both victims and perpetrators, innocent and guilty. "Old cadres from Xinyang told me: 'If you didn't beat others, you would be beaten. The more harshly you beat someone, the more firmly you established your position and your loyalty to the Communist Party. If you didn't beat others, you were a right deviationist and would soon be beaten by others.'"[69] Working according to his *minjian* method, Yang compiled many internal reports, personal memoirs, and documents that attest to both mass mortality and violence.

Southern People Weekly, a widely read liberal weekly, published a special issue in May 2012 with the title "The Great Famine" and an eloquent graph of production statistics for the years 1959–1961 on the cover. The lead editorial article is titled "Commemorating the Famine with Sincerity and a Moral Conscience"[70] and is backed up by four in-depth investigative articles. A witness of the famine in Guangshan County (Henan) was able to set up a commemorative stele in his village in 2004. A young village writer from Niuzhai (Fuyang County, Anhui), Niu Ben 牛犇, published a book based on oral history and local archives of the famine (*An Oral Record of the Great Famine* [*Dajihuang koushu shilu*, 2011]). A reporter interviews eighty-two-year-old Li Shengzhao 李盛照, a rightist from Sichuan University who for years wrote reports and petitions about the famine.[71] Finally, an interview with Liao Bokang 廖伯康, a former Chongqing Party secretary, explains how he reported the famine in Sichuan to Yang Shangkun 楊尚昆 in 1962 but was attacked by local party members and sentenced to two decades in labor camp. The most remarkable aspect of the whole report is that the official designation "Three Years of Natural Disasters" is no longer used at all and systematically replaced with "the Great Famine."[72] Although Yang's study is not directly referenced, its influence on the issue is obvious, showcasing the interplay between marginal publications and the mainstream public sphere, or the "centripetal" mechanism by which certain discussions find their way from specialized or overseas venues to the mainstream media on the mainland.

This issue of *Southern People Weekly* is perhaps the most critical account published to date in the mainstream media in China, and its circumstances deserve further elucidation. It was published a few months after Bo Xilai 薄熙來, who had tried to revive Maoist politics in Chongqing in an attempt to increase his chances to take a top party position in the Party Congress of 2012, was detained and accused of corruption in March 2012. Bo's supporters tried to drum up support by attacking Yang Jisheng and other critics of the famine on social media. On April 29, 2012, Lin Zhibo 林治波, the head of *People's Daily* Gansu Bureau, used his verified Weibo account (with 230,000 followers) to question the death toll of the famine between 1960 and 1962, denouncing a plot "to defile Chairman Mao by utilizing the exaggerated slander of millions of people dying of starvation."[73] This comment resulted in a protracted controversy that was allowed to play out on social media, in which many users posted about their own family history of the famine, and the issue generally received attention. The *Southern People Weekly* story was probably a reaction to this controversy, which was allowed to be published (in Guangdong, governed by Bo's rival Wang Yang 汪洋) to further discredit Bo Xilai's Maoist politics ahead of the Eighteenth Congress. In November of the same year, just after the Congress, the film director Feng Xiaogang 馮小剛 skillfully wove allusions to the Great Famine of 1959–1961 into his film *Back to 1942* (*1942*, 2012), adapted from a novella by Liu Zhenyun dedicated to the famine during the war: this can be seen as a typical example of a "hidden transcript."[74]

Although *Tombstone* was not directly or officially available in China, it received considerable attention there. Writing in a Hong Kong journal, the CASS philosopher Xu Youyu compared it to Aleksandr Solzhenitsyn's *Gulag Archipelago* (1973).[75] Yang's introduction, with its designation of the "totalitarian system" as the main cause of the famine, was widely posted on the Internet. Attention was further sparked by an academic controversy that played out in journals and online. Yang's calculation of the number of famine victims was challenged by the Marxist mathematician Sun Jingxian 孫經先 in *Chinese Social Sciences Today* (*Zhongguo Shehui Kexuebao* 中國社會科學報, September 2013), to which Yang published a long rebuttal in *Yanhuang Chunqiu* in December.[76] The two sparred in person at an academic conference convened in Wuhan in July 2014 at the invitation of He Xuefeng 賀雪峰, where Yang again gave detailed replies to Sun's critiques, but Sun subsequently tried to distort the gist of the discussion that had taken place.[77] The conference was widely discussed online and on WeChat, with the effect of drawing more readers' attention to *Tombstone*. Hong Zhenkuai 洪振快, another *minjian* historian writing for *Yanhuang Chunqiu* also subsequently sparred with Sun in the journal.[78] This mechanism illustrates the parallel channels by which works such as *Tombstone*, backed by a well-established publisher in Hong Kong, circulate among publics in China despite being banned. As Yang Jisheng noted in 2016 in a speech that had to be read for him at a prize-awarding ceremony he could not attend, "Pirated editions of *Tombstone* are being sold from the hinterlands of the Central Plains to the Yunnan-Guizhou Plateau to the Xinjiang frontier. I've received letters from all over China expressing their fervent and unwavering support. This shows the power of truth to break through bronze walls and iron ramparts constructed by the government."[79] *Tombstone*'s success in mainland China also showcases the centripetal mechanisms at work in China's embryonic public sphere.

The Folk Memory Project

Most of the previously mentioned projects are individual ones; by contrast, the Folk Memory Project stands out as a unique collective enterprise. Wu Wenguang, who made the first independent film on the Cultural Revolution in 1992, and his partner, the dancer Wen Hui 文慧, set up a new production base in Caochangdi art district northeast of Beijing in 2004, where they were able to enjoy for ten years the rent-free use of half a modern compound (designed by Ai Weiwei, whose studio was nearby) that had been leased by friends. From this position, Wu undertook several participative documentary film projects, including the China Village Documentary Project, which provided villagers with cameras and training to make films about issues they deemed relevant to their lives (the director Jia Zhitan 賈之坦 joined Wu's group in this manner and continued to work with him on the memory project).[80]

The Folk Memory Project (Wu's own English translation) includes the word *minjian* in its Chinese name: Minjian Jiyi Jihua 民間記憶計畫. After some exploratory work in 2009, it began concrete operations in 2010. Conceived as a participatory project, it assembled a core team of young artists in residence at the Caochangdi workstation, whose living and working costs as well as a small stipend were covered by the project. These core members included Zhang Mengqi 章夢奇, Luo Bing 羅兵, Shu Qiao 舒僑, Zou Xueping 鄒雪平, Li Xinmin 李新民, Wang Hai'an 王海安, and Guo Rui 郭睿, each of them bringing a different background and angle to the project. Most of them were recent graduates from (or students initially still enrolled in) art schools, in particular from Tianjin Academy of Fine Arts, where Wu taught every year.[81] However, Zhang Mengqi was trained as a dancer, Guo Rui was a history graduate, and Li Xinmin had come to

Beijing as a migrant worker to help with cleaning and cooking in Caochangdi but became interested in the project and decided to join. The social diversity illustrates the nonelite nature of the project. There were also more sporadic participants. Overall, "as of early 2014, more than 130 individuals had participated at various times, carrying out interviews with more than 1,000 elderly people in 19 provinces and more than 200 villages. These interviews, images and texts are now being transcribed and placed on the Folk Memory Project Blog to become part of a future Memory Archive."[82]

The project was initially devoted to hunger and the "collective eating" in the People's Commune canteens; most of the participants had no prior knowledge of the Great Famine, apart from the standard propaganda version taught in schools:

> The young people who set out to track down these "hunger memories" 50 years later, like the "standard youth" of this era, have been constrained by official textbooks to a macro-environment of "turning their backs on history and only looking forward." The vast majority of them were not only completely cut off from the "hunger history," but had almost no knowledge of China's true history during the 30 years following 1949. The pallidness and poverty of historical memory and a sense of uncertainty and confusion in the present have created a "spiritual hunger," and this group of people set off on their journeys in hopes of satisfying this hunger. This Hunger Project was the first phase of what one year later came to be known as the Folk Memory Project.[83]

After a period of collective discussion and research, the notion of "folk memory" (*minjian* memory) was identified as the project's main focus, and it was decided that each participant would set out to a village where he or she had family connections:

> Their initial move after returning to their villages was to open the "first door of memory" by recording old people's memories of the three-year famine. These elderly villagers, ever the "insignificant" and the "most voiceless," had always maintained their silence, no matter how tragic and painful their lives—in the past as well as the present. For this reason, history as they experienced it was likewise unspoken and blank. The returnees were therefore returning to the unspoken and blank, to the ordinary, and to common knowledge. Another

> important point was that returning to the villages in this way was not merely for the purpose of documentary production or a one-time "material-gathering safari" or "helicopter-style field investigation" with "withdrawal upon achieving the objective"; it was a process of planting their feet firmly on the ground, taking in the local essence, engaging in creation at the same time as participation, and combining their understanding of society with self-transformation. It was not only the documentary that was the work of art; the creator himself or herself was also a work in a constant state of self-training and self-molding. This was an encounter. In their search for elderly people with long-submerged histories, these young people had to bridge the ignorance of their parents' generation regarding the Great Famine. This meeting of grandparents and grandchildren spanned the mnemonic void of an entire generation.[84]

The aim of the project was somehow to cut through the many layers of contending discourses about the famine or obscuring the famine by returning to the grass roots ("common knowledge"), not as intellectuals who were instructing the people or even as intellectuals collecting evidence to rewrite the history of ordinary people for their own (political or career) purposes ("material-gathering safari"), but rather as participants in a collaborative project that aimed to reestablish a firsthand connection with China's rural history and thus to overcome the daunting barrier between urban elites and villagers erected by China's household registration (*hukou*) system. In this manner, investigating the famine also led back to the present: some villages remained in terrible poverty, whereas in other cases the relative improvement in economic conditions made the villagers unwilling to talk about bygone times of lack and suffering.

For this reason, the project encompasses four distinct aspects: in addition to collecting data (recording interviews, transcribing them, and publishing them on the project website or other venues) and documenting the witnesses of the famine, participants also used documentary films to question their own position with respect to village life and history and regularly staged theater and dance performances to reenact important moments they encountered in their fieldwork. They were often drawn into debates with villagers about the advisability of making documentary films about the famine, had to persuade villagers to talk to them, but also developed concrete projects that would have an impact on villagers' lives so as to "give back" something to the villages. The first such project was raising money to set up commemorative steles engraved with the names of those who died during the famine as well as collecting and double-checking their names and identity. Fieldwork further revealed that many villages had few working-age people, with old people and children making up a majority of the population. The second project therefore consisted in setting up a welfare fund for the elderly survivors, who sometimes had no one to rely one, and the third project was concerned with setting up reading rooms or small libraries for the children.

Some participants, such as Zhang Mengqi and Zou Xueping, made films every year, shooting footage over several months around the Chinese New Year, editing in Caochangdi in the spring and summer, and holding screenings, performances, and discussions in the fall. Workshops at Caochangdi were always well attended; in addition, several of the films from the project were screened in film festivals in China as well as overseas or in other venues.[85] Some participants took the topic of yearly activities (steles, libraries, care of the elderly) as the main theme for their films. Others devoted their research to a single topic; for instance, Luo Bing discovered that one of his neighbors in his village in Hunan, Ren Dingqi 任定其, had written a critical memoir of his life dating back to the foundation of the PRC in 1949. Luo's films retrace the process of slowly gaining the elderly man's confidence and helping him edit and publish the manuscript.[86] The unofficial and grassroots nature of the project is clearly illustrated in Luo Bing's method: just as *Spark* published an essay by a villager in 1960, he tried to bridge the gap between the "village intellectual" and the public realm.

Crucial to the spirit of the project was the unofficial but also entirely non-commercial nature of the Caochangdi collective and the work its members carried out. Freed from the burden of rent, they were able to cover daily expenses through income from screenings and performances as well as some grants. In this sense, they formed a kind of grassroots utopian community, shielded from both the control of the state (although their website was briefly closed down, they remained largely under the state's radar) and the commercialization of Chinese society. In August 2014, the ten-year lease of the Caochangdi premises came to an end, and the owners dramatically increased the rent, forcing the tenants to take back the half of the compound occupied by the workstation and sublet it for money. Wu Wenguang moved to Qinjiatun in the far northern suburbs, and other participants decided to stay closer to the center of Beijing and face the reality of making a living. However, to date, the project continues.

Minjian *Sociology*

At the same time as Caochangdi was established, some oral history projects were initiated in an academic setting. Despite this more formal context, they can nonetheless be understood as being carried out from a *minjian* standpoint. In the late 1990s and early 2000s, the Tsinghua University sociology professor Guo Yuhua began carrying out ethnographic investigations in a village in northern Shaanxi (which she calls Jicun 冀村). Guo's work deals with the entire period of land reform and collectivization, as well as touching upon the famine. Her project, highlighting the role of female *minjian* intellectuals, uses a gender perspective to challenge established methodologies. Women's memories of the Mao era and the Great Famine have become a subfield of study in their own right.[87] As in previous cases, although the full version of her study was published only in Hong Kong, several chapters were published in mainland journals as well as in a collection of articles published in China,[88] making her research available to fellow academics and drawing their attention to the book that was available in Hong Kong. Guo also discusses her research in events for the general public.[89]

To establish her own position, Guo relies on a strong theoretical framework that borrows from Gayatri Spivak and other South Asia scholars' "subaltern studies" and James Scott's concepts of "weapons of the weak" and "seeing like a state." In fact, she published an article in *Dushu* in 2002 introducing two of Scott's works that had not been translated into Chinese at the time, tying them in closely with her own work, as the title suggests: "*Weapons of the Weak* and *Hidden Transcripts*: A Subaltern [*Diceng*] Viewpoint of Peasant Resistance."[90] In the book she eventually published in 2013, she returns at length to the notion of subaltern, tracing it back to Gramsci and the notion of cultural hegemony. She argues that to rescue the anonymous masses from forgetting, the only method is to write a "counter-history" based on "body memory."[91] In his preface to the book, Sun Liping 孫立平 echoes this argument: "Writing subaltern history [*diceng lishi* 底層歷史] and the process of reconstructing history are a dialogical process of speaking and listening, understanding and reflecting, explaining and re-explaining."[92] Oral history is therefore not meant to supplement the gaps of history, but to open a space for autonomous narration by peasants excluded from history: as Guo Yuhua puts it, "making history from the everyday life of common people," or "providing a systematic folk transcript [*tigong yitao xitong de minjian wenben* 提供一套系統的民間文本]." Guo Yuhua concludes her introductory chapter by quoting Wang

Xiaobo's essay "The Silent Majority" and adding, "Oral history is precisely the voice of the silent majority; it is a bottom-up history of those groups that have been marginalized by historical records."[93]

No one died of starvation in Jicun during the Great Leap because, ironically, the government didn't try to extract grain from a poor mountain area, but people did suffer from edema. In the chapter devoted specifically to the years of the Great Famine, Guo collects several narratives demonstrating that the peasants clearly connected the People's Communes system with the famine. One interviewee exclaims, "If they had collectivized us for a few more years, there would have been nobody left! Another few years and we would have f—— starved to death, really."[94] In her conclusion to this chapter, Guo points out that the People's Communes were a utopia conceived by intellectuals and imposed on peasants who were not given a choice:

> After the dust settles on the Great Leap Forward and the People's Communes, what is really worth thinking about is . . . why [a beautiful utopia] brought only deep suffering and extreme disaster to the peasants?. . . The idea of collectivization originated in the cities and not in the villages; it was "seeing like a state" and not seeing like a peasant; the peasants never had their own subjectivity [*zhuti diwei* 主體地位]. The great unification under the People's Communes provoked a catastrophic destruction of the pluralism in society; just as Scott pointed out in *Seeing Like a State*, when the state reorganizes village life and completely changes the production model from the top downward, this is usually described as a process of civilization. I would rather call it . . . *social gardening* [in English].[95]

It is precisely because the large-scale "modernization" projects led by the state, with the support of many intellectuals influenced by Marxism, had such deadly consequences that it is important to view the historical events of the early Mao period from a *minjian* rather than an elite perspective. In this sense, Guo's conclusion is similar to that of the *Spark* writers.

DEBATING: SEMIOFFICIAL AND UNOFFICIAL JOURNALS

An important development in the early 2000s was the growth of unofficial journals devoted to the history of the Mao era. Most of these journals were run as volunteer associations by a few dedicated retired scholars; technical expenses and production costs were reduced to a minimum. They took a collaborative attitude toward the elaboration of historical knowledge, soliciting research manuscripts from readers as well as reactions to published articles.[96]

The first journals devoted to unofficial history were in fact not unofficial but can be described as "semiofficial." Semi-independent journals had already played an important part in the early 1990s: *Orient* was shut down after publishing a special issue on the thirtieth anniversary of the Cultural Revolution in 1996. *Yanhuang Chunqiu*, established shortly after the Tiananmen crackdown in 1991 by reformist officials inside the system who were determined to keep the flame of political reforms alive, benefited from support from both the military (General Xiao Ke and General Zhang Aiping 張愛萍) and the press and publication bureaucracy, which allowed the editors to take over the serial number of a defunct publication. Former editor Wu Si 吳思 describes the journal's unique status as follows: "In short, *Yanhuang Chunqiu* was both a publication of a state-owned unit and the journal of a private association; it was both a private publication and a circle publication [*tongren kanwu* 同仁刊物]. This makes it unique and impossible to classify; in other words, it resembled neither a work unit nor a company, neither a state-run company nor a privately run company."[97] The opening issue ran a critical piece on Mao Zedong by Li Rui 李銳, who had the personal protection of Xiao Ke. The journal also repeatedly commemorated Hu Yaobang 胡耀邦 (1915–1989) and pushed back against the Propaganda Department's attempts to curtail discussion of his ideas.[98]

Although the early issues of *Yanhuang Chunqiu* were devoted mainly to political debates, historical research gradually became a core concern. In 2014, liberal elder Zi Zhongyun published a programmatic article in which she called for a radical break with the format of dynastic history writing, which is always prone to political instrumentalization, and for an embrace of *minjian yeshi* 民間野史 (unofficial history) that focuses on the "people" (*min*) rather than on the party in power.[99] As mentioned earlier, under Wu Si's chief editorship, Yang Jisheng (a member of the editorial committee) published early results of his research on the Great Famine in the journal and sparred with famine deniers, which boosted sales; the journal even established a special column called "Records of Contention" ("Zhengming lu" 爭鳴錄). At its most successful, in 2014, *Yanhuang Chunqiu* reached a print run of almost two hundred thousand copies (of which about two-thirds were sent to subscribers) and 11 million followers on social media, through partnerships with all the major portals.[100] It remained inexpensive and simple (ending at ten yuan an issue in 2016) as well as easily accessible, with a number of articles posted for free on the journal's website. Until the journal was purged and effectively silenced in 2016, it played a central role as an interface between *minjian* historians and other critics and the mainstream media.

Another important pioneer was *Old Photos* (*Lao Zhaopian* 老照片), established in 1996, the year of the thirtieth anniversary of the Cultural Revolution, at Shandong Pictorial Press as a "journal published as a book [*yi shu dai kan* 以書代刊]" and originally sold for six yuan an issue (it is currently sold for twenty yuan). It was this journal that published early versions of Zhang Yihe's family memoir. One of the editors, Ding Dong 丁東 (a *minjian* historian who has taught in Shanxi for most of his career), notes that, in addition to features on some symbolic personalities (Zhang Naiqi 章乃器, Hu Yaobang for his ninetieth birthday, Lin Zhao, Yu Luoke 遇羅克, and others), the journal features material devoted to ordinary people:

> I valued memories of the common people, opening a dialogue with official history. In *Lao Zhaopian*, a large percentage of articles dealt with unknown people's recollections of the past, accompanied by their private photos, and this has become a distinctive feature of our journal. In general, common people seldom have the opportunity to record their memories, or to turn these memories into words and publicize them. But once these words and photos are publicized, they become history. From these private stories, readers find out that those who bring about tragic events are not always buffoons, nor are those who bring about happy events always heroes.[101]

Old Photos continues to publish on a monthly basis and to enjoy a stable circulation, drawing spontaneous contributions of photos and accompanying articles from its readers. In this way, individual, ordinary memories of everyday life can be discussed in a larger public forum.[102]

In the late 2000s, these semiofficial book-magazines were joined by a set of unofficial journals. Compiled as simple electronic files (usually Word or pdf files) and posted on the Internet or circulated by email, these journals have no registration and are provided for free to their readers. *Wangshi Weihen* 往事微痕 (Tiny scars of the past) was established on July 10, 2008, in Chengdu by Tie Liu 鐵流, a retired *Sichuan Daily* (*Sichuan Ribao* 四川日報) journalist, and circulated to former rightists in Chengdu, at first by post and then from 2011 electronically until it stopped being published when Tie Liu was detained in September 2014 and sentenced in February 2015 (at the age of eighty-one).[103] *Remembrance* was set up in September 2008 in Beijing by retired film scholar Wu Di 吳迪 (under the pen-name "Qizhi 啟之," the Enlightener) and He Shu 何蜀, the former deputy editor of a party history journal in Chongqing.[104] In 2012, He Shu left *Remembrance* to set up *Yesterday* (*Zuotian* 昨天) in Chongqing, with similar goals. Both journals more or less specialized on the Cultural Revolution. *Hei Wu Lei Yijiu* 黑五類憶舊 (Remembering the five black categories), edited by PKU journalism professor Jiao Guobiao 焦國標 (using a title calligraphy first by Xin Ziling 辛子陵, then by Mao Yushi 茅于軾), was published for about a year in 2010–2011 before Jiao was briefly detained and put under residential surveillance in 2012. Finally, the website Minjian History, established by the University Services Center for China Studies at the Chinese University of Hong Kong, also served as a forum that allowed many people to contribute and debate.[105]

In its first issue, *Remembrance*, defined as a "self-published, nonprofit, occasional electronic journal [*ziban de budingqi, feiyingli de dianzi kanwu* 自辦的不定期，非營利的電子刊物]," sets as its main task to change the anomalous situation whereby Cultural Revolution research takes place mainly overseas, and it follows the motto "Collect research results, offer academic news, establish a platform for exchange, encourage Cultural Revolution research." It vows to publish academic research; memoirs and oral history; original journals, letters, and other documents; and book reviews on the Cultural Revolution. The inaugural issue was a tribute to the historian Wang Nianyi 王年一 (1932–2007), author of *The Age of the Great Turmoil*, on the first anniversary of his death: he is eulogized in an article titled "From Official to *Minjian*—Wang Nianyi's Path and Its Meaning."[106] After a year of monthly publications, *Remembrance* began to be published bimonthly in 2009 because of the buildup of contributions, before returning to a once-a-month publication in 2011. When He Shu pulled out at the end of 2011, he was replaced by Dai Huang's daughter, Dai Weiwei.

Looking back on the first few years of *Remembrance*, Wu Di underlines in an essay addressed to his readers that not only is the journal run entirely by volunteers, but as the editor he often had to spend his personal money to invite contributors to meals, photocopy documents, and send books around: "*Remembrance*'s greatest expenses are to support *minjian* Cultural Revolution researchers and archivists—for example, when last July Tsinghua University held a conference, *Remembrance* paid the travel expenses for *minjian* participants, several thousand yuan. . . . [I explained to Mr. Zhang Qinglin 張清林 that] *Remembrance* is not a business, nor is it an organization, just one or two idle people who volunteer. Costs are very low, apart from [making] photocopies, sending documents, and buying some books."[107] Dai Weiwei not only is not paid for her work on *Remembrance* but has also spent her own money on subsidizing samizdat publications and collecting Cultural Revolution journals. Furthermore, the journal will not accept donations from overseas.

Wu Di sums up his argument:

> For these reasons, I define *Remembrance* as follows: it is a small-circulation publication, intended for ordinary [*minjian*] people, young people, colleagues [*tongren* 同仁; amateur researchers], not a nonprofit work unit that "serves the people." It is a platform for independent speech, not a charity that offers free archives. We don't pay but still require high-quality manuscripts. We voluntarily put up money and efforts, but we don't feel entitled to occupy the moral high ground for this reason, nor will we demand of anyone to show interest in the Cultural Revolution. We hope that more people can participate but don't demand that anyone reads *Remembrance*; even less do we count on foreign celebrities or domestic grand masters to do us the honor of contributing manuscripts.[108]

The essay "From the Chief Editor of *Remembrance* to Readers" makes several important points. First, it provides an empirical definition of Wu Di's work as a *minjian* intellectual: those who write for *Remembrance* are not part of the state system, nor do they use the leverage offered by a commercial publication to advance their agendas; rather, they choose a third road that is neither the market nor the state. Second, taking a cue from Wang Xiaobo's critique of intellectuals, Wu Di refuses to occupy the moral high ground: remembering the Cultural Revolution is not "better" than what others do or a moral obligation for everyone. He has no patience for "academic stars" and their unreasonable requirements (here he is referring to a controversy that took place between *Remembrance* and the Chicago scholar Wang Youqin 王友琴, to which Wu Di devotes a subsequent section of his essay). Finally, the journal follows only professional ethics: "*Remembrance* is a scholarly platform, any rationally argued article can be published. Otherwise, why would we have specified from the beginning that the articles published in the journal do not reflect the editors' viewpoint?"[109]

This comment was made in response to Wang Youqin and others who reproached the editors for publishing former Red Guard Song Binbin's 宋彬彬 article in one of the three special issues devoted to Beijing Normal University Girls School and the death of Bian Zhongyun.[110] In any case, these debates drew increased attention to the case of Bian's death, as did Hu Jie's documentary *Although I Am Gone*.[111]

Remembrance, too, has faced growing pressure from the authorities. Wu Di notes in this same article that the journal has had to make compromises: "In order to survive, *Remembrance* has reduced the number of people on its mailing list; it no longer convenes academic conferences and has turned down an offer to work with a foreign university to jointly publish a book."[112] In particular, as the state has stepped up regulation of the Internet, it has increasingly cracked down on mass emails, criminalizing certain types of messages if they are sent to more than five hundred addressees.[113] As Wu Di points out, *Remembrance* continues to publish books (on the Lin Biao affair, on the history of Tsinghua University) and continues to be archived overseas, in libraries, and on specialized websites (such as prchistory.org), so in this sense it has already made a great contribution. But no issues published after the end of December 2016 seem to be in public circulation.

In his introduction to *Hei Wu Lei Yijiu*, an online journal that printed collections of short narratives commemorating people who had been "labeled" in some way by the state, Jiao Guobiao provides an interesting definition of *minjian*. He begins by enumerating the five categories used under Mao—landlords, rich peasants, counterrevolutionaries, bad elements, and rightists (*di, fu, fan, huai, you* 地富反壞右):

> In theory, these are the five black categories. In reality, their children are also members of the five black categories. According to official statistics, China had 20 million "4-type elements," and half a million of the "fifth category" (rightists). Researchers conclude that the generation of children and grandchildren represent five or six times the original number, so that the total number of people affected by the five black categories is more than 100 million, about 15 percent of the population at the time. But not only their direct descendants were targeted. [If we count all types of family connections], people involved with the five black categories are not just 100 million, [but] up to half of Chinese citizens may be "tainted." President Hu Jintao's father . . . was a bad element. . . . Vice President Xi Jinping's 習近平 father was a counterrevolutionary. Former premier Zhu Rongji was a rightist. . . . The

> five black categories were the scapegoats for the entire Chinese people, a coming-of-age sacrifice for China to become adult; they have taken up the cross for the entire Chinese people. Thank you, Hei Wu Lei![114]

This approach strikingly echoes Wang Xiaobo's argument about the "silent majority." For many years, the significance of the victims of Mao's campaigns has been minimized in official discourse because it was claimed that these victims represent just a small number of groups, who previously enjoyed undue privileges. Jiao points out, however, that in fact almost everyone in China was potentially vulnerable to being labeled as somehow involved with these groups or even with a single member of these groups. To make his point, he even includes short pieces by real estate tycoon Pan Shiyi 潘石屹 and then vice president Xi Jinping about family members who became "black elements." The realm of *minjian* and the realm of the "five black categories" end up overlapping.

The fiftieth anniversary of the Cultural Revolution in 2016 marked an important moment of unofficial historical debate but also provoked a pushback from the authorities. Although practically no official commemorations took place, discussions were active in various *minjian* venues. There had been a considerable buildup of public apologies from former Red Guards and others guilty of violence during the Cultural Revolution, which played out largely in the pages of *Yanhuang Chunqiu*.[115] A special column "Record of Confessions" ("Chanhui lu" 懺悔錄) was set up that published a little more than twenty articles between 2008 and 2016. In an article published in 2012 in a special issue of *Remembrance* devoted to the events of August 5, 1966, Song Binbin offered her "reflections and apologies."[116] This article was followed by considerable criticism of her sincerity and a long controversy involving several respected scholars, including Wang Youqin. However, these apologies from former Cultural Revolution elites were possible only because of the existence of *minjian* publications. They peaked in a brief episode when several children of important leaders made public appearances to apologize in late 2013 and early 2014, including Chen Yi's 陳毅 son Chen Xiaolu 陳小魯 and Song Binbin. After a brief flare-up in the media, further discussion was actively discouraged.

Already under considerable pressure since Wu Si had resigned as chief editor in 2014, *Yanhuang Chunqiu* published a series of articles in the spring of 2016 to commemorate the Cultural Revolution anniversary, which directly led to the purge of its editorial team in July. After the Hong Kong–based journal *Leader* (*Lingdaozhe* 領導者), which was affiliated with the widely read website Consensus

Net (Gongshiwang 共識網), published a Cultural Revolution issue in July, the whole website was permanently shut down. *Orient*, Wang Xiaobo's favored journal, had encountered the same fate in 1996 when attempting to commemorate the thirtieth anniversary of the Cultural Revolution.[117] In the March 2016 issue of *Yanhuang Chunqiu* , an excerpt from a new book by former minister of culture Wang Meng pointed out that considering the Cultural Revolution as an expression of Mao's wish to democratize society was a terrible misunderstanding. Wang concluded by describing the need to research and reflect on the Cultural Revolution as China's and the party's responsibility to the world.[118] In the same issue, Shanghai-based historian Wang Haiguang 王海光 called for ethical reflection but also for a new direction in historical research on the Cultural Revolution, turning toward society, the periphery, and everyday history and away from elites, the center, and the state, turning toward academic research and away from politics.[119] These calls were echoed by the respected historian Ma Yong 馬勇, who called on intellectuals to step up academic research on the Cultural Revolution before all the witnesses had disappeared and to distinguish clearly between seeking revenge and clarifying facts.[120]

Yang Jisheng, closely involved with *Yanhuang Chunqiu*, marked the fiftieth anniversary by publishing a monumental study of the Cultural Revolution that had been ten years in the making. Despite reported threats warning him not to publish the book even overseas, it appeared under the imprint of Hong Kong's Cosmos books, the publisher of *Tombstone*. In it, Yang makes an argument he had been advancing for many years: the Cultural Revolution did not persecute the elite as much as it persecuted ordinary people. As Hu Ping noted in his review, Yang argues that the Cultural Revolution saw more repression than rebellion, more deaths provoked by the state apparatus repressing rebels than by rebels themselves. If, in Yang's view, the Cultural Revolution can be summarized as a contest between Mao, the rebels, and the bureaucracy, then the bureaucracy (whose rift with Mao is overestimated) won, and the rebels paid the price.[121] Yang Jisheng had been developing this argument for a number of years. As he wrote in *Remembrance* in 2013, "Unfortunately, the final winner of the Cultural Revolution was still the bureaucratic system. The bureaucracy controlled the power to hold people accountable, to lead Reform and Opening, and to redistribute the benefits of reforms." The bureaucracy spared the rebels of Red August (and their children) while punishing ordinary participants: "Actually, there were a thousand times more ordinary people who suffered persecution in the Cultural Revolution than cadres."[122] In this statement, Yang is echoing a point developed previously by the economic historian Qin Hui, who as early as 2004, in the article "How Should We Remember the Cultural Revolution?," argued that "compared to the short-lived (though of course cruel) attacks endured by the 'faction in power,' the suffering of those ten years [1966–1976] was sustained mainly by the lower rungs of society, in particular the outcasts [*jianmin* 賤民] (five black elements, rightists) who had continually been persecuted before the Cultural Revolution."[123]

A few months later, in the unofficial journal *Yesterday*, He Shu published an article summarizing research on the Cultural Revolution in China, which he concluded by pointing out how the historical narrative was changing:

> Previously, we often said: history is written by the winners. However, since we have entered the new century, a very striking phenomenon has appeared: the history of many political movements, especially that of the "losers" [*shibaizhe* 失敗者] of the Cultural Revolution—those high-level cadres, military commanders, or those rebels that were active for just one or two years before they were submitted to ten or twenty years of repeated investigation, attacks, or punishments, labeled as members of counterrevolutionary cliques, . . . all began to write their memoirs or to give oral history testimony. Whether openly published, unofficially printed, disseminated on the Internet . . . [these memoirs] sprouted like mushrooms after the rain.[124]

This is yet another possible definition of *minjian* history: the history not written by winners.

The *minjian* position tried to rethink the Cultural Revolution from the standpoint of ordinary people—understanding the "black categories" not as a name for a small group of outcasts but as a contagious label that could potentially contaminate anyone. In an episode that highlighted the ambiguity of these categories, when the venerable writer Yang Jiang died at the age of 104 on May 25, 2016, just at the time of the fiftieth anniversary, a fierce discussion ensued on Chinese social networks about the responsibility of intellectuals during the Cultural Revolution. Yang Jiang, her husband, Qian Zhongshu 錢鍾書, and the intellectual elite in general (who had often been labeled as counterrevolutionaries) were accused of complicity with the regime.[125]

The grassroots intellectuals discussed in this chapter engage in the field of history by three types of practices: commemorating, documenting, and debating. The impetus to challenge official history began by commemorating victims of the Anti-Rightist Movement, by organizing events at graves or prison camps, by screening films, and by republishing old writings as ways of rebuilding respect for victims whose causes have not been recognized. Having opened a social space for these personal, individual events, *minjian* historians have devoted themselves to reconstructing a more solid alternative narrative by documenting large-scale collective events such as the famine, whether through oral history interviews or the collection of public archives and private documents. In a third stage, these alternative *minjian* narratives are confronted with each other and are debated in unofficial forums and journals, thus engaging different memories and opening up spaces for confession and repentance.

In these practices, *minjian* historians intervene as specific intellectuals. Whether they are journalists, documentary filmmakers, or retired academics, they base their public discourses on specialized knowledge of the period that they have acquired as amateur—or sometimes even professional—historians. They turn to subaltern groups (*ruoshi qunti*) to reconsider the history of the Mao era and in so doing question the myth of social justice under Mao, reconsidering society from the viewpoint of the subaltern. Their investigations reveal that intellectual elites were often supportive of Maoist ideology, whereas peasants constituted many of its victims. They use these conclusions to question the structure of contemporary society and the legitimacy of party rule. Finally, their practices are noncommercial. Whereas it has long been a tenet of research on Chinese intellectuals that they must choose between the state and the market, *minjian* intellectuals define their position by hedging between the two and developing a third space of noncommercial practices, enabled sometimes by retirement pensions, the generosity of friends (Wu Wenguang), as well as the development of digital technologies that enable almost cost-free self-publication (pdf documents sent by email). *Minjian* history can be summed up as unofficial history of nonelite individuals and groups by noninstitutional historians with the aim of establishing knowledge rather than acquiring money or other benefits. Starting out from individual cases, *minjian* historians gather documentation to reconstruct alternative collective narratives and finally open up forums to foster a more pluralistic approach to history.

It is of course unfortunate but unsurprising that their endeavors have been met with an unprecedented crackdown on "historical nihilism" since Xi Jinping took power. Although censorship and various forms of pressure never ceased, the purge of publications that took place during the fiftieth anniversary of the Cultural Revolution marks an inflection for which Yang Jisheng, Hong Zhenkuai, *Yanhuang Chunqiu*, and Consensus Net all paid a price. "Historical nihilism" was singled out as a danger for party rule in Document Number 9 of 2013. The subsequent decision to include the act of defaming Communist heroes as a legal offense in the first civil code adopted in March 2017 confirms the threat that the party believes such activities pose to its rule.[126] However, ultimately *minjian* historians do not only challenge the institutions of the state. *Minjian* history also undermines the legitimacy of historical narratives based only on the stories of great men As Zi Zhongyun noted with reference to the traditional practice of *yeshi* (unofficial history), intellectual elites have long looked down on histories written not only for the rulers but also for the people.[127] In this sense, bringing the stories of ordinary people to the forefront may be just as challenging as questioning the role of political elites. Whereas the state may repress the more overtly political interventions of *minjian* historians, as a new practice of knowledge *minjian* history poses a deeper challenge to established authority that cannot be easily suppressed.

CHAPTER 4

Investigating and Transforming Society from the Margins

The Rise and Fall of Independent Cinema

In 2001, the First Independent Film Festival (Shoujie Duli Yingxiang Jie 首屆獨立影像節) took place at Beijing Film Academy (BFA), co-organized by the Practice Society (Shijian She 實踐社) and *Southern Weekly* under the banner "*minjian* independent film."[1] It was the first public film event not sponsored by a state entity and represented a significant institutionalization of the alternative spaces and publics that had begun to emerge after 1989, originally in artist villages or as loose film clubs or associations (Practice Society in Beijing, Back Window Films in Nanjing). The weekly newspaper published a kind of manifesto of the event under the title "The Meaning of *Minjian*," in which Yangzi 羊子, critic and programmer, rejected accusations that works in the feature-film selection were examples of "fake *minjian*" in fact connected to the Beijing Film Academy. Rather than defining *minjian* in an institutional manner, he presented the term as a form of individual expression:

> I must explain that the terms "independent" and *minjian* are not targeted at any particular "system"; advocating the independent spirit aims at furthering the self-contained artwork as a comprehensive idea and the self-sufficiency of the author who throws out commercial and other pressures. In this perspective, the student productions from BFA are not works that necessarily have to be called into question. Furthermore, I don't believe that *minjian* is something that can be achieved just by saying the word; I believe *minjian* has a kind of contract with independent spirit. Only individual expression can be considered truly *minjian*, while some *minjian* forms of collective conscience

> are in fact anti-*minjian*. Therefore, what we should emphasize is whether artworks express an individual conscience of quality.[2]

In laying out the five selection criteria for participating films, the organizers further connected *minjian* with an amateur approach that has not been excessively formatted by the official production system, calling to "foster and encourage *minjian* creation that has not gone through professional orthodox training [*zhuanye zhengtong xunlian* 專業正統訓練]."[3] Individualism, autonomy, and freedom from professional conventions appear to have been the central claims of this foundational event, which proved to be a great success among the small circle of people who took part.

From 2003, regular festivals also took place in Nanjing and Kunming (Yunnan), and from 2007 Beijing events settled in the eastern suburbs in Songzhuang. Independent cinema was further institutionalized in 2003 by the state's decision to lift its ban on unofficial directors, who began to apply for production and distribution visas: the most spectacular example was Jia Zhangke, whose film *The World* (*Shijie* 世界 2004) was approved for release. Seio Nakajima has documented a meeting on November 13, 2003, between Wang Xiaoshuai 王小帥, Jia Zhangke, Lou Ye 婁燁 and the Film Bureau, after seven directors had published a petition in *Southern Weekly* requesting that independent films be given a chance to enter the system. As a result, the State Administration of Radio, Film, and Television issued three simplified regulations in December 2003, including approval of production by its provincial offices on the basis of a synopsis, although the final cut still had to pass the central censorship committee and obtain a quota number from a state studio.[4] At the same time, unofficial distribution channels and publics also expanded, in particular on the Internet, and were fostered by liberal media through screenings, prizes, and competitions.[5] Independent film continued to develop until around 2013, when it came under increasing pressure from the state, pressure that culminated in a new film law, passed in late 2016, that significantly curbed its activities.

From its inception, independent cinema in China has been closely connected to the rise of *minjian* intellectuals. The term "independent" generally refers to films not produced, or at least not initiated, by a state studio or broadcaster, which are in this sense "outside the system" and therefore also generally underfunded and in resonance with grassroots society. In 1988, Wu Wenguang left his stable job and became a "free person" (*ziyou ren* 自由人). In the summer of that year, using equipment borrowed from China Central Television (CCTV) where he was working on a television documentary, he began shooting *Bumming in Beijing* (*Liulang Beijing* 流浪北京), arguably the first film produced outside a state studio since 1949. After he had finished shooting in late 1989, he used a friend's equipment in Kunming to edit the film. Focusing on five "drifting" artists afloat in Beijing before and after the Tiananmen crackdown, *Bumming in Beijing* documents both the idealism and illusions of the 1980s as well as the confusion and bleakness that followed the crackdown (although this event is never mentioned). Wu Wenguang documented a new lifestyle, which he and other directors shared with their subjects: the *mangliu* 盲流 or "drifters" who had cut ties with the work-unit system and made a living as freelance artists.[6] Subsequently, four of the five artists in *Bumming in Beijing* chose to leave China, as documented in the sequel *At Home in the World* (*Sihai wei jia* 四海為家, 1995).

As the first independent film in China, *Bumming in Beijing* not only established a foundational link with the democracy movement of 1989 but also opened a space dedicated specifically to reflecting on the failures of the movement,[7] the responsibility of the elite, and the lack of a "cultural democratization" that could reach the grass roots of Chinese society. The elite-reformist "theme film" (*zhuantipian* 專題片) *River Elegy* (*He Shang* 河殤, 1988), which had been broadcast on CCTV in 1988 and was seen to have foreshadowed the events of 1989, epitomized these defects. In almost every aspect, independent cinema took the opposite approach to *River Elegy* and the theme-film model.[8] Just as the May Fourth "turn to culture" became a vector for in-depth democratization after the failure of 1911, the turn to independent film can be seen as an attempt to reconnect the elite with the "grass roots" (*diceng*) after the failure of 1989. Lü Xinyu 吕新雨 argues that the production of *The Other Shore* (*Bi'an* 彼岸) in June 1993 represented a turning point for *minjian* intellectuals, who renounced utopias and focused on "this shore."[9] By reflecting on the disenfranchisement of those who had previously been sidelined by intellectuals, independent directors adopted a more "democratic" approach to film and thus began rethinking the notion of democracy itself.[10]

Focusing on the margins and before long living in the margins (in artist villages such as Yuanmingyuan and later Songzhuang) became alternative ways of challenging the authoritarian structures and inequalities in Chinese society of the 1990s. Geographical proximity with avant-garde painters and visual artists also offered some alternative funding opportunities. In this sense, independent film directors were immediately quintessential *minjian* intellectuals. Those who later became known as the "Sixth Generation" included Zhang Yuan 張元 (b. 1963), Lou Ye (b. 1965), Wang Xiaoshuai (b. 1966), and Guan Hu 管虎 (b. 1967). Indeed, Wang Xiaobo was associated with one of the earliest independent feature films, Zhang Yuan's *East Palace, West Palace* (*Dong gong xi gong* 東宮西宮, 1996), for which he cowrote the screenplay.[11] Jia Zhangke uniquely captured this original connection in an essay published in *Southern Weekly* in 2010:

> Political tumult was not yet in the distant past for Chinese people in the early 1990s. In the aftermath of trauma and engulfed by societal-wide depression, the so-called "Sixth Generation" directors used film to challenge the authorities. I was especially thrilled by the "independent" label that they carried. . . .
>
> From the 1990s we began to hear individuals' voices outside the official rhetoric, and they were injected with the independent spirit. Today, ordinary people can assert their self-esteem. Shouldn't we then thank the "Sixth Generation" directors for having directed their attention to the lower rung of society, representing marginalized people, and advocating the restoration of basic human rights to them?. . .
>
> When we see young people today with dyed hair moving freely in the cityscape and having the freedom to choose their sexual orientation, do we ever think of Zhang Yuan's banned feature *East Palace, West Palace*? Yes, the film was made possible thanks to the book by Wang Xiaobo and the academic research by Li Yinhe. Their combined efforts spent in organizing events and making speeches brought about the freedom that people can enjoy today. But what about Director Zhang Yuan? During the reform era, many people were marginalized because they lacked power and money. Which of our films told the stories of these people? Which [among] them induced society to acknowledge their existence—helping the weak gain recognition? The Sixth Generation directors' films did. To me, their films are the gems of Chinese culture of the 1990s.[12]

Looking back more than a decade later, Jia Zhangke finds that independent films, often derided by their critics as marginal and insignificant, have in some significant ways transformed mainstream society.

The first independent documentaries were quite closely connected to the group of directors working in television because they had access to equipment, which was costly and complex to use. The first collective event, a symposium with several screenings, was held in the winter of 1991 at Beijing Broadcasting Institute.[13] However, in 1997, digital video (DV) cameras became widespread in China, dramatically lowering the entry barrier to the profession and allowing a virtually unlimited number of people to make films at minimal cost. Although inexpensive DV equipment did not provide the original impetus for the emergence of independent film in the early 1990s, it was a decisive new development at the end of the decade. It empowered a second wave of film directors, who further investigated the margins and the "vulnerable groups," emphasizing the new term *diceng* (lower strata). Jia Zhangke (b. 1970), Zhao Liang 趙亮 (b. 1971), and Du Haibin 杜海濱 (b. 1972) as well as the slightly older directors Wang Chao 王超 (b. 1964), Wang Bing (b. 1967), and Pema Tseden 萬瑪才旦 (b. 1969) all turned their cameras away from big cities and toward ordinary lives in China's countless remote industrial county towns, often drawing strongly on documentary aesthetics. They generally rejected the name "Sixth Generation," situating their role not within the state-sponsored production system, in which successive "generations" of directors had been fostered, but "among the people" (*minjian*). Their films, produced and distributed through noncommercial channels, were devoted to documenting everyday life in spaces outside the control of the state. In the early 2000s, this new interest combined the urge to investigate social realities, the will to intervene in social debates, and an aesthetic reflection on how to ethically represent social issues.

This chapter focuses on the place of independent film with respect to elite and subaltern groups in society, to the state and the market, as well as to discourses of social knowledge. It begins by examining how independent directors defined their position in self-reflexive discourses, before looking at how these positions were expressed in the filmic texts they produced and finally at how the *minjian* practices of independent film connected to alternative publics that formed in the marginal spaces of artist villages such as Songzhuang.

INDEPENDENT DIRECTORS AS *MINJIAN* INTELLECTUALS: MANIFESTOS AND INTERPRETATIONS

Although it is relatively easy to compile a list of films and directors working outside the state-owned studio system since the early 1990s,[14] trying to gather these productions under a conceptual definition has proved challenging and inevitably controversial. Two of the earliest articulations came from two key directors in the respective areas of documentary and feature film.[15]

Jia Zhangke: Amateur and Minjian

After graduating from the BFA, Jia Zhangke published several influential texts at the same time as he was making his first films, placing his work under the two banners of "amateur" and *minjian* cinema. In one of his first articles, "My Focal Point," published in *Avant-garde Today* (*Jinri Xianfeng* 今日先鋒),[16] he took issue with the shortening attention spans induced by television and the growing commercialization of cinema and argued: "If professionalization of art is only in order to feed your family, I by far prefer to be a carefree and unrestrained amateur director because I don't want to lose my freedom. When the camera starts to run, I hope to ask myself: Is everything in front of your eyes what you really think and feel?"[17] It is clear from this early pronouncement that Jia's critique is directed as much against the market as against the state and defines "amateur" cinema as part of a "third realm."

Expanding on this theme, Jia's essay "The Age of Amateur Cinema Is About to Return" appeared in *Southern Weekly* in 1998. Based on his remarks at a forum on independent cinema at the time of the Asian crisis, held at the Busan International Film Festival in 1998 (where the film *Xiao Wu* 小武 received the New Currents Award), the essay criticizes "professional" productions as stereotyped and formulaic, inducing homogenization of culture in Asia:

> That's when I proclaimed: the age of amateur cinema is about to return.
>
> Amateurs are a group of people who love cinema, who have an irrepressible desire for cinema.... Because they don't pay attention to the so-called professional style, they find more possibilities to create. Because they refuse to abide by the established standards of the profession, they find a plurality of ideas and values. Because they have broken out of outmoded conventions, their horizon is boundless. Because they safeguard the integrity of their conscience as intellectuals, they can achieve sincerity [*tashi houzhong* 踏實厚重]....
>
> And today? Why shouldn't a Chinese Tarantino emerge from the crowd jostling in pirate VCD [video compact disc] stores, or a present-day Ogawa

> Shinsuke among the young people who use digital cameras? Cinema should no longer be reserved for a minority; it should belong to the masses. . . . I have always disliked the attitude of professional superiority, while the amateur spirit includes equality and fairness as well as a concern with human fate and solicitude for ordinary people.[18]

In this context, the term "amateur" refers not to lack of professional training but to a refusal to abide by the twofold norms of the film industry: political correctness and commercial success. It also highlights the concern for ordinary people and for equality between filmmaker and subjects. Whereas such a position was all but impossible in the 1980s, when state studios controlled equipment and film, by the late 1990s it had been made possible by new technologies and had the potential to democratize film production.

In another early essay, Jia singles out VCDs and DV cameras as decisive innovations. After buying cheap VCDs of *Battleship Potemkin* (Sergei Eisenstein, 1925) and *Citizen Kane* (Orson Welles, 1941), his thoughts return to the decades when such films were available only as "internal reference screenings":

> Making film screenings dependent on people's administrative rank and professional affiliation is no doubt a great Chinese invention. Watching films became a special privilege, predicated on contempt for ordinary people's intelligence and suspicions about their level of morality. The words "internal reference" immediately introduced a distance between cinema and ordinary people. . . . Now things have changed; finally we can enjoy films on an equal footing. . . . The appearance of DV cameras made filming simpler, more flexible, cheaper. It allowed more people to overcome financial and technical constraints and to express their feelings though moving images.[19]

Like many of his peers, Jia highlights the decisive role of technical progress in democratizing both film viewing (VCDs) and filmmaking (DV cameras) as well as in removing films from the control of the authorities. He critiques China's Communist regulations in the name of equality: they made the possibility of art dependent on administrative hierarchy (for viewing) and on co-optation into a state unit (for producing). By contrast, new technologies have an equalizing effect that empowers ordinary people to express their personal feelings, speak for themselves rather than for a class or social group, and address their audience through feelings rather than through a theory of society. This is the deeper sense of Jia's reclaiming of the label "amateur."

In an interview with producer and critic Lin Xudong 林旭東, first published in *Today*, Jia also claims the status of *minjian* for his own work. He begins by emphasizing his rural origins and the importance of popular, unofficial culture for his work: "Compared to the education I received in school, I was lucky that in the early years of growing up, I had the opportunity, through some ordinary people living at the grassroots of Chinese society, to come into contact with resources that are deeply embedded in China's *minjian* culture." In conclusion, he defines himself as "a *minjian* director from the grassroots of Chinese society [*yige laizi Zhongguo jiceng de minjian daoyan* 一個來自中國基層的民間導演]."[20] In this manner, Jia significantly subordinates his national identity, often deemed central in the cinema of the 1980s, to the "grassroots" (*jiceng* 基層) identification of an ordinary person, an "unofficial" (*minjian*) director, whose work is not justified by his status or qualification, an "amateur" (*yeyu* 業餘) in the noblest sense.[21]

This position is echoed by the important female director Ji Dan 季丹, who was trained in Japan:

> I suddenly realized I was among the "lower rungs" of society, those people we see trapped in a mine shaft or whose house burnt down on the evening news, that abstracted "other" that arouses our curiosity and ignites our anger against injustice. Actually the "lower rungs" are much more far-reaching and profound than I originally thought. They are not the dark thing we find underneath our shoes. They are beside us and inside of us. They are part of the ruins of society and humanity. The compassion and kindness of strangers are not guardian angels to them. These ruins are resourceful enough to regenerate on their own.[22]

For Ji Dan, independent film came about through the realization that directors are part of the subaltern groups in society: making films is not simply a form of compassion for "others," but also a form of self-recognition.

Jia Zhangke has continued to explain and detail his stance as a *minjian* director and *minjian* intellectual. The central impetus of this stance stems from his experience of watching official films for many years without ever seeing "anything related to my life."[23] This experience determined a preoccupation with filming ordinary people and everyday life, which is expressed most remarkably in his choice of amateur actors and local languages:

> Using non-professional actors was a form of revolt against the film world I had experienced, in which actors were never natural, everything was rehearsed. They spoke Mandarin, and a form of Mandarin that was specifically achieved through actor's training, like television presenters. So why did I use [the actor] Wang Hongwei 王宏偉? Because his body is always slouching, just like all of us in life are always slouching, no one stands straight all the time like an actor. Non-professional actors can speak local language. Mandarin is a very violent thing. Each local language is some people's mother tongue.... [A]t the time I shot *Xiao Wu*, the Film Bureau censorship rules had a provision stipulating that in order to promote Mandarin we should not film in dialect. If we had to use dialect, we had to write a report. At the end, only Mao Zedong was allowed to speak dialect. And Zhou Enlai 周恩來. Nobody else could speak their mother tongue. This was another form of autocracy.[24]

This emphasis is of course a direct rebuttal of the aesthetics of propaganda and official films, as illustrated by the negative reactions Jia's films have elicited among officials.[25] It is further expressed in his aesthetic preference for a fragmented style, which avoids smooth editing and uses long takes that allow his characters to roam freely (Jia argues such takes have a "democratic quality"[26]).

Jia Zhangke's cinema focuses on individuals. He has often mentioned in interviews how he measured the historic shift of the end of the Mao era through music: whereas Communist songs were sung in the plural ("We are the heirs of socialism"), Teresa Teng's 鄧麗君 lyrics, smuggled in from Taiwan on fishing boats, were phrased in the first person ("The moon stands for my heart"). Discussing the directors of the early 1990s (Zhang Yuan, Wang Xiaoshuai), Jia Zhangke argues: "They are no longer spokespeople for a generation. In fact, no one has the right to represent the majority of people anymore; you only have the right and the ability to represent yourself. This is the first step in breaking away from our cultural fetters; it is a kind of skill, a way of life.... We have no right to explain other people's lives."[27] Individual stories are not representative in the sense that socialist aesthetics tried to define the meaning of individual characters by class: independent films refuse the tenet of representativity or symbolism that pervaded the cinema of the 1980s.[28]

This means that even marginal or subaltern characters have universal significance: "Afterward people told me that choosing a pickpocket as the main character [for *Xiao Wu*] was a choice lacking in universal meaning [*pubian yiyi* 普遍意義], unsuited to the creative project of recording this era. I believe that the question whether a character in a film has universality is not determined by the character's social status but rather by whether you are able to handle this character from a human perspective."[29] In this area, too, Jia expresses a break not only with Marxist aesthetics but also with the entire representation of society pervasive until the late 1980s: as it was for Wang Xiaobo, his interest in the subaltern (in the case of Xiao Wu, a small-time delinquent in a county town in Shanxi) is invested with a different meaning than the classic representation of the proletariat by elite intellectuals.[30]

Indeed, Jia Zhangke repeatedly emphasizes that he, just like Wang Xiaobo, has no sense of mission as an intellectual and an artist:

> I have never felt that I had any kind of responsibility to shoot any kind of film. I also don't think I can represent these people. Actually, this is also a very personal situation: I myself grew up in this environment. I was the child of the most ordinary kind of Chinese family in the most ordinary kind of Chinese county town. . . . So I did feel I had to film our lives, but I don't like to describe it as a responsibility, or a mission. When people talk about a mission, it's usually to assert their own power, their discursive power, which is something I reject.[31]

This argument directly echoes Wang Xiaobo's critique of "speaking out" and intellectuals' habit of occupying the moral high ground in the name of their "responsibility for all under heaven." Just like Wang Xiaobo, Jia's responsibility is first and foremost to himself. Like any director, he hopes that more people can see his films (and for this reason chose to work through the official distribution system after 2003), and he often participates in public debates (for example, delivering a famous speech at PKU after *Still Life* [*Sanxia hao ren* 三峽好人] received a prize in Venice in 2006), but he is not deterred by people who believe that his films are of no interest to the subaltern people he films. Rather, he argues that although independent films may not be seen by many people, they have gradually entered a form of "public consciousness [*gonggong yishi* 公共意識]," which ensures greater attention to ordinary or marginal people: "people today no longer dare to say: we can simply overlook ordinary people."[32]

Wu Wenguang's Xianchang 現場*: On the Scene*

In another early manifesto, Wu Wenguang advances similar arguments. After the success of *Bumming in Beijing*, Wu was invited to screen his film first in Hong Kong (his passport application was not approved in time) and then in Yamagata in 1991, where he came in contact with works by Ogawa Shinsuke and Frederick Wiseman, whom he was later able to visit and observe at work.[33] Reflecting on his experience filming a traveling performance troupe (in *Jianghu, Life on the Road* [*Jianghu* 江湖, 1995], the first film he shot in DV), he mentions both the *diceng* subject matter and the amateur approach:

> Here I do not want to talk about what material I filmed or what I discovered about the "lower rungs" of society or that kind of thing. Rather, I would like to talk about how the feel of this project was totally different than the very "professional" kind of documentary filmmaking I had done before. With this project, I just carried the DV camera with me like a pen and hung it out with the members of the troupe. Every day my ears were filled with the rough sounds of Henan dialect. . . . I have become an individual with a DV camera, filming anything I please that happens to wander into my line of vision, whether or not it has anything to do with the theme of the film. . . . [I]t was DV that saved me, that allowed me to maintain a kind of personal relationship to documentary making, and made it far more than just an identity.[34]

For Wu, the "nonprofessional" nature of his work, which also deals with marginal or subaltern groups, is connected to the contingency of events shot "in the present and on the spot [*xianzaishi he zaichang* 現在時和在場]"[35] and of course greatly enhanced by the arrival of DV cameras. He has also defined his work as "individual visual writing [*geren yingxiang xiezuo* 個人影像寫作]."[36] As Luke Robinson argues, the term *xianchang* can be defined as "liveness": rather than by "realism" (with its prescriptive criterion of "representativeness"), it is characterized by contingency; the primacy of *xianchang* dictates the progression and structure of the film. Reality is unpredictable, and only by capturing its randomness can the director be true to the individuals who populate it and whose stories he or she is telling.[37] This randomness precludes the "metonymic or metaphorical mode" that is inherent in socialist realism. in the words of the director Hu Xinyu 胡新宇, "poetry rejects metaphor, so too does documentary."[38] In this way, *xianchang* becomes an ethical problem: narrative structures that make historical contingencies into necessities driven by a teleological vision of progress are rejected in favor of contingency and particularity.[39]

The notion of *xianchang* was central to one of the first collective publications about the new cinema. Wu Wenguang published three volumes of what was presented as a journal, *Xianchang* (English subtitle: *Document*) in 2000, 2001, and 2005. Organized by "files" (*dang'an* 檔案) , these volumes explicitly aimed to document the new cultural practices without the constraints of any preconceived or narrowly genre-oriented definition. The first volume contains the entire screenplay of Jia Zhangke's film *Xiao Wu* as well as material related to Kang Jianning's 康建寧 documentary *Yin Yang* 陰陽; the second volume dedicates a "file" to Du Haibin's film *Along the Railroad* (*Tielu yanxian* 鐵路沿線, 2000). These works are thus situated within a larger group of literary, artistic, and more largely cultural productions, such as oral history. What they share is not spelled out but is suggested by the eclectic juxtaposition: *xianchang* refers to a symmetry between the real scene and the film set, documentary and fiction, codified cultural practices and ordinary narratives told by migrant workers, labeled as "oral history." Referring to both the "real" scene and the film set, *xianchang* denotes a preoccupation with directness, contingency, improvisation but also with a public space of performance. The last scene of Jia Zhangke's film *Xiao Wu* epitomizes the space of independent cinema: a street scene in a small town where the police have chained the protagonist to an electric pole, but even as more and more passers-by stop to gape, no one speaks out to question his arrest.[40] The main square of a gritty county town becomes the epitome of an "ordinary" space.[41] In this sense, *xianchang* is a place where the individual stories told by independent cinema encounter society and raise questions about common values, an "unofficial" (*minjian*) space where alternative discourses enter "public consciousness."

In 2005, Wu Wenguang was commissioned by the Ministry of Civil Affairs under a grant from the European Union to run a film project introducing villagers to the practice of village elections. This project became an experiment in participative documentary, in which ten villagers were given cameras and collaborated in making short films. Wu describes this work as a way of empowering ordinary people: "In the course of our work, I realized that what was the most exciting for these people who had never held a camera in their lives was finding a way to express themselves. Filming gave them the status of someone who can speak out and will probably be heard. Previously, they felt ignored by the media.... With this participative system, they are able to express themselves on their own, and this allows them to discover their status as citizens. Being able to focus on politics in their village awakened their civic consciences."[42]

A similar understanding of documentary film as a form of civic empowerment is developed by Ai Xiaoming, who also focused on village elections and the social movement they sparked in Taishicun (Guangdong) in 2005: "What I want to do in my films is not to give a passive representation of people, but to show their agency and how they can change their destiny through their own means. This is what documentary is for in my mind.... When we shoot a documentary, we become one with our protagonists. When I film peasants, I let them tell me what I should show or not. I simply consider myself a volunteer in the service of their cause, as someone who provides them with technical tool that they have not mastered."[43] In this approach, the notion of *xianchang* is further broadened from a place of visual documentation to a forum for participative intervention.

Critical Discussions: Independent, Avant-garde, Realist

After directors such as Jia Zhangke and Wu Wenguang published their manifestos, active and often critical discussion of independent films by academics and journalists took place in journals and other media, while at the same time directors and other practitioners undertook collective publications that established groups with varying perimeters. In China, *Avant-garde Today* was an important forum. Hong Kong publications played a role, with early discussions in Bei Dao's exile journal *Today* and in *Twenty-First Century (Ershiyi Shiji* 二十一世紀). By this time, just as Zhang Yuan had come out of "banishment" by working with a state studio on *Seventeen Years* (*Guonian huijia* 過年回家) in 1999, Jia Zhangke and others had taken advantage of the reforms in the state production system in 2003 to "come out of silence" and speak out within the system. This important development marked a decisive shift from "underground" (*dixia* 地下, a term initially often played up by overseas critics) to "independent," suggesting that independence was more than simply working outside the state production system.[44]

BFA professor and well-known liberal scholar Cui Weiping's 崔衛平 essay in *Twenty-First Century* in 2003, "A Space for the Growth of China's Independently Produced Documentaries," established "independent" as the preferred term to designate the new type of film.[45] Lü Xinyu traces the origin of the term "independent" back to a meeting at Zhang Yuan's home in late 1991, attended by Wu Wenguang, Duan Jinchuan 段錦川, Jiang Yue 蔣樾, Wen Pulin 溫普林, Shi Jian 時間, Hao Zhiqiang 郝智強, and Li Xiaoshan 李小山, who provides the explanation: "The notion of 'independent' actually meant two things: first, working independently; second, thinking independently: I can express myself without other people interfering. But if you want to achieve this, you have to work independently, you can't take other people's money. This was mainly Wu Wenguang's view, the others supplemented it."[46] Cui connects independent film with "unofficial avant-garde art [*minjian xianfeng yishu* 民間先鋒藝術],"[47] in the tradition of the Stars exhibition of 1979, echoing an earlier publication of documents using the term "avant-garde," *xianfeng*, in its title (which also controversially asserted "my camera doesn't lie").[48]

The term "avant-garde" did not stick, and "independent" subsequently became the preferred label used by most directors to define their own work, including documentary productions, as highlighted in a collection published in 2004 under the title *Archives of China's Independent Documentaries*, edited by members of the Practice Society, which had organized the first independent festival in 2001. It also uses the notion of *minjian* to refer to both documentary directors and their productions: "Documentary films, from the perspective of Chinese culture, are always hesitating on the two-sided boundary-line between state discourse and *minjian* narratives. The former construct grand narratives of history, in which documentaries become visual footnotes to official history; the latter originate in individual initiative, searching for a form of memory different from the mainstream ideology, authentic and self-aware."[49] Another characteristic of documentary, they argued, is that the people on both sides of the camera share a marginal position: "In the environment of Chinese society, the lack of status of documentary filmmakers to a large degree determined the subject matter of their films. As they looked around, because of their purely *minjian* status, it seemed that focusing on people with even lower status then they—peasants, migrant workers, drifters, retirees or their own friends—would allow them to shoot from a close distance. . . . To an extent their role as spokespeople for the vulnerable was imposed on them."[50]Finally, DV cameras brought a kind of liberation from the weight of both the film camera and the state apparatus that controlled access to it. Zhu Jingjiang 朱靖江 argues that the big equipment used by television documentarists was alienating because it made them into a part of the machine, whereas DV was self-redeeming: "As a renewed tool for individual image creation, DV for the first time allowed a *minjian* voice to enter official history."[51]

As Yangzi, one of the organizers of the Practice Society, put it in an interview, the two slogans of the new type of documentary were "Defend cinema's right to think" and "Advance the *minjian* turn of visual expression."[52] In another collection of documents edited by activists based in Songzhuang, the editors argued that new documentaries' focus on "marginal groups" was aimed at providing the "silent majority" with an opportunity to express themselves:

> In the course of the development of documentary film, quite a few people also expressed doubts, for example saying that documentaries in China paid too much attention to marginal people, that they were not mainstream enough, and so on. A brief explanation is in order here. Actually, the majority of people in the lens of our documentary films are not marginal, including peasants or disabled people: in our population of more than one billion, they represent a majority. . . . This sort of conscious or unconscious way of establishing oneself as the mainstream will only provoke further misunderstandings.[53]

In this perspective, it is in fact the mainstream entertainment films that focus on an "unrepresentative" minority of characters. Although the title of Cui Weiping's article explicitly refers to documentary, she also includes feature films in her argument: in her view, the role played by marginal groups in the filmic narratives, the difficulty of working with TV producers, and the problems posed by state control were all common traits shared by features and documentaries.[54] This view was developed more fully in a more extensive collection of material, published shortly after Cui's article by two influential critics and producers of independent cinema, Zhang Xianmin 張獻民 and Zhang Yaxuan 張亞璇, who focused on DV films and argued that the new technology transformed documentary into "one-person cinema."[55]

Shanghai media scholar Lü Xinyu, by contrast, put forward the term "new documentary movement": she viewed the documentaries produced since the early 1990s as a homogeneous set of texts based on an aesthetic (and even philosophical) "consensus" that rejects the utopias of the "other shore" and plunges head on into the reality of "this shore."[56] In her view, this "movement" developed simultaneously inside and outside the system: among directors working for television as well as among those who no longer had a work unit; therefore, in her opinion most directors understood "independence" as a far-off ideal rather than as a reality.[57] Highlighting the simultaneous critique of and nostalgia for utopia expressed in many of these films, Lü defines them by an aesthetic of critical realism that denounces social injustice, connecting with the longer tradition of socially critical art in twentieth-century China in the context of the rise of discourses critical of capitalism and globalization.[58] The aesthetic preoccupation with reality, defined either as an "ism" (*xianshi zhuyi* 現實主義, which has a long history in Chinese propaganda discourse), in Lü's manner, or as a looser "style" (*xieshi* 寫實, a word borrowed from literati painting, or *jishi* 紀實, "recording reality"), was echoed by overseas scholars but often led them to overlook the decisive break operated by independent film with the Fifth Generation and all previous generations who also claimed realism as their approach. By contrast, Jia Zhangke and his peers tend to emphasize "authenticity" (*zhenshi* 真實) rather than realism.[59]

Critic Wang Xiaolu 王小魯 takes issue with Lü's label, proposing to restrict the name "new documentary movement" to the new style that emerged in television documentary; independent documentary, by contrast, is an unprecedented phenomenon that in his view cannot be described as a "new" articulation of an old form. He further notes that Lü Xinyu predicted that DV would be swamped by commercialism, but in fact the contrary took place: the 1990s inaugurated an age of relative freedom and self-expression. This self-expression is, in Wang Xiaolu's view, not simply solipsistic but can result in a strengthening of subjectivity: "For documentary directors to find their own angle and operate a selection among the boundless reality and complex social materials and to edit it into something shapely, the creating subject must have a notion of society, a moral training, an aesthetic gaze, as well as the ability to mobilize."[60] Independent documentaries thus appeared as a way of investigating society.

In a long analysis of Wang Bing's three-part film *West of the Tracks* (*Tiexi qu* 鐵西區, 2003) , Lü Xinyu makes a complex argument for a neo-Marxist reading of the film as a nostalgic invocation of the working class created by Mao (and ultimately an elegy for Maoism itself): "Its subject is epic—the dusk of an entire social world, together with all the hopes and ideals that created it." Noting both antiutopian and utopian aspects in the film, she finds in working-class subjectivities evidence of a nostalgia for the industries built under Mao as symbols of "Third World resistance to the domination of Western capitalism." In a suggestive conclusion, she describes the coming dawn at the end of the film as "the twilight before history is clarified."[61] Wang Hui has similarly argued that the work of the Sixth Generation of filmmakers is "epic," by contrast with the "lyrical" quality of the Fifth Generation. In a revised version of his presentation at a symposium on Jia Zhangke's film *Still Life* organized by the journal *Dushu* in December 2006 in Jia's hometown Fenyang,[62] Wang Hui also highlights the potential for social change embedded in Jia's film: "The film has a nostalgic flavor, but nostalgia is not its true theme. The setting of the film is ruins, but not those found in European Romantic paintings, music, and literature, and not the ruin-like industry and city that appeared in modernist works. Rather, these are ruins that contain the potential of forward change. The ruins represent an end, but more so a beginning. The theme of change extends from these ruins: the past is already determined, but the future is indeterminate."[63] Both Lü's and Wang's Lukácsian training shines through their interpretive endeavors to imbue the independent documentaries with a historical teleology and political undertones that directors are often uncomfortable with.[64] Wang Bing, for example, has taken issue with the idea of a utopia, arguing in an interview: "These factories were not a dream, they existed. The workers had a life, despite the bad management and bad working conditions. They made 300 yuan a month. It's not for me to say whether those factories should have been kept open."[65] Wang Bing's rejoinder is characteristic of the reticence among *minjian* intellectuals in general and filmmakers in particular to engage in abstract theorizing.

Some of the tensions between the more traditional Marxist view and the practice of independent cinema came to light during a forum held in Nanjing in 2011. Discussing the recurrent question of "how the subaltern can be responsibly represented in film," Lü Xinyu developed the view that there is a radical disconnect between the subaltern at the "lowest levels of society" and other classes and that therefore the former "cannot meaningfully consent to the agenda of those who are more powerful." This idea of course contradicts the position that evolved from Wang Xiaobo's essays—that *minjian* intellectuals and subaltern groups can be reunited within a "silent majority." Distinguishing between the filmmakers' different positions (populist, realist, carnivalesque) with respect to subaltern groups, Lü Xinyu endorsed the "populist mode" whereby filmmakers "express their admiration for the dignity and nobility of people at the bottom of the society, and expose the injustices and grievances of these people."[66] In response, the filmmakers in attendance, reacting against this asserted theoretical position, drafted a manifesto entitled "Shamanism-Animal," arguing that "documentary is the opposite of theorization." Ji Dan, praised by Lü as a "populist," argued for a definition of documentary film as "shamanism," in which the "other" can speak through the director as shaman, thus implicitly rejecting Lü's label.[67] This shamanism metaphor is not unlike the approach favored by Ai Xiaoming, which, according to Dan Edwards and Marina Svensson, is "built on a relationship with on-screen subjects that is at once instinctive, emotional, even spiritual—and at the same time resolutely politicized and concrete. It involves an 'encountering with other souls' in a 'concrete historical context,' as Ai puts it."[68] Both approaches are based on an unmediated expression of the standpoint of the subject.

In 2010, in connection with the release of Jia Zhangke's film *Still Life*, the journal *Today* published a special issue on independent film, which also appeared as a book edited by the poet Ouyang Jianghe 歐陽江河 under the title *Chinese Independent Cinema: A Collection of Interviews* (*Zhongguo duli dianying: Fangtan lu*) and with the English subtitle *On the Edge: Chinese Independent Cinema*. Bringing together interviews with ten feature directors born in the 1960s and the 1970s (Jia Zhangke, Wang Chao, Li Yang 李楊, Li Yu 李玉, Zhang Ming 章明, Lou Ye, Zhu Wen, Pema Tseden, Li Hongqi 李紅旗, and Han Jie 韓傑), it marked a strong assertion of collective existence. In the introduction, Ouyang notes the contributions of the Sixth Generation (Lou Ye, Zhang Ming) but dwells at length on the significance of Jia Zhangke and other directors' work after 2000 in the context of the decline (*moluo* 沒落) of the Fifth Generation and on the need to find a space for noncommercial films in China and in the world.[69] Ouyang further argues that since the late 1990s a group of young directors had "gradually formed a common understanding of the new independent Chinese cinema, a common direction and aspiration: using film to pay attention to reality [*guanzhu xianshi* 關注現實], to document reality [*jilu xianshi* 記錄現實], to represent reality [*chengxian xianshi* 呈現現實], and to intervene in reality [*jieru xianshi* 介入現實]. This is why their practice of cinema achieved a form of visual texture blending testimony and reflection, an epic gaze, and a contemporary narrative language that the Fifth and Sixth Generation lacked."[70] Although all the directors in the volume may not share Ouyang's aesthetic characterization (in particular the epic dimension), his discussion of independence as a kind of immersive recording of and critical intervention in reality clearly sets this genre apart from the productions of the Fifth Generation. Implicit in his call to define space for noncommercial cinema is the *minjian* position of independent cinema.

In a more recent study by director Huang Wenhai (Wen Hai), Zeng Jinyan argues that a new type of "citizen-director" is emerging, who defines his or her work according to four positions: as a member of the critical intelligentsia, as an artist, as a social activist, and according to his or her gender. As intellectuals, these citizen-directors take inspiration from Edward Said's endorsement of the "amateur" who follows only his or her own interests. As artists, they turn toward the margins, which provide them with the necessary distance from mainstream society. As social activists, they contribute to helping the subaltern gain their own voice. Working from a gendered position, they investigate the modes of gendered domination at work in society. In this configuration, Zeng Jinyan sees the potential both for a new practice of film and for a new civic identity.[71]

Debates on definitions reveal important fractures. The choice of *minjian* as an aesthetic, ethical, and political program that includes highlighting narrative contingency, refusing authorial responsibility, and paying attention to social marginality has often met with contestation on the part of critics who view aesthetics and the role of intellectuals from a Gramscian perspective. Just as Wang Xiaobo's essay "The Silent Majority" challenges the understanding of class in Chinese society, independent documentary challenges the Lukácsian conception of the epic artwork that is widely shared among mainstream critics in China and overseas.

INDEPENDENT DOCUMENTARY AS A DISCURSIVE AND VISUAL PRACTICE

Independent filmmakers established themselves as *minjian* intellectuals on the basis of representations of society that were very similar to the ones Wang Xiaobo referred to in his essays.[72] Just like *minjian* historians, filmmakers also expressed this self-understanding in their textual practice: in their case, the practice of producing visual texts that encapsulated certain discourses on and representations of Chinese society. The film scholar and Yunfest organizer Yi Sicheng 易思成 underscores that independent documentaries focus on previously invisible "minority" groups in society but consider them without traces of "exotic orientalism," thanks to the aesthetic approach of modernist storytelling, including improvisation, lacunary narrative, and nonprofessional actors. In this way, he argues, independent film has done away with the need for a grand symbolic dimension.[73] This section analyzes the filmmakers' practices and its cognitive as well as aesthetic characteristics.

Far too many independent films have been produced since the early 1990s to give anything resembling a comprehensive overview;[74] instead, this section tries to point out three main characteristics that are broadly shared across this large body of visual texts. The analysis focuses on documentary films because they form a relatively more homogenous body of work, but it could be extended to feature films. Each of the three characteristics is both an aesthetic principle that guides the visual representation and a methodological discourse that implicitly advocates a certain way of understanding society. First, independent cinema has focused on the textuality of reality rather than on ideology or theory, in a direct break with "realism" as it was understood in Chinese cinema and literature before the 1990s. As Huang Wenhai puts it, "I oppose the whole idea of 'grand narratives'; the expression makes me think 'fake, big, empty'; it's a megalomaniac idea."[75] Or as Ying Qian 錢穎 puts it, "Instead of letting ideology lead the camera, contemporary filmmakers prefer to face the world with minimal a priori knowledge, allowing the lens to wander and observe what unfolds."[76] Second, independent cinema represents history as contingent time, breaking with the discourse of teleology that underpins not only visual and literary representations but also much of the historical or sociological work that is undertaken within the boundaries of Chinese academia and Marxist theory. Third, independent cinema focuses on characters envisaged as individuals rather than as "representatives" of a class or social group.

First, an example of how directors emphasize the textuality of reality rather than ideology is their interest in the theme of trains and the railway system, which frequently appear in independent documentaries. The railway grid almost inevitably stands for the "system": the strictly regulated, centralized, and severely policed state-run grid, a state within the state, which provides stable employment and transportation to many Chinese citizens[77] but long remained out of bounds to people outside the system: rural migrants, people without household registration, criminals, "hooligans." However, it is significant that the political system is viewed through concrete images rather than as a philosophical abstraction. Three films made in 2001 capture the contrast between the system and the marginal groups that survive at its borders. This engagement with reality does not rely on ideology or theories of society, Marxist or otherwise; rather, it observes the details of social texture and provides subaltern groups with an opportunity to "come out of silence."

Du Haibin's film *Along the Railroad*, which won the top prize at the first Beijing Independent Film Festival (BIFF) in 2001, focuses on teenagers living on the margins of a railway network that has become the symbol of a system that excludes them, an opening to other spaces that remain always out of reach. While the entire Chinese population is squeezing into trains—a symbol of the economic development of the country and the new opportunities for migrant workers—to return home for the New Year festival, the group of marginal youths who sleep near the Baoji station have no money to board the trains that speed past—by reversing angles rapidly, the camera suggests they are surrounded by the tracks and the trains speeding home along them. The director takes time to talk to these characters—some of them escapees from various types of penal institutions, one of them bereft of his official identity by the loss of his identity card: there is no social agenda in these conversations, no discourse about the roots of the problems portrayed, but simply a focus on the everyday events of the protagonists' lives, completely at odds with socialist realism. This film, ostensibly about the railroad, thus focuses on the appearance of marginality on the borders of a system characterized by its institutions of ordering and control. "Rails" ("Tielu" 鐵路), the last part of Wang Bing's film *West of the Tracks*, which deals with a scavenger living off the railway tracks and his son, who must fend for himself when his father is arrested, can also be viewed as a displacement from the study of the factory in part 1 to the study of individual people on the margins of the system in part 3.

The director Huang Wenhai, who has worked with Wang Bing on several films, argued for a similar reading of his own film *We the Workers* (*Xiongnian zhi pan* 凶年之畔, 2017):

> We used to see migrant workers as the silent majority. But during our conversations, they showed sharp judgment and a good understanding of life. Some had graduated from high schools and could write well. Some of their experiences struck a chord with me. Unlike public intellectuals, these workers can not only write, but also organise protests and mobilise and train each other. In the film, I used a lot of their monologues. I feel I am portraying a group of

> humans . . . in this age. I want to change the stereotype of factory workers as a social class under socialism and present them as who they are: people.[78]

Contrary to previous documentaries, the aim is not to present a social analysis of the working class, but to understand them as individuals and to establish a sense of equality and dialogue between the subjects of the film (the no longer silent majority) and the director.

Ning Ying's 寧瀛 documentary *The Railroad of Hope* (*Xiwang zhi lü* 希望之旅, 2001) is another reworking and deconstruction of the railroad motif. It follows female migrant workers traveling from Sichuan to Xinjiang for the cotton harvest. Shot with a nonrechargeable hand-held camera during a single journey from Chengdu to Ürümchi, it probes the personal lives of female migrants through direct interviews, in which the director raises questions not usually put to migrant workers, such as the meaning of happiness. As Ning Ying said in an interview, "I didn't want to explore social problems through this film. Some people criticised this film for 'asking a lot of questions that peasants wouldn't think about.' My response is that this very comment shows their own ideological constraints: 'Don't you see that all the peasants are answering my questions?'"[79] Ning Ying thus highlights that within the socioeconomic system symbolized by the railways and mass labor migrations, there is no lack of human subjectivity.

Jia Zhangke's short documentary *In Public* (*Gonggong changsuo* 公共場所, 2001) is another example of how textuality replaces ideology. Against the background of the drab, industrial landscapes of Datong, swathed in coal smog, the camera takes abode first in a train station, then at a bus stop, and finally at a long-distance bus station, waiting at length for something to happen, producing a reflexive meditation on the work of the documentary artist. As Jia argues,

> For example, if you take a train, it is not only a train, an opportunity for travel, but also an extremely powerful space: for example, if you are not able to buy a ticket, and you board the train and need to look for the conductor to obtain a seat, then you are really in a direct relationship with power. It's not at all like being in contact with a transportation company, it is, after all, the railroad ministry! So you will see all the negative aspects of power. When people cross through public spaces, by observing their appearance, their demeanor, you will get a very good idea of the relationship between an individual and the entire public system. For example, when we were shooting *In Public*, we

> shot the Datong train station. There was someone there fast asleep, apparently exhausted. But I noticed a detail: although he was sleeping, he was still tightly grasping his bag with two hands, holding on to the zipper. So by looking at his hands you could observe the dangers of travel, the chaos in society, the stealing right and left. So from an individual gesture, an individual reaction you can understand the phenomenon of power.[80]

It is by observing the details of reality that the documentary draws conclusions about the system. All the characters of *In Public* are waiting, just like the director himself: a man expecting a woman at the train station, a woman who rushes into the camera angle to catch a bus but misses it, and a mafia-like character with dark glasses observing the movements at the long-distance bus station. Jia Zhangke has described his attitude when filming as a fascination with the lives of characters "floating among the dust."[81] This short film can therefore also be read as a reflection on contingency: the contingency of successful and missed connections as well as the contingency of the work of filming itself, symbolized by the woman who rushes into the shot, finally creating an "event" in the film. In this sense, independent documentaries are often not actually "about" anything. Their subversion of the classical tenets of socialist realism serves as a starting point for investigating and reflecting on the texture of reality.

Second, the view of history that informs independent documentaries is in many ways diametrically opposite to the Marxist or Lukácsian understanding of history as an epic movement underpinned by the unstoppable laws of socioeconomic development.[82] As noted earlier, Lü Xinyu reads Wang Bing's film *West of the Tracks* as the expression of such a Hegelian teleology, which she paradoxically links with the decline of Western industrial capitalism: "The same historical rationality appears to unfold remorselessly across space and time, and no-one can escape its compulsion. As Lukács put it, in a dialectical and historical sense industry is the object of a social-natural law. It is in the spirit of this objectivity that Wang Bing constructs a narrative of the factories of Tiexi."[83] For Lü Xinyu, Wang Bing's film takes the factory as its protagonist, situating itself in the tradition of industrial cinema, in which individuals appear as interchangeable and anonymous, simple toys in the hands of the great law of history which has decreed the end of the working class, whose "majesty" (Lü's term) survives onscreen.

Although Wang Bing's tribute to industrial cinema is undeniable—for example, in the steel-smelting scene in "Rust" ("Gongchang" 工廠), the first part of *West of the Tracks*, there is little evidence for Lü Xinyu's assertion concerning the laws of history. Rather, the closure of the steel works and state-owned industries of the Northeast are presented in the film as an incomprehensible contingency. The economic justification for the closure—that they are not profitable—is hardly a new development; what is new is the sudden decision by the government to abide by the law of profit rather than to follow the logic of socialist construction. It is this absurd reversal of fortune and the sacrifice of individuals in the name of this unexplained state policy that stand at the forefront of Wang Bing's film: the workers in the lead plant who have been contaminated by their contact with the metal, one of whom commits suicide in the sanatorium; the young men and women in "Remnants" ("Yanfenjie" 艷粉街), the second part of *West of the Tracks*, who live in the residential quarters where demolition and expropriation (*chaiqian* 拆遷) in the name of "modernization" parallel the destiny of the factories. "Remnants" follows a young man named Zhao Bo 趙波, who tries to invent a love story for himself by having his mates present Valentine's Day flowers to Zhang Na 張娜, accompanied by the tune of a sentimental song titled "Ai ni wan nian 愛你萬年," thus presenting a striking contrast between the old collective lifestyle and the new culture of consumerism (this contrast is similarly illustrated in the film's opening scene, where a laid-off worker wins a car in a lottery but seems indifferent to his "luck").

The workers express no nostalgia for the factories that were so closely bound up with their lives—or for the work with heavy metals that so often imperiled them. On the contrary, the zinc worker in "Rust" who is telling his life story to the camera when someone bursts into the room to announce the closing of the factory—a typical trope of historical contingency—seems resigned and expressionless, just as the long call for a person named "Tianhai" at the end of "Remnants" remains unanswered. There is no utopian ideal here that might imbue history with meaning, neither in the collectivist past nor in the consumerist future. "Rails," the last part of the film, is also the most individualized, telling the "story" of a father and his son caught up in historic changes they can make no sense of: this is a further argument against viewing this film as collective, industrial cinema, where individuals have no place. Rather, the structure of the film, moving from the monumental impersonal factories of the first part to the collective living areas in the second and finally to the individual story of marginal characters living along the railroad tracks, follows a clear narrowing trajectory from collective to individual narration.

Jia Zhangke's film *24 City* (*Ershisi cheng ji* 二十四城記, 2008) echoes Wang Bing's interest in the dismantling and privatization of state-owned industries by turning to a former arms factory in Chengdu that has been bought by a Hong Kong real-estate developer. As Jia Zhangke writes, "The momentous transformation from a state-owned, top-secret factory to a commercial development was presented as the fate of the land, but what of the life and death, the rise and fall in fortunes, and the memories of countless workers? Where would these memories be placed?"[84] Again there is no overarching narrative; rather, the director strives to record individual stories and to encapsulate lives that are caught in an incomprehensible maelstrom of absurd politics: the factory originally stood in Manchuria, from where it was moved to the "third line of defense" after the Sino-Soviet split of 1960, uprooting thousands of workers and sending them on an odyssey across China, some of them even losing their children on the way. In the film, they are laid off once again in the name of the country's higher interests. Against the background of collective politics as a realm of uncontrollable, arbitrary forces unleashing destruction and reconstruction on a titanic scale, the film uses interviews to search for the value of the individual.

Ruins are often used in independent documentary films as ironic images of modernization. In the implicit historical narrative, modernization is not a linear progression but rather a contingent blend of creation and destruction. In Li Yifan 李一凡 and Yan Yu's 鄢雨 documentary on the Three Gorges Dam, *Before the Flood* (*Yanmo* 淹沒, 2005), the camera wanders around the town of Fengjie months and weeks before it is to be permanently flooded to make way for the dam, recording the stories and grievances of many an inhabitant. The narrative of a Korean War veteran, who has survived several historical crises of the People's Republic, only to see his home flooded and himself bused away to an artificial town, underlines the contingency to which individual lives are subject. Jia Zhangke also echoes many of these themes in his feature film *Still Life*, a story of missed connections and broken-up families that unfolds around the flooding of Fengjie in preparation for the opening of the dam. In these investigations, the construction of the dam is envisaged as an expression not of human progress but rather of how individuals are forgotten by the grand narratives of modernization.

Perhaps the ultimate expressions of history as a mound of ruins are the many films about the Sichuan earthquake. Wang Libo's film *Buried* (*Yanmai* 掩埋, 2009) uses interviews with Earthquake Bureau officials about the Tangshan quake in 1976 to highlight the duplicity of the state's discourse. Ai Xiaoming's film *Our*

Children (*Women de wawa* 我們的娃娃, 2009) uses footage from cell phones of victims in Sichuan to highlight the contrast with the Olympics propaganda that saturates the official media and to reflect on the role of independent reporting. Ai Weiwei's film *4851* (2009) is simply a list of names of confirmed children victims of the earthquake. Pan Jianlin's film *Who Killed Our Children* (*Shei shale women de haizi* 誰殺了我們的孩子, 2008) is an investigation of one school and the reasons for its collapse. Du Haibin's film *1428* (2009) is both a meditation on ruins and rubble and a series of interviews of ordinary people, officials, and victims' families, all of whom make contradictory statements. The figure of the fool (*fengzi* 瘋子), dressed in tatters, who at first appears to be an actor but turns out to also be connected to the events, a surviving ghost among all those who have not survived, also symbolizes the incomprehensible nature of the event that has taken place. This event cannot be invested with any collective meaning, whether as an act of divine vengeance or as a test of the steadfastness of the Chinese nation, as government propaganda would have it, without risking the obliteration of the memory of its individual victims.[85]

Yu Jian's film *Jade-Green Station* (*Bise chezhan* 碧色車站, 2004) focuses on the old tracks built by the French colonial administration in Indochina to connect Kunming with Hanoi. Working by free association, Yu Jian subverts the rational, linear design of both the colonial train system and the modern capitalist trade route that has now taken its place, highlighting personal memories of French presence, village anecdotes, faded slogans from the Cultural Revolution, and a form of parallel history. As Yu Jian writes, the camera is a violent tool, like a weapon, that fragments the world: "weapons smash the world into pieces, and the camera too cuts off fragments of the world that was previously an indistinct whole."[86] His film is not reportage; rather, the only intermittently visible railway track becomes a poetic metaphor for the meaningless and unpredictable course of history, in which the town of Bise, which gives the film its title, today a forgotten backwater on a dead-end railway line, is also remembered in a half-mythical, reconstructed manner as "Little Shanghai." Far from offering the official historical narrative of liberation from "imperialism" and foreign encroachment, Yu Jian's images show how Bise went from being a cosmopolitan commercial hub at the intersection of empires to a rural backwater, forgotten by history.

The third aspect of the aesthetics of independent documentary is its interest in individuality rather than in the representativity that gives socialist realism its meaning and justification. To commemorate the PRC's sixtieth anniversary and as a counternarrative to the collectivist pageant staged in Beijing, Zhang Ming's documentary film *60* (2009) focuses on a single character, a Chongqing *minjian* intellectual named Wang Kang 王康, whose life, though bound up with the twists and turns of Chinese politics, is hardly representative of the official narrative. A former high school teacher and expert on the Soviet economy, Wang Kang became caught up in the aftermath of the movement of 1989 and had to spend ten years in hiding; he was finally saved only by a high-placed politician who was able to wipe his record clean.

Similar comments can be made about certain films devoted to the Mao era. In the opening sequence of Wang Bing's film *He Fengming* 和鳳鳴 (2007), the camera follows the former rightist He Fengming, seen from behind, through the snow in the dusk. Without turning around, she leads the camera and the audience into her small apartment in an old-style red-brick compound, which we later understand to be in Lanzhou, sits down in front of the camera, and begins talking. One might read this beginning sequence as a manner of counteracting the grand narratives in which a particular character is interviewed because of the outstanding meaning of his or her testimony, which can symbolically stand for a whole nation. Here, the camera literally seems to pick up He Fengming in the street, focusing on a random passer-by, whom it follows to her home, only to discover the travails of her life story. There is no attempt at symbolic totalization in the film—for example, through the use of voiceover or archival material or other interviews. Although we know that this interview was one among a series that Wang Bing undertook in preparation for his film *The Ditch*, there is no juxtaposition with other testimony putting it into perspective. The path the individual traces for herself in history, just like He Fengming's shuffling through the snow in the opening scene, although it may seem ordinary, is unique and incommensurable. The story He Fengming tells is private; there are no lessons to be learned for the community.

Among the many documentaries that focused on the private sphere in this period, Liu Jiayin's 劉伽茵 *Oxhide* (*Niupi* 牛皮) series, filming mundane moments of discussion in a family setting, stand out for their attention to the apparently most uneventful routines: making a leather bag in *Oxhide* (2005), making dumplings in *Oxhide II* (2009). As Liu said,

> I think these daily routines are interesting in themselves. I don't have to add anything else to these moments in order to make them interesting to me. I

> don't think you need somebody to catch fire, or for somebody to die, to make them worthy of observing. So daily routines aren't backdrops in my films—they're the subject, and that's very important. Nothing is simply a backdrop, just like in life. I can't just say "today wasn't really that interesting so I'll cut that out," that this day wasn't really part of my life, or it was simply part of the backdrop of something else that was more real. . . .
>
> It all exists, it's all equal. So this is a way of looking at life, and if you take this way of looking at life and put it into a film it becomes a new method of filmmaking. And that's what I'm trying to do. . . .
>
> I'm sure my values can be seen in my films, but I don't want to make any great statements about society. I don't want to try to represent anyone or pose any arguments about how society should be. . . . In China today, most filmmakers seem to think they need to represent somebody in order to give their films weight. A film has to represent a certain class or profession. I think if I can manage to represent myself then I'm already doing quite well![87]

The extreme attention to the cinematic technique, using fixed frames, an extra-wide lens, a rigid structure where the camera turns by a certain angle between every shot in *Oxhide II*, contrasts with the apparent vacuous quality of the film itself. This focus on "representing herself" and on filming the ordinary and the everyday can be seen not only as a mannerist aesthetic experiment but also as a form of bringing the camera back into the world of *minjian* authenticity and amateur video.

Even when the ostentatious subject of a film is a "social" topic, independent directors often deliberately avoid a "representative" approach and focus on both the individuality and the ordinariness of the people they depict. Two films on the topic of petitioners particularly stand out. For more than ten years, from 1996 to 2009, Zhao Liang visited the petitioner village near Beijing's South Railway station and filmed the people he met there, becoming as engaged in his project as they in their petitions. The long version of *Petition* (*Shangfang* 上訪, 2009) is divided into three parts: "The Masses" (Zhongsheng 眾生), "Mother and Daughter" (Mu nü 母女), and "Beijing South Station" (Beijing Nanzhan 北京南站). The first part consists of a series of monologues of petitioners presenting their cases to the camera as if the filmmaker were also part of the petitioning system. In the second part, the director gets closely involved in the individual story of one mother–daughter family, even serving as an involuntary messenger for the daughter when she decides to run away. The third part puts the story of the film's protagonists back into the historical context of the modernization of Beijing and preparations for the Olympic Games, with the inauguration of the new South Station built on the ruins of the petitioner village to serve the national high-speed rail system and the fireworks for the Olympics inauguration ceremony.

As Jie Li has noted, Zhao Liang is at pains to take the perspective of the "powerless" to make visible a community of people who are rarely seen, whether onscreen or in life, and to show them under the surveillance of ubiquitous state institutions.[88] But Zhao Liang is also determined to give a form of agency back to the petitioners who have been deprived of it. There is no omniscient discourse to qualify petitioners' claims and explain their existence in collective terms. Rather, he repeatedly shows that each petition is an individual project; petitioners need it because it is a form of political agency, paradoxical as this may seem given the almost inexistent chances of success. They do not petition because they hope to achieve recognition but because petitioning gives meaning to their lives and leaves open the possibility that they do not have to accept whatever injustice has befallen them; they will not let the system define their lives. Zhao Liang repeatedly shows petitioners engaging in political discussion and claim making. After a female petitioner commits suicide by lying down on the train track, her friends organize a demonstration in the petitioner village, calling for democracy, human rights, and the end of one-party rule. In part three, another petitioner carefully analyzes the reasons for the "dictatorial" (*ducai* 獨裁) nature of the Chinese government. A young man studying a book with the title *Democracy Reader* (*Minzhu jiaocheng* 民主教程) argues that a democracy must show tolerance and hence open up to other political forces than the United Front parties. Throughout these sequences, Zhao Liang tries to use his film to allow ordinary people to express the political ideas that find no place in the public sphere. In an interview, Zhao Liang explains how the dignity he tries to bestow on his characters translates into an aesthetics: "The characters in this film are very elegant. To see elegance and grace from the petitioners is exactly what I want to express. . . . I'm like a fish, swimming in the reality of Chinese society. My deepest feelings and thoughts are about the institutional system. I'm touching it all the time and all I want to express is related to it. . . . My fear for it is deeply rooted in me."[89] His occasional aestheticism is therefore not designed to ignore the institutional context, which is always present, but rather to be used as a tool to give his subjects a dignity the system denies them.

Part 2 of *Petition* represents a kind of counterpoint: the mother Qi Huaying 戚華映 has petitioned for more than twenty years by the end of the film (and been committed to a mental institution several times), and her daughter, Xiaojuan 小娟, has had no choice for much of her life. When she learns that she is an adopted child, she tries to find a way out. After escaping with the filmmaker's tacit complicity, she ironically ends up being taken in by a Letters and Visits Bureau official in Taizhou, who adopts her and officiates as the father at her wedding while using her story to bolster his career thanks to an official CCTV documentary. However, Xiaojuan ends up feeling remorseful and, under the gaze of a different type of camera controlled by the independent filmmaker Zhao Liang, goes back to Beijing to ask for her mother's forgiveness.

Throughout the project, Zhao Liang seems to have been interested in showing that petitioning is a universal form of meaning making, which does not differ in nature from other people's lives:

> There was a phase where I would set up the camera and have them talk. They could talk about whatever they wanted. I filmed a lot of these interviews. At the time I was thinking about doing a large scale installation, perhaps putting up several dozen screens with these people talking about their experiences simultaneously. Work began on the new South Railway station around 2006, and this marked the impending end of a chapter in the lives of the petitioners living there. I had a feeling that the film should end with the opening of the new railway station, so I also started filming the construction there. Interestingly, as the railway station expanded, a boss of one of the petitioner hotels also became a victim of forced demolition, and he ended up building a shack and petitioning. I remembered something that the petitioners often said: today I'm the one petitioning, but tomorrow it could be you.[90]

The original project to create an installation with petitioners occupying the entire space around the viewer was Zhao's first idea to express the mirror-image relationship between the petitioners and the audience. He ends up translating this project from a spatial into a temporal schema, showing that anyone who refuses to submit to injustice can be caught up in the dynamics of petitioning. At a post-screening discussion in Songzhuang's Fanhall Café organized by Zhu Rikun

朱日坤, the sociologist Yu Jianrong drew a direct connection between the problem of petitioning and the nature of the Chinese political system. The famous art critic Li Xianting 栗憲庭 noted its allegorical meaning for the whole of Chinese society, which is trapped within a system where the only hope for many people is one day to meet an upright official (*qingguan* 清官).[91]

Ma Li's 馬莉 (b. 1975) film *Born in Beijing* (*Jingsheng* 京生, 2011) is built around a similar idea: the main character in the film, Hao Wenzhong 郝文忠, is a former petitioner who becomes the boss of a petitioner hostel. Having petitioned for thirty years (she began in 1977 on the first anniversary of Mao's death), she has spent twelve years in prison and been locked up countless times in a mental ward. Like Xiaojuan, Hao's daughter Jingsheng, who gives her name to the film, was born while Hao Wenzhong petitioned. Just like Xiaojuan, Jingsheng feels "wronged" (*weiqu* 委屈) by her mother, who is keeping her away from her own small children and husband. A young man from Chongqing who is petitioning because of a forced vasectomy tells Ma Li that although he has no hope of finding an "upright official," he cannot stop petitioning because it is about his "lifelong happiness [*yisheng de xingfu* 一生的幸福]." Here, too, the director brings out the paradox of individual lives that are both invaded by and defined by their petition cases, which give their lives meaning but end up crowding out any alternative life. Petitioners are individuals before they are a social phenomenon.

What defines *minjian* cinema can be summarized as the close attention to documenting realities (in particular those unknown to mainstream society), the rejection of any form of teleology, and of the canonical realist ideal of representativity. Marginality, contingency, and individuality are instead brought to the fore. What brings these three strands together is their contribution to an open-endedness that points in the direction of the audience. As Ying Qian writes, independent cinema seeks to "break the state's monopoly on the interpretation of the physical and social world and return that right to ordinary people."[92] The questions raised in these films—about the interpretation of social reality, the reading of history, and the respective value of the individual and the collective—aim to bring about a much-needed discussion on the common values of Chinese society.

MINJIAN SPACES ON THE MARGINS: FESTIVALS, ARTIST VILLAGES, UTOPIAN COMMUNITIES

The reaffirmation of aesthetic autonomy as a form of professional ethics by *minjian* directors did not result in privatization and commercialization of independent film (as Lü Xinyu predicted), but rather in the opening of new spaces and counterpublics. Zhang Xianmin distinguishes three types of "spheres of reception" of independent documentary: the filmmaker and his or her private circle (dominant from 1990 to 2001), a "controlled group communication" (film clubs, social groups, etc., dominant from 2001 to 2008), and the mass media. He argues that Chinese documentary knowingly avoided mass-media communication and focused instead on a sphere of "limited community": "I would call this the 'see audience,' the communicative effect of which is an exponentially increasing process of informative achievement, contrary to the effect of mass media."[93]

In the early 1990s, the first "spaces" for independent films were situated overseas (the third Yamagata Documentary Film Festival screened six Chinese films in 1993;[94] the Busan International Film Festival hosted Jia Zhangke's early films) or in Hong Kong (the Hong Kong International Film Festival played a central role beginning in the early 1990s),[95] but in the late 1990s the practice of *minjian* film created new spaces in China itself. The first among these spaces were film clubs, such as Office 101 in Shanghai, Southern Film Forum in Guangzhou, Back Window Films in Nanjing, the Box Bar in Beijing. Many of them held screenings or discussions in cafés, university facilities, and art spaces or at exhibitions.[96] These spaces were followed by the establishment of independent festivals: after the first independent film festival held at the BFA in 2001 (which continued in different locations in the following years), the biennial Yunfest devoted to documentary was launched in Kunming in March 2003 under the Yunnan Academy of Social Sciences; the DOChina Festival was held in Beijing in April 2003; and the China Independent Film Festival was held in Nanjing in September 2003.[97] A little later, the BIFF began to be held in Songzhuang from 2006, joined in 2009 by the China Independent Film Archive festival held in the Iberia Art Center in Beijing's 798 Art District. Counterpublics networked online, using video-posting sites such as Tudou and Youku as well as social groups such as Douban, although there were frequent disputes about copyright. As noted in a recent study, the practice of independent film transformed China's public culture by opening new spaces of social commentary and critique.[98] This section studies the case of one of these *minjian* spaces, the artist village in Songzhuang, which became a center of China's independent film and film festival culture in the early 2000s, and in so doing suggests that the *minjian* quality of independent film is not only a political agenda of directors or an aesthetic characteristic of filmic texts but also a marker of the counterpublics that formed around independent film.

Artist villages as marginal spaces first appeared in the 1980s and further developed in the aftermath of 1989 as control over work units weakened and the *mangliu* (drifter) developed as a halfway accepted cultural model for aspiring artists. Yuanmingyuan, the Old Summer Palace just beyond Peking University in Northwest Beijing, was the first area in which, beginning in 1986, artists—including future directors Zhao Liang and Hu Jie, who began as visual artists—rented inexpensive houses from villagers and pursued their work in relative freedom and marginality.[99] In the early 1990s, they were joined by migrant workers, who for lack of a Beijing residence permit, were not able to rent legitimate lodgings. The settlement reached a peak population of two to three hundred around 1992. In the following years, they were increasingly harassed by the police, and in 1995 the village was completely torn down, compelling the artists to move to a different district altogether.

Xiaopu 小堡 village in rural Songzhuang township, Tongzhou District, about twenty kilometers east of Beijing's second ring road, was the home of one of the students who frequented Yuanmingyuan, Jin Guowang 靳國旺. He introduced several artists—including Fang Lijun 方力鈞, Yue Minjun 岳敏君, and the influential art critic Li Xianting—to Xiaopu and made the connection with the village leader, Cui Dabo 崔大柏. Because Xiaopu was poor due to bad-quality soil, the village committee was eager to rent or sell plots and courtyard houses to the artists.[100] Cui, a mason with a high school diploma and military experience who built houses for several artists, understood the benefits the artists could bring to the village and protected them against attempts at repression from the township government. The artists, initially challenged by the lack of infrastructure, raised money for street lamps, which in turn pleased the villagers.[101] A modus vivendi was established.

In the late 1990s and early 2000s, the encounter of marginal groups—peasants, migrant workers, and artists—gave rise to a new type of community before commercialization and development began increasingly to estrange artists and peasants: "Farmers-village collective-artists, in Li Xianting's eyes, this was the normal structure of the Xiaopu village ecosystem." For Li, the early years can be seen as a kind of utopian experiment: "That the goal of achieving a professional lifestyle could serve as a rallying point for artists is in itself a remarkable cultural phenomenon. It meant that to become an artist you had to choose the path of freedom and independence. . . . From this perspective, Yuanmingyuan was a manifesto, Songzhuang was the practical experiment."[102]

The CASS rural sociologist and *minjian* intellectual Yu Jianrong moved to Xiaopu in 2002 and bought and rebuilt a house that he called "Eastern Study" (Dong Shufang 東書房), in which he set up his personal archive of petitioner files. He took a particular interest in the village:

> Songzhuang culture is a pluralistic social phenomenon. On the one hand, it is a traditional northern Chinese village, inhabited by peasants who have cultivated the land for many generations. At the same time, it is the frontline of avant-garde art, where a whole bunch of idealistic artists have congregated. . . . After I settled in Songzhuang, I repeatedly forced myself to forget my meaningless status as an investigator and researcher and to live like Songzhuang people. Therefore, for many years, I became a Songzhuang peasant. Just like villagers of my generation, I built a house, planted vegetables, kept dogs, burned coal for heating; and at the same time, I also defined myself as an artist. Together with artists from all directions, I painted, wrote lyrics, held rambling conversations, shot films. I made this free and unrestrained life into the reality of my existence. I often forgot my original profession, not to mention academic pursuits or the scholar's responsibility.[103]

In addition to being an academic working on the subject matter of petitioners and migrant workers, Yu incarnated the cultural melting pot of artists and villagers that Songzhuang stood for.

After a promoter unsuccessfully attempted to buy the entire Xiaopu village in 2002, the artists' presence there was increasingly acknowledged and institutionalized by the state. In 2004, the Songzhuang township government, persuaded by the increase of income in Xiaopu, launched a "revival through art" plan complete with a gigantic museum and designated Xiaopu as a development site for creative industries, a decision confirmed by the Beijing municipal government in 2006.[104] In 2005, the Association for the Promotion of Art was set up to monitor the artists.[105] In 2008, when the commercial weekly *Sanlian Shenghuo Zhoukan* published a detailed report on Li Xianting and Songzhuang, Xiaopu village had a nonresident population of six thousand, four times the number of registered inhabitants; eighty-eight art galleries; a gross domestic product of 600 million yuan; and a tax revenue of 20 million yuan, which made it the most affluent of Songzhuang's twenty-two natural villages. Later, when Songzhuang was rezoned as urban land and the development company owned by the township government undertook "demolition and relocation,"[106] Xiaopu was able to successfully resist the rezoning process and remain a rural village, thanks to a "coalition" of the artists and the village authorities.[107] Nonetheless, rents have continued to increase exponentially, and Xiaopu is increasingly in danger of becoming a consumerist theme park, like the 798 Art District.[108] The township's policy, using artist villages to promote cultural industries, was not a wholehearted endorsement, but rather a form of "limited tolerance in order to create a better global image for itself." It can be argued that such limited tolerance also served to "quarantine" artists from the rest of society and to control them.[109]

Li Xianting was an influential academic and art critic who was known for curating an exhibition on "boredom art" (*wuliao yishu* 無聊藝術) after 1989 and for discovering many future stars in Yuanmingyuan. He moved to Songzhuang in 1995 and was interested in promoting independent cinema, in particular documentary film. He recruited Wu Wenguang and the curator Zhang Yaxuan for a new journal to be titled *New Wave: Archives of On-location Art* (*Xinchao: Yishu Xianchang Dang'an* 新潮 藝術現場檔案) in 2000. Zhu Rikun, a PKU banking major, arrived in Songzhuang around 2001 and set up Fanhall (Xianxiang 現象) in December 2001, originally a film club on the model of the early film-lover associations and later also a café and screening venue. Zhu also organized DOChina (also known as China Documentary Film Festival [Zhongguo Jilupian Jiaoliu Zhou 中國紀錄片交流週]), an annual festival that took place for the first time from March 29 to April 1, 2003, at Beijing Normal University (screening Wang Bing's *West of the Tracks* as the opening film). It was held for a second year at the Millennium Monument (Shijitan) on June 21–25, 2004, provoking a crackdown by the venue management.[110] As a consequence of this crackdown, it proved impossible to organize DOChina in 2005, but in 2006 it took place on April 18–22 at the China University of Science and Technology in Hefei, far from Beijing.

Li set up the Li Xianting Film Fund in 2006 and entrusted the management of it to Zhu Rikun; it was registered as a company in 2008.[111] Well-known artists and business people provided support.[112] The fund had four components: the DOChina Film Festival, which Zhu brought with him; the BIFF; the Film Archive (established in 2006) and the Film School (from 2009).[113] Starting from its fourth edition in 2007, DOChina took place in May in the Fanhall Café in Songzhuang.[114] BIFF was set up in 2006 with Li as artistic director and Zhu as program director (with Wang Bing), and the first festival was held in October as part of the Songzhuang International Arts Festival curated by Li Xianting at the Songzhuang Museum.[115] Sections for student works, experimental works, and animation were progressively added. In 2009, Zhu Rikun described BIFF's mission as an antidote to dominant discourses:

> Often there are people who discuss the "power to speak," but no matter who controls this power, it seems as if his/her position changes extraordinarily fast. Those in the past who shot "underground films" are now busy shooting government propaganda films; those who before catered to foreigners now hurry to cooperate with domestic businesspeople. That is to say, film festivals are unwelcome affairs, seeming to be out of tune and superfluous to society. As a result, film festivals appear luxurious to many people; however, this "superfluous" work must continue. Luckily, cinema is still emerging. Even though the lens doesn't have a tongue, it seems to communicate in ways that exceed the mouth. Everyone says his/her camera doesn't lie, so lying is certainly a human affair.[116]

Taking up the role of remaining on the margins of both politics and commercial cinema, Zhu highlights that cinema, in contrast to mainstream society, is silent or cannot make itself heard.[117] Here again, we may read an echo of Wang Xiaobo's reflections on contesting the hegemony of discourse.

In 2010, the BIFF encountered its first major interference from the authorities and had to move to Chengdu.[118] The Li Xianting Film Fund was repeatedly investigated, and Zhu Rikun had to separate himself from it in 2010, at which point Wang Hongwei (Jia Zhangke's favorite actor, who had played the character Xiao Wu) took over the role of the festival's artistic director.[119] In 2011, the eighth DOChina in May was interrupted by the authorities; some documentaries were shown at the sixth BIFF in October, but the organizers again endured harassment and had to move the festival to Yanjiao in nearby Hebei, which is under a different provincial jurisdiction.[120] In the catalog for this sixth festival, Li Xianting reaffirmed the *minjian* nature of the festival, the tenet of independence, and underscored that it did not challenge those in power:

> Yet there is no need for those involved in independent film to emphasize their marginal identity, and even less of a need to oppose the industry and ideology of mainstream film or even the present system. We only want to make the films we like! This is a society gradually moving towards pluralism, presenting views that are growing more diverse. . . . Relative to the business and ideological message in cinema, we only care about the expression of independent spirit. This kind of independence emerges from the loyalty with which the individual filmmaker follows his/her feeling, and from exploring and experimenting with forms of expression. . . . This is a forum with almost no relation to mainstream society; it is for the people [*minjian*], self-funded and self-determined.[121]

Despite the affirmation of the festival's harmless and grassroots character, the authorities continued to intervene.

In 2012, the two festivals merged under the name "Beijing Independent Film Festival," retaining the numbering of the older DOChina series (so that the festival in 2012 was the "ninth BIFF," even though the BIFF in 2011 was the "sixth BIFF"). The organizers received more than one hundred submissions, and more than five hundred spectators attended the opening.[122] This time, Li Xianting's introduction theorized the necessary emergence of alternative spaces:

> At a time when the whole of mainstream culture is tending towards consumerism and entertainment, at a time when we can neither change the wider environment with anger, nor fully express our anger, I believe what we can do for our culture is to promote the formation of unofficial "small environments" [*xiao huanjing* 小環境] in all social arenas. This is a constructive effort; it builds culture from [the] bottom up. The immaturity of Chinese modern culture has put several generations of us in an awkward in-between position. We do not know what is the best culture, but we know that turning everything into entertainment is rotten culture. Anger may not be the best way to halt this rotten culture; instead each person should take up a simple and straightforward attitude to confront one's true self. The coming together of authentic selves, like the convergence of small streams, can help us move from "small circles" to "small environments," and even to the wider environment.[123]

However, such "small environments" and counterpublics were perhaps exactly what the authorities wanted to nip in the bud. The opening screening of the ninth BIFF, under heavy police surveillance, was interrupted by an electricity blackout. "Guerilla screenings," moving nimbly from place to place, eventually took place in Fang Lijun's and other artists' workshops. In November 2012, the sixth Nanjing festival was also shut down.

In 2013 and 2014, the BIFF was disrupted and entirely shut down, respectively, and a decade of archives, computer files, and DVDs were confiscated and lost forever.[124] The Film School was also raided in 2013, and students were taken home or to Beijing train stations by the police.[125] Public activities all but came to end, although the Film School continued to operate in always changing locations. In the catalog for the BIFF in 2014, Wang Hongwei echoes Zhu Rikun's earlier point about speech and silence, noting that *minjian* directors are in danger of being pushed back into silence:

> I don't know whether black ear fungus, shaped like human ears, could actually help recover one's hearing. . . . Can Chinese independent cinema rid us from the so-called "spineless symptoms" widespread in mainstream pictures? On and off the silver screen, many of us have already lost our hearing. Or to be more accurate, we have lost our ability to speak. The emergence of the sound picture is the greatest milestone in film history. However, in a "voiceless" era, everybody needs to fix their non-functioning ears.[126]

Minjian society is voiceless among mainstream discourses and images controlled by the state and the market, and independent film is the only way for some individuals to preserve their "spine." Although some independent film activities continue, in particular at the school, the public space that had emerged around the Songzhuang festivals, was reduced to silence.[127] As Wang Hongwei notes, the issue is not scraping together the 200,000 yuan needed to organize a festival but to find a stable status for the Film Fund. Despite (or because of) Songzhuang's unique community, he is not optimistic that the festival can continue.[128]

There are a few other examples of similar communities or publics, each with its own distinctive characteristics. Yunfest, held in Kunming every two years from 2003 to 2013, grew out of an anthropological film tradition at the Institute of Anthropology, Yunnan Academy of Social Sciences, where the organizers Yi Sicheng and He Yuan 和渊 held positions. There was no artist village in Kunming comparable to Songzhuang (although some lived in Dali), but Yunfest stood out by its high standards and artistic tradition, which also defined a community: "Its [the documentary genre's] originality stems from its simplicity and plainness. . . . While the entire film industry attempts to make film into a dream factory . . . only independent documentary presents itself unadorned, proudly and with self-respect preserving the independent thinking and judgment of 'I think therefore I am' and dedicated to 'my hand writes my mind,' safeguarding the ancient principle of truth, goodness and beauty."[129]

Yi Sicheng argued that Chinese independent documentary is a specific phenomenon, which cannot be reduced to the Western concept of "cinema vérité" or "direct cinema." Rather, it expresses "the knowledge system of this entire generation, their aesthetic experience, and even the influence of Chinese aesthetic tradition on this form of expression."[130] Independent documentary is, in this view, an alternative way of understanding the world. After several instances of harassment, in 2013 Yunfest was first moved to Dali, then shut down completely, with participants passing around DVDs and watching them in their hotel rooms. Yi Sicheng ascribed this harassment to a decision made by the national security bureaucracy rather than to a local issue.[131]

A different kind of artistic community, less connected to cinema, was set up by Ou Ning 歐寧, a music promoter from Shenzhen and underground publisher, and Zuo Jing 左靖 in the Bishan Commune in rural Anhui in 2011,[132] where Ou moved with his family in 2013. Referring to the rural reformer James Yen (Yan Yangchu 晏陽初) and the Russian anarchist Peter Kropotkin, Ou set out an agenda of reviving the sense of rural community and questioning urbanization, development, and the expropriation of farmland. Bishan members were recruited through the Internet, and all decisions were to be taken through consensus democracy. He claimed a distance from both the Mao era and hypercapitalist development, choosing to use the term "community" (*gongtongti* 共同體) rather than "commune" (*gongshe* 公社, the term used for the Paris Commune).[133] However, Bishan, too, ran into difficulties with the authorities and was closed on May 2, 2016.[134]

From the 1990s, filmmakers defined themselves in ways significantly different from their predecessors. As *minjian* intellectuals, independent directors have carved out a space, both geographically and intellectually, that is neither part of the state institutions nor directly connected to the commercial circuit (although some individuals may move in and out of both the former and the latter) but is rather a kind of "third sector." Their aesthetics is not simply a matter of form but defines a specific methodology and a system of knowledge production that does not reflect the dominant norms of academic or journalistic inquiry: it is open-ended, egalitarian, sometimes confusing. This mode of inquiry (and indeed of life) places them in a social and geographical position that is in close proximity to their subjects, at the margins of big cities, in artist villages, and in rural enclaves. These filmmakers have developed their own way of understanding society and of situating themselves among the silent majority, which would seem quite unfamiliar to most elite intellectuals working in academic positions. Their empirical approach defines a new methodology of inquiry, which is significant of how critical discourses are embedded in Chinese society (rather than being only in the eyes of the Western observer[135]).

Throughout its twenty years of existence in China, independent film has never really enjoyed a loosening of state controls. When independent films appeared in the 1990s, the state still had a full-fledged monopoly over film production, theater distribution, and television broadcasting. All productions were supervised by the Film and Television Bureau (set up in 1986), which was merged with radio into the State Administration of Radio, Film, and Television in 1998 and with press and publications into the State Administration of Press, Publication, Radio, Film, and Television in 2013. The first reforms of the state system took place in 1995, when provincial studios were authorized to produce films, and private coproducers were allowed to invest capital if they could fund 70 percent of costs.[136] These reforms resulted in a culture of mainstream blockbusters largely guided by state priorities but with significant amounts of private funding. A further round of reforms took place in 2003, when independent directors were given an opportunity to be inducted into the system. Documentaries not produced through the television system remained generally in a gray zone, although a very small number were approved for theater distribution.[137]

However, this space was not durably institutionalized. In November 2016, the Film Industry Promotion Law was passed, containing further measures to simplify and generally strengthen the mainstream film industry through subsidies and support for theater distribution of domestic films. It also strongly reaffirmed ideology: the need for films to "spread core socialist values," to serve "the people and socialism, [to] prioritize social benefit, and [to] coordinate social and economic effects."[138] It made it an offense to partner with overseas entities whose views are considered "harmful to China's dignity, honor and interests, harm social stability or hurt the feelings of the Chinese people,"[139] and reaffirmed in law the common practice of imposing five-year bans on directors who show unauthorized films at foreign festivals.[140] Finally, Article 35 of the law makes the organization of any type of film festival or film "exhibit" dependent on approval from the Film Bureau or its local administration. Article 49 bans public screening or festival screening of any films that have not obtained an official permit.[141] These provisions practically make all the independent film activities that have taken place in China over the past twenty years illegal. Whereas some critics remain optimistic about independent filmmakers' ability to create new niches to continue their work in the gaps in the system,[142] these directors may well be pushed so far to the margins as to disappear from sight altogether.

CHAPTER 5

Professionals at the Grassroots

Rights Lawyers, Academics, and Petitioners

On March 20, 2003, Sun Zhigang, a recently graduated designer without a local residence permit, was found dead in the clinic of a Custody and Repatriation Center in Guangzhou after being detained and suffering torture. The incident was reported in *Southern Metropolis Daily* (*Nanfang Dushi Bao* 南方都市報) and caused an uproar among intellectuals and especially lawyers. After a letter written by three young legal scholars to the National People's Congress, the custody and repatriation (*shourong qiansong* 收容遣送) system, officially set up to prevent migrant workers from settling in cities, was abolished in June. Sun Zhigang's status as a university graduate rather than an "ordinary" migrant worker undoubtedly played a role in drawing attention to this vulnerable group that *minjian* intellectuals had been trying to work with and raise awareness about.

This event marked an as yet unequalled high point in the use of legal means to roll back some of the most contested political arrangements within the system. Since the 1990s, lawyers and legal scholars had been playing an increasingly prominent role in challenging the government. The failure of the student movement in 1989 led critically minded intellectuals in the 1990s to step back from efforts at changing the regime and instead to focus on more concrete projects.[1] This approach was in sympathy with the democracy movement, but it also introduced a critical distance from the previous generation. Trying to use the letter of the law to change political practices was both a more practical and restrained approach (limited to circumscribed problems rather than challenging the system as a whole) and a concrete way of attempting to deal with many problems within Chinese society. The law was increasingly seen as a tool to advance the liberalization of society, when legal professionals gradually understood that rights-based arguments could be effective.

This evolution also signaled the rise of the professions as economic reforms proceeded throughout the 1990s. Lawyers were needed for China's economic development, and they articulated a professional ethos that both limited their area of intervention and empowered them to intervene within (and later expand) their sphere of competence. In this sense, some of the legal activists of the 1990s and 2000s may be seen as specific intellectuals. Furthermore, in comparison to discussions in the 1980s, these efforts were strongly reoriented toward the grass roots. Legal activism emerged as a reply to problems such as forced eviction and uncompensated expropriation related to land development and rezoning, residency status (access to health care and schooling for migrants and their children), discrimination, labor law abuses, and requests for reparation and compensation for political persecution during the pre-reform era or among Falungong practitioners. In turn, prominent rights-defense cases contributed to developing a form of rights consciousness among ordinary citizens, which led them to turn more systematically to lawyers and legal scholars for help. In this sense, the "specific intellectuals" that emerged through the rise of professions were not only experts beholden to the state or the market but also *minjian* intellectuals who grounded their social legitimacy in the work they undertook with disenfranchised communities. As a whole, legal professionals were also less beholden to the state than were other categories of society.[2] The law became a new tool to deal with political problems in a concrete (rather than theoretical) manner and on the basis of specialized knowledge.

THE SUN ZHIGANG INCIDENT AND THE NEW APPROACH OF "RIGHTS PROTECTION"

After the relaunch of economic reforms in 1992, the 1990s were a period during which the state supported continued professionalization of legal work in step with the growing role of the market economy. At a speech to senior officials in 1996, the year the new Law on Lawyers was adopted (ostensibly removing them from state employment and creating a bar association), Jiang Zemin put forward the notion of "governing according to the law" (*yi fa zhi guo* 依法治國) as a means to buttress confidence in the party and the Reform and Opening policy.[3] The notion of *weiquan* 維權, "protecting rights," originated within the framework of the party-controlled discourse on rights granted by the state as a useful safety valve for popular discontent whose use could be controlled.[4] However, some legal scholars appropriated this concept to "demonstrate the power of the law and protect the rights of the party concerned, to call on the government to abide by the law, to expose the unlawful actions of officials, to use the court of public opinion to monitor law enforcement departments when necessary, or to defend civil rights through legal arguments in court."[5] Eva Pils argues that this interpretation of *weiquan* opened up the possibility to "vernacularize" the idea of human rights, an important notion in a context in which abstract critiques of the political system are often dismissed as irrelevant to ordinary people.[6] In any case, it resulted in an improvement of the perception of lawyers in society that was in step with an increasing professionalization of lawyers as a group bound not only by common knowledge but also by common standards and norms.[7] At least one of the subgroups among lawyers developed a strong argument for the importance of the autonomous rules of the profession.[8]

It was against this background that the Sun Zhigang affair marked a turning point. Sun Zhigang, who had been living in Guangzhou without a temporary residence permit, was taken into custody on March 17, 2003, and discovered beaten to death on March 20 in the clinic of a Custody and Repatriation Center. *Southern Metropolis Daily*, a newspaper from the liberal Southern Media Group, edited by Cheng Yizhong 程益中, reported the death on April 24, sparking an outcry.[9] On May 14, three Ph.D. graduates from PKU Law School, Xu Zhiyong 許志永, Teng Biao 滕彪 and Yu Jiang 俞江, published an open letter under the title "Proposal on Reviewing the *Measures for Internment and Deportation of Urban Vagrants and Beggars*," which was reported in the official newspaper *Legal Daily* (*Fazhi Ribao* 法制日報). As Teng Biao recalls, after intense discussion, they decided not to reference Sun's case directly or to list the human rights violations incurred but instead to focus on the PRC Constitution and the recent Law on Legislation, challenging the constitutionality of a regulation that served as legal basis for the detention. Their goal was both to provoke the repeal of the State Council regulation and to initiate a constitutional review system.[10] Xu Zhiyong insisted that the letter be framed not as a petition but as a legal document.[11] Although the National People's Congress ostensibly ignored the letter, on June 16, 2003, the State Council repealed its regulation and transformed the Custody and Repatriation Centers into "Social Aid Centers." Through this face-saving repeal, the State Council avoided having its regulation struck down as unconstitutional by the National People's Congress, yet for the first time the authorities implicitly acknowledged that an unconstitutional legal rule was not legally valid. However, in Teng Biao's view, the case's main contribution was in raising awareness about rights:

> The Sun Zhigang incident has increased popular concern for rule of law, constitutionalism, and human rights. The movement has made these large, abstract goals more concrete and relevant for individual persons who fight for their rights in their daily lives. This is why an increasing number of average people have joined the movement, including lawyers, netizens, writers, intellectuals, farmers, students, and petitioners. While these average people try to resolve the issues affecting their own lives, they also fight for greater, more abstract rights. . . .
>
> Some of these ideas—freedom of political organization, the right to vote, a free press—had been raised by intellectuals, students, and activists during the democracy movement in the 1980s and 1990s as they protested official corruption. In the rights defense movement, however, these ideals remain, yet the focus has moved more to individual cases of injustice in order to broaden their appeal for ordinary people. This has helped in constructing a larger narrative for the movement from many small narratives—the thousands of cases in which ordinary people have fought for their rights, and it has forged a closer connection between liberal intellectuals and ordinary people.[12]

Weiquan lawyers can therefore be characterized by their attention to the thousands of "small narratives" of ordinary people confronted with injustice.

The Sun Zhigang case to a large extent determined the roadmap of the emerging "rights-protection" movement. Teng Biao notes that at first scholars referred to 2003 as year one of the civil rights mobilization (*minquan xingdong yuannian* 民權行動元年).[13] *Minquan* is of course a significant term because Sun Yat-sen used it to convey the notion of "democracy" by a word with strong Chinese flavor.[14] It was only afterward that more people switched from *minquan* to *weiquan*, which at first seemed a less sensitive choice because the government had occasionally used it. The use of *weiquan* was in particular popularized by the Hong Kong magazine *Yazhou Zhoukan* 亞洲週刊 (Asia news weekly), which selected fourteen "*weiquan* lawyers" as collective "person of the year" in December 2005.[15]

It should be noted here that *weiquan* is different from though related to the notion of "rightful resistance" developed by Kevin O'Brien and Li Lianjiang. Whereas *weiquan* may be one strategy or form of rightful resistance, the latter is defined more broadly as "a form of popular contention that (1) operates near the boundary of an authorized channel, (2) employs the rhetoric and commitments of the powerful to curb political or economic power, and (3) hinges on locating and exploiting divisions among the powerful."[16] In this context, legal norms are combined with legitimating myths or norms that are not based on the letter of the law (sometimes they are borrowed from the Mao era, for example). *Weiquan* later evolved toward a broader conception of contention, in particular drawing on natural law and human rights, but it started out in a more legalistic mindset.

At the outset, *weiquan* was defined by two characteristics: concrete action and a nonconfrontational stance. *Weiquan* addressed a common set of grievances: "criminal process wrongs such as torture, wrongful conviction and extrajudicial incarceration, forced evictions, housing demolitions and land expropriations, food and medicine poisoning, forced abortions, discrimination, internet censorship, labor rights violations, law enforcement abuses, psychiatric and other medical abuses, official corruption and dereliction of duty, and pollution of the air, soil or groundwater."[17] This mindset was arguably shared across a wider set of social practices at the grass roots: Anthony Spires has argued that grassroots NGOs were able to articulate their work as not opposed to but complementary to the state's approach. Understandable neither as sprouts of a Tocquevillian civil society nor as corporatist government-organized NGOs, these organizations were able to survive through a "contingent" and sometimes short-lived tolerance by local authorities based on the social legitimacy of the concrete work they were carrying out.[18] In rights defense, too, political questions were not presented through "big" theories (of democracy or human rights) or as alternative constitutional arrangements (as in 1989 or later in Charter 08, discussed later in this chapter), but as a set of issues that were relevant to ordinary people's everyday lives and that could be pursued within the present constitutional framework.[19] Mo Shaoping 莫少平, who as a young lawyer had defended some of the June Fourth participants, was often understood to have pioneered this approach of "turning political problems into legal problems."[20]

Teng Biao has provided a detailed analysis of the relationship between the democracy movement of the 1980s and the *weiquan* movement. Teng recalls a discussion with Wang Tiancheng 王天成 (jailed for five years in 1992 for his involvement in the Tiananmen protests), in which Wang argued that the protesters of the 1980s "failed" to make the larger issues relevant to ordinary people. Teng replied that it is mainly the social environment that has changed: "*Weiquan* and the democratic movement have a common pursuit; while pursuing this common goal, each one diligently did as much as permitted by the circumstances in the system."[21] In another essay, Teng quotes a distinction proposed by Hu Ping: "*Weiquan* demands the resolution of some concrete problem, whereas the democratic movement demands the realization of a universal principle."[22] However, Teng notes that it is often the government that tries to establish a watertight border between these two complementary approaches. For this reason, he does not want to overemphasize the differences between them. In fact, he ended up addressing the twenty-fifth anniversary commemoration of the June Fourth massacre in Hong Kong.[23] As Jerome Cohen notes, defending rights within the current system does not preclude working for legislative improvements to the system, although it precludes direct challenges to the CCP's monopoly on power.[24] In any case, *weiquan* brought a new angle to citizen activism, not least through its engagement with grassroots and marginal groups.

Representing "vulnerable groups" (*ruoshi qunti*), those whose lives are the most affected by the various dysfunctional aspects of the Chinese political and legal system, was therefore a core concern from the start of the *weiquan* movement. This focus in turn led to an empowerment of these groups: "laid-off workers, dispossessed peasants or jobless veterans have organized themselves to pursue collective interests. Lawyers and other social activists are playing an increasing role in helping them."[25] Rachel Stern connects this concern for marginal groups with China's socialist heritage.[26] However, Teng Biao takes issue with this argument: "For us, human rights are the rights of weak and persecuted people. . . . In China, the old or new Left never showed any interest in vulnerable people. Only liberals showed interest in them. Their social and economic rights were attacked just as much as their political rights; in fact, they were compromised because of their political situation. . . . For example, the question of equal access to education [for migrant children without a residence permit] is a problem of constitutional equality, not a problem of social protection."[27] Indeed, although socialism is still the official "system" of the PRC, there are few attempts to deal with marginal groups except reluctantly and under pressure. In this perspective, the emergence as a group of rights protection activists can be closely connected with the reevaluation of the position and status of intellectual discourse in the post-1989 context. In a break with a certain type of elitist intervention, rights activists increasingly adopted a bottom-up perspective, working together with ordinary people to better understand and articulate the forms of domination and marginalization that they are victims of. In his typology of *weiquan* activities, Teng Biao mentions courtroom defense, various forms of investing public spaces, participation in local elections, impeachment of local leaders, and Internet-based activism.[28]

Another example is the case of women's rights activism. Although the Chinese state has officially always endorsed gender equality, feminist intellectuals nevertheless often risked bureaucratic rivalry with the official government-organized NGO in charge of women's issues, the All-China Women's Federation. Ai Xiaoming,[29] who was closely associated with Wang Xiaobo and appears in almost every chapter of this study, has noted the seminal role of both the Sun Zhigang case and the Huang Jing 黃靜 rape case that coincided with it (Huang's death occurred just one month before Sun's, but it was publicized more slowly). The Huang Jing case sparked a new form of independent women's activism outside the Women's Federation, with NGOs such as the Stop Domestic Violence Network (Fandui Jiating Baoli Wang 反對家庭暴力網).[30] Ai Xiaoming was active in both cases, posting essays on Sun Zhigang to her blog after newspapers refused to publish them and becoming closely involved in the campaign to appeal against the acquittal of Huang Jing's boyfriend in 2004: "The Sun Zhigang case awoke a lot of expectations—that slow, step-by-step, qualitative change was possible. When I started I also thought I wanted to change society. I had a strong urge to change society, but now [when] I think back on it, that was childish."[31] The new approach to political activism could therefore be used in different areas, including gender rights.

Together with Huang's mother, Ai set up an advocacy website, published articles, and eventually made her first documentary film, *Garden in Heaven* (*Tiantang huayuan* 天堂花園), working with Hu Jie despite some disagreements with him (she had seen his film *Looking for Lin Zhao's Soul* in 2003).[32] Ai was particularly interested in expressing herself as a female director: "Not many women make films. And women who make films about social problems are even fewer."[33] Ai has consistently maintained this attention to approaching social issues from a woman's standpoint, even as many of the problems she investigated were not gender specific, such as the village revolts in Taishicun (2005) or the Sichuan earthquake and the children who died in collapsed schools. Working with the female director Xie Yihui, she defined her involvement in the Sichuan events as a form of independent investigation:

> Many deep conflicts in Chinese society had accumulated in the earthquake zone—environmental issues, conflicts between economic projects and human

> rights, children's rights to live, citizens' pursuits of social justice, as well as government responses to media coverage and the civil rights movements. . . . I understood how important it was to document these realities, before they disappear. With these images, we can record the pulse of social change in China. . . . Ai Weiwei and others encourage the idea of facing the authorities, emphasizing the rights of citizens to film and scrutinize their actions. This was a huge breakthrough, not in terms of content, but in attitude: the documentarian no longer runs away, but instead stands up, insists on filming to the end, facing the opponent's camera.[34]

It was through her original attention to the issue of women's rights that Ai gradually developed her position as a specific *minjian* intellectual who refuses to back down in the face of intimidation by the authorities.

Ai maintains a critical view of intellectuals, whom she sees as often compromised by the establishment, in contrast to ordinary people. "Most people, very many people, are really terrible, they're afraid of losing things. I don't mean ordinary people. In fact, ordinary people are often quite clear about the system. I mean, a lot of people in universities, a lot of intellectuals, they know. But the pressure is so great. A lot of people don't want to sacrifice because being inside the system has a lot of advantages."[35] By contrast, she prefers to define herself as an artist: "I'm at the front. I'm on the Web. I pay attention to intellectuals' discussions. But I don't do research, I document."[36] She has continued to teach and work on a variety of gender issues. A topless photo of herself, with a large pair of scissors approaching her breasts, in a disturbing suggestion of veiled violence, was circulated to great effect on the Internet in 2013 in protest against sexual violence against children, sparking a movement of "grassroots feminist protest."[37]

GONGMENG, A NEW TYPE OF *MINJIAN* THINK TANK

The most prominent and original example of this new approach to intellectual interventions was the social organization Gongmeng 公盟, an abbreviation of the full name Gongmin Lianmeng 公民聯盟 (Citizen Alliance), known in English as the Open Constitution Initiative, which was founded in October 2003 by the three scholars who drafted the open letter on the Sun Zhigang case and the lawyer Zhang Xingshui 張星水. Originally registered as the Sunshine Constitutionalism Social Science Research Center (Yangguang Xianzheng Shehui Kexue

Yanjiu Zhongxin 陽光憲政社會科學研究中心), Gongmeng was established to provide logistical support for petitioners and to further develop the strategy of defending rights within the current legal system.[38] After the business registration of the Sunshine Constitutionalism Center was cancelled in March 2005, it registered again in June under the name "Gongmeng" (Beijing Gongmeng Zixun Youxian Zeren Gongsi 北京公盟資訊有限責任公司), still as a business incorporating a law research center (Gongmeng Falü Yanjiu Zhongxin 公盟法律研究中心) as a subsidiary.[39] Its new name was inspired by the American Civil Liberties Union, which Xu Zhiyong encountered as a visiting scholar at Yale in 2004–2005. On the day Sunshine was deregistered, Xu wrote an essay, stating, "We are not critics, we are proposers."[40] In Teng Biao's description, Gongmeng brought together scholars, lawyers, and journalists, "quite resembling a think tank." It took interest in a variety of "issues" (*yiti* 議題), mainly but not exclusively legal, sponsoring research or holding seminars on topics such as Reeducation Through Labor. When Xu Zhiyong ran for the Haidian District People's Congress in 2004, Gongmeng organized a series of election forums, training independent candidates (eighteen of them were elected), explaining the People's Congress system, and inviting representatives to join discussions.[41] Xu Zhiyong's election to the Haidian People's Congress epitomized Gongmeng's strategy of working for change inside the system.

As opposed to the salons of the 1980s, Gongmeng was oriented toward "action" (*xingdong* 行動) rather than simply toward discussion and was based on empirical research and concrete policy proposals, another sign of the professionalization and specialization of post-2000 intellectual discourse. In particular, Gongmeng developed as a structure to support and provide legal aid to petitioners. The association of *minjian* scholars, journalists, and lawyers, with a strong proportion of volunteers, including young graduates from Beijing's top universities, to work with petitioners and grassroots activists was a particularly original one. Gongmeng combined the aims of producing knowledge outside the official system through firsthand investigation, disseminating that knowledge through public reports, and using its in-house results to formulate policy recommendations that were in keeping with the letter of China's Constitution. It further strategically leveraged the legal knowledge of its in-house professionals to provide practical support to grassroots groups involved in protests. From 2007, it also published *Citizen Monthly* (*Gongmin Yuekan* 公民月刊), an unofficial journal distributed electronically.[42] As Teng Biao put it, "Among Chinese NGOs, Gongmeng is a rarity that has clear political aspirations, pays close attention to rule of law and human rights, actively engages in social movements, and has gained the support of a large number of intellectuals working inside the system."[43]

There are a few other examples of comparable structures.[44] Under the regulations on social organizations adopted in 1989 and revised in 1998, it was possible to register one "nongovernmental" (*minjian*) organization per sector of activity with a supervisory unit (*zhuguan danwei* 主管單位) and the Ministry of Civil Affairs. Among the first were Liang Congjie's Friends of Nature and Unirule, an early model for the research-driven "legalist" advocacy practiced by Gongmeng. Unirule was established on July 6, 1993, by a group of prominent academic economists (Sheng Hong 盛洪, Mao Yushi, Zhang Shuguang 張曙光, Fan Gang 樊綱, Tang Shouning 唐壽寧) as a research institute in economics that advocated market reforms in the aftermath of 1989 and Deng's relaunch of reforms. It registered as a consulting firm and a nonprofit organization affiliated with the Beijing Commission of Science and Technology. In 1999, it separated into a for-profit consulting business and a private think tank that appeared as an administrative subsidiary of the consulting firm.[45] This arrangement has protected Unirule quite effectively from political interference. In a recent interview, Mao Yushi explained Unirule's position, which he describes as a "*minjian* think tank": "we discovered that real scholarship cannot be sold for money; it cannot be commercialized; no one will buy it. . . . But we slowly understood that our real advantage was our independent scholarship."[46]

However, it should be noted that despite the high-profile interventions by several of its founders or prominent members (such as calls to abolish the Reeducation Through Labor system and Mao Yushi's involvement in a series of calls to remove references to Mao Zedong from China's Constitution, originally published in *Caixin* in 2011[47]), Unirule's basic activities have remained confined to the realm of economic reforms, which is a much less sensitive area than working with marginal populations. Nonetheless, as the last standing independent think tank, it too has come under increasing pressure since 2013, with the authorities preventing it from holding conferences, shutting down its Chinese and English websites in January 2017, and pressuring the landlords of its office to terminate its lease in 2018.[48] Sheng Hong published a characteristically legalistic open letter, pointing out lack of due process in the closure of the website and reiterating Unirule's mission to work with the government for better-informed policy making and to advance a plurality of ideas in Chinese society, but to no effect.[49]

Another forerunner of *minjian* think tanks was the group Yirenping 益仁平, founded by Lu Jun 陸軍, who was chosen as one of *Southern Weekly*'s top-ten people of the year in 2005 for his work advocating against discrimination of hepatitis B carriers (estimated at 100 million in China). He registered Yirenping as a company in 2006, arguing, "I came to feel strongly that this kind of anti-discrimination work is very important for vulnerable groups, but at that time there wasn't any domestic groups specifically working in this field."[50] Yirenping became the most respected public-health NGO in China before eventually being investigated in April 2015 for "illegal activity."

The Transition Institute (Chuanzhixing 傳知行), established by Guo Yushan and others in 2007, similarly produced firsthand research, in particular on migrant-worker issues, which it combined with legal advocacy. In her study of the institute, Zeng Jinyan describes its activities as follows:

> Transition Institute (TI) defines itself as an independent think-tank focusing on research into social and economic transition. Its research topics included the informal taxi market, tax reform, the Three Gorges Dam and related environmental issues, rural health care reform, and educational equality. Its research has two intended audiences: the first consists of economic theorists, both domestic and overseas; the second, Chinese policy-makers. . . . [W]hat TI has attempted is to put forward their own ideas on the basis of their local experience, even though they have yet to make a theoretical breakthrough. Still, such indigenousness is precisely what TI should be most commended for. TI attempts to explain their research findings in a language that makes sense to Chinese policy-makers. To some extent, both their interviewees and the Chinese government should be thankful to TI, because they have built a platform for dialogue between the government and those at the very bottom of society, without taking a penny from the state's coffer.[51]

The key components of the *minjian* spirit are reunited in this description: a bottom-up, empirical approach, the use of "indigenous" language that ordinary people can understand, the attention paid to vulnerable groups. Guo Yushan argued in favor of maximal "depoliticization" of the institute's activities: "Guo disagreed with fellow activist Teng Biao's assertion that human rights lawyers take either a 'politicized' (that is, expressing political ideals and identifying the case as part of a broader movement) or 'depoliticized' approach to their defense cases, and Teng's implication that the cause of human rights in China can only be advanced through the former. In response, Guo argued that a lawyer should always prioritize the client's interests, irrespective of his or her—or the client's—political intention."[52] Despite its striving to avoid being perceived as politically antagonistic, the Transition Institute's business registration was revoked in 2013, and Guo Yushan (who had been prominently involved in Chen Guangcheng's 陳光誠 "escape" to the U.S. embassy) was arrested in October 2014 for illegal business operations, including the management of foreign funding.[53]

Petitioners were instrumental in the evolution of Xu Zhiyong's political thinking. As a Ph.D. student, Xu traveled to Liaoning in 2001 to provide legal assistance to petitioners detained by the local government (in an expropriation case to build a highway) and was nearly disciplined by PKU.[54] Earlier yet, during the summer after completing his undergraduate studies, he offered legal advice to villagers in a conflict in his hometown in Henan (four villagers had been killed in a conflict over land confiscation by a state-owned farm). Before being admitted to his Ph.D. program, Xu planned to study grassroots democracy in villages in Henan and had found a job at the Zhengzhou Academy of Social Sciences.[55] After graduating, Xu both taught at university and worked at *Caixin*'s monthly magazine *China Reform* (*Zhongguo Gaige* 中國改革), where he and a group of colleagues would meet with petitioners every weekend.[56] Teng Biao also specifically mentions the influence of the rural reformer James Yen on Xu, in addition to Martin Luther King Jr. and Mahatma Gandhi.[57]

To better understand the petitioning system, Xu Zhiyong lived from March to May 2005 in the Beijing petitioner village near Yongdingmen: "China's petitioners mostly belong to the most vulnerable groups [*zui ruoshi de qunti* 最弱勢的群體] in society; they have no money and even less power; their clothes are mostly old and worn, and they carry backpacks full of their petitioning documents; painful memories are etched on their faces; such groups are of course very easy to recognize on the streets of Beijing."[58]

Teng Biao described Xu's motivations as a kind of immersion into the grass roots:

> He believed that these people were the best mirror of the Chinese reality. On the one hand, he wanted to help them; on the other he wanted to learn about the social reality through their experiences. He visited them not in the same way as an [official] writer would to "collect materials for writing." Not at all.

> He hoped to feel their pains and share their experiences first hand, and he often stayed in the petitioner villages, where petitioners came to congregate and live, for days on end. Petitioners get beaten up a lot, and to change the situation, he insisted on going to these Letters and Visits offices on a regular basis, knowing that he could be harassed too. When he went, he mingled with petitioners and he didn't say, I'm a university teacher with a PhD. Those sent by local governments to intercept petitioners from their jurisdictions would think he was a petitioner and beat him up too. If he witnessed petitioners being manhandled, he would confront the assailants. . . . Deep inside, he doesn't have a thing called "superiority."[59]

This description closely matches the characteristics of *minjian* intellectuals as first set out by Wang Xiaobo. Xu was not engaging with the petitioners as a theoretician in a class struggle against dominant groups (that is, as an organic intellectual of the working class), nor was he considering the petitioners' situation as a detached object of study. Rather, his interest was part of an understanding that the different groups belonging to the silent majority share a similar disenfranchisement. Breaking with the elite position of producing political or constitutional blueprints that had little connection with ordinary people's lives, he instead tried to find practical solutions to social problems.

Gongmeng rose to prominence through the quality of its work on petitioners, black jails (where petitioners intercepted in Beijing by local authorities from their hometowns were held before being taken back to their place of official residence), forced evictions, Tibetans, and migrants' children's rights, among other things. It progressively got involved in a number of cases, setting up "case-specific lawyer teams" or concern groups for certain types of cases.[60] As early as 2004, Xu Zhiyong and Teng Biao became involved in the four death penalty cases of Chengde, an intervention that resulted in deferred death penalty and life imprisonment sentences on appeal. Gongmeng provided assistance in the case of children migrant workers in 2006 in Beijing, in the case of the "black" brick kilns of Shanxi in 2007, and in the Sanlu tainted-milk scandal just after the Olympics in 2008. It also provided legal defense for the blind activist Chen Guangcheng in Shandong and for the journalist Cheng Yizhong (who was prosecuted in connection with the Sun Zhigang article). In 2008, it offered legal help to Tibetans implicated in the March uprising. Teng Biao was closely involved in the death penalty case of Xia Junfeng 夏俊峰, a street vendor beaten by *chengguan* 城管

(urban-management officers who often harass street vendors) in Shenyang.[61] In 2009, Gongmeng was directly involved in the campaign to elect the leaders of the Beijing Bar Association.[62] As Andrew Nathan notes, Gongmeng was the first organization in China to devise an impact-litigation strategy that used egregious cases in order to challenge blatantly unjust rules and initiate discussion in the media.[63]

Gongmeng's most unusual activity was perhaps its publication of research reports. A report devoted to human rights developments in China provoked some controversy.[64] But the one that gained the most attention was devoted to petitioners.[65] Three counties were selected in Henan, Fujian, and Hubei for deeper investigation. As noted earlier, Xu Zhiyong went to live in the petitioner village near Beijing's South Railway station for two months. Having heard of the report, Chen Guangcheng visited the Gongmeng office near PKU South Gate in Summer 2005 and obtained help from Teng Biao and Guo Yushan in investigating excesses in enforcing birth control, which eventually led to Chen's escape from China and Guo Yushan's arrest. In Teng Biao's description, "Upon the completion of the project, Gongmeng invited well-known scholars in the area as well as government officials across China to attend a large-scale seminar on the petitioning system. The report was widely circulated at the time, resulting in the public paying more attention to this special group of people know as petitioners as well as [to] the reality of China's so-called Letters and Visits system."[66] The final two-hundred-thousand-character report was published in 2007, and a contract was signed with a commercial publisher but then cancelled. The report concluded that the entire petitioning phenomenon was a result of China's undemocratic system and proposed to reform it by implementing direct elections at the county (*xian*) level and advancing the independence of the judiciary.[67]

The other report prepared by Gongmeng that achieved great publicity dealt with the social causes of the uprising in Tibet in March 2008. Public opinion was starkly divided, with many intellectuals taking the side of the central government in denouncing the "ungratefulness" of Tibetans, who they felt had benefited from many years of government subsidies, and the double standards of foreign public opinion in siding with the Tibetans and using these events to call for a boycott of the Beijing Olympics. A few liberals, especially in the metropolitan press, criticized Han nationalism and singled out the problem of ethnic discrimination as a cause of the riots. Gongmeng strived to strike a balanced position, informed both by moral principle and empirical research. First, it offered pro bono legal aid to Tibetans arrested during the crackdown.[68] Second, in order to provide more substantial material for a critical assessment of policy, Gongmeng set up a research team led by a Tibetan graduate student in the PKU Department of Journalism, Fang Kun 方堃. The report's first premise was already at odds with the Chinese mainstream media's understanding of the uprising as having been incited from outside Tibet:

> Such a large social contradiction could not have been created solely by external factors; there must be internal causes, but media reports have given little detailed consideration to investigating the social roots of these violent incidents. Under the influence of nationalist sentiment, there were some reports that even broadened mistrust and mutual criticism between the nationalities. The lack of field research into the living conditions of Tibetans has been detrimental to clearly understanding the nature of the social contradictions in Tibetan areas on a theoretical level and has been detrimental to resolving problems on a practical level.[69]

Gongmeng argued for the ability of professional and sincere research, carried out on the ground, to propose solutions rather than relying on purely theoretical and ideological constructions, in keeping with its position as a specific, professional, *minjian* think tank. The report provides detailed analysis of a number of factors explaining the uprising: resistance to modernization, a subjective feeling among Tibetans of being discriminated against, the rise of a new elite in Tibet based on clientelistic networks (which Wang Lixiong had designated as the "bureaucratic elite"), and the increasing exclusion of Tibetans from economic life since the 1980s.[70] Xu Zhiyong summarized these conclusions from the perspective of a concerned Chinese citizen:

> Against the general background of modernization, although the Tibetan economy achieved strong development, in comparison with other provinces, other countries, or even other nationalities within Tibet, Tibetans lagged behind; combined with the experience of the wealth amassed by people from other provinces who came to Tibet, this entailed a feeling of relative disenfranchisement. At the same time, traditional religious culture was shaken by modernization; many young Tibetans belong to a confused and disoriented generation. Furthermore, the top-down power structure produced a group

> of local Tibetan cadres who used the privilege of the power they received from above to form murky networks of local connections; in this manner economic support from the state was largely channeled into projects for the political gain or personal enrichment of a minority, [and so] ordinary Tibetans felt more deprived than supported by state subsidies and, like many people in other provinces, developed strong resentment against local officials.[71]

When Gongmeng received no response from the administrations it sent the report to, it published the report online. Individual conclusions in the report were sharply critical of Chinese policy in Tibet, in particular raising doubts about modernization: "When the land you are accustomed to living in and the land of the culture you identify with; when the lifestyle and religiosity are suddenly changed into a 'modern city' that you no longer recognize; when you can no longer find work in your own land and feel the unfairness of lack of opportunity; and when you realize that your core value systems are under attack, then the Tibetan people's panic and sense of crisis are not difficult to understand."[72]

Finally, the report's conclusion brings Gongmeng's work in Tibet into resonance with its work throughout China: "[Recommendation no. 7] Promote rule of law in governance processes in Tibetan areas. Urge the introduction of laws and regulations as represented by ordinances in the Tibet Autonomous Region and other autonomous areas, to change the current status quo of a lack of lower laws since the promulgation of the Regional Ethnic Autonomy Law. Regulate the ownership rights and disposal rights of key natural resources. Encourage participation by experts in advising and discussing all aspects of policy in Tibetan areas."[73] Formulated in Gongmeng's usual style as a policy recommendation, the report emphasizes giving legal substance to the Law on Regional National Autonomy and more generally remedying the lack of rule of law in Tibetan areas through a strengthened legal framework. The report also proposed using Buddhism as a means to reestablish connections between Tibetans and Chinese.

Noting that the American Civil Liberties Union was formed around the protection of minority rights, Xu Zhiyong provides an interesting discussion of Gongmeng's function:

> China and the United States are different. We are very far away from the luxury of being able to pursue the rights of minorities; even when we pursue

> rights that the majority strongly identifies with and supports, we often cannot achieve success. The individual cases we choose are usually the most extreme, the ones most likely to achieve broad sympathy and strong support, and we remind ourselves at every moment that we stand on the side of the public [*gongzhong* 公众]. . . . Even legal techniques become unimportant in this situation; the essential thing is to use the sunlight of public opinion to rescue respect for the law.[74]

Although public discourse is dominated by official language that paints rights defense as the work of a small minority, Xu Zhiyong understood his legal advocacy work as bringing the voice of a silent majority into the public sphere. In this sense, majority rights and minority rights are not contradictory or in tension, as they may be in the U.S. context, but are intertwined. In this sense, although Xu Zhiyong alleged not to have time for such a "luxury," by turning to petitioners and Tibetans as research objects for Gongmeng's two main reports, he precisely advanced an understanding of legal rights based on the rights of minorities as constitutive of the rights of the majority. As Eva Pils and Joshua Rosenzweig noted in an op-ed, "In the process of taking its protests outside the system, the New Citizen Movement allowed disadvantaged segments of society to express their sense of injustice in more coordinated ways, and to derive new courage and power from their status as citizens with rights. In this respect, it is particularly worth noting the work of Mr. Xu and his colleagues with China's petitioners."[75] Anecdotal evidence suggests that with the help of the liberal media and Internet communication, Gongmeng's work did find an increasing echo within society. For example, Christoph Steinhardt argues that there was a discursive shift toward framing incidents in terms of *weiquan* through competition between state and commercial media.[76]

Gongmeng's final major project before Xu Zhiyong's arrest was devoted to migrant-worker schools, "equal access to education," and reform of the household registration (*hukou*) system. It advocated normal operation of schools for the children of migrant workers and the abolishment of household registration requirements for high school and college entrance exams. Beginning its work on this project in 2009, it achieved some success: by August 2012, twenty-nine provincial-level administrations promised to allow nonlocal *hukou* holders to register for the examination to enter university (*gaokao* 高考).

The authorities began to pay close attention to Gongmeng in 2009: the Beijing tax office opened an investigation and raided Gongmeng's offices on July 14, 2009. Xu Zhiyong was accused of tax evasion and detained.[77] When a fine of 1.42 million renminbi was imposed, Gongmeng decided to pay and began a citizen subscription (more than half was paid by the Internet entrepreneur Wang Gongquan 王功權).[78] Finally, the case was closed on August 22, 2010.[79] Gongmeng was able to register again in the fall of 2009, but it now began to use the name Gongmin 公民 (Citizen).[80] Pressure never really dropped, and in 2012 Gongmeng again lost its offices. This eventually led to a complete change in the nature of Gongmeng's mission, a change that Xu Zhiyong again justified by referring to the group's duties toward petitioners and other vulnerable groups: "Before March [2012], we had a fixed office. Every day we had at least one person available to receive petitioners. I would go there twice a week to read their documents. Perhaps there were many cases we could not handle, but at least we could offer some advice. We spent a lot of time doing this concrete work. But after March, you shut down our office. A lot of underprivileged people couldn't find us. So we shifted the emphasis of our work to promoting people's awareness of their identity as citizens."[81]

Prevented from doing practical work, Gongmeng turned back to the theoretical elaborations that were more characteristic of the style of the democracy movement in the 1980s. Although Xu Zhiyong had not signed Charter 08, both to protect Gongmeng and presumably also because an open letter requesting a new constitution was somehow in tension with his previous strategy and stance, Gongmin now increasingly developed a discourse of "citizenship" that started out on a philosophical and individual level but eventually also led to rethinking China's institutional structure.[82]

YU JIANRONG AND THE PETITION SYSTEM

Petitioning in many ways represents the flip side of the legal system and as such provides a useful window into how intellectuals and ordinary people relate to the issues of the law and rights defense. It is no coincidence that Gongmeng and *minjian* legal scholars became particularly involved in the question of petitioners. While human rights lawyers may be few,[83] petitioners are unquestionably many; they can be seen as the silent majority of China's legal system. Petitioning, which has some premodern precedent, existed throughout the Mao period at both the central level and the provincial level. Before 1979, it was used mainly as a channel for denunciations or for authorities to root out rightists or other critics. In the transition period from 1979 to 1982, petitioning played an important role in dealing with requests for rehabilitation. Since 1982, its role has been ambiguous because it became a safety net and catch-all for cases rejected by the courts.[84] Carl Minzner describes the Letters and Visits (Xinfang 信訪) institutions as "multi-purpose governance tools" that allow citizens a degree of input into government policy as well as providing to the government a stream of information about citizens' discontent and a tool for monitoring officials. Deriving their influence from the discretionary power of the party, these institutions "represent the rule of man (or Party), not the rule of law."[85]

From the 1990s, when the quickening pace of economic development created new types of conflict that the law was ill equipped to deal with, the Xinfang system was swamped with requests. Between 1992 and 2000, the number of letters received by general State Letters and Visits Offices (not counting those received by specific administrations) increased on average by 10 percent per year, reaching 10 million in 2000,[86] despite new State Council Regulations issued in 1995 to reduce the number.[87] As Isabelle Thireau and Hua Linshan note in their study, "The space for speech linked to the Letters and Visits Administration has become the main venue for those who believe they are victims of injustice to express themselves."[88] A significant reason why the petitioning system continues to exist is the courts' unwillingness to file certain cases, despite a new law that discourages that practice.[89] As the authorities became more anxious about protest, they put pressure on local cadres to reign in petitioners, thus incentivizing the "interception" of petitioners by local police, who are sent to Beijing specifically for this purpose, and the proliferation of "black jails," often situated in provincial representation offices in the capital.[90] Officials also did not hesitate to use judicial psychiatry to get rid of insistent petitioners, a practice that was famously defended in 2009 by a PKU professor of judicial psychiatry, Sun Dongdong 孫東東.[91] Ching Kwan Lee and Yonghong Zhang consider petitioning a form of "bureaucratic absorption" of protest: it causes petitioners to "disappear" inside the system, which neutralizes their energies and prevents them from mobilizing.[92] After the Hu-Wen administration was installed in 2003, the number of petitioners reached a "high tide" because they assumed they would be tolerated by the new leadership.[93]

It is important to note that petitioning relies on a premodern representation of (in)justice captured in the term *yuan* 冤 (grievance), "a concept that is part of the popular counterculture of ordinary people, petitioners seeking justice"[94] and that encompasses a duty (*yi* 義) to seek redress. Eva Pils thus understands the *weiquan* movement as the encounter between two strands in Chinese intellectual history: the liberal political philosophy of the late nineteenth century and the vernacular tradition of *yuan*, which traces its roots to traditional conceptions of natural justice found in popular literature.[95] In this configuration, *yuan* is embedded in *minjian* representations rather than in official (*guanfang*) state Confucianism. This is probably a reason for the very strong resilience of petitioners' trust in the top leaders, sometimes despite several rounds of failed petitions.[96] Pils notes that the *yuan* character is often inscribed on petitioners' leaflets, banners, headbands, imparting a moral depth to their legal claims (for this reason, Yu Jianrong refers to them as a kind of tribe, *yuanmin* 冤民).[97] *Yuan* plays a central role in the popular comprehension of petitioners and their social position, who are understood to be treated unfairly by the state, which opens a space for legitimate intervention by *minjian* scholars or activists. Although, not unlike the *weiquan* lawyers, petitioners often refer to discursive categories preferred by the authorities, as highlighted by Thireau and Hua, they also use their own ethical and moral standards to question and reinterpret the categories of official class identities used by the government and thus redefine their own collective identities; they request dignity and respect not as personal favors but on the basis of shared values.[98]

In 2004, Yu Jianrong, a lawyer and at that time recent Ph.D. graduate just hired by CASS, published a report on the Xinfang system based on an analysis of 20,000 petitioner letters and 632 questionnaires filled out by petitioners: *The Systemic Shortcomings of the Letters and Visits System and Its Political Harm*.[99] The original files were stored in his residence in Songzhuang and could be consulted by interested parties. In this way, Yu was trying to exert influence, in a legalistic manner possibly inspired by Gongmeng and the Sun Zhigang case, on the upcoming new State Council regulations regarding petitioners. The most widely reported figure in his report was that only 0.2 percent of petition cases meet with a successful conclusion, so the system could therefore not be seen as viable in redressing grievances. Yu argued for the progressive abolition of the system, proposing to delink cadre evaluation from petitions, to shift responsibility to local People's Congresses, to give courts more power to deal with petition cases, and to give public opinion more space to express dissatisfaction.[100] He also noted that petitions were generally brought by poor manual laborers, especially migrants. Yu pointed out that behind the system's inefficiency, it also had a close connection with a political situation in which officials, occupying the dominant position, hold unchecked power in the system (*guan benwei zhidu* 官本位制度).[101] However, Yu's report failed to influence the authorities: on the contrary, the regulations approved in 2005 reaffirmed the Xinfang system, obliging all administrations to create Letters and Visits Offices and strengthening leader responsibility, although they did introduce a recommendation to solve cases according to laws and regulations.[102] Yu has since then continued to advocate for substantial reform and eventual abolition of the Xinfang system.[103] The petitioner system also closely informed his research on the Reeducation Through Labor system (to whose camps petitioners are often sent), which he advised officials to abolish in 2012, and his project, conducted with the support of National Social Science Foundation funding, to reform China's *hukou* system.[104]

Yu Jianrong, born in 1962 in Hengyang, Hunan, is in many ways the epitome of a *minjian* intellectual. Eva Pils and Marina Svensson describe him as "a socially and politically engaged scholar advocating on behalf of people on the margins of Chinese society."[105] One of his book editors writes that he is "one of the rare fourfold big shots [*dawan'r* 大腕兒]—in politics, scholarship, art, and *minjian*—on the contemporary intellectual scene."[106] His father, a cadre who was labeled a "bad element" during the Cultural Revolution, incurred a revocation of the family's household registration, with the result that Yu Jianrong was denied schooling because he was an unregistered "nonperson."[107] In the end, Yu was nonetheless able to obtain a place to study politics and law at Hunan Normal University in 1979 and became a journalist after graduation. After being fired from the newspaper he worked for in the antiliberalization campaign of 1987, he became one of the first people to obtain a license to practice law in 1991 and chose to begin by making money through commercial litigation in Hainan from 1991 to 1996. This practice gave him the financial basis for all his other activities, and he has often declared that he does not fear termination of his employment or similar forms of retaliation for his work: "I made a promise that I would first solve the issue of livelihood, but that the goals in my life were (1) to become clear about what made a 'yellow-skinned' child turn into a 'black' person; and (2) to find methods so that none among our next generation would become a 'black' person the way I did. So . . . my purpose to earn money at the time [wasn't] the money itself—it [was] to obtain freedom, because without money you have no freedom."[108]

Having achieved financial security, Yu enrolled in a PhD program from 1997 to 2001 and wrote a dissertation devoted to an anthropological study of a village in Hunan.[109] After graduating, he joined CASS as a sociologist at the Rural Development Research Institute. In 2003, he bought a house in Songzhuang (under an uncertain land-rights regime), which brought him into proximity with other *minjian* activists. In addition to social media, he now routinely uses film, video, and painting to publicize important issues, such as the situation of petitioners and kidnapped child beggars.

In an important text that Yu Jianrong has presented as a lecture and as an essay that gives its title to one of his books, he establishes his "lower-class standpoint [*wode diceng lichang* 我的底層立場]": "The underclass [*diceng*] requires us to take its situation, its needs and aspirations as the departure point for understanding society's development and objectives. For this reason, our political research cannot be confined to the activities of the political elite. . . . Carrying out analysis from the perspective of methodology, using 'underclass' as a social research method requires the researcher to understand social phenomena from the perspective of the underclass."[110]

He reaffirms what this study has identified as the classic stance of the *minjian* intellectual, who refuses to analyze from a position of superiority but merges with the social phenomena under examination. This means that both the rural peasants and the urban workers need to be considered differently. On the one hand, Yu urges that the peasant resistance movements be taken seriously, arguing that "peasants are by no means too ignorant to distinguish what is in their interests and modern society should allow for the existence of a lower-class politics."[111] On the other, he argues that the Chinese working class has lost its political identity because of the overwhelming role played by the party:

> After the revolutionary Communist Party seized political power, the working class became the "ruling class" in mainstream political discourse and was subjected to gradual organizational structuring by the regime. As China's working class became endowed with an unparalleled sacredness, it ultimately became a class that lost itself in revolutionary mobilization and political struggle.

> . . . [T]he workers' organizations engendered through this revolutionary mobilization were not political organizations arising from among industrial workers, but rather a political party's tools of political mobilization. Thus, in the early stages of its formation, China's working class came under the control of external theory and demands. . . . Second, reform and opening caused revolution to lose its legitimacy . . . and the rapid changes in society, the economy and politics led to the ideologically diluted working class being cut up into separate groupings[,] [resulting in] a series of non-class related rights defense movements that became a very serious social problem. . . .
>
> Third, if China's workers are to become a class in the genuine sense, they must be liberated from their illusory status as the "ruling class" and build a class consciousness based on the status of "laborer," organizing their class ranks under the banner of protecting workers' rights and interests. . . . I feel that protecting the interests of the most disadvantaged workers is the fundamental principle of modern civilized society.[112]

Yu criticizes the CCP's top-down mobilization of passive workers and suggests the need to start with the workers' own experience. For Yu, a true working-class consciousness, encompassing the laid-off industrial workers in state-owned enterprises as well as the rural migrants on temporary contracts, can be achieved only on the basis of a shared condition of disenfranchisement.[113] This argument can also be read as a critique of the position of Marxist intellectuals, who purport to provide the self-consciousness for the working class to realize its historical role, but in doing so contribute to manipulating the working class for the party's political ends. For example, Pun Ngai and Chris Chan argue that "[Yu Jianrong's] good intentions of protecting the fruition of the Chinese working class by not being hijacked [*sic*] by some utopian intellectual project have trapped him in a theoretical and empirical cul-de-sac from which he argues that the Chinese working class was ontologically a lost one." They believe that Yu "underestimates the capability of the Chinese working class to make sense of its class positions in relation to capital, state and its counterparts [the middle class]."[114] Yu, by contrast, doubts that intellectuals can play the Marxian role of assigning a class identity to "vulnerable groups" who do not share a common understanding of their status and political role.

Highlighting the significant social transformations of the Reform and Opening period and the work of critical establishment sociologists (e.g., Lu Xueyi,

Sun Liping) to redefine social strata in a situation of growing inequalities, Yu proposes his own definition of the "underclass" (*diceng*) as people who have no state-sponsored positions, make a living not through capital but through labor, live at subsistence or near-subsistence level, and cannot easily achieve social mobility. He proposes to take this underclass as the reference point in studying society: "In terms of values, I feel that to a very great extent, the idea of the underclass as an expression of value orientation requires us to use the situation, demands and aspirations of the underclass as the point of departure in understanding society's development and objectives."[115] A substantive engagement with the marginal or excluded groups is therefore necessary to achieve a better understanding of contemporary Chinese society. Yu argues that this engagement requires paying attention to the underclass as "individuals" endowed with their own interests and rationality, an approach he compares to the methods of "India's Subaltern studies group."[116] This approach is definitely post-Marxian and implicitly acknowledges "petitioners" as a kind of identity group.

In this spirit, Yu receives petitioners in his Songzhuang study whenever they care to come. For each visit, he takes a photograph and video-recording of the content of the petition and sometimes also paints portraits of petitioners.[117] Yu contrasts his approach with the mainstream view among intellectuals and political elites, whose only interest in poor and marginalized populations stems from their potential to affect the "stability and unity" of society. This disinterest is, in his view, what prevents adequate understanding and management of the petitioner system.

Over the years, Yu Jianrong has consistently intervened in the public sphere based on his own specialization and firsthand knowledge of the issues. He was one of the first to support setting up retirement funds for migrant workers returning to their hometowns.[118] He pointed out the predicament of peasants experiencing the "three withouts" (no land, no work, and no social security) and proposed creating a market for their land-use rights to generate income.[119] He repeatedly endorsed autonomy of village government and peasant organizations and the need for graduated oversight of local government.[120] In his view, politics should be returned to the grass roots: "For a long time, politics has been seen as an elite affair, because it is connected with power, domination, and governance . . . , whereas the lower levels have no politics—this elitist political view keeps influencing people's analysis and judgment on politics. . . . But, actually, low-level politics is also closely connected to real policies."[121] In Yu's view, society does not function along two tiers, in which only the elite are endowed with political agency; rather, lower-level society also has its own agency and modes of political intervention.[122] He has also drafted practical proposals for reforming political institutions. While constituting a kind of blueprint for institutional reform, these proposals remain very concrete (when compared, for example, with Charter 08, which he did not sign, as discussed later in this chapter) and gradualist: because judicial independence is impossible, he argues that more fairness can be achieved by subjecting local courts to oversight by a jurisdiction one rank higher or by liberalizing county-level people's congress elections.[123]

In 2008, Yu expressed the positive view that "increasingly when their rights are infringed upon, the masses, especially vulnerable groups, will no longer remain silent."[124] He traces an evolution from using "weapons of the weak" and "everyday resistance" (James Scott) to "resistance through law [*yi fa kangzheng* 以法抗爭]" in order to highlight the progress in civil conscience of human rights. In a lecture to the Beijing Lawyers Association in 2009 about the rising number of mass incidents, Yu argued for the need to move from "rigid stability [*gangxing wending* 剛性穩定]" based on violence to a more flexible stability based on the Constitution (at the beginning of his talk, Yu says that the title he originally planned to use was "Let the Constitution Become the Baseline for Social Stability").[125] When Gongmeng was closed down, although Yu expressed regret that it was so difficult to register a *minjian* organization in China, he encouraged Xu Zhiyong to use "Gongmeng's own methods to solve Gongmeng's problem within the legal system."[126]

Yu Jianrong has also developed a comprehensive critique of China's intellectuals:

> The problem with intellectuals striking a pose is that once they find a so-called theoretical command point, they too easily come up with something nonsensical. . . . I haven't joined any organization or signed any petition, I'm a completely independent individual. . . . I position myself very simply as an ordinary scholar, I don't consider myself a personality, because I'm not one. . . . Intellectuals do what they're able to do, little by little revealing the truth; translators translate more things, I do more of my surveys, you in the media write more about what you think is right—that's the best way. . . . I couldn't care less about what CASS thinks—if they fire me, it doesn't matter. I'm not dependent on a salary—I don't even take any notice of it. Ten years

> ago, I earned all the money I'll need for the rest of my life.... It's only when you don't have to worry about making a living that you dare to speak up.[127]

The object of his criticism is the typical figure of the traditional universal intellectual who uses "theory" to take a stance on issues he or she has not studied empirically. By contrast, Yu defines himself both as an ordinary person and as a specific intellectual who only does his "job" like everyone else, based on specific empirical knowledge. Finally, he highlights his financial independence from the state administration that employs him, bringing together three key traits of the *minjian* intellectual: specific, nonelite, and self-funded.

This stance is further enabled by Yu's direct access to readers through social media:

> With a microblog, finally I have the same opportunity for expression as you. You can't steal my microphone. Current technology has altered the social environment. Everyone has a microphone. Everyone is a news headquarters. Now it's easy to find friends. You can instantly find a comrade when you post an essay. For so many years, intellectuals have never had much power of speech. Or you could say, few people possessed that power. In the past, one had to gain a kind of status/identity in the system before getting some power in their words or writing. Now you can create an identity by doing something. Intellectuals can also solve the problems of their reliance on the system. I can make money through entirely different means.[128]

Whereas China's public sphere is dominated by the rules of status and state affiliation (reserved for people "inside the system"), social media provides a platform to *minjian* intellectuals. And, indeed, at the peak of his use of Weibo in 2011, Yu had 1.8 million followers.[129]

However, Yu also continued to intervene in more traditional ways open to intellectuals "within the system," such as lecturing to cadres, although he combined these methods with social media in a unique way. For example, after a lecture in Wanzai County, Jiangxi, in which Yu appealed to local officials to consider the legitimate demands of petitioners who had been expropriated, a controversy developed with a local party secretary who exclaimed over lunch, "If county party secretaries don't carry out demolitions, what will intellectuals eat?"[130] Yu Jianrong, taking exception to this berating, punched the party secretary, left the scene, and uploaded the whole incident to Weibo, creating a backlash for the secretary, who had to apologize. During the crackdown on "big V's" (verified Weibo users with many followers) in 2013, Yu expressed solidarity with "public intellectuals" while still maintaining an ironic distance: "I also cannot be considered an intellectual, but now that public intellectuals are being smeared, let me admit to being one. From today, I am a Big V and a Public Intellectual. If you want to detain me or scold me, just do it. It is just like the Anti-Rightist campaign at the time."[131]

More fundamentally, Yu Jianrong embraces what the self-proclaimed postmodernist thinkers discussed by Gloria Davies reject: the notion of a pluralism of academic inquiry. In an essay reflecting back on thirty years of academic life in China, Yu notes that social conditions have rarely permitted the autonomy of intellectual pursuits in China, citing Cai Yuanpei's 蔡元培 (1868–1940) endeavors to promote a new model of the pursuit of truth. However, truth is not everything, Yu argues:

> Of course, every scholar's investigation and research of history and reality have their own goals or instrumental aspects. For this reason, scholars with different perspectives and philosophical preoccupations, when examining a social or historical problem, can produce completely opposite "truths." But as long as they don't use "scholarship" as a means to obtain advantages, they all are worthy of respect. Because it is only when research in social sciences is not simply a profession but also a part of the researcher's life that the value and meaning of scholarship become apparent. . . . Those scholars and their works who direct their interests toward people who endure suffering or who speak out for subaltern groups may not be well regarded or may even be persecuted for this reason, but the spirit of contributing to the pursuit of truth will surely gain the people's lasting respect.[132]

He concludes that it is only by confronting the problems of society that scholars can produce "truly great social theory [*zhenzheng weida de shehui lilun* 真正偉大的社會理論]": "How to connect the creative concepts and conclusions of Western theory with Chinese reality, to create in a true sense the most interesting theory of this time, this is the great opportunity that this era presents to Chinese scholars as well as a responsibility that cannot be shirked."[133] Yu Jianrong represents another example of the *minjian* intellectual, one who is interested in producing specific knowledge at the grass roots rather than in theory and ideology, who defines himself by opposition with the academic elite, but who at the same time advocates a methodological plurality that the elite often eschews.

A similar shift in perspective can be observed in other works dealing with petitioners. The writer Liao Yiwu became famous when his book *Interviews with the Underclass* was banned in 2001 and a dialogue between Liao and the journalist Lu Yuegang 盧躍剛 published in *Southern Weekly* coincided with a major purge in the newspaper.[134] Liao, an avant-garde poet in Chengdu in the 1980s, had been imprisoned for four years in Chongqing after writing and disseminating the poem "Massacre" after the June Fourth crackdown. In prison, he became fascinated with the stories of *diceng* people and completely changed his approach to literature, devoting himself to series of interviews with marginal groups.

Liao Yiwu's collection of interviews with petitioners, published in 2005, is similarly written from the standpoint of the subaltern. As Hu Ping, an intellectual of the old school, writes in the preface, "Ever since June Fourth, Liao Yiwu has become the duty-bound proxy [*daiyanren* 代言人] of China's underclass—or to be more precise, he has become their spokesperson [*fayanren* 發言人] because he considers himself a member of the underclass."[135] Whereas the term *daiyanren* conveys the idea that someone outside the group speaks for the group, the term *fayanren* denotes a member of the group speaking with the group. Hu Ping describes the massive phenomenon of petitioning as a microcosm of Chinese society, where rights infringements at every level give rise to a "public opinion" that can be expressed only in the Letters and Visits system. Liao Yiwu and the Gao brothers 高氏兄弟 (well-known contemporary artists whose father had gone through the petition system for a rehabilitation) undertook several expeditions to Beijing's petitioner village in the spring of 2004, and Liao Yiwu stayed with a family for one month. The book is a collection of interviews, firsthand material collected from petitioners (mainly open letters to the top leaders) and critical essays by artists, activists, and scholars. Although this book could not be published in China (in particular because of testimony from Falungong petitioners) and did not achieve large circulation on the mainland, the end of Liao's introduction is relevant to the argument about reconfiguring elite-*minjian* relations: "As for making a writer live for one month in a petitioner village, you can give it a try to see whether your nerves can hold up. Does the silent majority really want to be silent? No, if you make them speak, day after day their voice will be louder and stronger than any elite who is empowered to speak, and noisier. People, even insects or ants, do not naturally want to keep silent."[136] Liao reappropriates Wang Xiaobo's trope of the silent majority and redefines his stance as that of an enabler who empowers members of the silent majority to speak (albeit with some irony about living with petitioners, doubtless intended to mock elite intellectuals). His collection sparked a whole genre of "lower-class literature" (*diceng wenxue* 底層文學), generally understood as dealing with "vulnerable groups" in a realist, critical manner.[137]

FROM THE TURNING POINT OF 2008 TO THE NEW CITIZEN MOVEMENT

The year 2008 represents a kind of turning point in the evolution of China's *minjian* society and its relations with the state. The Tibetan uprising and Olympic Flame controversy were followed by the Sichuan earthquake. After a wave of citizen participation in rescue and reporting efforts, the state prioritized cracking down on investigations providing evidence that the high count of casualties was due to man-made causes rather than to the disaster itself, a crackdown that curbed the newfound enthusiasm of civil society to work with the state and dampened international sympathy. The Olympics were a popular success but also coincided with a continued crackdown on social organizations. Jessica Teets argues that this juncture marks a turn away from civil society's regulatory role with respect to the state (leading to democratization) and toward a "consultative authoritarian" arrangement in which NGOs function both as service providers to the state with "operational autonomy" and as tools of social control, improving governance and ultimately making authoritarianism more efficient.[138] This turn, which was further sharpened after 2012, proved detrimental to the further development of legal activism. As Carl Minzner argues, the party-state now "sought to close down rhetoric (constitutionalism), channels (court trials), and social forces (lawyers) that activists had used to mobilize for greater change."[139]

In December 2008, Liu Xiaobo and Zhang Zuhua 張祖樺, along with a group of leading liberal intellectuals, launched Charter 08, a call for institutional reform modeled on Václav Havel's "Charter 77" in Communist Czechoslovakia.[140] Intellectuals on the left or at the center criticized Charter 08 for sacralizing private-property rights and paying insufficient attention to social equality: the charter reaffirms equality as a fundamental principle but contains only a general call to do away with the household registration system and to establish social security. Nonetheless, Liu was immediately arrested, and signatories around China were harassed by the police.

Certain reactions to Charter 08 perfectly illustrate the gap between the more traditional view of the intellectual and the *minjian* position. The economic historian Qin Hui and the literature professor Qian Liqun, two leading voices among critical elite intellectuals, refused to sign because of the charter's lack of attention to social protection. Yu Jianrong also refused to sign, even although Liu Xiaobo had drafted part of the charter in Yu's Eastern Study in Songzhuang. As Yu explained in his personal obituary for Liu, "I must say that I agreed in principle with your main points. However, an opinion I repeatedly expressed is that I dislike the way in which great narratives [*hongda huayu* 宏大話語] completely overlook the individual, especially those vulnerable groups [*ruoshi qunti*] who today survive in the most precarious situation. To put it another way, I cannot agree with those who hope that the oppressed will be subjected to even more cruel persecution in the expectation of provoking a revolution."[141] In characteristic fashion, Yu preferred concrete, specific problems and the individual approach to the theorizing and lofty constitutional principles expressed in Charter 08, even though he agreed with them in principle.

Qin Hui similarly argued that the roots of democracy in China are too shallow (compared with the situation in Czechoslovakia when Charter 77 was published), that the method was too top down, and that it was not wise to criticize the state at a time of economic crisis (especially considering that this crisis seemed to be affecting liberal democracies more harshly than China):

> In China today, rather than the spirit of democracy being inspired by the declarations of principle of a few courageous souls, the case for constitutional democracy needs to be argued. It can be said that the need for profound intellectual debate in China today goes far beyond the need for signing things. . . . If Charter 08 is only about political rights and leaves out the economy, so be it—as stated above, this can be understood as avoiding differences of opinion. Since it has been raised, in addition to demands for economic freedom (such as private ownership of land) there should also be demands for welfare and public services.[142]

Qin Hui's insistence on not separating political freedom and social protection (arguing that opposing the two is precisely one of the false dichotomies of CCP discourse) is a long-standing position. As he argued in another essay, "Why should China, the overwhelming majority of whose population (the peasantry) have had next to no social security *or* freedom (witness the ubiquitous situation of 'expelling migrant workers!')[,] not move toward having 'more welfare state *and* more laissez-faire?'"[143] This is part of Qin Hui's general stance of intervening in public discussions on the base of specialized knowledge as an economic historian and an economist.[144] He further developed his argument in another essay:

> The root cause of such problems [welfare state versus laissez-faire imbalance] lies in the absence of mechanisms of people-delegated power to rule and linkage of power and responsibility—mechanisms of constitutional democracy which provide a common basis for both "laissez-faire" and the "welfare state." Without these, consistently "leftist" or "rightist" governments with excessive power and inadequate responsibility are unavoidable. Abuses accumulate in both. . . . Most abhorrent of all is unrestricted power that now turns "left," now "right." Relying on autocratic power at all times, it first robs in the name of being "left" and then divides up the spoils in the name of being "right"; turning ordinary people's private property "public" in the name of "socialism," and reconverting it into the private property of influential officials in the name of the "market economy." In this "cycling of left and right," the state-owned sector becomes a primary accumulation pump: the powerful engine of unrestricted power is used to pump the private property of ordinary people into the treasury on one side, and from there into the private pockets of influential officials on the other.[145]

Qin develops here his critique of the left/right dichotomy and underlines the need to look at concrete issues. Given China's situation in 2008, the reforms suggested in Charter 08 may appear too abstract to deal with the most deep-rooted problems. Although Qin is a prominent academic, his position can be described as typically *minjian*: when society is viewed from the margins, there is not so much concrete difference between collectivization and privatization, both of which are always carried out to the profit of the elite.

Although Xu Zhiyong may indeed have refrained from signing in order to "protect Gongmeng,"[146] while of course Teng Biao was among the original 303 signatories, there is clearly some resonance between Xu's approach and Qin Hui's critiques of Charter 08. The approach developed by Gongmeng valued informed argument more than "signing things"; it also considered all issues from the standpoint of the marginalized subordinate groups, who Qin Hui also believes have been left out of the discussion.

In April 2010, the Citizens' Commitment Pledge (Gongmin Chengnuo 公民承諾) campaign took off on the Internet. Gongmin/Gongmeng now called on every Chinese person to "be a citizen" by defending justice and righteousness both in private and in their professional capacities in order to change China. Although the organizers (among whom the entrepreneur Wang Gongquan took a prominent role) never mentioned any divergence of views, this initiative can be seen as affirming Gongmin's difference with Charter 08: rather than asking ordinary people to sign off on an institutional blueprint that had little probability of being translated into reality, it asked them to pledge commitment to certain principles that would truly transform their daily lives. Of course, this pledge also provided Gongmin with a useful database of email addresses.[147] Noting that the "rule of law" had already been written into the Constitution but continued to be flaunted by widespread corruption and special privileges, the signatories "resolve to mutually abide by the principles of conscience, duty, democracy, the rule of law, and the concept of the 'modern citizen'; to protect the people's rights and livelihoods; to promote good laws and leaders." This promise is detailed in nine points, all of which call to uphold either legal or moral standards (including guaranteeing the quality of produce or services and refusing any form of corruption) and to further a culture of citizenship. The pledge references the Constitution, in which the term "citizen" (*gongmin*) appears explicitly (although it has disappeared from official discourse), and does not endorse any activities beyond the boundaries of legality, but it does contain a provision to "strive to push forward the rule of law so that government departments, political parties, and social groups in China are bound by the rule of law" as well as a pledge to support legal and other forms of activism targeting illegal or corrupt activities by government departments.[148]

Eva Pils argues that the pledge to hold private and public activities to the same ethical standards provides the link between lawyers as professionals and ordinary people. This connection is conceptualized as the notion of the "citizen" (*gongmin*). This reading further provides a justification for lawyers both acting within the courtroom as professionals and continuing their activities outside the courtroom as advocates because in both cases they are acting as citizens.[149] More generally of course, the pledge is an attempt to make the principles of political activism relevant to ordinary people's lives by highlighting the connection between everyday practices such as corruption and the area of politics, although the issue is framed in terms of individual morality rather than institutional change. Pursuing professions authentically and fairly and changing social practices in a bottom-up way regardless of unfair practices in the system are ways of improving "small environments" and making political commitment relevant to ordinary people. A close reading of the pledge would suggest that China's political system could be made to work fairly if every citizen could be persuaded to apply its laws and principles fairly.

The citizen pledge, which achieved a measure of success online, was followed by Xu Zhiyong's full-fledged theoretical elaboration that launched the New Citizen Movement.[150] On May 29, 2012, Xu Zhiyong published an essay defining it as a political (antiauthoritarian), social (against privilege and inequality), and cultural (new spirit of love) movement, inspired by a progressive and peaceful ideal summarized in the slogan "Freedom, justice, love" (*Ziyou, gongyi, ai* 自由, 公益, 愛):

> China needs a new citizens' movement. This movement is a political movement in which this ancient nation bids utter farewell to authoritarianism and completes the civilized transformation to constitutional governance; it is a social movement to completely destroy the privileges of corruption, the abuse of power, the gap between rich and poor, and to construct a new order of fairness and justice; it is a cultural movement to bid farewell to the culture of autocrats and subjects and instead create a new national spirit; it is the peaceful progressive movement to herald humanity's process of civilizing.[151]

This movement advocates democracy in politics, equality in society, and a civic culture of morality and responsibility, with at its center a notion of the citizen (*gongmin*) rather than of the subject (*chenmin* 臣民), defined by an ideal of individual authenticity: "Freedom means the independent pursuit of belief, thought, expression by an unrestrained, autonomous, authentic self."[152]

There is a perceivable evolution in this manifesto with respect to earlier discourses articulated within China's constitutional framework in that it clearly labels China's present government as "authoritarian" and calls on an evolution toward constitutional governance (presumably still based on the letter of the current constitution[153]). It was accompanied by a set of new attributes, some of which were already used nonsystematically and all of which were designed to present the movement as a structured political initiative, if not outright as a party. Xu now envisaged a process toward institutional change: "We emphasize a constructive approach and emphasize freedom, justice, love; these are our credos. The most ideal form of change in China would be a constitution-drafting process through negotiation between forces inside and outside the system; our mission is to end authoritarian rule through constructive methods, and we will maintain a benevolent attitude toward any individual." Although Xu Zhiyong insisted that no one should impose "violent revolutionary ideas and standards," the new concept marked a clear shift beyond the borders of the present constitutional order.[154]

The New Citizen Movement used as a logo Sun Yat-sen's distinctive calligraphy of the characters *gongmin*, establishing a connection with older political movements, as in the original idea of a *minquan* movement. The characters in the logo allude to the passage in the *Classic of Rites* (*Liji* 禮記) from which Sun borrowed the famous expression "the world under heaven belongs to all" (*tianxia wei gong* 天下為公) and to premodern conceptions of "the public" and "justice." Signatories of the pledge addressed each other as "Citizen XXX." Finally, there was great enthusiasm for demonstrations of civic virtue, and in particular the American manual *Robert's Rules of Order* was widely referred to in meetings and debates to emphasize the procedural requirements of civic culture. This emphasis connects with the late-nineteenth-century liberal tradition in China, which took inspiration from Anglo-American thinkers. Bringing together classical Chinese thought and cosmopolitan liberalism, Xu argued that "'citizen' is an idea that is broader even than democracy, rule of law and such ideas" in that it encompasses personal civic virtue in addition to institutional democracy and freedom.[155]

Yet, as Xu explains in another essay, the New Citizen Movement still retained a distinctive focus on marginal and vulnerable groups, who provide the justification for citizen action:

> Every place has its own social problems: domineering, corrupt officials; *chengguan* who beat people; a polluted environment; injustice; land grabs; and arbitrary fines and illegal charges, to name a few. We need to cast our attention downwards, sincerely care about the underprivileged, and help them protect their rights and interests. Citizen groups should do things that offer

> genuine help to the people. Only if we help many, many people can we take root in society and gain broad support, so that we can promote the development of a democratic and constitutional government in China. Politics should serve the public. At present, there are a lot of opportunities to serve the people in China.[156]

This point was sharply reaffirmed in "Open Letter to Mr. Xi Jinping," published on the day the Eighteenth Party Congress closed and Xi Jinping was appointed as secretary-general:

> This is not a normal society. In an internally split country, behind the incomparable pomp of the [closing] ceremony [of the Eighteenth Congress] lies the despair and helplessness of the vulnerable. Some are the oppressing class; they rely on power, on the barrel of the gun, on prosecutorial law, on the mafia, devoting all their efforts to advance their private interests, before sending their assets and children overseas. Others are the oppressed class, without power or influence, bullied by everyone, deprived of equal opportunities, without universal rights and dignity; even the slightest form of social protection is a black hole for the powerful to encroach and embezzle. . . . Ten years already, and in fact I am still a reformist because I fear that if society changes too radically, innocent, vulnerable people will pay too big a price; I worry that this country will split up.[157]

It is hard to gauge whether Xu's deference to Marxist rhetoric such as "serve the people" or the dichotomy of the oppressors and the oppressed is a mitigating strategy, an attempt to hold the party to its own standards (as Xi Jinping's anticorruption campaign unfolded, Gongmin increasingly called on officials to disclose their assets, launching a petition in November 2012) or a shift in Xu's own understanding of social structures. Most characteristic, however, is his fear that, in case of revolutionary change, the most vulnerable would once again pay the price, a fear that strengthens his reformist stance.

The citizen agenda was most memorably translated into concrete action over the citizen meals (*gongmin jucan* 公民聚餐) that began in 2012. With the idea of lowering the threshold for ordinary people to participate in activities critical of the government and strengthening the notion that "everyone is a citizen," these dinners were organized all around China and could bring together between a dozen and more than one hundred participants. For example, a citizens' dinner took place in Songzhuang in November 2013.[158] The expression *tongcheng fanzui* 同城飯醉 became popular, meaning "eating and getting drunk in the same city" but also by homophony "committing crimes in the same city." Discussions were held according to *Robert's Rules of Order* in order to create a culture of equality where everyone could feel entitled to speak out. In Xu Zhiyong's words, "Only when we let go of our obstinate egos and follow democratic rules can we achieve unity. No matter how senior you are or how much you have accomplished, at citizens' dinners we sit as equals and speak as equals. When we disagree, we can engage in public debates and resolve them by vote."[159] Joining such a dinner means both sharing citizenship in common and retaining differences that can be democratically discussed: "You recognize, first, that you are a citizen and, second, democratic principles: so we all are sitting here together, sharing a common platform that does not belong to any particular person, that does not belong to a particular 'hill' but rather is a common one that belongs to all of us and that is a union of free citizens."[160] This attitude is very different from the traditional position of the elite intellectual who would feel entitled to a special position if taking part in such meetings. On one day in 2013, citizen meals reportedly took place in thirty cities, with hundreds of thousands of participants.

From March 2013, however, the crackdown on rights lawyers began: Wang Gongquan, who had been instrumental in promoting the citizen meals, became one of the first to be detained on public-order charges. The preferred charges were "inciting subversion," "unlawful assembly," and "gathering a crowd to disrupt social order." The wave of arrests was apparently triggered by the activists' call for officials to declare their assets: "On March 31, 2013, Yuan Dong 袁冬, Zhang Baocheng 張寶成, and two others gave a speech at Xidan, Beijing, in which they called on government officials to make public their property holdings. They were arrested on the spot. This was the official prelude to the authorities' repression of the New Citizens Movement and [of] the civil society. Within a year, throughout China no fewer than two hundred human rights activists were arrested and incarcerated."[161] Xu Zhiyong himself was arrested in August and tried in January 2014 for "gathering a crowd to disturb public order." The famous editorialist Xu Zhiyuan wrote in the Hong Kong magazine *Yazhou Zhoukan*, "An ever-stronger feeling of failure is rising all around, and you feel that, in the face of this regime, you are completely powerless. . . . I am not sure what challenges Xu Zhiyong will face next, a new round of repression has already started. For an individual and a society, external pressure and cruelty are indeed terrifying, but even more terrifying is the generalization of moral numbness. I can feel the onset of this numbness, but I am not sure I can free myself from it."[162]

Xu Zhiyong's final statement to court, after he had remained silent throughout his trial, brought together all the most important strands of his writing and thinking. He began by enumerating the many concrete issues he had worked on (providing education for all, allowing migrant children to take university exams, demanding that civil servants declare their assets): "You have accused me of disrupting public order for my efforts to push for rights to equal access to education, to allow children of migrant workers to sit for university examinations where they reside, and for my calls that officials publicly declare their assets. . . . The New Citizens Movement advocates a citizenship that begins with the individual and the personal, through small acts making concrete changes to public policy and the encompassing system."[163]

He reaffirmed a gradualist approach to ensuring that citizens can exercise the rights guaranteed in the Constitution: "Of course we hope that the sacred rights enshrined in the Constitution will be realized, but reform requires stability, and social progress requires gradual advancements. As responsible citizens, we must adopt a gradualist approach when exercising our constitutionally guaranteed rights and when advancing the process toward democracy and the rule of law."[164] Finally, he returned to the inspiration he took from working with the vulnerable groups at the margins of society, alluding to Havel's notion of "living in truth":

> I am forever proud of that moment, and we will not give up our promise to the vulnerable [*ruozhe* 弱者] even when we ourselves are in trouble. . . . Petitioning is rights defense with Chinese characteristics. . . . Having chosen to stand alongside the powerless, we have witnessed far too much injustice, suffering and misfortune over the past decade. . . . China's biggest problem is falsehood, and the biggest falsehood is the country's political system and its political ideology. . . . Political lies know no bounds in this country and 1.3 billion people suffer deeply from it as a result. . . . Although I possess the means to live a superior life within this system, I feel ashamed of privilege in any form. I choose to stand with the weak and those deprived of their rights, sharing with them the bitter cold of a Beijing winter the way it feels from the street or an underground tunnel, shouldering together the barbaric violence of the black jail.[165]

He concluded by contesting every detail of the charges brought against him, but he was of course nonetheless sentenced to four years in jail. The *weiquan* and New Citizen movements were undoubtedly uniquely successful in articulating concrete social claims and a vision for democracy. However, in the end they remained confronted with the difficulty of articulating change within the system except on the basis of individual ethics and civic virtue.

The crackdown continued after Xu's trial. On May 5, 2014, the police detained Pu Zhiqiang 浦志強 and charged him with inciting ethnic hatred and disturbing public order on the basis of a series of text messages sent in connection with the Ilham Tohti case.[166] During the lead-up to International Women's Day on March 8, a traditional day of celebration in socialist countries, repackaged by a group of women activists to raise awareness about sexual harassment, domestic violence, and lesbian, gay, bisexual, transgender (LGBT) rights, the police detained the "feminist five" (*nüquan wu jiemei* 女權五姐妹) for several weeks.[167] These activists, including Li Tingting 李婷婷, who was then working for Yirenping, had also largely adopted the *weiquan* approach of targeting specific issues in creative and nonconfrontational ways—for example, in the "Occupy Men's Toilets" campaign to protest against a lack of women's restrooms and in the act of exposing their breasts to denounce domestic violence.[168] On July 9, 2015, the authorities stepped up the crackdown with a wave of detentions targeting the Fengrui 鋒銳 law firm, well known for its defense of petitioners and public-interest cases.[169] Interestingly, one of the first arrests, that of Fengrui's director Zhou Shifeng 周世鋒, took place in Songzhuang.[170] When more than one hundred lawyers signed a petition to protest the arrests, they were detained, too. At the center of the case were two lawyers known for their offensive tactics in mobilizing public opinion: Wang Yu 王宇 and Wu Gan 吳淦 (a.k.a. "Super Vulgar Butcher," a name he chose to mock "so-called elites who theorize too much and do too little"). Wu, who had made a name in the Deng Yujiao 鄧玉嬌 case (involving a sex worker who stabbed two cadres when they became violent after hiring her services), developed a technique of online fund-raising, publicizing details of cases on trial, and presenting performance art, which he called a "hog-butchering technique" to skin officials.[171]

The grassroots lawyers, academics, and activists discussed in this chapter illustrate the new position occupied by *minjian* intellectuals: favoring concrete problems rather than theoretical discourses, positioned in a third realm outside the state and the market, they rely on their unique connection with the disenfranchised and the vulnerable to justify their public speech and action. For a group of young lawyers, the Sun Zhigang case served as a model for how to make the abstract demands of the democracy protests of 1989 more relevant to ordinary citizens by drawing on their everyday experience. Gongmeng was set up as a new type of organization that would both produce knowledge outside the official framework of academic investigation of social strata and combine this specific knowledge with action. It produced several reports that challenged both the central tenets of China's domestic policy as well as the findings by previous scholars on petitioners and ethnic policy. Yu Jianrong, a *minjian* scholar who relies on his own wealth to take certain liberties with his unit of academic affiliation, also used his specific investigation of petitioners to challenge Marxist theories of class in favor of ethnography and to reject the avant-garde role of intellectuals in favor of a more modest position among those people who are most vulnerable. After 2008, the New Citizen Movement evolved toward a more openly political stance but also attempted to go further toward the grassroots and the everyday, using tools such as citizen meals and *Robert's Rules of Order*. In comparison with other groups, such as amateur historians or documentary filmmakers, legal scholars and activists are more likely to explicitly designate their activities as related to their status as "citizens."[172] However, they also share some basic traits of *minjian* intellectuals: specific knowledge, the derivation of legitimacy from concrete work with subaltern groups, epistemological pluralism, and a determination to work neither for the state nor for the market.

The strategy chosen by the New Citizen Movement was ultimately unable to open a space for further contentious action. Eva Pils notes that in legal advocacy, even an insistence on adherence to the law can become subversive of state power: because the system prevents the formation of a professional community and common professional ethics, it pushes lawyers outside the system to identify with their clients and petitioners.[173] Similarly, Wang Chaohua argues that the authorities were caught off guard by this new group of *sike* 死磕 lawyers ("sticklers") and their "use of unpolitical causes to turn the regime's own slogan about the rule of law against it."[174] In any event, the systematic repression of the *weiquan* movement and rights lawyers more broadly suggests that the new approach taken by *minjian* lawyers and academics, relying on greater specialization and nonpolitical solutions to practical problems, has exhausted its potential for tolerance by the state authorities and will now be actively eradicated. Nonetheless, the figure of the *minjian* activist and the alternative body of social knowledge that has already been constructed may represent a deeper long-term challenge to elite authority than is currently apparent.

CHAPTER 6

Journalists, Bloggers, and a New Public Culture

The Lhasa protests on March 14, 2008, directed mainly against Han and Hui residents, resulted in a significant number of deaths and injuries.[1] Mistakes in the use of images by CNN and other Western media sparked a backlash in Chinese public discourse, with the creation of online groups such as Anti-CNN.[2] The events also coincided almost exactly with the launch of the Olympic torch relay in Greece on March 24, leading up to the Beijing Olympics in August. On April 5 and 6, the relay was disrupted in London and Paris by protesters supporting Tibet and free-speech groups. This led to a further nationalist backlash in China, where student groups and bloggers called for a boycott of French and other firms, in particular the supermarket chain Carrefour on May 1.[3] These events, which were grave enough in their own right, also resulted in epic controversies in the Chinese media and on the Internet, highlighting the role of a new generation of *minjian* journalists and bloggers. Independent journalists had become increasingly active since the late 1990s, followed by bloggers, who often made a name for themselves in relation to protest events in the early 2000s. The controversy in 2008 represents a benchmark for the implication of *minjian* journalists and bloggers in a debate about nationalism and freedom of expression in which they eclipsed traditional elite intellectuals.[4]

The investigative journalist, editor, and columnist Chang Ping 長平, who had already courted controversy through his earlier reporting for *Southern Weekly*, was now working at *Southern Metropolis Daily* and wrote a column for *Financial Times Chinese* (*FTChinese*) on April 3, 2008, in which he reacted to attacks on Western media reports by questioning the reliability of domestic media:

> If the netizens genuinely care about news values, they not only should be exposing the fake reports by the Western media [but] should also be challenging the control by the Chinese government over news sources and the Chinese media. There is no doubt that the harm from the latter is even worse than the former. When individual media outlets make fake reports about real events, it is easy to correct because just a few meticulous Chinese netizens can do the job. When media control is exercised by the state authorities, the whole world is helpless. . . . The biggest harm to news values by these fake reports is that many people have chosen to abandon their trust in objectivity and fairness and hence seek refuge in narrow nationalism. They draw the conclusion that talk of universal values is all a deceptive trick used to cover up underlying national interests.[5]

Chang Ping's argument revolves around the question of double standards, pointing out that it is paradoxical for Chinese netizens to criticize CNN for a mistake in its coverage of events that the Chinese government was actively concealing, while at the same time not questioning the state-controlled reporting in the Chinese media. Tellingly, this argument is grounded not in a political position, but in a professional ethos of journalism, which is harmed both by incorrect or misleading Western media reports and by China's state system of misinformation. Against the perception that media everywhere are simply tools in the hands of governments and national interests (hence legitimizing and normalizing the practices of Chinese state media), he suggests that professional ethics provide a reasonably objective standpoint to examine controversial discussions as well as a source of legitimacy that does not rely on state co-optation.

He then expands the argument against double standards to the question of nationalism:

> But I also see that many Chinese people have taken this opportunity to engage in broader discussions and deeper thinking. They found out that the bigotry of the Western people against China is based on a sense of cultural superiority. The warning message is that when the Han people are facing the ethnic minorities, do they also have the same cultural superiority that leads to bigotry? The distorted Western reports about China came from an unwillingness to listen and understand because they are too engaged in the sort of

> Orientalism that Edward Said wrote about. But what about us and the ethnic minorities? If we use nationalism as the weapon to resist the Westerners, then how can we persuade the ethnic minorities to abandon their nationalism and join the mainstream nation building?[6]

Chang Ping's argument is a kind of generalization of the journalist's methodology to address the larger problem of nationalism. Examining the issue from two sides—both the viewpoint of Chinese nationalists dissatisfied with Western media reporting on Tibet and the viewpoint of Tibetans dissatisfied with the reporting of Chinese media—he points out the logical contradiction in legitimizing Han nationalism while denying legitimacy to discourses of Tibetan nationalism.

In return, he was violently attacked by name as "Southern Metropolis Chang Ping" and described as a "trendy crispy chicken [*danghong zhaziji* 當紅炸子雞]" in an op-ed by Mei Ninghua 梅寧華, the publisher of *Beijing Evening News* (*Beijing Wanbao* 北京晚報), published by the Beijing Municipal Propaganda Department, writing under the name Wen Feng 文峰. The gist of Mei's argument was that Chang Ping and the Southern Media Group were in fact agents of "westernization" operating under the cover of a radical conception of free speech that condoned slander and violence.[7] Of course, the fact that Chang Ping's column was published by a foreign media venture in China (*FTChinese*) was in itself part of the background that eventually led to his dismissal from the Southern Media Group.[8] The simple fact that foreign media set up Chinese-language reporting and translation offices within China, even though some of their websites were later blocked, changed the media environment by offering influential columnists, such as Chang Ping and Xu Zhiyuan, alternative sources of income that were not dependent on state control.

A week later, Han Han, who was then already a well-known blogger and racer, posted several widely shared comments on his Sina blog in which he made fun of nationalists and nationalism and deflated the bombastic rhetoric favored by the online nationalists and official discourse. "Boycotting Carrefour, I feel, is not patriotism, but a game for losers. An action that is truly patriotic requires you to put your money where your mouth is. . . . Why is our national self-respect so fragile and superficial? When others called us a mob, we cursed them and appeared to be aggressive. And then we claimed, 'We are not a mob.'"[9] Three days later he further attacked nationalist arguments in a "Q&A with Chinese Nationalists":

Q: The motherland—that's your mother.
A: The motherland is the motherland, my mother is my mother.
Q: How can you possibly think you're doing the right thing for this land of yours?
A: I own no land, and neither do you.

. . .

Q: Patriotism is a virtue, a fine tradition; it comes with us when we are born.
A: If, given the chance to be born a second time, you chose to be born once more in this country, I agree this would show true patriotism and excellent moral fiber.

. . .

Q: We must resolutely boycott Carrefour. Shockingly, you are prepared to let foreign powers humiliate our great nation. If everyone was as cowardly as you are, our country would have been swallowed up long ago.
A: Oh yes, you're strong and brave, you're not afraid to die—because you're so daring as to refrain from shopping at a supermarket, because you're so bold as to put Carrefour ice cream on a shopping cart and let it lie there melting while you go off without paying, because you're so fearless as to stand by the exit to the supermarket and curse the emerging shoppers as traitors, because you have the gumption to burn the Dutch flag as a warning to France.[10]

Whereas Chang Ping's critique is connected to the affirmation of a professional ethos, Han Han's discussion of nationalism is *minjian* in another sense. Rather than talking about big issues in a theoretical (and bombastic) manner, he deflates each question by returning it to a concrete problem: nationalist bloggers are cowards who do not practice what they preach. The relationship with the "motherland" and the "land" has been hijacked by the government, which eagerly trumpets that the Chinese people "own" it but which will not grant them property rights.[11] Officials extol patriotism but transfer their money to Hong Kong and send their children overseas for study. Han Han uses metaphors taken from ordinary discourse to deflate these claims. His arguments are all the more effective as he describes himself as a former nationalistic youth.[12] An interesting aspect is Han's attitude toward consumerism. Unlike other *minjian* intellectuals who emerged in the 2000s, celebrity bloggers are generally uncritical of capitalism and consumption, continuing in the vein of writers such as Wang Shuo and Jia Pingwa in the 1990s. However, in this post Han Han also slips in some critique of consumerism: by highlighting that for nationalist bloggers boycotting a supermarket is the summit of political activism and underscoring that in a country where consumption of foreign goods is ubiquitous they do not put their money where their mouth is, he also mocks the importance that consumption has taken on in contemporary China.[13]

When a few weeks later the Sichuan earthquake struck, nationalist bloggers attacked Sharon Stone for insensitive remarks about "karmic revenge" for the persecution of Tibetans (she eventually apologized). Han Han again denounced double standards: "A country needs friends, but our people seem to want only friends who can say nice things about us. . . . Our criticism of [Sharon Stone] is far more extreme than our criticism of the people behind the shoddily built schools and hospitals that collapsed in the earthquake. This demonstrates once again how selective we are in our tolerance of things: We can endure suffering caused by natural disasters and the bitter fruit of man-made disasters, but what we cannot countenance is foreigners criticizing us."[14]

He also points out that Chinese forums are full of posts invoking karma in connection with natural calamities in Japan, Indonesia, and the United States.[15] Han Han, who traveled to Sichuan after the earthquake, made donations, and complained about being endlessly bothered by "patriotic" journalists asking how much money he had donated, again takes the position that real problems of everyday life are often obscured rather than illuminated by abstract discourses about the nation. The issue of substandard construction in Sichuan is of course a case in point. However, Han's essays also raise the question of the significance of his editorializing: Are they simply intellectual by-products of the cultural marketing of Han Han himself? Or do they contribute to the rise of the *minjian* sphere and its engagement in political debates?

In some respects, Chang Ping's and Han Han's interventions marked a new mode of public engagement. Microblogs, the instant coverage of events allowed by smartphones, and the instant access to information they provided to huge groups of readers marked a distinct moment in the rise of *minjian* intellectuals, preceded and prepared by the rise of commercial media in the 1990s, email and blogs in the 2000s and then followed by WeChat and social media in the 2010s. The newfound professional ethos of journalists gave an editorialist the credibility to make an independent contribution that was sufficiently widely disseminated and discussed that it warranted a violent rebuttal from a very senior propaganda official. Bloggers such as Han Han grounded their credibility and *minjian* status in freedom from state employment and in a critique of traditional "serious" intellectual discourses, which is implicit in Han's satirical style. These vectors more generally gave rise to a new type of *minjian* or popular culture: not traditional "folk" culture, but a form of mainstream, everyday culture that incorporates consumerism, global "pop" references, and domestic culture produced outside the state's remit.[16]

Of course, the state has kept a very vigilant eye on the new spaces that have emerged on- and offline and in most cases has quickly developed technological tools that have allowed it, after a brief time lag, to restore the level of control it exercised on cultural and intellectual products before the Internet and marketization. At the same time, it has also tried to use these new spaces as a tool to transmit its message by positively investing mainstream culture with the party's values and historical narratives.

THE RISE OF COMMERCIAL MEDIA AND THE PLURALIZATION OF PUBLIC DISCOURSE

In some ways, the media may have been one of the fields that was least conducive to nurturing *minjian* intellectuals. Traditionally a fortress of establishment intellectuals, such as Deng Tuo (1912–1966), the first chief editor of *People's Daily*, who transposed the Confucian literati ethos to a new role as thought-worker cadres, the field was very rapidly commercialized in the 1990s. As Chang Ping argued, "Before Deng Xiaoping's Southern Tour, the media was on the one hand a propaganda machine for the government, on the other the stage for literati who 'use writing to transmit the Way.'"[17] This evolution left little space for journalists who identified neither with the many state-centered tasks that official journalists traditionally carried out (public reporting but also preparing internal reports for officials and taking part in propaganda work) nor with the sensationalistic market-oriented reporting. Despite commercialization, the party's ideology and propaganda bureaucracy maintained strong controls over any type of media, especially because the state still remained wary of journalists, who had organized a separate demonstration during the democracy movement of 1989 under the banner of freedom of the press. Therefore, the new role of the media in the reforms era—summed up in the phrase "supervision by public opinion" (*yulun jiandu* 輿論監督), endorsed by Zhao Ziyang 趙紫陽 in his report to the Thirteenth Party Congress in 1987 and highlighted by some critical newspapers of the 1980s (e.g., Shanghai's *World Economic Herald*)—largely disappeared after the Tiananmen crackdown. It was replaced in official discourse by "channeling public opinion" (*yulun daoxiang* 輿論導向) under Jiang Zemin and then by the more proactive policy of "leading public opinion" (*yulun yindao* 輿論引導) under Hu Jintao at the very same time as the commercialization of the media field took place.

In 1992, the General Administration of Press and Publications announced a new policy of "responsibility for losses and gains" (*zifu ying kui* 自負盈虧), which led many major media outlets (including *People's Daily* and other party newspapers) to create commercial subsidiaries to boost their profits. The same year, the Hong Kong businessman Yu Pun Hoi, who had recently taken control of the *Mingpao* from Louis Cha 查良鏞 (Jin Yong 金庸), launched the first major media joint venture in China, the Guangzhou weekly *Modern People* (*Xiandairen Bao* 現代人報), which lasted for three years before being shut down.[18] Shortly thereafter, he recruited the Hong Kong writer and editor Chan Koonchung as well as film producer Nansun Shi 施南生 (Tsui Hark's 徐克 partner) to set up a new media conglomerate in Beijing. However, plans to publish *Life Weekly* and *China Business Times* 中國工商時報 got stuck in red tape, and Yu eventually withdrew.[19] Commercialization of the press offered unprecedented opportunities to editors who were willing to use the commercial subsidiaries of official press organs to challenge the boundaries of self-censorship, whether in the area of lifestyle, entertainment, or politics. Of course, it also entailed a trivialization of journalism and an increasing drift toward entertainment, which scholars have criticized. Zhao Yuezhi, for example, points out that the brief golden age of investigative journalists ("watchdogs") quickly gave way to a new structure in which they became a tool in the hands of powerful capitalist interests ("lapdogs").[20] However, this somewhat binary approach may pay insufficient attention to the journalistic ethos that emerged from the transition, which echoes the preoccupations of *minjian* intellectuals.

Southern Weekly (its official English name was *Southern Weekend* until 2006) was probably the most successful and the most influential of the new commercial media. Established in 1984 as a four-page weekend cultural supplement to Guangdong's official provincial daily under the editorship of Zuo Fang 左方 (Huang Keji 黃克驥, b. 1934), in the 1990s it became the reference for a new style of investigative journalism, with the support of provincial leaders, in particular when the Guangdong Party secretary saved it from a closing order by the Central Propaganda Department in 1993. This incident defined the professional ethos of *Southern Weekly*: in an article titled "The Issue of Fact-Based News Reporting: To Writers," the newspaper stipulated that reporters must be eyewitnesses to the scene, adhere to the principle of truth, provide documentation and verification for all news reports, and establish trust with their readership.[21] From then on, the notion that standards of journalism should take the highest priority became the newspaper's trademark.

Southern Weekly early on developed a tabloid style that ensured its commercial success and reached a circulation of 475,000 copies in 1991 (in its original four-page format). After it expanded to a fully independent newspaper, its circulation reached 1 million in 1993 and a peak of 1.3 million in 1997.[22] Another tabloid spin-off from the official Guangdong daily newspaper, *Southern Metropolis Daily*, increased its sales from 40,000 copies a day in 1997 to 1.4 million in 2003.[23] As Li-fung Cho notes, many of the investigative reporters at *Southern Weekly* were hired under "outside the system" (*tizhi wai*) arrangements, meaning they did not have a formal status as state employees. The newspaper increasingly compensated them with attractive salaries, thereby achieving a situation in which journalists were both well paid and relatively insulated from political pressure. In this sense, *Southern Weekly* can be seen as the first *minjian* newspaper. This quality was quite evident in the approach promoted by Jiang Yiping 江藝平, who took over from Zuo Fang as chief editor in 1996 and was joined by Qian Gang 錢鋼 (previously editor of *Sanlian Shenghuo Zhoukan*) as deputy chief editor from 1998. This approach was famously illustrated in the editor's New Year's column "Give Strength to the Weak, Let the Pessimists Move Forward" in 1999:

> Looking back at the last 365 days and nights, all our efforts have been directed at proving that "we are journalists." . . . Some people say that fulfilling one's professional duties is a way of achieving happiness. Others say that it is more like repaying debts because it will never give us much personal satisfaction. How could the professional duty of a journalist not be a form of "repayment" to the public? They tell people the news that happened in the world. They also tell people about the truth behind the news. . . . Just as the survival of plants depends on displaying their green leaves, the survival of journalism is guaranteed by truth. . . .

> Yes indeed, we hope that we have never abandoned the weak [*ruozhe*]. We hope that they are us ourselves.[24]

Although the assertion of professionalism and the value of truth (which was also made necessary by the incident in 1993, in which *Southern Weekly* was almost closed down) may seem banal today, these guidelines were entirely at odds with the principles that were supposed to guide journalists in the Leninist system (in one passage, the editorial explicitly notes that *Southern Weekly* reporters have "eliminated the notion of 'reporting pleasing news, not worrying news' [*bao xi bu bao you* 報喜不報憂]"). This professional ethos is presented as a duty, an imperative for survival, and even a source of personal satisfaction. Finally, the conclusion underlines that this ethos is understood as a contribution to helping the weak and vulnerable, resonating with previous assertions in the *minjian* spirit. One year later, rather than send reporters to the Pacific Islands to witness the dawn of the new millennium, *Southern Weekly* sent reporters and editors to their home villages to discuss with the villagers the historical changes that had taken place in China over the past decades.

Despite repeated editorial changes, this ethos was kept alive by several senior editors, such as Chang Ping, as well as by the chief editor of *Southern Metropolis Daily*, Cheng Yizhong (who publicized the Sun Zhigang affair and was sentenced for corruption in 2004), and by reporters such as Zhai Minglei 翟明磊 and Xiao Shu 笑蜀. Similar themes were repeatedly taken up in subsequent New Year's editorials: "Prosperity and Fairness" (2003), "One Sentence of Truth Is More Important Than the Weight of the Whole World" (2006), "Raise High the Flag of Freedom and Openness" (2008), "There Is No Winter That Cannot Be Overcome" (2009).[25] In an editorial published shortly after the Tibet controversy and discussing *Southern Weekly*'s new slogan "Read us to understand China," Xiao Shu argued, "What is our basic professional ethics? In as far as possible, it is to satisfy the citizens' right to know and to allow information to circulate between people as unobstructedly as possible."[26]

Chang Ping joined *Southern Weekly* in 1997 and reported widely on social topics. In 1999, a major ideological rectification took place at the newspaper, after which he became director of the news department. As he remembers, "At the time, we tried to record change in Chinese society using methods from anthropology and sociology. For example, we chose a village, a township, a street in the heartland. . . . [O]ur plan was to revisit the same place at the end of every year for ten years to record its changes."[27] It was through this mindset that Chang Ping got embroiled in the Zhang Jun 張君 scandal: when a notorious mafia murderer was arrested in Chongqing by police chief Wen Qiang 文強, Chang Ping undertook an investigation in Zhang Jun's home village that highlighted the social factors that had led him down the path of crime.[28] This article as well as three others brought on another purge of the *Southern Weekly* editorial room, and Chang Ping was first demoted and then left the paper.[29] After briefly working for CCTV and a private newspaper in Shanghai, *Bund Illustrated* (*Waitan Huabao* 外灘畫報), he returned to the Nanfang Group as deputy chief editor of *Southern Metropolis Daily*. It was while working there that in 2008 he published his commentary on the Tibetan uprising on the *FTChinese* website. The upheaval around his column eventually again resulted in his demotion, followed by the termination of his contract.

After that, Chang Ping moved to Hong Kong and then to Germany, from where he edited the Hong Kong weekly *iSun Affairs* (*Yangguang Shiwu* 陽光時務).[30] Published in Hong Kong by media tycoon Chen Ping 陳平 for a little more than a year, *iSun* in many ways continued the tradition of the popular media in the vein of the Southern Media Group, briefly bringing together a set of journalists who had contributed to changing the Chinese media before being pushed out of the mainland.[31] The highlight of its short lifespan was its reporting on the protests in Wukan in the fall of 2011, mainly by Zhang Jieping 張潔萍, who later became the chief editor of *Initium* (*Duan* 端). *Initium* was funded by Cai Hua 蔡華 (Will Cai), a corporate lawyer in Hong Kong who, like Chen Ping, sought to continue the tradition of "saving the country through private entrepreneurship [*shiye jiuguo* 事業救國]."[32] Similarly, Zhai Minglei, a Shanghai native who wrote for *Southern Weekly* from 2001 to 2003 and made a name for himself through his investigation of Project Hope in 2001, left the paper to work on training NGO workers and set up the journal *Minjian* at Guangzhou's Sun Yat-sen university as a free online publication that did not require registration. When *Minjian* was shut down in 2007, he launched the blog *1 Bao* 一報 (One man's journal).[33] In this manner, the philosophy of *Southern Weekly* continued to develop and expand.

Hu Shuli, a star journalist who began at the *Workers' Daily* (*Gongren Ribao* 工人日報) in the 1980s, had been involved in the media protests in 1989 and had written for *China Business Times* in the 1990s, established *Caijing* 財經 (Finance and economics) in 1998 with the support of financial reformers within the bureaucracy. Owned by SEEC Media (Caixun Chuanmei 財訊傳媒), controlled by the Stock Exchange Executive Council (Zhongguo Zhengquan Shichang Yanjiu Sheji Zhongxin 中國證券市場研究設計中心), a think tank set up by a group of technocrats around Wang Boming 王波明,[34] *Caijing* was officially established to protect shareholders' interests and expose financial scandals.[35] Two cases made it famous: its revelations regarding the broad circulation of the SARS virus in China in 2003 and its investigation of the Shanghai pension funds scandal in 2006. After these incidents, it became extremely profitable. As Cheng Yizhong notes, Hu Shuli has always positioned herself as a loyal critic inside the system,[36] which has protected her from persecution, although others see her as the voice of financial markets.[37] Nonetheless, Hu Shuli was eventually forced to leave the paper over an incident related to the coverage of the Ürümqi protests in July 2009.[38] She took up a position at Sun Yat-sen University in Guangzhou and subsequently founded a new media group, *Caixin*, registered with the Zhejiang provincial government, which generally continued the line she had taken at *Caijing*.

In both *Caijing* and *Southern Weekly*, it is significant to note the formation of a professional ethos (*zhuanye zhuyi* 專業主義) that characterizes specific intellectuals, increasingly structured around a culture of fact verification, and a separation of investigative and editorial functions of the press, which of course ran counter to the historic mission of the media in the Communist context.[39] As Li Datong 李大同, the editor of *Bingdian* 冰點 (Freezing point), a commercial supplement to *China Youth Daily* argued, professionalization was a way of advancing the agenda of journalism, using "professional techniques to publish articles that were outside the official agenda."[40] It is hard to overestimate the influence of *Southern Weekly*'s attention to *minjian* society: whether it was amateur historians investigating the Mao era, the new genre of independent documentary, or the lawyers and NGO workers dedicated to working with subordinate groups, *Southern Weekly* was always involved in reporting, publicizing, and organizing various contests, prizes, or public events that would enable it to reach more readers.

Zhao Yuezhi concludes that throughout the reforms of the media system, journalists remained part of the ruling class: although they might sometimes ally with reformers within the system, they were unlikely to take the side of subaltern groups, who were historically always excluded from the public sphere.[41] By contrast, Liu Qing 劉擎 and Barrett McCormick, although recognizing that the party retains a considerable capacity to channel the media, argue that professionalization and the normative autonomy it entails enabled a transition away from a "monopolistic public sphere" of discursive homogeneity and exclusivity (state ownership of all media, the party as monistic authority holding a superior truth, co-optation of journalists within the state apparatus, assertion of the party's ideology as spoken in the name of the people) and toward a more "pluralistic" though still tightly controlled sphere: "Just as we should not overestimate the impact of still closely supervised media, so we should not underestimate the importance of the expectation that journalists and intellectuals will have at least the appearance of autonomy."[42] This qualified pluralism resulted in a relative diversification of discourses, making space for interventions by "the most disadvantaged and underrepresented groups such as peasants and laid-off workers. . . . While direct and explicit criticisms in opposition to the core of the official ideology are restricted, a large volume of a wide range of indirect and implicit discourse that contains alternative political vocabularies, ideas and perspectives is available in the public sphere."[43] Because such discourses are tolerated, their legitimacy is implicitly recognized although they may not appear in the official media.

Nonetheless, the position of *minjian* media remains very precarious: a newspaper such as *Southern Weekly*, which is neither a propaganda organ (although it remains under the supervision of the propaganda bureaucracy) nor a simple object of consumption and profit like the entertainment press (even though it relies on its economic profitability to keep the state at arm's length), but a newspaper relying on its professional ethos and investigation of specific issues to connect with ordinary readers, is always at risk. For its New Year's editorial in 2013, taking a cue from a speech made by Xi Jinping in December shortly after taking up the party leadership, in which he endorsed "governing the country according to the Constitution," Dai Zhiyong 戴志勇 and other editors at *Southern Weekly* drafted a piece describing the "China Dream" as a "constitutionalist dream." The editorial may also have been inspired by the "Proposal for Constitutional Reforms" published by seventy-one intellectuals on Christmas Day 2012.[44] For the first time in the history of New Year's editorials, this editorial was submitted to the Propaganda Bureau before publication, resulting in a long bargaining process and its ultimate scrapping. It was replaced, well after the editorial deadline and under direct orders of the Guangdong Propaganda Bureau head Tuo Zhen 庹震, by a hastily compiled text that incorporated several quotations from Xi Jinping (as well as several embarrassing factual errors) and was published under a title taken directly from the *People's Daily* New Year's editorial, "We Are Now Closer to Our Dreams Than at Any Time Before."[45] This incident triggered a protracted strike by *Southern Weekly* journalists and eventually an exodus from the newspaper. It also led to a full-fledged controversy around constitutionalism throughout the spring and summer of 2013: the call for constitutional government was repeatedly endorsed by publications such as *Yanhuang Chunqiu*, *Caijing*, and the website Consensus Net as well as by individuals such as law professor He Weifang 賀衛方, until he had to close all his social media accounts at the end of the year.[46] On the other side, the campaign against constitutionalism in the party press was underpinned by the publication of Central Document Number 9 (in which constitutionalism was identified as one among seven "unmentionables"), endorsed by a series of scholars such as political scientists Wang Shaoguang and Hu Angang throughout the spring, and reached its climax with Xi Jinping's speech on August 19, 2013. Rogier Creemers describes this pushback as a manifestation of Xi Jinping's "anti-constitutionalist" agenda.[47] The New Year's editorial incident in any case shows the precarious position of the *minjian* press and the party–state's ability to reaffirm its full ideological control over the media when it is so inclined.

THE DEVELOPMENT OF THE INTERNET AND INTELLECTUALS AS BLOGGERS

China first linked up to the Internet in 1993, and access became more widely available beginning in 1996. By January 2017, the number of Internet users in China was estimated at 731 million (53 percent of the population).[48] The state regulated the development of the Internet but inserted responsibility for it into pre-existing structures rather than creating a new regulatory apparatus. Generally, the state seems to have viewed the Internet primarily as a propaganda platform, only gradually realizing its subversive potential. Responsibility for technical regulation of Internet providers was first given to the telecom authorities (the Ministry of Information Industry, which became the Ministry of Industry and Information Technology in 2008), with the Ministry of Public Security responsible for surveillance (modeled on the regulation of telephone lines), while content providers were inserted into the propaganda system (under the overall coordination of the CCP Propaganda Department). Connections to the international network were routed through a small number of backbone networks, such as the one developed by China NetCom (which enjoyed the backing of Jiang Zemin's son Jiang Mianheng 江綿恆). The Ministry of Public Security was first given responsibility for surveillance in a regulation adopted in February 1994; it issued detailed rules for access providers, including specifications of nine types of forbidden content in December 1997, and launched the Golden Shield project (Jin dun Gongcheng 金盾工程) in 1998 to monitor the Chinese Internet (the "Great Firewall" to block foreign content was developed within the Golden Shield project). The first form of online discussions that encountered enthusiastic (though numerically limited) popular success were the online forums known as BBSs (Bulletin Board Systems), which were particularly active in the controversy around the bombing of the Chinese embassy in Belgrade in 1999.[49] Subsequently, in 2000 and 2002, the Ministry of Information Industry adopted a series of regulations for content providers and consumers, including a registration system for the BBSs, as well as the first form of keyword filtering.[50] Under Hu Jintao, the state gradually developed a discourse on "cybersovereignty," legitimizing its regulation of the Internet to create a "healthy and orderly" online environment. The Fourth Plenum of the Sixteenth Central Committee in September 2004 set new rules and instituted more proactive surveillance through a system of "online commentators" (*wangluo pinglunyuan* 網絡評論員). State intervention was now summarized under the catchword "soft management" (*rouxing guanli* 柔性管理).

The early years of Hu Jintao's first term corresponded with the great popular success of blogs, especially in the aftermath of the Sun Zhigang affair. One of the most comprehensive compilations of Chinese blogs, edited by the former *Southern Weekly* journalist Zhai Minglei, describes the phenomenon as "the power of *minjian* discourse in the era of new media."[51] This somewhat breathless evaluation is backed up by the figure of 181 million blogs for 338 million Internet users in June 2009, and closer analysis shows that bloggers with large followings are extremely diverse in terms of geographical location, age, profession, and education, ranging from primary or middle school graduates to university professors.[52] Ying Chan describes them as "public intellectuals" on the basis of their "public criticism" (*gonggong piping* 公共批評) and refers to Edward Said's notion that intellectuals do not practice systematic criticism as much as they seek a balance between individual problems and public speech.[53] The seventeen "bold" bloggers in Zhai Minglei's edited collection *China's Bold Blogs* are classified as either "individual critics" (Ai Weiwei, Han Han, Xu Zhiyong, Ran Yunfei 冉雲飛, Chang Ping) or "platform publishers" (Qianliexian 錢烈憲, Luo Yonghao 羅永浩 at Bullogger.com, shut down in 2009).[54] Several grassroots bloggers became famous in connection with certain "mass incidents," such as Lian Yue 連岳 and Tiger

Temple 老虎廟 (the Xiamen PX environmental protest in 2007[55]), Zeng Jinyan (Hu Jia's 胡佳 arrest), Zola 佐拉 (the Chongqing nail household incident in 2007). A more academic study of blogs hosted on Chinese providers similarly concludes that despite a high level of surveillance and filtering, there is a considerable degree of variation in the rigor with which providers apply censorship rules, thus creating opportunities for users.[56]

Hu Jintao's second term corresponded with an increasingly restrictive regulation of the Chinese Internet and the development of microblogs, known as *wei boke* 微博客 or *weixing boke* 微型博客 and commonly abbreviated as *weibo* 微博. Twitter became available in 2006, and its Chinese spinoff, Fanfou, in 2007; however, it was closed down after the Ürümqi protests of 2009, at the same time as Facebook and Twitter were blocked in China, a series of blogs and other websites were closed, and the government announced a plan to preinstall Green Dam (Lüba 綠壩) software on all computers sold in China. As an alternative, Sina Weibo was launched in August 2009 and became the most successful microblog service provider, and it was followed by Netease, Sohu, and Tencent in 2010. Of course, these new media platforms were not exempt from the general trend of commercialization and trivialization of the media: on Sina Weibo, as opposed to Twitter, entertainment celebrities were recruited to attract netizens and "pitch" discussion topics chosen by the company.[57] After the Wenzhou High Speed Rail crash of 2011, microblogs were severely limited, even as the state tried to co-opt influential bloggers. A full-fledged crackdown on "Internet opinion leaders" (the so-called big Vs for "verified accounts") followed in 2013. As a consequence, when Tencent launched a new instant-messaging application named WeChat (Weixin 微信) in 2011, following the model of WhatsApp (which had appeared in early 2009), many users migrated to WeChat. While Weibo content was generally publicly available to any registered user, public content was strictly limited on WeChat, restricted to sharing through groups (*weixinquan* 微信圈, limited to five hundred members and to no more than four groups per individual). WeChat Public accounts (Weixin Gongzhong Hao 微信公眾號) were restricted to registered entities, limited to one posting a day, and their content was closely monitored.[58] This allowed the state, working closely together with the private developer Tencent, to push sensitive content out of the public sphere while retaining the ability to monitor that content through WeChat groups.

In China, just as in other political settings, the Internet had a transformational impact on the public sphere, but at the same time it did not durably change the balance between freedom of information and prevalence of control. As Yang Guobin noted in 2009, the Internet provided an unparalleled platform for citizen activism, which the state at first had to adapt to. In particular, it allowed ordinary people to become "knowledge producers," hence broadening the space for citizen discourses.[59] By contrast, Rebecca MacKinnon, noting the efficiency of China's system of "intermediary liability" in exercising political control in an imperceptible way, argues that direct manipulation of content allowed the state to exercise the same level of control but users to feel freer.[60]

An important aspect of the early development of the Chinese Internet was the interaccessibility of Chinese content posted from different areas, in particular China, Hong Kong, and Taiwan. Although there had already been a longstanding tradition of textual circulation between these territories (as well as Hong Kong-based satellite television broadcasters such as Phoenix, which became increasingly available in China), exchange was greatly enhanced by the new technical capabilities of the Internet, creating a "transnational Chinese cultural sphere,"[61] made up of news sites, journals, discussion groups, and online publications. This virtual space encouraged the emergence of a new kind of pan-Chinese textual ecosystem made up of press and media groups (*iSun* TV and weekly magazine, Phoenix, and, later, *Initium*), publications (Yang Jisheng's books published by Cosmos), bookstores in Hong Kong, and a group of pan-Chinese intellectuals who increasingly spoke out on a broad range of issues cutting across different territories: Lung Ying-tai, Leung Man-tao 梁文道, Qian Gang, Chang Ping.

One of their preferred discussion forums was Consensus Net, a broad Internet platform established by Zhou Zhixing 周志興 in 2009. Zhou Zhixing (b. 1952 in Jiangsu) was a typical intraparty reformer: he met Liu Shaoqi's 劉少奇 personal secretary, Liu Zhende 劉振德, in a factory in the 1970s, who then later had him transferred to the party's Central Literature Research Office to work on the Liu Shaoqi Research team in 1980. Zhou Zhixing later played a role in establishing the Central Documents Publishing House (1987), produced the official CCTV documentary on Deng Xiaoping, and edited Deng Rong's 鄧榕 biography of her father.[62] In 1996, Zhou "dived into the sea," becoming a producer at Phoenix TV and then taking charge of setting up *Phoenix Weekly* (*Fenghuang Zhoukan* 鳳凰週刊, 2000) as well as its website, ifeng.com. After leaving Phoenix TV, he established a glossy, Hong Kong–registered magazine titled *Leader* (*Lingdaozhe*) in 2004, which served as the springboard for Consensus Net in 2009. Although Zhou fully endorsed Consensus Net's traditional approach as a "spiritual home of the elite,"[63] he conceived it as an open forum inspired by the U.S. Constitutional Convention of 1787, which eventually produced sufficient agreement among participants to lay the foundation for a new system of government.[64] In this perspective, "consensus" referred less to achieving agreement of opinion than to developing greater mutual understanding among differing voices, in particular between "court and society" (*chao ye gongshi* 朝野共識).[65] Consensus Net, too, was eventually shut down in 2016.

Without doubt, one of the most popular blogs from 2006 until it was shut down in 2009 was Ai Weiwei's blog at sina.com.cn. It is tempting to portray Ai Weiwei, born in 1957, as a typical universalist intellectual in the traditional sense, using the prestige he had accumulated as an internationally recognized artist to speak out on just about every topic under the sun. In his study of Ai Weiwei as an intellectual, William Callahan portrays him as essentially working "with or against the state, but always for the good of China": an enlightenment figure—albeit updated for the Internet age—who combines "classical liberal ideas" with twenty-first-century high-tech tactics and the art of turning the state's weapons against the state (a tactic Callahan compares to those described by Sun Tzu). He also describes Ai as a "princeling" and hence an "insider" (because his father was an important Communist poet, although he spent several decades exiled far from Beijing), who was invited to join the Chinese People's Political Consultative Conference, and a "broker" between East and West (for example, through his work on the Bird's Nest stadium as consultant to Swiss architecture firm Herzog and De Meuron). Finally, Callahan concludes that Ai is a "citizen intellectual" who supports "living in truth" and contributes to fostering civil society by setting up informal groups, such as the volunteers who collected the names of Sichuan earthquake victims.[66]

It is clear that Ai is a maverick who will not, in any event, be easily pigeonholed. However, a careful study of his blogs also suggests that he can more precisely be described as a specific intellectual, who is preoccupied not with "the good of China" but with using his own specific knowledge to see the world from the perspective of the subaltern. Ai is one of the few Chinese artists and intellectuals who were exposed to counterculture in the West as early as the 1980s (he lived in New York's East Village from 1981 to 1993). Returning to Beijing in 1993, he joined the underground art scene in Beijing's "East Village" (Maizidian area), before settling in Caochangdi in 1999, where he designed a studio for himself to great acclaim (as well as the one used by Wu Wenguang and his group). His most famous artworks deal with the issues of the early twenty-first century: migrant workers and their status in relation to the revolutionary "masses" in *Fairytale* (*Tonghua* 童話, shown at the Documenta 12 in Kassel in 2007);[67] the victims of the Sichuan earthquake and the state's lack of construction norms in *Remembering* (*Jizhu* 記住, shown at the exhibit *Ai Weiwei: So Sorry* in Munich in 2009); and an ironic commentary on the rise of nationalism in *Circle of Animals / Zodiac Heads* (*Shi'er shengxiao touxiang* 十二生肖頭像, 2010), showing oversize "reinterpretations" of the original heads made by eighteenth-century Jesuits for the gardens of Yuanmingyuan, which were plundered by Western armies in the late nineteenth century and were transformed into a cause célèbre by early-twenty-first-century nationalists, who wanted to buy them back.[68]

From the time Ai Weiwei began publicly expressing himself, he represented a *minjian* voice that was not reliant on income from the government or on a state-funded university position. When he first began blogging in 2005, he devoted a series of texts to art, in particular photography and architecture, which he had become interested in since designing his studio in Caochangdi in 1999 and then working on the Bird's Nest.[69] When Ai started to write, he, like other *minjian* intellectuals, established a public stance based on his specific ethos as an artist:

> Art is an artist's business. The ultimate relationship between artwork and spectator is difficult to judge, and is sometimes entirely separate from the artist's original intention. . . . The core beliefs of middle-class society have been formed by a mainstream, orthodox consciousness, a sense of security, and various attempts to aestheticize these. . . . Interesting artworks effectively disturb tradition, this popular and vulgar aesthetic, and social ideology. . . . An artwork unable to make people feel uncomfortable or to feel different is not one worth creating.[70]

In this post, Ai affirms the autonomy of artistic practice and its prerogative to refuse mainstream aesthetics and to distance itself from and challenge social norms. Even when art is "public," its norms cannot be dictated by the public.

Two themes connect his interventions in the spheres of blogging and art: his challenge to the alleged authenticity of tradition (in particular when it is mobilized in the service of nationalism) and his public use of artwork to take the standpoint of the vulnerable or subaltern. Much of Ai's early artwork challenged the sacralization of cultural artifacts, from *Han Dynasty Urn with Coca-Cola Logo* (*You kekoukele biaozhi de Han guan* 有可口可樂標誌的漢罐, 1994), *Dropping a Han Dynasty Urn* (*Han ping shishou* 漢瓶失手, 1995), and *Whitewash* (*Xi bai* 洗白, 1993–2000), in which a series of old urns are painted over, to *Fragments* (*Suipian* 碎片, 2005), the series of deconstructed Ming dynasty furniture, in which table legs stand against the wall and stools are cobbled together. As the curator Philip Tinari writes, "The furniture works find their maker generating contemporary art from the destruction of ancient objects, simultaneously sending up the antitraditional cultural mandate that grounded the vandalism of the Cultural Revolution and the full-speed-ahead economic mandate that justified the demolitions of the '90s."[71] Ai deliberately remains ambiguous about whether he is endorsing or mocking this "productive" way of transforming cultural relics into modern profits. In his blog posts, however, he sometimes takes a clearer stance—for example, when discussing how his family courtyard house in Beijing was altered when "a giant hand had come down and had plastered everything with concrete, eliminating all traces of history and memory at the same time,"[72] almost as if the urban workers were imitating Ai Weiwei's own work on the Han urn:

> The alleged "preservation of Beijing's old city" actually means plastering over the walls with cement and then redrawing the outlines of bricks, irrespective of the building's age, history, or ownership, whether they are private or public ownership, ancient or modern. A brand-new fake city—a fake world—has been created. In a city like this, how can we even begin to talk about culture? . . . Spare the homes of the common people; if you can't help them then leave them some peace. Keep your distance from them, and please do not try to speak for them, let them quietly, silently, pass away. Continue the corruption of large-scale projects, of the banks and the state-owned industries, but don't paint the faces of the common people. This nation, our home, has been whitewashed so many times, we can't even recognize our faces, or perhaps we simply never had a face at all.[73]

This essay, "Different Worlds, Different Dreams," rooted in a discussion of urban architecture, connects several important themes in Ai's work: the government endlessly intervenes in ordinary people's lives to erase and falsify the past, even as at the very same time it uses this reinvented past to fuel nationalistic discourses of Chinese exceptionalism. In this sense, Beijing as a city and China as a whole have become "fake" antiques (Ai Weiwei is particularly enamored of this term, which he uses in English as well as in pinyin, *fake* 發克, to rhyme with an English expletive, as the name of his registered company). Furthermore, this erasure of authentic memories is particularly targeted at the ordinary people who used to live in these courtyard homes (and have now been displaced mainly by high officials). The renovations that the government likes to justify in the name of improving ordinary people's livelihood are, in Ai's view, a way of whitewashing and painting over the faces of ordinary individuals, making them conform to a sanitized but inauthentic national narrative. In fact, Ai generalizes this conclusion to the political organization of the post-Mao state and Deng's notion of "Chinese characteristics": "Thirty years of reforms with 'special characteristics' are only a *shanzhai* 山寨 [fake] version of phony government ideals that unsympathetically pass the country's political and moral crisis off onto the weak."[74] The metaphor taken from architecture and cultural artifacts is here successfully translated into the realm of politics, where Deng's (reinvented) "Chinese characteristics" serve only to render meaningless such notions as "democracy" and "socialism."

The Wenchuan earthquake of 2008 also spoke to Ai Weiwei's creative imaginary, perhaps because the very heavy mortality rate was directly connected to an issue of public architecture: a large number of children died because the schools they were in when the earthquake struck in the early afternoon proved to be less resistant than government or commercial buildings.[75] The death toll and the authorities' efforts to conceal it raised questions that Ai Weiwei noted on his blog:

> Within any other system, the majority of weak populations has difficulty gaining protection. Only in democratic societies is it possible to return power and dignity to the weak and impoverished. Don't make decisions on behalf of the people; let them take their own initiative. To give them back their rights is to take responsibility and return their dignity to them.
>
> Who will answer for China the question of exactly how many students died as a result of these tofu-dregs schools? And to the villains in Sichuan: Does this really require concealing state secrets? Is it really so hard to tell the truth, about even such things?[76]

Characteristically, Ai does not present democracy as an abstract system, but as a concrete question: "How many people died?" Answering this question became a necessity for ordinary people to recover their dignity.

As a consequence of his question, Ai began working on a commemorative installation, which eventually became *Remembering*, an installation of nine thousand schoolbags shown in Munich in 2009. At the same time, he initiated a "citizen investigation" (*gongmin diaocha* 公民調查) to compile a list of names of child victims, which eventually reached a total of 5,212,[77] and produced a film with the names. "Those children who perished in the earthquake are not an unknown figure, they are not the result of a 'stabilized' nation. Those children have parents, dreams, and they could smile, they had a name that belonged to them. . . . Reject the failure to remember, reject lies. To remember the departed, to show concern for life, to take responsibility, and for the potential happiness of the survivors, we are initiating a 'Citizen Investigation.' We will seek out the names of each departed child, and we will remember them."[78] The installation and the citizen investigation were therefore two translations of the same impetus to do something "unofficial" (*minjian*), concrete but meaningful and authentic, that would restore to the public record the individuality expressed in each child's name and erase the anonymity of a simple statistic. Ai explained his aim by stating, "We hope that the dignity of the deceased can be restored bit by bit."[79]

Subsequently, the authorities stepped up surveillance of Ai Weiwei: his blog was suspended on May 28, 2009, and he was beaten up during the trial of Tan Zuoren 譚作人 (another activist advocating on behalf of victims) in Chengdu in August 2009, which triggered a blood clot in his brain that was discovered later. After another episode involving the demolition of his Shanghai study in November 2010, during which he was put under house arrest in Beijing, he was detained at Beijing airport on April 2, 2011, on suspicion of tax evasion (he was eventually fined 2.4 million renminbi) and held until July 2011. He left China for Germany in July 2015.

Taking architecture as a point of reference, Ai developed a stance that used his knowledge of public architecture and his understanding of urban heritage to challenge the official discourse, both explicitly through his blog posts and implicitly through his sarcastic artworks. In so doing, he positioned himself less as a citizen intellectual (speaking out as a citizen in favor of a political program) than as a *minjian* voice relying on his own knowledge to take the side of subordinate groups. Although many observers may see him as a cultural elite and be irritated by his constant self-promotion, it should be recognized that the topics he engages with are quite different from the mainstream topics discussed by the most well-known contemporary Chinese artists.

If there is one blogger able to outshine Ai Weiwei, it is no doubt Han Han, the man whose blog boasts more than 500 million visitors. Giorgio Strafella and Daria Berg describe him as a "new type of celebrity" who combines the images of "rebel, opinion leader, and cultural entrepreneur."[80] However, Han Han also shares several key traits of most *minjian* intellectuals. First, ever since dropping out of high school at age seventeen in 1999 with the intention to "live off royalties" (his first book *Triple Door* eventually sold more than 2 million copies, making it the best-selling work of literature in China since the early 1990s[81]), he has been the epitome of the individual who works "outside the system." As he noted in an essay about the school system, "It's fair to say that many people's experience of telling lies starts with writing essays, just as their limited experience of telling the truth starts with writing love letters."[82] Second, being *minjian* implies financial independence. Han Han's ability to make a living through car racing placed a significant part of his income out of the state's reach, even though his income from advertisements (he has at various times embodied Johnnie Walker whisky, Hublot watches, Nescafé, Subaru cars), which he defends as a source of independence,[83] or even his presence in the public sphere would not be possible without the state's tacit consent. He refused to join the Writers' Association in 2007 or any other official body, in contrast to his rival, Guo Jingming 郭敬明. Car racing represents a step farther along the spectrum of autonomy from the state when compared with intellectuals who simply rely on income from private publishing, such as Wang Shuo, but are still vulnerable to state control of culture and media. Han Han's income as a race car driver, solidified by his multiple wins in the China circuit championship, is further removed from the reach of the Central Propaganda Department.[84] Third, his antielitist stance also places him within the realm of *minjian*. Although (now) certainly a member of the economic elite, Han Han likes to emphasize his humble origins and common sense.[85] His critiques are presented as "non-ideological" and "reasonable and moderate."[86] Establishment intellectuals are sometimes a target of his sarcasm—for example, when he opines, "Public intellectuals are just like public toilets, both are used to vent anger."[87]

Although Han Han has been praised by most liberal intellectuals (ranging from the founder of Gongmeng Xu Zhiyong to the cultural critic Leung Man-tao and the Shanghai literature professor Chen Sihe[88]), especially those who advocate a stronger role for the market in advancing political liberalization, his critics are not limited to proponents of state ideology and include some well-known liberal commentators, such as Xu Zhiyuan and the antiplagiarism activist Fang Zhouzi

方舟子, who highlights Han's connection with consumer culture and his alleged lack of elite knowledge. Xu Zhiyuan, in particular, ascribes Han's success to the "mediocre masses" and makes the argument that Han's sarcasm is a "sugar-coated" form of criticism that anesthetizes its readers rather than mobilizing them.[89]

Among scholars of contemporary China, the same divide can be identified. On the positive side, William Callahan sees Han Han as one of the "citizen intellectuals" who are able to negotiate a critical stance that accommodates the state's agenda.[90] Indeed, many liberals praised Han's savvy (non)comment on the award of the Nobel Prize to Liu Xiaobo.[91] He has managed to strategically refer to June Fourth without being censored.[92] He was named Person of the Year 2009 by both the Hong Kong–based newsmagazine *Yazhou Zhoukan* and *Southern Weekly*. On the other side, Strafella and Berg perceptively characterize Han Han's stance as the acceptance of the status quo (in particular pointing out his endorsement of the value of Chinese culture and the importance of maintaining stability) coexisting with a spectacular and highly commercialized staging of "calculated rebelliousness."[93] In their view, his criticism of official corruption and the absurdity of propaganda discourse is satirical rather than denunciatory; his irony can therefore both corrode the authority of the state but also undermine the indignation of citizens because of its superior or cynical mindset.[94] This reading is supported by essays in which Han Han tries to downplay his own influence: "Writers [*wenren* 文人] are only writers. If they could really change something, it would take a long time. . . . If you think of everything as fun, then you won't feel so powerless."[95]

Indeed, Han Han displays characteristics of both *minjian* and elite intellectuals, which is the core of the controversies revolving around him. In fact, many of his most widely discussed essays can be understood as dealing with the contested role and status of Chinese intellectuals. On the *minjian* side, Han Han always finds ways to criticize political elites who use their power to bend the rules and use their office to pursue personal profit. He has devoted widely read essays to the suicides among migrant workers in the Foxconn factory ("Youth" ["Qingchun" 青春])[96] and to petitioners,[97] and (after a kindergarten killing) he echoed Lu Xun's call to save the children, who he argues are always the first victims in a society whose members tend to take revenge on the "weakest."[98] Han's best-selling novel *1988: I Want to Have a Talk with This World* is about a sex worker who is infected with HIV. The Hong Kong newspaper *Mingpao* praised his ability to "investigate China's *minjian* reality" while criticizing "the 'elites'

[who] left the masses to join the vested interests . . . [and] relinquished independence for blind obedience."[99]

Points that Han Han repeatedly argues are that China lacks pluralism and that censorship undermines the educational and cultural foundations of a more democratic society by fostering ignorance. The topic of censorship is of course directly related to his own claimed status as a writer,[100] and speaking out against it serves as his main justification for intervening in the public sphere: "I hate politics, I love literature. It's just that I dislike my beloved literature being blocked by the politics I hate."[101] Politics indeed interfered with his literary projects when he tried to launch his own magazine in 2009 by using the usual system of purchasing a book number for each issue. After some difficulties and delay, due in particular to a cartoon of a naked character hiding his private "central" parts with a gun (which can be read as a pun on "party central" [*dang zhongyang* 黨中央]) and a tattooed phrase mentioning Japan in a comic strip that caused the first print run to be pulped, the first issue was published on July 6, 2010, by Shanxi Press and Shuhai Press, with the title *Chorus of Soloists* (*Duchang tuan* 獨唱團) and the English subtitle *Party*. It sold 100,000 copies on the first day and more than 2 million copies in all.[102] A typical "pure literature" journal, it contained mainly fiction, with an autobiographical essay by the folk singer Zhou Yunpeng 周雲蓬, a story by the Hong Kong film director Pang Ho-cheung 彭浩翔, a scan of Ai Weiwei's brain (after the Chengdu blood-clot incident), a reader forum, as well as a part of Han Han's novel *1988*. However, despite the absence of explicitly political content, the second issue was stopped in the middle of its production in December 2010. Han later ironically reflected on how the implicit censorship system had replaced the accusation of being "counterrevolutionary" with that of being "downbeat."[103]

However, Han's critique of censorship also encapsulates a more ambiguous strand according to which the lack of broader knowledge and understanding in Chinese society is an impediment to democratic reforms because the masses remain too ignorant. His critiques of Chinese nationalism are similarly ambiguous, often highlighting that the Chinese culture that people should be rightly proud of has been lost in China and is preserved only in Hong Kong and Taiwan. In a famous speech at Xiamen University, he argued that China was prevented from becoming a cultural superpower because it always places "uncultured" officials in top positions. Because of their ignorance, these officials develop a fear of culture that further encourages censorship. In this situation, patriotism should consist of "protecting the country against the government."[104] In an interview with Taiwan's *CommonWealth* (*Tianxia* 天下) magazine, he similarly argues that Shanghai cannot be a great cultural city because its pluralism has been rooted out since 1949, when the cultural elite fled to Hong Kong and Taiwan, and should be described as "an adventurer's paradise, but the people's hell."[105] In the essay "The Pacific Wind" discussing his first trip to Taiwan in 2012, he describes what he sees as a moral collapse in China, which contrasts with a perceived moral exemplarity of the open and free society in Taiwan, which has successfully preserved Chinese culture:

> As a mainland writer, I'm dejected. . . . I am dejected by the environment we're living in, where people were taught to be cruel and to go to war with each other during the first decades, and turned selfish and greedy in the decades that followed, and who sowed the same seeds in the bones of many of us. Dejected because our forebears destroyed our culture, destroyed traditional moral character, destroyed trust between people, destroyed faith and common understanding, and did not build a new, more beautiful world in its place. . . . Dejected because, when someone treats me kindly, my first reaction is that there's some kind of conspiracy. . . . I have to thank Hong Kong and Taiwan for protecting Chinese culture, preserving the positive traits of the Chinese people, and keeping many essential things free from disaster.[106]

In this way, Han Han implicitly endorses the traditional view of the intellectual as moral exemplar and criticizes the lower classes for being morally lacking. In the interview by *CommonWealth*, he argues that Chinese people have "traded their rights and dignity for money" and are more likely to "request benefits, not power [*quanyi bushi quanli* 權益不是權力]," making it easy for the government to buy them off. For this reason, he defines his own role as avoiding to challenge the system while writing more so that the culture will slowly change and people will become more educated and thus, in his reasoning, less easy to buy off.[107]

This argument is developed most fully in three controversial essays on politics (popularly referred to as "Han's three essays," "Han san pian" 韓三篇) published on December 23, 24, and 26, 2011, in which Han Han argues that heroic dissidence is useless in present-day China because society needs to democratize first in a bottom-up manner before more freedom can eventually be granted by the government. All three are written in dialogue form and ostensibly presented as a response to summaries of some of the many questions Han Han receives from netizens, no doubt a good way of suggesting that bringing up such sensitive topics was not his own idea.

In "Discussing Revolution,"[108] Han Han argues that a revolutionary uprising in China is not only impossible but also undesirable. First, it is impossible because of the state's overwhelming power. Han Han is fully aware that the entire world of online debate can have its plug pulled by the government at a moment's notice: "all the government has to do is shut down the Internet and block cell phone signals, and I bet that without the government even mobilizing its stability-maintenance machine those angry protestors will be so devastated by their inability to chat with their friends through instant messaging or play games on the Internet or watch recordings of soap operas that they'll crush us in no time at all." Second, a revolution is undesirable because of the lack of civic culture: "In the eyes of most Chinese, freedom has nothing to do with publishing, media, and culture, or with personal expression, elections, and politics, but with public standards of behavior. Even people with no social connections feel free to make an uproar, jaywalk, and spit, while people with even the slightest connections ignore regulations, take advantage of loopholes, and engage in all kinds of malfeasance." In a vein going back to Liang Qichao and echoing a century of elite intellectual discourse, Han Han takes the stance that ordinary people lack the civic culture necessary to make democracy work and will oppose democracy because it restricts their freedom to flaunt public morals. In this context, he further argues, democracy will translate into an oppression of the elite: "There's no way that students, ordinary people, the social elite, intellectuals, peasants and workers can all reach a common understanding." Referring to the Taiping and White Lotus uprisings, he argues that "the kind of leaders that young intellectuals would favor would be kicked out within a week" and that the revolution will become an opportunity for poor people to appropriate the property of the rich: "in the eyes of an egalitarian, looting is legitimate." The super-rich have already stashed their assets abroad, so "the ones who suffer will be the middle class, the quasi-middle class, and even the quasi-affluent."[109]

Furthermore, Han Han is not ignorant of the numbing effect of consumer capitalism: "Even if social contradictions were ten times more intense than they are now and even if we had ten Václav Havels giving speeches simultaneously in ten different cities, and if we imagine too that the authorities don't interfere, ultimately these speeches will end up becoming advertisements for sore throat lozenges delivered in the Haidian Playhouse." As a consequence, if elections are held, they will be taken hostage by the CCP, with its unlimited funding abilities, or by one of China's new capitalists, such as Pony Ma 馬化騰, who will leverage his direct messaging service to canvas for votes, by which point he "will have joined the Communist Party." The only answer, therefore, is to cultivate the people's moral qualities and educational level: "When everyone knows to dim their headlights when they pass another car on the road, then we'll be ready for a revolution. But a country like that doesn't actually need a revolution at all. When the people's personal caliber and educational level reach that point, everything will just happen automatically."[110]

These well-rehearsed arguments place Han Han within the mainstream of intellectual elitism that has endured in China throughout the twentieth century, with its parallel fear of the "uneducated" and morally inferior masses depriving the intellectual elite of its influence and fear of "capitalism," which ensures that elections are only a scam controlled by financial interests. Indeed, he often uses the classical term *wenren* (literati, writers) to refer to intellectuals. In an interview, he notes in connection with his previous critiques of popular nationalism and more recent critique of revolution, "I have always stood on the opposite side of the people. But the opposite side in those cases was relatively speaking more readily acceptable to the liberals or the elites. Today I may be standing on the opposite of these liberals or relatively radical elites."[111] It is precisely the kind of position that other *minjian* intellectuals described in previous chapters have taken issue with. However, on one point, Han Han stands out from his predecessors: he is no longer confident in the ability of intellectuals to play a central role in any political change or in his own ability to significantly affect the political culture, as further elaborated in the second essay.

Similar arguments are presented in the second essay, "Speaking of Democracy." The Czech Velvet Revolution cannot serve as a model for China because of the low "quality of the people [*suzhi* 素質]," which would bring about a "low-quality democracy." Han Han ironically acknowledges, using the dialogue form, that he may be suspected of taking "a kickback from the government's stability maintenance budget" and specifies that in his view the arrival of democracy is inevitable. Nonetheless, he reaffirms that the ordinary people in county towns he meets during car-racing events may be dissatisfied, but "their resentment of authoritarian government and corruption does not lead them to ask: 'How can we limit and monitor these things?' but rather 'Why can't I, or why can't my family, have what bureaucrats have?' ... So long as the government gives them adequate compensation, they'll be satisfied."[112] This is a reformulation of his idea of the people's preference for benefits rather than rights. He also highlights the overwhelming presence of the party, whose 80 million members (300 million including relatives) pervades the whole system.[113]

However, in this essay Han Han also emphasizes the critical role of writers (*wenren*) who "should sit on the fence but turn their faces against the wind [*fanxiang qiangtoucao* 反向牆頭草]." "Writers need to have a sense of justice, but shouldn't be wedded to a single position; the more influential they are, the less they should take sides.... Thus, if China has a revolution in the future, I will stand by whoever is the weaker [*ruoxiao* 弱小], and if they become strong, I'll side with their rivals. I'm ready to sacrifice my own view in order to see different sides coexist."[114] In this unexpected conclusion, Han Han takes inspiration from Wang Xiaobo's endorsement of the vulnerable groups, in defiance of the elite tradition of remaining closely affiliated with a faction in power in order to influence the powerful. This is the *minjian* aspect of Han Han's complex politics.

The third essay, "Claiming Freedom," again makes the case for the need to lift the restrictions on the freedom of expression and creation in order to allow Chinese culture to flourish. The whole essay is rhetorically presented as a petition: whereas the other two essays serve to renounce abstract and unachievable ideals, the third one is intended as a forceful plea requesting a concrete right that is closely connected to the author's own profession:

> In my last essay I said that democracy and the rule of law involve a process of bargaining. No matter how big the markdown in the Christmas sales, you're not going to get something for nothing. So now I need to start to do some bargaining. For a start, as someone involved in culture, in the coming New Year I demand a freer hand in literary creation. I'm not putting it in terms of freedom of this or freedom of that, because those two expressions will only provoke wariness and alarm in certain quarters, even if these freedoms have always been written into our constitution. In reality, they have never been well implemented. At the same time, on behalf of my colleagues in the media, I need to demand more freedom for the press, since the news is always subject to such rigid controls, and freedom also for my filmmaking friends, who have a terrible time.[115]

He restates his arguments about the connection between censorship and Chinese culture's lack of global impact. While promising to respond to increased freedom by steering away from sensitive issues, he also jokingly threatens to take his protest to "every congress of the Writers' Association or the Federation of Literary and Art Circles" and concludes: "Such, then, are my demands, reflecting my own professional background."[116] Han Han has also spoken out on other issues linked to his profession, in particular copyright, leading a successful legal challenge against the Chinese tech company Baidu's attempt to offer its own version of Google Books.[117] The affirmation of a professional ethos can again be connected with a critique of the traditional universalist intellectual and the rise of specific intellectuals as an alternative. Han Han has even used this stance to make explicit political demands: "first, opening freedom of speech; second, expanding personal rights and protecting society; third, eliminating the so-called crime of subverting the state."[118]

In a speech delivered at Peking University less than a year later, which was widely posted online, Li Chengpeng 李承鹏 voiced similar demands for freedom of expression, linking it with the forced silence under Mao's rule. Just like Wang Xiaobo, he noted that "during the great famine, our entire nation lost its tongue. . . . You couldn't say 'I'm hungry,' you couldn't say 'I love you,' and you could even less tell the truth, as your alumna Lin Zhao experienced." He concluded his talk by arguing that "what is most terrifying in a country . . . is when the population loses the right and the ability to speak. . . . In a country that created the most beautiful language in the world . . . 'speaking' has become a grave problem: everyone lives in an impoverished, boring, sterile linguistic environment: we repeat lies, nonsense, and absurdities that everyone knows. . . . I will never stop criticizing this country or having hope for it."[119] Li's lecture closely echoes Wang Xiaobo's reflections on speech as a tool of power under the Mao era and the need to "come out" of silence.

In a New Year's essay written a few days after the three political pieces, Han Han again couched his argument in terms of professional ethos:

> Some years ago, I was a committed revolutionary, believing that all one-Party dictatorships had to be overthrown, that there had to be a multiparty democracy, direct elections, a tripartite division of power, and a nationalization of the armed forces. . . . But gradually I realized that this attitude doesn't differ very much in its emotional tenor from a dictator's offhand attitude. . . .

> Therefore, I have no aspirations in other directions, but I will continue demanding all the constitutionally permitted freedoms that have a bearing on my work.[120]

He attributes this change to the uncompromising attitude of some liberals who sometimes bend facts to their beliefs.[121] Han Han argues that he is more interested in facts than in ideologies and depicts as elitist the liberal intellectuals who criticize his gradualist stance on democracy:

> They look down on me, because I did not have advanced education and I am not doing academic research. Therefore, I am unqualified to discuss democracy and freedom. In theory, I must have read more books than ordinary citizens. If they look down on me, they must be looking down on ordinary citizens even more so. Yet they want the people to stand behind them. . . . [T]he current problem is that the elites and the intellectuals are even more stupid than the people. They have merely read a few books. They don't even know who the people are or where the people are.[122]

This is the contradiction at the heart of Han Han's stance: a *minjian* intellectual who criticizes both the people for its moral shortcomings and the elite for not listening to the people.

After Han Han published these three essays, attacks against him only increased. In 2012, the liberal science blogger Fang Zhouzi accused him of signing work written by others (among them Han Han's father, Han Renjun 韓仁均, and his literary agent, Lu Jinbo 路金波).[123] After Xi Jinping took power, restrictions on the Internet increased, and in 2013 Han Han became a collateral victim of the campaign against "Big V's": his blog practically came to a stop, although most previous posts remained and continue to remain accessible. He turned to films, achieving respectable success with his first production, *We Won't Meet Again* (*Hou hui wu qi* 後會無期) in 2014. He was subsequently attacked by the PKU professor Xiao Ying 肖鷹 for copying previous films, and there were renewed accusations of literary plagiarism. The elitist streak in the attacks is quite clear: writing in the official *China Youth Daily*, Xiao notably accused Han of being uneducated and speaking out of turn as a high school dropout, of being the spokesperson for big capital, and of taking up the role of an antiknowledge hero in the vein of the Cultural Revolution.[124] Han's second film, *Duckweed* (*Cheng feng po lang* 乘風破浪, 2017), though also successful, triggered accusations of a male chauvinist bias. All in all, the public controversies, some of them doubtlessly supported by important vested interests, have taken a toll on Han Han's ability to speak out to a large public.

Han Han's contribution to the discussion about the status of the intellectual has several salient points. First, his interventions evince a resolve to deflate pompous or vacuous discourses, whether they come from government propaganda organs or from traditional elite intellectuals who like to pontificate about abstract concepts. He is always eager to mock hypocrisy as well as those who deform or take liberties with facts for their own ends, in particular the censors. By contrast, he prefers to discuss concrete issues, many of them related to his ethos as a writer or to his daily experience. Rather than devising grand blueprints, he prefers to put forward concrete claims. This preference does not appear to be simply a tactical way of avoiding censorship, but a substantive choice. Despite his doubts about the degree of civility of the population and the possibility of finding common interests among different social classes, he likes to take the position of the "ordinary people" and criticize any form of privilege. In this manner, he even sometimes ends up defending public intellectuals: "Yes, I am an intellectual. I consume politics, I consume current events, and I consume hot-button issues. I consume the vested interests of public power. . . . Wouldn't it be great if everyone was concerned about the world, criticized social injustice, condemned heinous deeds when they are revealed, and celebrated when corrupt officials are taken in?. . . We should encourage everyone to become a public intellectual."[125]

Although recognizing the toll taken by consumerism and social media formats on the quality of critical discussion, Han Han ultimately defends "public intellectuals" against "opinion leaders" controlled only by the private interests that fund them. As an intellectual, he represents a complex mix of *minjian* and elitism.

PUBLIC SPACES: THE EXAMPLE OF ONE-WAY STREET

Among critics of the new Internet culture, there were also attempts to revive the old model of the bookstore, the salon, and the public discussion of literature by bringing them into the *minjian* sphere. There was a tradition of such venues, represented by several prominent bookstore-salons such as Sanwei 三味 Teahouse in Beijing, which was a vibrant meeting place in the 1980s; All Sages (Wansheng 萬聖) set up by Liu Suli 劉蘇里 in 1993 in Beijing's university Haidan District; and Jifeng 季風, established in Shanghai in 1997. The most interesting attempt to build on this tradition and set up a new type of space was the creation of One-Way Street (Danxiangjie 單向街), a library/bookstore and cultural journal established by the journalist and writer Xu Zhiyuan (b. 1976) as a privately funded cooperative in 2006. A graduate of PKU's Computer Science Department, Xu first wrote about cultural changes among the new generation and became an influential columnist for the *Economic Observer* (*Jingji Guanchabao* 經濟觀察報) in 2001, then for *FTChinese* after it was set up in 2005 and for *Yazhou Zhoukan* in Hong Kong. He established the popular blog *The Pleasure of Thinking* (*Siwei de lequ* 思維的樂趣, with the English title *Think Again*), named after Wang Xiaobo's essay. In 2001, Xu published his first book of essays, *All the Sad Young Men*, which made some people call him "the spiritual leader of a generation of China's literary youths."[126] In the preface, he identifies as an intellectual, despite the mockery and doubts that this word inevitably provokes. But, he writes, "I am a common intellectual [*tongsu zhishifenzi* 通俗知識分子], a person wandering between the peaks of thought and the lowlands of reality, trying to establish closer connections between these two lonely extremes. Such connections are of the highest importance."[127] This was Xu's way of incorporating the critique of elitism that had been gaining impetus since the early 1990s.

In late 2005, Xu and a dozen like-minded colleagues from journalism and business, including Yu Wei 于威 (a journalist at *Bloomberg Businessweek*), contributed 50,000 renminbi each to set up a private bookstore on a cooperative basis, which Xu described as functioning "like an NGO" and for which "each of us used our income to support our interests."[128] Situated in Yuanmingyuan, using as its name a phrase taken from an essay by Walter Benjamin, One-Way Street, functioned both as a library where books could be exchanged, an independent bookstore, and a free cultural salon that anyone could join, with talks given by Hung Huang 洪晃, Chan Koonchung, Yan Lianke, Liu Wai-Tong 廖偉棠, Mo Yan, Yan Geling 嚴歌苓, and others.[129] It was not a commercial venture but was instead described by its owners as "an idealist's utopia," as illustrated in its English-language slogan "We read the world." When Yuanmingyuan became too expensive, the bookstore's cultural prestige was attractive to the managers of new shopping malls, and it made an advantageous move to the Blue Harbor (Lanse Gangwan 藍色港灣) mall in 2009, then to another mall in Chaoyang in 2012. Between 2006 and 2014,

One-Way Street organized 660 salons, which attracted approximately 110,000 participants.[130]

Xu was able to capture the naive enthusiasm sparked by the Internet boom of the late 1990s:

> It was as if we had seen a new world. To hell with the problems of politics, ideology, moral stance; they were completely out of date. We had Apple computers and Google, international travel, plentiful job opportunities, and sex; we could discuss the respective merits of the Silicon Valley spirit and the rock-and-roll spirit, comment on 911 and US foreign policy, and even occasionally quote James Joyce. We could calmly and confidently say: "Farewell to Revolution," China needs gradual progress; let's stop criticizing and be constructive; morals are stupid because they lead to disaster; we are intelligent, trendy, we think we know everything, maybe we're even quite cool . . . We are the generation of China's economic miracle.[131]

However, despite recognizing the new spaces opened up by the market, Xu was critical of the commercialization of life: "Our status as homo economicus has delivered us twenty years of enlivening activity and freedom. It's been far more joyous than our previous role as homo politicus. But aren't we increasingly aware that we want to live in a community, a society, and not just exist in a company? But a community requires trust, security, compassion, literature, art, poetry, and not just stockbrokers, managers, salesmen and pop stars."[132] The cooperative and cosmopolitan bookstore could thus be seen as an attempt to build a community in the third realm that is not defined by profit or politics.

Along with the bookstore-salon, there was also the literary and intellectual journal *Danxiangjie*, which published five issues between 2009 and 2014 under the motto "Documenting, investigating, critiquing" (*Jilu, tansuo, piping* 紀錄探索批評), each as a separate book with a purchased book number and different publishers. The special topics for each issue sketch out a coherent editorial line. The first issue was titled "The Most Foolish Generation: How the Internet and Commodification Destroyed the Brains of a Generation" (July 2009). It was followed by "Is the Avant-garde Dead? There Are No Great Masterpieces, Only a Mediocre Generation" (March 2010). The third issue was devoted to gender: "Complexity/Gender: Understanding the National Sentiment/Understanding Sex Life" (October 2010). The fourth issue discussed exoticism: "Foreign Land: Looking for the Coordinates of Life" (March 2012). The last issue, titled "An Anti-intellectual Epoch," was published in 2014. A critique of anti-intellectualism is a clear thread that runs through the journal, in which Xu Zhiyuan and the editors seek to defend a kind of elite position for intellectuals that is more reminiscent of the enlightenment of the 1980s than of the *minjian* intellectuals of the 2000s. As a journalist noted, Xu himself could be quite unrepentant about this stance in interviews: "When people say that his essays are too full of citations, he answers, 'Don't people need to understand more? Sometimes readers are really too ignorant.' When people say his way of discussing China resembles that of an outsider—as suggested in the title of his book *Stranger in the Motherland* [*Zuguo de moshengren* 祖國的陌生人]—he again replies, 'Do they understand their own country? They probably haven't read any of my books and don't know what I have written.'"[133] In another essay, he defends the accomplishments of intellectuals: "Every moment in the twentieth century when China was free and showed promise was connected to the educated elites."[134]

Xu made this argument the most fully in an essay on Han Han, published in 2010 in response to Han's nomination by *Time* magazine for the list of one hundred most influential people in the world:

> Nobody can deny Han Han's charm. . . . He has managed not to sell out either to the government or to any corporations. And he has accomplished all this at the age of twenty-seven. . . . He is not only sarcastic, he also strives to create new meaning, even though Han himself is not sure exactly what that meaning is. . . . People claim he is the hero of his generation and a symbol of the power of thought as well as opposition to the regime. But that's not who he is. The more people claim that he should have this identity, the more it becomes clear that this is an era of shouting people, of idiocy, frailty and cowardice. In some respects, Han's success was not his own, but that of the emerging era of the masses. . . .
>
> He can race cars, write and perform. He also subconsciously recognizes the strengthening anti-intellectual trend in China, and his writing is plain. He writes about topics that aren't too deep, in a style that is easy to understand, and he never mentions facts that you might not know. His ironic and provocative style makes him sound witty. He knows what he can get away with, and he never says anything that offends the government. If he is anxious or confused, he never shows it. He is so cool. . . .

> Freedom requires not just resistance but a clear argument, which in turn requires intellectual and emotional maturity. We would have to be ready to deal with the consequences of our decisions. The enthusiastic praise for Han Han is a sign that society refuses to pay the price for true freedom. Every time we delight in a few sound bites of satire, we deceive ourselves into thinking that we have contributed to the dissolution of this abhorrent system of power. In actuality nothing has changed, and the satire just sugar-coats the reality. . . . He can put up a symbolic resistance on the fringe of things and then exit the stage as if he had just gone shopping at the market.[135]

Xu Zhiyuan's critique of Han Han is twofold: it targets the shallowness of Han's writing, which does not bring any new knowledge to the discussion, and his lack of risk taking and moral engagement, which in Xu's view make his critique of the regime toothless. For Xu, the mindset captured in Han's blogs encapsulates the contradiction in Chinese society, which is happy to indulge in superficial critiques of the regime as part of the new consumption culture as long as it does not have to pay the political price for its criticism. At a more substantive level, Xu's position reflects deep doubts about the Internet: "The public opinion that has gathered steam on the Internet has never translated into real social progress; it is only done for the spectacle. . . . People allow themselves to express deeply personal emotions, which turn a public space into a forum for private thoughts, so that a private argument or personal emotion can quickly blow up into an Internet-wide issue."[136] At the same time, though, Xu's critique of Han is somewhat disingenuous. He compares Han to Liu Xiaobo, while admitting that the comparison is unfair. The description of Han's blogging could well be applied to Xu himself, who in an essay published in 2010 recognized that "when Miklós Haraszti asked me directly [whether I write two versions of my essays], I had to confess that I, too, self-consciously self-censor."[137] Xu's preference for academic complexity minimizes the impact of Han Han's admittedly more simplistic satire on broad groups of readers.

In 2014, One-Way Street was recapitalized through a trust fund of U.S.$10 million and renamed One-Way Space (Danxiang Kongjian 單向空間); Yu Wei became its CEO, and the nature of the enterprise changed. Taking its cue from the Taiwanese culture and lifestyle chain Eslite and the Japanese bookstore chain Tsutaya, it added several locations and included lifestyle products and the news app WeZeit, designed on the model of Buzzfeed. The journal *Danxiangjie* was renamed *Dan Du* 單讀 (Reading alone), edited by Wu Qi 吳奇, and again published in book form, initially by Guangxi Normal Press in the "Imaginist" series, which had already published several issues of *Danxiangjie*, then by Taihai Press beginning in 2016 after "Imaginist" ran into trouble.[138] In parallel, another journal appeared in 2013 edited by a similar group of people: *Oriental History Review*, a stylish paper publication in book format (subtitled *Historical. Critical. Aesthetic* [*Lishide Pipande Shenmeide* 歷史的批判的審美的]) that was financially supported by the Oriental Culture group and printed in the "Imaginist" series at Guangxi Normal Press. Subsequent volumes were published as books with separate book numbers purchased from different publishers. Several issues of *Oriental History Review* encountered some sort of trouble, and the print publication was held up for several years: after issues 9 and 13 appeared in 2016 with China Broadcasting Press, it took two years for an issue on Meiji Japan (no. 10) and another one edited by the historian Ma Yong titled "On the Eve of Collapse: From 1884 to 1894" (no. 11) to appear in early 2018 from another publisher. In the interval, much of the content moved online, first to the journal's website and Weibo, then to a public WeChat account (Oriental History Salon or Dongfang Lishi Shalong 東方歷史沙龍).

Around this time, Xu Zhiyuan described a feeling of helplessness when faced with the evolution of society: "When you realize that the changes of society and history are not going in the direction you had hoped for, and your interventions are more and more ineffective, because you need to keep backtracking and protecting yourself, you really feel helpless. Of course, sometimes we exaggerate our own impotence and failure because this exaggeration covers up our own lack of ability and courage: I am very worried about being stuck in this situation."[139] Xu justified marketizing the bookstore and journal by the need to sustain diversity: "I have confidence in social diversity. Diverse information is most likely to stimulate people's abilities."[140] The new One-Way Space was indeed a commercial success. With three venues, more than five hundred events a year, and a great deal of online activity, it attracted more than 500,000 visitors a year and 2 million subscribers to the website in the first two years. From 2016, it established a set of book prizes. A quote from Yu Wei on the website suggests the type of branding that enabled this success: "This is not only a bookstore but rather a utopia created by idealists. Here, you can escape the narrowness of everyday life, light up your spirit, and meet your intellectual peers."[141]

Although Xu Zhiyuan was now sometimes described as a "businessman-intellectual" (*jingshang de zhishifenzi* 經商的知識分子),[142] he continued to defend his stance: "Of course I am a public intellectual: Why shouldn't I be? This is a very important force in society for thinking about problems that go beyond private interest and concern public interest. . . . Just because they have been slandered in China, you cannot just accept that they are tainted. . . . People who slander intellectuals are very foolish, and they will pay a price for it. . . . The pestilential atmosphere in society is closely connected to the disappearance of intellectuals."[143] Noting that Liang Qichao, whose biography he began working on in 2016, was also an entrepreneur, Xu Zhiyuan sets out a positive project for One-Way Space and *Dan Du*. In a context in which the media has lost all independence because of the growing influence of business, setting up an all-round cultural enterprise provides a form of independence, which allows intellectuals to speak out. *Dan Du* can be both a commercial success and remain an independent platform. When asked whether One-Way Space could become "mainstream," he replied, "Of course this would be a good thing, perhaps not for me personally, but for society as a whole it would be excellent. Perhaps [the Taiwanese chain] Eslite is no longer as avant-garde as before, but having fifty shops like this in Taiwan, exercising a tremendous influence on Taiwan society, isn't this a wonderful change? It improves the whole quality of living; of course I hope we can become mainstream!"[144] In this sense, the project of One-Way Space and its publications can somehow be described as *minjian*: although it pays tribute to the traditional elitism of Chinese intellectuals, it also emphasizes widely spreading the "pleasure of knowledge," in the vein of Wang Xiaobo. Although it relies on increasingly commercial activities, it tries to use them to build an independent intellectual platform. And ultimately its aim is to build a new type of mainstream culture in which critical thinking and diverse reading can be brought to the mainstream thanks to the attractiveness of cultural products.

Of course, this is a somewhat idealized narrative, as Xu Zhiyuan is well aware. Since 2009, he has published a series of increasingly anguished collections of his newspaper essays in Taiwan under the titles *The Totalitarian Temptation* (2010), *Stranger in the Motherland* (2011), and *Rebels* (2013).[145] Some of the essays, including "The Totalitarian Temptation" (on Western intellectuals and the Soviet Union) were included in a collection published on the mainland by Guangxi Imaginist in 2012 under the title *A Scarecrow of the Times*. The latter title alludes to a children's fairy tale written by Ye Shengtao 葉聖陶 in 1923 about the ineffectiveness of intellectuals, as Xu explains in the collection's eponymous essay: "If you preserve your independence of thinking and pursue some kind of social critique, then you are a 'superfluous man.' The state and the masses have decided that you are a challenge to their way of thinking. Whether in the name of state interest, nationalism, or the humiliated majority, they all collectively, intrinsically, hate the individual."[146] In such times, the intellectual becomes a scarecrow or a strawman.

Despite this principled elitist stance that critically confronts the "silent majority" rather than embraces it, Xu Zhiyuan also endorses a critique of the elite, as laid out in the preface to the collection:

> Blaming the hollowness of the times, or the blind obedience of the masses, while trying to establish a kind of cultural standard, is of course not wrong, but constituting an ossified enlightenment elite is equally dangerous. It must have been Lionel Trilling who said, "Guided by some contradiction in our nature, one day we take our compatriots as the object of our enlightenment efforts, then we take them as an object of commiseration, then they become the target of our wisdom, until eventually they become the object of our coercion." When held up to the mirror of China's twentieth-century history, it seems like a déjà-vu. . . .
>
> How does change happen? What I bemoan is not the mediocrity of the masses (they are generally like that), but the general decadence of the elite. Fewer and fewer people are willing to take the narrow middle road of critiquing the ossified power—regardless of how it appears—while retaining a sufficient measure of self-awareness—reflecting on the limitations of the self. The elite is not only unprepared to lead this era, it has become its most loyal follower, terrified that it will be discarded by the revelry of the masses.
>
> It is very possible that I am the classic example of what I am criticizing. These unbalanced essays are the best evidence. In them, I keep oscillating between firm criticism and hurt powerlessness. Therefore, all of these essays are clearly dated, so that you may judge for yourself whether I have become more mature or more narrow-minded.[147]

Despite his reluctance to embrace the "masses," Xu Zhiyuan is also able to critically distance himself from the elitist position of the "enlightenment" intellectual and its twentieth-century history of abetting social engineering as well as to point critically to elite intellectuals' inability to meet the challenges of the times. This dual critique of course raises the question of his own position.

In an essay published in Hong Kong in January 2016, Xu introspectively examined his self-censorship strategies and his fear of becoming a dissident "fixated by forbidden zones" to the point of "ignoring all other major social issues" and in this way becoming irrelevant by his own device. He describes the year 2009 as a turning point, when one of his friends involved in civil society organizations was arrested: "I became aware of my previous self-deceit, of having wasted time and energy honing an ambiguous writing style, part and parcel of my self-censorship. Up until then, I'd imagined I was wrestling with an anaconda. I'd tried grabbing it by the throat and pushing it away. Instead, I found myself entangled in its coils. I'd now woken with a start."[148] The friend is very probably Xu Zhiyong, about whom Xu Zhiyuan wrote several essays. In another essay, Xu Zhiyuan had previously endorsed Xu Zhiyong's position among the "silent majority" as an alternative for intellectuals:

> The elite pays [*sic*] little attention to petitioners; they would much rather hype up the topic of China's global leadership and economic growth. The weak are simply regarded as unavoidable victims in the process of development. . . . The strength of the powerful, far from making them feel compassion and responsibility for the vulnerable, simply makes them arrogant and indifferent. The vulnerable feel angry and resentful and, perhaps because they have lost all sense of self-respect, they'll do whatever it takes to get redress. Somewhere between these two extremes is the majority: those who share neither the arrogance of power, nor the humiliation of being at the bottom of the heap. They take a generally flippant and scornful attitude to the predicaments of others, but beneath that lies a deep sense of helplessness. Reality is hard to change, so they tacitly accept it. Xu Zhiyong and his fellow lawyers were a beacon of hope. They refused to follow the traditional trajectory of intellectuals who imagine they can change China by writing manifestos about freedom, democracy and the constitution. They were well aware that freedom, democracy and constitutional government are no more than empty words unless they are given meaning through concrete changes in the law. They never expressed political opinions by openly challenging government because they favoured a pragmatic approach . . . But even this approach got them into trouble.[149]

By distancing themselves from the elite, paying attention to the vulnerable, and concentrating on concrete measures, Xu Zhiyong and others appealed to the silent majority. Xi Zhiyuan particularly emphasized Gongmeng's symmetrical distance from state and market: "After thirty years of reforms, we have seen the rapid rise of the market but not the maturing of social forces. Only a healthy and robust civil society can foster pluralist values and bring people both to resist powerful political forces and to guard against simply being reduced to producers and consumers, to become a healthy citizen. . . . Gongmeng is the quintessence of the evolution of China's legal sector: how a group of young people used the weapon of the law to help ordinary people obtain fundamental rights and respect."[150] Xu Zhiyong's arrest provoked a kind of paralysis in Xu Zhiyuan: "It makes you lose any kind of sensitivity; it makes any kind of distorted thing seem normal to your mind, and because it is normal, you lose the anger to resist."[151]

Xu Zhiyuan ended up developing a "two-version" strategy, as Miklós Haraszti predicted; rather than self-censoring everything, he continued to write essays avoiding red lines for the Chinese audience but uncensored essays on websites or in the press outside the mainland: "In the global Chinese world, I write freely and publish politically sensitive work, while in Mainland China I produce non-political prose."[152] After Xi Jinping's rise to power in 2012, control of public expression tightened, and Xu eventually received a call from a friend informing him that his name was on a list of writers banned from publishing anything in the mainland. Rumors swirled that there was a connection between the list and Hong Kong's Umbrella Movement (the protests for universal suffrage that took place over a period of three months in the fall of 2014):

> The irony is that even if the ban on me is never officially confirmed, no one will dare publish me, even the writing I do that is completely apolitical. I'm simply taboo. It doesn't matter that nobody knows how the taboo came about, or how it might end. . . . There's another unsettling fact: I'm concerned that, at some point in the future, my status as a public intellectual will hurt our brand. I'm no longer just me, I'm responsible for a whole team and a company. In China, everyone knows: to be successful in business, you need to be politically submissive. . . . As a result, in effect I've abandoned my critique of politics and current affairs, and I've even distanced myself from some of my dissident friends. . . . I've become insensitive to political violence in China. Since I can't criticise or analyse it, I've come to pretend that it simply doesn't

> exist. It seems that I'm content with this new kind of self-deception: I turn a blind eye to China's authoritarian system: the "elephant in the room." . . . I feel humiliated; I'm ashamed of my cowardice. For the first time in my life I've started keeping a diary. In it I try to record my alienation from myself; I hope that this might act as a balm to my sense of alienation.[153]

There is a measure of self-castigation in this essay that operates, just as Xu previously pointed out in the writings of others, to atone for many intellectuals' feeling of helplessness. However, there is also in it a coherence with Xu's project of trying sustain his platform through commercial ventures that can nurture a public space for cultural discussion rather than to force a face-off with the system. In a way symmetrical with Han Han, Xu Zhiyuan is both "among the people" and attached to the elite.

THE CRACKDOWN ON THE INTERNET

After the new party leadership took office in 2012, deep-reaching changes on Internet policy were announced. Under Hu Jintao, despite increasing censorship, as Rogier Creemers puts it, "the internet [*sic*] became a vibrant space for social interaction and public exchange,"[154] but under Xi Jinping the state's policy goals changed with a heightened emphasis on security and a more comprehensive all-round strategy for the Internet. With the new Leading Small Group for Cybersecurity and Informatization, technical control, propaganda function, and economic regulation of the Internet were brought under the umbrella of one coordinating authority. After Document Number 9 identified the open Internet (under the heading of "Western notions of journalism") as one of seven "forbidden" topics, Lu Wei 魯煒, appointed as head of the Wangxinban (Office for Cybersecurity and Informatization) in the spring of 2013 (which became the Cyberspace Administration of China in April 2014), published "seven baselines" for online discussion. In a secret speech delivered on August 19, 2013, Xi Jinping identified the Internet as one of two battlefields of the party's new public-opinion war (together with the "traditional" battlefield of the media). Throughout the fall of 2013, several "Big V's" were arrested (most prominently Charles Xue Manzi 薛蠻子, but also Murong Xuecun 慕容雪村 and many others[155]), many more accounts were shut down, and the Supreme People's Court issued a new interpretation transposing the notions of "picking quarrels" (*xunxin zishi* 尋釁滋事) and "spreading rumors" (sending messages to more than five hundred people or being retweeted by more than five thousand) to the online sphere.

New rules on real-name registration were promulgated, enforced strictly, and further strengthened and made more comprehensive (including phone lines, websites, social media) throughout 2014 and 2015. Ultimately, the Supreme People's Court imposed liability on service providers who are unable to provide the identity and contacts of Internet users in legal cases.[156] This decision accelerated the migration of users to private group-based social media such as WeChat.[157] An important characteristic of WeChat is that it is not fully interoperable with the Internet: for example, public WeChat accounts are not included in search engines. This has increasingly cut Chinese users off from the rest of the world. In March 2014, there was a further crackdown on WeChat public accounts (which were already limited to publishing one post a day). Finally, a campaign was launched for the "sinicization" of operating systems (government computers were no longer to be equipped with Windows, and foreign service providers were compelled increasingly to communicate source codes and user data to the Chinese regulators). In March 2015, Xi Jinping summed up these developments under the heading "Internet Plus."

Although some people adapted their discourse or were able to find more protective channels, the bloggers and journalists, whose rise was a unique characteristic of the first decade of the new century, accelerated by the momentous events of 2008, generally lost their prominence. Nonetheless, their activities durably transformed the relationship between the elite and the *minjian* realm. A critical public emerged among *minjian* bloggers and writers on the Chinese Internet that to some extent became mainstream among the younger generation. The *minjian* ethos of relying on specific knowledge, keeping a distance from both state and market, and paying attention to the situation of vulnerable groups was to an extent in sympathy with the technology of the early Internet. By contrast, although popular nationalists are often connected to the *minjian* space, they stand apart from other *minjian* intellectuals because they receive significant support from the state, which encourages and facilitates public expressions of nationalism.[158]

In a recent exchange about Han Han triggered by the publication of a collection of English translations of his essays, Zeng Jinyan replied to a charge by the blogger Mo Zhixu 莫之許, who criticized intellectuals for placing high hopes in

Han Han even though it was clear he would be unable to change the system. Zeng argues that on the one hand this expectation is setting the bar too high (not all of society's problems can be blamed on intellectuals), while on the other hand Han Han's original voice has already been drowned out. A product of the short-lived age of blogs, Han Han was unable to survive in the time of social media, when readers have already isolated themselves into small groups with similar ideas. Because the Chinese government impugns and attacks intellectuals, many have left the system, and others have become cynical and excessively critical. By contrast, Zeng believes that engaging in concrete actions within the system is still the only alternative: not because these actions will change the system, but because they are meaningful. "We may not be able to change politics, but at least we can refuse to be changed by politics. A life and history without illusions bring only stagnation and deadly silence."[159]

The new public culture that emerged with the Internet was crucial to the rise of *minjian* intellectuals. The development of the commercial media not only allowed the pluralization of public discourse that *minjian* intellectuals rely on but also created a space for what *Southern Weekly* termed a *minjian* press: a press not only striving for profit but committed to a professional ethos that adequately addresses the concerns of ordinary readers. The Internet created further opportunities for *minjian* bloggers and journalists, whether they were ordinary citizens or "Big Vs" such as Ai Weiwei and Han Han. But more traditional public spaces, such as bookstores and print magazines, could also offer new possibilities, as shown by the example of One-Way Street. It is noteworthy that tensions between grassroots loyalties and residual elitism continue to inform some of the most famous commentators: elitist representations persist even when individuals define themselves as antielite. Han Han purports to speak for ordinary people and takes pride in deflating "big ideas" such as nationalism while at the same time dwelling on what he sees as the public's moral deficit. Xu Zhiyuan criticizes anti-intellectualism and takes pride in producing high-quality cultural content, while at the same time taking issue with the hypocrisy of the elite. In this sense, *minjian* intellectuals predictably have not solved the dilemmas that many of their predecessors struggled with throughout the twentieth century.

Conclusion

The introduction to the present study outlined a new group of intellectuals sharing some combination of freelance position, unofficial status, and grassroots connections. Not all of them check all three boxes, and each criterion is subject to interpretation. Nonetheless, tentatively defining this group as *minjian* intellectuals, this study has argued that they can be heuristically characterized by their mobilization of specific knowledge, their subaltern identification, their endeavor to pluralize public forums, and their critical attitude toward both the political control of the state and the new hegemonies inherent in the market economy. Joseph Levenson famously argued that in some measure the *tianxia* ethos of the Confucian literati was reincarnated in the intellectuals who advocated communist universalism in the 1950s. Even the democracy activists of the 1980s still broadly shared the same universalist stance and strived for official status and recognition from the state. Today, elite intellectuals in top universities and think tanks broadly continue to embrace co-optation by the state, although they have tended to tone down their universalist competence and embrace a new role as experts in the service of the state (and, often in their free time, also of the market). By contrast, the *minjian* intellectuals of the 1990s began to challenge the state-dependent model of the universal intellectual in significant ways. Their critique of the elitism ingrained in previous generations led them to examine more concrete problems at the margins of Chinese society. Referring to themselves as part of the "silent majority," they argued that it was time to "come out of silence" and to assert the views of the many disenfranchised groups. By framing their public interventions as those of ordinary citizens (rather than invoking the privilege of intellectuals), they challenged not only the historical model of the literati but also the avant-garde role of intellectuals in the widely shared Marxist conceptualization of a class society—or its post-Marxist variant with Chinese characteristics, the "strata society," where intellectuals are expected to be spokespeople for a class.

This study has attempted to provide a relatively broad sample of grassroots intellectuals. By virtue of their specific status, they address different publics, although some, such as Ai Xiaoming or (in a very different way) Han Han can also to some extent cut across the boundaries of specialization. Wang Xiaobo was the first freelance writer to leave his university job in 1992 and invoke his connection with the "vulnerable" or subaltern groups as the basis for his public interventions in the new commercial media. Li Yinhe and Ai Xiaoming continued his work in the area of sociology and gender studies. Writers such as Zhu Wen and Yu Jian advocated *minjian* literature and poetry.

In the aftermath of the fortieth anniversary of the Anti-Rightist Movement in 1997, amateur historians questioned the official narrative of the revolution. Shen Zhihua had already pioneered archival collection and research from a position outside academia. Guo Yuhua carried out oral history on the early PRC from inside academia. Hu Jie's film on Lin Zhao awakened many people's interest in both unofficial history and independent documentary. Yang Jisheng's book on the Great Famine provoked a full-scale public controversy that ended with the purge of the journal he edited, *Yanhuang Chunqiu*. As noted earlier, in this instance *minjian* history refers to an unofficial history of nonelite individuals and groups by noninstitutional historians, which tries to establish knowledge rather than obtain material or symbolic benefits.

Independent cinema provided a new channel for intellectuals outside the system to engage with important social issues and to disseminate their findings to alternative publics. Jia Zhangke was the most eloquent advocate for the legitimacy of this alternative form of knowledge production, and Wu Wenguang worked the most closely with grassroots communities to investigate village life and village memories of the Great Famine. After the first independent film festival took place in 2001, the artist and filmmaker communities in "urban villages" such as Caochangdi and Songzhuang provided directors such as Ma Li and Zhao Liang with the space to work on large-scale documentary projects with disenfranchised communities such as petitioners while minimizing financial pressure.

When Teng Biao and Xu Zhiyong successfully challenged the constitutionality of "repatriating" rural migrants lacking urban residency permits after the Sun

Zhigang incident in 2003, they opened the way for a new type of legal and non-profit work to advance the interests of subaltern groups such as petitioners. Yu Jianrong and other scholars set up grassroots organizations to support petitioners even as they lobbied the government from within academia. Although their studies were not purely detached and academic, Xu and Yu did not enroll petitioners under their banner in the style of organic intellectuals seeking to establish a new theoretical hegemony. Breaking with the elite position of producing political or constitutional blueprints that had little connection with ordinary people's lives, they instead tried to find practical solutions to social problems.

In the aftermath of the Tibet protest, the Sichuan earthquake, and the controversial Beijing Olympics in 2008, *minjian* nationalism blossomed on the Internet, often with the open support of the state. In response, journalists and bloggers such as Chang Ping and Han Han employed new strategies to contend for the support of the silent majority. Other writers, such as Xu Zhiyuan, criticized the new forms of populism and attempted to open spaces such as One-Way Street to foster a better-informed and more cosmopolitan reading public.

Although individuals play a role, this study has tried to avoid the overly personalized approach of traditional intellectual history, focusing instead on intellectual spaces and networks: unofficial journals, commercial newspapers, bookstores, artist villages, social media. It attempts not to draw heroic portraits of a few individuals but to document a social phenomenon, which leads to a redefinition of who can be considered an intellectual in today's China. Being intellectual no longer implies a traditional education (e.g., high school dropout Han Han) or a well-established, stable socioeconomic position, as in premodern, May Fourth, and Marxist contexts. Furthermore, whereas previous incarnations of Chinese intellectuals were overwhelmingly male, this gender hierarchy, like other hierarchies, has been challenged, as attested by the prominent role of some female grassroots intellectuals such as Ai Xiaoming, Li Yinhe, Guo Yuhua, Ma Li, and Zeng Jinyan. Rather than presenting a systematic theory, this study has attempted to extrapolate from a broad set of case studies to establish a trend. It does not argue that this is the only significant trend in contemporary Chinese society. However, in the increasingly fragmented field of contemporary China studies, there is also a need for academic studies to claw back larger arguments in a heuristic manner. Evolutions on the margins often trigger centripetal dynamics that end up redefining, if not transforming, the mainstream.

The material is also structured by an implicit set of intellectual controversies that often played out across the borders of different publics. Amateur historians debated the number of famine victims and the sincerity of Red Guard apologies, thereby engaging with the unwritten chapters of early PRC history. Documentary filmmakers were drawn into controversies over the political meaning of representing laid-off workers or other subaltern groups and over how to present their own position with respect to these groups without being co-opted or manipulated by state discourses, in particular when their films were screened to foreign audiences. Legal activists debated whether focusing on concrete issues within the framework of the Constitution meant forgoing any challenge to the system. Qin Hui and others argued that the liberal/New Left dichotomy excessively focused on artificial "isms" that masked the actual "problems" of Chinese society, in which state and market often worked hand-in-hand against ordinary people. Rather than using the old framework of state versus market, they argued that considering how state and market are often on the same side of a tension with *minjian* society may yield new insights.

The challenges to China's Olympic Games in 2008 sparked an acrimonious and still ongoing debate about double standards and whether China is being held to a different benchmark by the international media. Han Han's moderate pleas for reform provoked a protracted debate about the alleged limitations of media intellectuals. As in liberal democracies, the shift to social media provoked a new form of polarization of public debates within narrow circles of like-minded publics. Although many of the debates touch on larger issues that are often framed within the liberal/New Left dichotomy, the actual debates generally displace intellectual boundaries and reconfigure the ideological alignment in the context of concrete issues.

This study uses the term *minjian*, which many of the players studied here use to refer to their own stance and activities, rather than a term or concept taken from Western theory. This choice also challenges the notion that Chinese society should be viewed only through the (often Marxist) categories favored by the Chinese state. However, like most terms that are widely used in ordinary discourse, *minjian* tends to be quite ambiguous. Although an attempt has been made to sketch out its semantic boundaries, it is probably impossible to define it in overly rigorous terms because it takes on different meanings in different contexts and continues to evolve. Throughout the articulations studied in the previous chapters, recurrent themes are associated with *minjian*: the silent majority, the need to speak out, the critique of the state and the market, grassroots and nonelite status. However, *minjian* is not coterminous with an articulated civil society or a substantive understanding of citizenship. Similarly, in a recent study of opposition groups in Russia, Mischa Gabowitsch argues that protest against the government has not necessarily advanced a liberal conception of the individual or rights but rather forms of nonviolent civic engagement that foster solidarity and build on human relationships in communities.[1] The term *minjian* therefore also highlights that citizenship remains conditional in present-day China.

The term *minjian* does emphasize paying attention to subaltern groups and questioning the speaker's stance in relation to these groups; *minjian* intellectuals tend to ground their interventions in shared experience and the firsthand collection or elaboration of knowledge among such groups. It should be emphasized that the elite and the grass roots remain engaged in a productive discussion. Chapter 6 sketches out some of the tensions generated by the parallel critiques of traditional elite intellectuals and state-sponsored anti-intellectual populism. More broadly, this study has tried to foreground the existence of a significant group of "crossover" intellectuals who move back and forth between academic or professional settings and grassroots work. The *minjian* role should therefore not be seen as exclusive. However, this new dynamic also challenges the generally accepted notion that grassroots individuals have no autonomous intellectual life or are productively studied only as consumers or as elements within the socialist state and its new mainstream culture. An examination of intellectual productions through the scope of the notion of *minjian* makes it clear that Chinese society contains many different forms of critical engagement that generally challenge the tenets of earlier models of dissidence. Although many of the individuals studied in this book also continue to work both within the system (as many people in China have always done) and around or outside it, the significant development is that the old ways of opposing the establishment are now increasingly criticized as overly theoretical, elitist, and disconnected from people's lives. By contrast, a new set of critical discourses have developed that are ingrained within broader social practices, such as legal procedures and the use of social media. Although the current regime may offer "consistent, practical results for the majority," as one commentator recently put it,[2] critical discourses are also increasingly likely to be relevant to ordinary people's lives. The "silent majority" shares a sense of disenfranchisement that is a well-recognized source of anxiety for broad sections of Chinese society.[3]

This realignment represents a reconfiguration not only of the tradition of Chinese intellectuals but also of Marxist representations of society. In official discourse, since intellectuals were rehabilitated by Deng Xiaoping, they are considered a stratum (*jieceng*) within the working class. At the same time, post-1992 marketization has undeniably provided many "intellectuals" (in particular academics and professionals) with the opportunity to embrace a middle-class lifestyle. Zhidong Hao has consequently argued that intellectuals could constitute their own class in the new Chinese social pyramid. The rise of disenfranchised groups questions the existence of a clear-cut class structure within Chinese society and more profoundly undermines the epistemological monism of mainstream Marxist theory. Emphasizing the *minjian* status of intellectuals as part of a "silent majority" suggests that society is not aligned along class lines but rather polarized between vested interests (including the political and economic elite) on the one hand and a mosaic of disenfranchised groups with diverging agendas on the other. For many neo-Marxist critics, this representation of society is undesirable or even erroneous. They generally deny intellectuals the legitimacy to intervene as members of the silent majority and insist either that intellectuals should align with the working class against economic elites or that the working class should generate its own organic intellectuals to advance its class interests. Echoes of this critique can be discerned in several interventions discussed in each of the chapters here. Lin Chun rebuts Wang Xiaobo's essay on the silent majority by arguing that intellectuals are by definition an "awakened minority." Lü Xinyu's insists that Wang Bing's documentary *West of the Tracks* is a nostalgic plea to save the working class created by Mao. Wang Hui reaffirms the need to foreground class struggle in the study of PRC history. Pun Ngai and Chris Chan critique Yu Jianrong's indictment of the party–state's instrumental "reification" of the working class. Zhao Yuezhi argues that marketization of the media has provoked corruption and manipulation by capitalist interests.

This book is also about the social construction of knowledge. On an epistemological level, the *minjian* view is a pluralistic one and implicitly defines a new methodology of inquiry, which can be viewed within the larger timeframe of a slow reconstruction of social and human sciences after the end of the Mao era.[4] After an examination of Wang Xiaobo's critique of the status and role of the intellectual in chapter 2, the following chapters dealt with three major areas of empirical inquiry: about the past (minjian history), about present-day society (documentary film as ethnography), and about citizen rights and China's political system (grassroots politics). The last chapter deals with the publics that read and circulate the knowledge produced in these alternative spaces. In this sense, this study has also attempted to offer an alternative to discussing China in terms of "postsocialism." Whereas the "post-ist" intellectuals of the 1990s were still strongly indebted to notions of a single truth informed by Marxism's scientistic approach to the study of society as well as to a linear, Darwinist view of history based on modernization, *minjian* intellectuals generally make a case for the need to individualize and pluralize the construction of knowledge. Amateur historians have tried to foster platforms for open debate of contentious historical events. Documentary filmmakers investigate social phenomena in an empirical, individual manner. Social scientists such as Yu Jianrong have pleaded for plurality of theoretical approaches. Many of these trends can be traced back to Wang Xiaobo's argument that intellectuals should separate cognitive issues from normative issues and embrace value neutrality. As Zygmunt Bauman noted, this more modest form of self-understanding, in which neither class structure nor historical evolution can be prescribed, also means that the proletariat can no longer function as the intellectuals' Pygmalion. Or, as Wang Xiaobo put it, intellectuals now write to educate themselves rather than to educate others.

Returning to the classic theories of intellectuals, we may ask whether the rise of *minjian* intellectuals can challenge our understanding of what makes an intellectual. Chapter 1 began by contrasting Pierre Bourdieu, who argues that the public authority by which intellectuals speak out is a product of their prestige within a field, with Michel Foucault, who makes the case that specific intellectuals can speak out on the basis not only of prestige but also of their engagement with knowledge production in specific locations in society. Knowledge can therefore translate into both heteronomous experts and autonomous specific intellectuals. *Minjian* intellectuals are predictably Foucauldian in that any prestige they may have is generally hard to reconcile with a position of authority within a field. Many of the discourses analyzed in this book highlight that *minjian* intellectuals reject the sense of social responsibility that defined previous generations of literati. As the filmmaker Ji Dan affirms in her reply to Lü Xinyu, the role of independent directors with respect to the subjects they investigate is like that of a shaman. *Minjian* intellectuals embrace empirical approaches and do not usually purport to play a leading or avant-garde role in theorizing, mobilizing, and leading the grass roots, or indeed any class, toward an alternative vision of society. This inflexion translates into a broader rejection of notions of class representativity, historical teleology, and realist aesthetics. *Minjian* intellectuals are neither proponents of a class-based neorevolutionary agenda nor mouthpieces for various interest groups fighting for "recognition." Rather, they are engaged with the politics of knowledge construction at the grassroots level. The new forms of knowledge are elaborated both on the basis of ethnographic investigation as social science and on a form of sensibility to the subjects under investigation, which gives a greater role to personal experience and engagement. In the methodology pioneered by independent documentaries, quotidian practices are more important than great narratives. As Yu Jianrong emphasizes in his retrospective assessment of three decades of scholarship, the most urgent task in his view is to facilitate and embrace the pluralism of methods of inquiry and knowledge. This profound turn away from academic Marxism can of course only be a cause for concern to the state, as suggested by the growing repression of *minjian* platforms, whether film festivals, unofficial history journals, legal support groups, or individual bloggers and microbloggers. Although the space for social autonomy has continued to shrink over the past few years, Chinese society continues to diversify, and the undermining of monistic discourses about society and politics may contain more profound challenges for the party. The marginalization of traditional academic intellectuals may yet be conducive to a greater plurality of approaches, which would also facilitate "mainstreaming of Chinese thought in Western academia."[5] Nonetheless, it remains an open question whether *minjian* society can resist the further encroachments of the growing surveillance state.

Viewed through an even wider lens, the rise of *minjian* intellectuals can also be seen as part of a worldwide set of efforts to advance citizen knowledge and to rethink the connections between expert advice, citizen knowledge, and political decision. As the traditional intellectual elite in liberal democracies have been increasingly co-opted by multinational corporations and rebranded as "thought leaders,"[6] there is a need to rethink the position of intellectuals as the producers of specific knowledge that is neither the simple application of a universal (or partisan) stance to a concrete problem nor the commodified expertise provided to economic and political elites. Rethinking the relationship between academia and the grass roots appears to be a pressing task in most societies around the world. In this sense, paradoxical though it may seem, *minjian* intellectuals in China may represent a fruitful example of how the reconstruction of citizen knowledge can serve as the starting point for a new type of intellectual.

APPENDIX

Minibiographies of Thirty Minjian *Intellectuals*

This volume argues that individuals are less significant to understand the intellectual dynamics in contemporary China than they were in previous decades. Associations, publications, informal networks may be more relevant objects of study. With that caveat, this list—limited to thirty individuals—is presented simply for the reader's convenience as a shorthand reminder of some of the main figures discussed in the book. Many more equally deserve to appear here. Therefore, this list should be viewed as a kind of index rather than as a representative sample.

1. Ai Weiwei 艾未未 (b. Beijing, 1957): visual artist, blogger. He investigated the victims of the Sichuan earthquake, to which he devoted a film and an art installation. He was detained for tax evasion in 2011 and moved to Germany in 2015.
2. Ai Xiaoming 艾曉明 (b. Wuhan, 1953): professor, documentary filmmaker, women's rights activist. She pioneered teaching gender studies at Sun Yat-sen University (Guangzhou); after her involvement in the Huang Jing rape and murder case in 2003, she began to make activist documentaries on social protests, the AIDS epidemic in Henan, and forgotten events of the Mao era.
3. Chang Ping 長平 (Zhang Ping 張平; b. Sichuan, 1971): investigative journalist and editorialist. He rose to fame in the Southern Media Group in the early 2000s, notably through his investigation of the Zhang Jun case in 1999 and later for his editorial for *FTChinese* at the time of the Tibet uprising of 2008. He moved to Germany in 2011.

4. Guo Yuhua 郭于華 (b. Beijing, 1956): professor of sociology at Tsinghua University. She devoted her research to rural society; her book *Narratives of the Sufferers* (*Shoukuren de jiangshu*, 2013) used oral history sources to investigate rural society under Mao.
5. Guo Yushan 郭玉閃 (b. Fujian, 1977): NGO activist. After receiving a master's degree in political economy from Peking University, he took part in the NGO Gongmeng before setting up his own think tank, the Transition Institute (2007–2013). He was arrested in 2014 and released on bail in 2015.
6. Han Han 韓寒 (b. Shanghai, 1982): blogger, novelist, and sports-car racer. After dropping out of high school, he became a best-selling novelist. He wrote an extremely influential blog between 2008 and 2012 and frequently commented critically on political issues. After his magazine *Party* ran into difficulties, turned mainly to producing films.
7. Hu Jie 胡傑 (b. Shandong, 1958): visual artist, documentary filmmaker. After working in the People's Liberation Army and for Xinhua, he became an independent director. Based in Nanjing, he is particularly well known for his series of investigative films on the traumatic events of the Mao era.
8. Ji Dan 季丹 (b. Heilongjiang, 1963): documentary filmmaker. After graduating from Beijing Normal University, she studied in Japan and lived in Tibet, producing a series of films on contemporary social issues, including migrant workers.
9. Jia Zhangke 賈樟柯 (b. Shanxi, 1970): filmmaker and producer. Leading filmmaker among the first generation working outside the state system (*Xiao Wu*, 1997), he was later able to secure state approval for his films while still dealing with topics often ignored by the mainstream.
10. Li Xianting 栗憲庭 (b. Jilin, 1949): curator and art critic. After curating the exhibition *China Avant-Garde* in 1989, distanced himself from the system, settling in Yuanmingyuan, then Songzhuang. There, he established the Li Xianting Film Fund, which was instrumental in running the independent film festivals in Songzhuang until 2016.
11. Li Yinhe 李銀河 (b. Beijing, 1952): sociologist and social activist, married to Wang Xiaobo until his death in 1997. As a CASS scholar, she pioneered research on homosexuality in China and activism on LGBT and gender issues.

12. Ma Li 馬莉 (b. Zhejiang, 1975): journalist, documentary filmmaker, based in Songzhuang until 2017. Her films have investigated sensitive social issues such as petitioners (*Born in Beijing*, 2011) and mental institutions (*Inmates*, 2017).
13. Qian Liqun 錢理群 (b. Chongqing, 1939): After taking part in the Hundred Flowers activities in Peking University as an undergraduate in 1957, he spent several decades in Guizhou teaching in vocational schools. As a professor of literature at PKU, pioneered research on the Anti-Rightist Movement after its fortieth anniversary in 1997.
14. Qin Hui 秦暉 (b. Guangxi, 1953): professor of economic history at Tsinghua University. A leading proponent of social democracy, he was instrumental in criticizing the overriding importance given to "isms" and the lack of interest in "problems" among China's elite intellectuals.
15. Shen Zhihua 沈志華 (b. Beijing, 1950): professor of contemporary history at East China Normal University. After being imprisoned for spying as a graduate student, left academia and made a fortune in the gold trade, which allowed him to purchase a large trove of Soviet archives and to set up his own relatively independent research institute.
16. Teng Biao 滕彪 (b. Jilin, 1973): lawyer, NGO worker, and civil rights activist. After the Sun Zhigang case in 2003, advocated constitutional review and established the independent NGO Gongmeng (2003–2009) for research and advocacy. After being detained in 2011, he moved to the United States in 2014.
17. Wang Bing 王兵 (b. Shaanxi, 1967): documentary filmmaker. Steering clear of all institutional connections, he has worked mainly with foreign producers to complete projects on the privatization of state-owned enterprises (*West of the Tracks*, 2003), the Jiabiangou labor camp, and other vulnerable social groups.
18. Wang Xiaobo 王小波 (b. Beijing, 1952–1997): novelist and essayist. After accompanying his wife, Li Yinhe, to the United States in the 1980s, he began publishing fiction and essays in the early 1990s. One of the first freelance writers in the reform era, also became an influential essayist and social commentator.
19. Wu Di 吳迪 (b. Beijing, 1951): retired film scholar and amateur historian of the Mao era. He began publishing the unofficial journal *Remembrance* in 2008, entirely devoted to popular memories of the Mao era.

20. Wu Si 吳思 (b. Beijing, 1957): journalist and essayist. After working for a variety of newspapers, he served as editor of *Yanhuang Chunqiu* for seventeen years, until the end of 2014. Now holds a leading position at the Unirule Institute.
21. Wu Wenguang 吳文光 (b. Yunnan, 1956): documentary filmmaker. His film *Bumming in Beijing* (1990) was the first independent documentary produced in China since 1949. Based in Caochangdi until 2014, he pioneered participative documentary in projects with rural villagers and migrant workers and in the Folk Memory Project devoted to the Great Famine since 2010.
22. Xu Zhiyong 許志永 (b. Henan, 1973): lawyer, NGO worker, and civil rights activist. With Teng Biao, instrumental in the Sun Zhigang case and in establishing Gongmeng, researching petitioners and migrant-worker schools in particular. After Gongmeng was shut down in 2009, he launched the New Citizen Movement, was arrested, and served four years in prison until 2017.
23. Xu Zhiyuan 許知遠 (b. Jiangsu, 1976): journalist, essayist, cultural entrepreneur. An influential columnist for *FTChinese* and *Yazhou Zhoukan*, he established the bookstore One-Way Street in Beijing and several associated journals from 2005, including *Oriental History Review*.
24. Yang Jisheng 楊繼繩 (b. Hubei, 1940): retired journalist, amateur historian. After a career with Xinhua, devoted his retirement to gathering unofficial and archival material on the Great Famine and the Cultural Revolution, served briefly as chief editor of *Yanhuang Chunqiu*, and published his study *Tombstone* in 2008 in Hong Kong.
25. Yang Xianhui 楊顯惠 (b. Gansu, 1946): journalist and novelist. After experiencing the labor camps of Gansu, devoted his retirement to interviewing survivors of the Jiabiangou camp, where several thousand victims of the Anti-Rightist Movement starved to death, which he published as *Chronicles of Jiabiangou* (2003).
26. Yi Sicheng 易思成 (b. Yunnan, 1976): anthropologist and film critic. After receiving a Ph.D. in visual anthropology, he was instrumental in establishing and running the documentary film festival Yunfest from within the Yunnan Academy of Social Science until the festival was shut down in 2013.

27. Yu Jian 于堅 (b. Yunnan, 1954): poet, documentary filmmaker, local culture activist. An important advocate of *minjian* poetry in the 1990s, he also made several independent documentaries on popular memories and village life and took part in the Yunfest community.
28. Yu Jianrong 于建嶸 (b. Hunan, 1962): sociologist, blogger, social activist. After making a fortune as a commercial lawyer, ha was able to maintain a degree of independence from his academic institution, CASS. Particularly active in advocating for petitioners.
29. Zeng Jinyan 曾金燕 (b. Fujian, 1983): scholar, blogger, gender-equality activist. With her then husband, Hu Jia, wrote about and filmed their residential surveillance. Received a Ph.D. in gender studies from Hong Kong University in 2017 and produces documentary films.
30. Zhu Rikun 朱日坤 (b. Guangdong, 1976): documentary film producer and director. Established the Fanhall Café and website in Songzhuang and contributed to organizing the Songzhuang film festivals. In later years, he also made several documentaries related to civil rights.

Notes

INTRODUCTION

1. Timothy Cheek, "Xu Jilin and the Thought Work of China's Public Intellectuals," *China Quarterly*, no. 186 (June 2006): 403.
2. Throughout this volume, Chinese periodicals with an English title that is official (e.g., when it appears in the publication, such as *Orient*) or is widely used (e.g., *People's Daily*) are designated by their English title, with the Chinese title provided only in the first reference. For publications without an official or widely accepted English translation (e.g., *Yanhuang Chunqiu*, *Caixin*), the Chinese title is used throughout, with an English translation provided only in the first reference. Chinese characters are provided in the main text (but generally not in notes) for personal names, journal titles, and important concepts.
3. Wang Xiaobo, "Chenmo de daduoshu" (The silent majority), in *Siwei de lequ* (The pleasure of thinking) (Kunming: Yunnan Renmin, 2006), 10. See also the English translation by Eric Abrahamsen, "The Silent Majority," *Paper Republic*, https://media.paper-republic.org/files/09/04/The_Silent_Majority_Wang_Xiaobo.pdf.
4. Michel Foucault, "La fonction politique de l'intellectuel" (The political function of the intellectual), in *Dits et écrits*, 4 vols. (Paris: Gallimard, 1994), 3:109–114.
5. Richard Posner, *Public Intellectuals: A Study in Decline* (Cambridge, Mass.: Harvard University Press, 2001), translated into Chinese as *Gongggong zhishifenzi: Shuailuo zhi yanjiu*, trans. Xu Xin (Beijing: Zhongguo Zhengfa Daxue, 2002). See also Nicolai Volland, "Fifty Influential Public Intellectuals," Heidelberg University Database, February 13, 2006, http://www.zo.uni-heidelberg.de/boa/digital_resources/dachs/special_collections/fipi_en.html, and David Kelly "The Importance of Being Public," *China Review*, no. 31 (2004): 28–37.
6. See David Herman, "Thinking Big," *Prospect Magazine*, July 24, 2004, http://www.prospectmagazine.co.uk/2004/07/thinkingbig/.
7. "Shei shi gonggong zhishifenzi?" (Who are public intellectuals?), *Nanfang Renwu Zhoukan*, no. 7 (September 8, 2004), http://business.sohu.com/20040907/n221927429.shtml.
8. "Shei shi gonggong zhishifenzi?"

9. See Ji Fangping, "Touguo biaoxiang kan shizhi—xi 'gonggong zhishifenzi' lun" (Discerning the substance behind the surface: An analysis of "public intellectuals"), *Jiefang Ribao*, November 15, 2004, reprinted in *People's Daily*, November 25, 2004.
10. Joseph Fewsmith, *China Since Tiananmen*, 2nd ed. (New York: Cambridge University Press, 2008), 260. Two members of the list (Mao Yushi and Wang Yi) were also banned from publishing in the mainland media, along with four other people not on the *Southern People Weekly* list.
11. Ian Johnson, "The People in Retreat: An Interview with Ai Xiaoming," *New York Review of Books Daily*, September 8, 2016, http://www.nybooks.com/daily/2016/09/08/people-in-retreat-chinese-filmmaker-ai-xiaoming/. A form of anti-intellectualism is popular among grassroots intellectuals, which is reflected in the success of Thomas Sowell's book *Intellectuals and Society*, translated as *Zhishifenzi yu shehui*, trans. Zhang Yayue and Liang Xingguo (Beijing: Zhongxin, 2013).
12. See, for example, Yang Jun, "Chongjian zhishifenzi jingshen" (Rebuild the intellectual spirit), *Nanfeng Chuang*, no. 2 (January 16, 2007): 24–25. The party opened to all groups within society by adopting Jiang Zemin's notion of "three represents" in 2002. The notion of "ruling party" (*zhizheng dang*) appeared in a leaked internal document as early as 1991. See *Zhongguo Qingnianbao* Sixiang Lilun Bu (Department of Thought and Theory of the *China Youth Daily*), "Sulian zhengbian zhihou Zhongguo de xianshi yingdui yu zhanlüe xuanze" (Realistic responses and strategic choices for China after the coup in the Soviet Union), September 9, 1991; see also Anne-Marie Brady, *Marketing Dictatorship: Propaganda and Thought Work in Contemporary China* (Lanham, Md.: Rowman and Littlefield, 2008), 47, 62 n. 52.
13. Ouyang Mijian, "Ai yu cheng quewei de xin qimeng" (A new enlightenment lacking in love and sincerity), *Nanfeng Chuang*, no. 12 (June 6, 2012): 53.
14. Li Beifang, "Gong zhi yu wei shi" (Public intellectuals and fake literati), *Nanfeng Chuang*, no. 12 (June 6, 2012): 54–56.
15. Feng Shiyan, "Zhishifenzi de tizhi bing: Huadong shifan daxue lishixue xi jiaoshou Xu Jilin fangtan," (The system sickness of intellectuals: An interview with East China Normal University History Department professor Xu Jilin), *Nanfeng Chuang*, no. 12 (June 6, 2012): 57–59.
16. Shi Yong, "Shehui bianle, zhishifenzi bianle ma?" (Society has changed, but have intellectuals?), *Nanfeng Chuang*, no. 12 (June 6, 2012): 46–50.
17. Yang Fudong, *The First Intellectual*, color photograph, 1999–2000, and interview in Hans Ulrich Obrist, *The China Interviews* (Beijing: ODE, 2009), 375. Yang has commented repeatedly on the contemporary role of intellectuals, most notably in the multipart video project *Seven Sages in a Bamboo Grove* (2002–), which explores how intellectuals can gradually return from "utopia" to contemporary city life.
18. Shi Yong, "Shehui bianle, zhishifenzi bianle ma?" 46. Yang Guobin notes a similar evolution when he describes the shift from initial enthusiasm about "netizens" (*wangmin*) who spoke out about issues of social injustice to an Internet that has become flooded by government-controlled astroturfers such as "50 centers" and "little pinks" ("China's Divided Netizens," *Berggruen Institute*, October 21, 2016, http://insights.berggruen.org/issues/issue-6/institute_posts/143).

19. Qin Hui, "Wang Xiaobo and the Fate of Critical Realism in Contemporary Literature" (1998), in *Wang Xiaobo yanjiu ziliao* (Materials for research on Wang Xiaobo), 2 vols., ed. Han Yuanhong (Tianjin: Tianjin Renmin, 2009), 1:333. On "splitting the family home," see Qin Hui, "Dividing the Big Family Assets," in *One China, Many Paths*, ed. Chaohua Wang (London, Verso, 2003), 128–159.
20. Shi Yong, "Shehui bianle, zhishifenzi bianle ma?" 50.
21. Yang Guobin, "Liang Congjie, Public Intellectuals, and Civil Society in China," *China Beat*, December 10, 2010.
22. See Pun Ngai and Chris King-chi Chan, "The Subsumption of Class Discourse in China," *boundary 2* 35, no. 2 (2008): 75–91.
23. Geremie Barmé points to this trend when he notes how "non-aligned intellectuals, professionals (in particular lawyers) and social activists attempted in a myriad of ways—through private, small-scale charity projects, covert foundation activities, legal cases and so on—to engage actively in civic actions that would benefit their fellows" ("The Revolution of Resistance," in *Chinese Society: Change, Conflict, and Resistance*, ed. Elizabeth J. Perry and Mark Selden [London: Routledge, 2000], 307).
24. See also Perry Link, Richard Madsen, and Paul Pickowicz, eds., *Unofficial China: Popular Culture and Thought in the People's Republic of China* (Boulder, Colo.: Westview Press, 1989), *Popular China: Unofficial Culture in a Globalizing Society* (Lanham, Md.: Rowman and Littlefield, 2001), and *Restless China* (Lanham, Md.: Rowman and Littlefield, 2013).
25. See Edward X. Gu, "Social Capital, Institutional Change, and the Development of Nongovernmental Intellectual Organizations in China," in *Chinese Intellectuals Between State and Market*, ed. Edward X. Gu and Merle Goldman (London: Routledge, 2004), 21–42.
26. For example, "*minjian* society" is not included among the types of civil society discussed in Roger des Forges's overview "States, Societies, and Civil Societies in Chinese History," in *Civil Society in China*, ed. Timothy Brook and Michael Frolic (Armonk, N.Y.: M. E. Sharpe, 1997), 68–95.
27. "2010 nian yingxiang Zhongguo shidai jincheng 100 ren pingxuan jiexiao" (100 influential personalities of the times in China 2010: Selection revealed), *Shidai Zhoubao*, December 10, 2010. These "influential personalities" included the melamine-milk powder whistleblower Zhao Lianhai, the blogger Bei Feng, the environmental activist BasuoFengyun (Panyu incinerator), the environmental journalist Feng Yunfeng, the journalist and self-taught lawyer Liu Changhan, the citizen reporter Lu Ningping, the Guangzhou urban activist Zhong Jizhang, the nationalistic fishing boat captain Zhan Qixiong (who was held by the Japanese Coast Guard near the Senkaku/Diaoyu Islands), Zhang Zi'an (unidentifiable), and expropriation victim Zhong Rujiu.
28. See Yang Weidong, *Lici cunzhao* (For the Record), 4 vols. to date (Hong Kong: Suyuan Books, 2012–2014), vols. 1 and 2 on intellectuals, vol. 3 on "Red descendants," and vol. 4 on Hong Kong. See also Ian Johnson, "A Father's Death Sets Off a Quest to Delve Into China's Soul," *New York Times*, August 12, 2016.
29. David Kelly, "Citizen Movements and China's Public Intellectuals in the Hu-Wen Era," *Pacific Affairs* 79, no. 2 (2006): 183–204.
30. William Callahan, "Citizen Ai: Warrior, Jester, and Middleman," *Journal of Asian Studies* 73, no. 4 (2014): 915. Callahan draws on Václav Havel's idea that a community

of people "living in truth" can form an alternative polis, offering the following definition: "Citizen intellectuals are 'independent voices' not because they are in opposition to state power, but because they take advantage of China's new social and economic freedoms to choose when to work with the state, and when to work outside state institutions" (William Callahan, "Shanghai's Alternative Futures: The World Expo, Citizen Intellectuals, and China's New Civil Society," *China Information* 26, no. 2 [2012]: 253).

31. Callahan, "Citizen Ai," 914. Callahan also refers to Robert Weller's notion of "alternate civilities" as a foundation for the emergent civil society (*Alternate Civilities: Democracy and Culture in China and Taiwan* [Boulder, Colo.: Westview Press, 2001]).
32. See, for example, Michael Frolic, "State-Led Civil Society," in *Civil Society in China*, ed. Brook and Frolic, 46–67. In a recent publication, Eva Pils puts forward the less-controversial concept of "liberal communities" ("Discussing 'Civil Society' and 'Liberal Communities' in China," *China Perspectives*, no. 3 [2012]: 3).
33. Tsinghua political scientist Zhu Xufeng makes a similar argument about the emergence of "civic activism" by public intellectuals who may use their expertise or not but participate in activism as citizens (they may in addition use their fame, but not all were well known before engaging in activism) as well as about cases in which citizens develop their own expertise (Xufeng Zhu, "In the Name of 'Citizens': Civic Activism and Policy Entrepreneurship of Chinese Public Intellectuals in the Hu-Wen Era," *Journal of Contemporary China* 25, no. 101 [2016]: 748).
34. Ching Kwan Lee and You-tien Hsing, "Social Activism in China: Agency and Possibility," in *Reclaiming Chinese Society: The New Social Activism*, ed. You-tien Hsing and Ching Kwan Lee (London: Routledge, 2010), 1–13.
35. David Palmer, *Qigong Fever: Body, Science, and Utopia in China* (London: Hurst, 2007); Sébastien Billioud and Joël Thoraval, *The Sage and the People: The Confucian Revival in China* (London: Oxford, 2015).
36. Zeng Jinyan, "Zhaohuan gongmin zhishifenzi" (Invoking citizen intellectuals), in *Zhongguo nüquan: Gongmin zhishifenzi de dansheng* (Chinese feminism: The birth of a citizen intelligentsia) (Hong Kong: City University Press, 2016), xxxi–xxxv. On the "superfluous men," see the postface "Jia Jia, wangluo shidai duoyu de ren" (Jia Jia: A superfluous man of the Internet era), 225–229. Zeng argues that these "superfluous men" are traditional elite intellectuals who are frustrated with the political stalemate but have become alienated from social activists and have drifted into art for art's sake and aestheticism (227).
37. Zeng Jinyan, "Dang women tanlun duli dianying shi, women tanlun shenme" (What are we talking about when we discuss independent film?), in Wen Hai, *Fangzhu de ningshi: Jianzheng Zhongguo duli jilupian* (The banished gaze: Chinese independent documentary) (Taipei: Tendency, 2016), 9–23.
38. For some examples, see discussions of Wang Hui's role as chief editor of *Dushu*: the Cheung Kong prize controversy (Geremie Barmé and Gloria Davies, "Have We Been Noticed Yet?" in *Chinese Intellectuals Between State and Market*, ed. Gu and Goldman, 75–108) and Wang Hui's replacement as editor in July 2007 ("*Dushu* Zazhi huanshuai fengbo: Dangshiren Wang Hui shouci jieshou caifang" [Controversial change of guard at *Dushu*: Protagonist Wang Hui's first interview], *Nandu Zhoukan*, July 27, 2007).

39. On the gender stereotypes inherent in traditional representations of the intellectuals, see Zeng Jinyan, "Daolun" (Introduction), in *Zhongguo nüquan*, 6.
40. Li Hsiao-t'i, "Making a Name and a Culture for the Masses in Modern China," *Positions* 9, no. 1 (2001): 29–68. See also Chang-tai Hung, *Going to the People: Chinese Intellectuals and Folk Literature, 1918–1937*, East Asia Monographs (Cambridge, Mass.: Harvard University Press, 1985), and Mark McConaghy, "Printing the Voice of the People: *Geyao Zhoukan* and the Heterogeneity of Minjian Culture," paper presented at Academia Sinica, Taipei, December 11, 2017.
41. Luo Zhitian, "Shifts of Social Power in Modern China: The Marginalization of Intellectuals and the Rise of Marginal Intellectuals," in *Inheritance Within Rupture: Culture and Scholarship in Early Twentieth Century China*, trans. Lane J. Harris and Mei Chun (Leiden: Brill, 2015), 185.
42. Li Hsiao-t'i, "Making a Name and a Culture for the Masses in Modern China." See also Li Hsiao-t'i, *Qingmo de xiaceng shehui qimeng yundong, 1901–1911* (Lower-class enlightenment in the late Qing period, 1901-1911) (Taipei: Institute of Modern History, Academia Sinica, 1992). In another essay, Li simply uses the phrase *minjian wenhua* to translate the notion of "popular culture." See Li Hsiao-t'i, "Shangceng wenhua yu minjian wenhua" (Elite culture and popular culture), *Jindai Zhongguoshi yanjiu tongxun*, no. 8 (1989): 95–104.
43. Chen Sihe, "Minjian de huanyuan" (The restoration of *minjian*), *Wenyi Zhengming*, no. 1 (1994): 53–61, especially the discussion of *Farewell My Concubine*, 59–60; Chen Sihe, "Minjian de chenfu" (The ups and downs of *minjian*), *Shanghai Wenxue*, no. 1 (1994): 68–80.
44. Gan Yang, "Minjian shehui gainian pipan" (A critique of the concept of *minjian* society), in *Beiju de Liliang: Cong minzhu yundong zouxiang minzhu zhengzhi* (The strength of a tragedy: From the democracy movement to democratic politics), ed. Lin Daoqun and Wu Zanmei (Hong Kong: Oxford University Press, 1993), 141–153.
45. Zhu Xueqin, "Sixiangshi shang de shizongzhe" (Those who vanished from intellectual history), *Dushu*, no. 10 (1995): 55–63.
46. Sun Yu, "Yuanqu de qunluo" (The faraway tribes), *Dushu*, no. 8 (2005): 81; Xu Xiao, *Ban sheng wei ren* (Half a life to become a person) (Beijing: Tongxin, 2005).
47. Qian Liqun, "Minjian sixiang de jianshou" (The resistance of *minjian* thought), *Dushu*, no. 9 (1998): 7–14. I thank Li Yuyang for drawing my attention to the essays by Zhu and Qian. Qian's project includes thinkers such as Gu Zhun, Tan Tianrong, and Yu Luoke. Interestingly, Yu Jianrong also drew attention to Yu Luoke as an important thinker of the Mao years ("Faxue boshi bu zhi Yu Luoke shi yizhong yihan" [It's a shame if a doctor of law does not know Yu Luoke], *Xinjingbao*, April 11, 2009, reprinted in Yu Jianrong, *Diceng lichang* [Shanghai: Shanghai Sanlian, 2010], 283–285).
48. Qian Liqun, "Gaige kaifang hou de zixiaershang de 'minjian shehui minzhu yundong'" (The bottom-up "democratic movement of *minjian* society" after Reform and Opening), interview by Chen Yizhong, June 25, 2008, originally posted on Chen's blog (now defunct), currently available on the Mingjing History website, http://www.mingjinglishi.com/2012/01/blog-post_7443.html.
49. Pierre Bourdieu, "The Intellectual Field: A World Apart" (1985), in *In Other Words: Essays Towards a Reflexive Sociology* (Stanford, Calif.: Stanford University Press, 1990), 144.

50. Foucault, "La fonction politique de l'intellectuel." See the detailed discussion and typology in chapter 1.
51. It could be argued that writers in the 2000s suffered from perceptions of growing commercialism and corruption of the literary field. See Julia Lovell, "Finding a Place: Mainland Chinese Fiction in the 2000s," *Journal of Asian Studies* 71, no. 1 (2012): 7–32. It can also be argued that mainland fiction has been gradually overshadowed by writing in Chinese produced outside the mainland. See David Der-wei Wang, introduction to *Chinese Literature in the Second Half of a Modern Century: A Critical Survey*, ed. David Der-wei Wang and Pang-Yuan Chi (Bloomington: Indiana University Press, 2000), xiii–xliii.
52. For a slightly different view of Fang, see Timothy Cheek, "From Priests to Professionals: Intellectuals and the State under the CCP," in *Popular Protest and Political Culture in Modern China*, ed. Jeffrey Wasserstrom and Elizabeth Perry (Boulder, Colo.: Westview Press, 1994), 198–199. Cheek argues that Fang was the first to articulate the project for intellectuals to form their own class, echoing George Konrád and Iván Szelényi's theory in *Intellectuals on the Road to Class Power* (New York: Harcourt, 1979).
53. Foucault, "La fonction politique de l'intellectuel," 110.
54. Qin Hui, "Zixu" (Author's Preface), in *Wenti yu zhuyi: Qin Hui wenxuan* (Problems and isms: Selected essays by Qin Hui) (Changchun: Changchun Press, 1999), 1–6.
55. David Kelly, "Guest Editor's Introduction," special issue on Qin Hui, *The Chinese Economy* 38, no. 4 (2005): 6.
56. Qin Hui, "Lun xiandai sixiang de gongtong dixian" (preface to the Korean translation of *Tianyuanshi yu kuangxiangqu* [Pastorals and Rhapsodies]), translated as "The Common Baseline of Modern Thought," trans. David Kelly, in special issue on Qin Hui, *The Chinese Economy* 38, no. 4 (July–August 2005): 19.
57. Qin Hui, "Zhongguo zhishifenzi dadou zai taolun jia wenti" (Chinese intellectuals are mostly discussing fake problems), *iFeng*, January 19, 2015.
58. See the discussion of Gloria Davies's study *Worrying About China: The Language of Chinese Critical Inquiry* (Cambridge, Mass.: Harvard University Press, 2007) in chapter 1.
59. See Gayatri Chakravorty Spivak, "Can the Subaltern Speak?" in *Marxism and the Interpretation of Culture*, ed. Cary Nelson and Lawrence Grossberg (Urbana: University of Illinois Press, 1988), 271–313. I thank the anonymous reviewer who pointed out how Spivak transformed Gramsci's adjective *sublaterno* (comparable in its use to *minjian*) into the collective noun "the subaltern" (comparable to *ruoshi qunti*). Guo Yuhua discusses Spivak and Gramsci in her study on rural collectivization, *Shoukuren de jiangshu: Jicun lishi yu yizhong wenming de luoji* (Narratives of the sufferers: The history of Jicun and the logic of civilization) (Hong Kong: Chinese University of Hong Kong Press, 2013), 2–3. Yu Jianrong mentions the Indian Subaltern Studies Group in his essay "Zhongguo de diceng shehui: Wode yanjiu he lichang," July 29, 2008, http://www.aisixiang.com/data/20274.html, translated as "China's Underclass: My Research and Standpoint," trans. Stacy Mosher, *Contemporary Chinese Thought* 45, no. 4 (2014): 41.
60. The possible appearance of such a linkage between students and workers in 1989 may have been a factor in the authorities' decision to use force.
61. Merle Goldman, "The Role of China's Public Intellectuals in the PRC," in *The People's Republic of China at 60: An International Assessment*, ed. William Kirby (Cambridge, Mass.: Harvard University Press, 2011), 334. Goldman dates this change to the links between

intellectuals and workers during the Tiananmen protests. Although Goldman believes that Charter 08, a call for institutional reform (discussed in chapter 5), is emblematic of this social diversification of public advocacy, the present study takes the view that Charter 08 is still strongly influenced by universalist "elite discourse," which led some intellectuals such as Qin Hui not to sign it.

62. Bourdieu, "The Intellectual Field," , 140–149. This question is further elaborated on in chapter 1.

63. Guo Yuhua, *Qingting diceng: Women ruhe jiangshu kunan* (Listening closely to the underclass: How we describe suffering) (Guilin: Guangxi Imaginist, 2011), 1–10 (originally published in *Dushu*, no. 6 [2008]). See also Pierre Bourdieu, *La misère du monde* (Paris: Le Seuil, 1993).

64. Qin Hui, "Women gai zenyang fansi wenge" (How should we remember the Cultural Revolution?), in *Wenti yu zhuyi*, 10–12. Gloria Davies highlights the importance of this short essay in *Worrying About China*, 216–217.

65. See, for example, a graph of the political spectrum in Fewsmith, *China Since Tiananmen*, xvii.

66. For a full discussion of these debates, see Timothy Cheek, David Ownby, and Joshua Fogel, "Mapping the Intellectual Public Sphere in China Today," *China Information* 32, no. 1 (2018): 107–120, as well as the five more detailed studies in *China Information* 32, nos. 1 and 2.

67. Qiu Zhijie, *From Huaxia to China*, 2015, ink on paper, https://www.artsy.net/artwork/qiu-zhijie-from-huaxia-to-china. This painting is part of Qiu's larger *Mapping the World* project and appears on the cover of this book.

68. Merle Goldman and Timothy Cheek, "Uncertain Change," in *China's Intellectuals and the State: In Search of a New Relationship*, ed. Merle Goldman and Timothy Cheek (Cambridge, Mass.: Council on East Asian Studies, 1987), 17.

69. Han Han, "Jue bu jiaru Zuoxie" (I will absolutely not join the Writers' Association), *Nanfang Zhoumo*, December 18, 2007, http://www.infzm.com/content/6948. The Writers' Association underwent structural reforms in 1992 and was downgraded from a *dang-zheng jiguan* (party-state organ) to a *shiye danwei* (administrative unit); the tenure system was reduced, and private profits (through commercial publishers) were encouraged. See Kong Shuyu, *Consuming Literature: Best Sellers and the Commercialization of Literary Production in Contemporary China* (Stanford, Calif.: Stanford University Press, 2005), 149.

70. Edward X. Gu and Merle Goldman, "Introduction: The Transformation of the Relationship Between Chinese Intellectuals and the State," in *Chinese Intellectuals Between State and Market*, ed. Gu and Goldman, 12.

71. Yuezhi Zhao, "Underdogs, Lapdogs, and Watchdogs: Journalists and the Public Sphere Problematic in China," in *Chinese Intellectuals Between State and Market*, ed. Gu and Goldman, 73.

72. See Anthony Spires, "Contingent Symbiosis and Civil Society in an Authoritarian State: Understanding the Survival of China's Grassroots NGOs," *American Journal of Sociology* 117, no. 1 (2011): 1–45; Fengshi Wu and Chan Kinman, "Graduated Control and Beyond: The Evolving Government-NGO Relations," *China Perspectives* 3 (2012): 9–17.

73. These developments demonstrate an interesting tension with the situation in post-Communist central and eastern Europe. Noting that after 1989 "the long glorified 'society' whose side dissidents took in their struggle against the communist state turned out to be the source of much antidemocratic nostalgia and emotion," Vladimir Tismaneanu underlines the need for "citizen-scholars"—that is, specific intellectuals who are critical of both the state and society ("Democratic Intellectuals Under Post-communism," in *Between Past and Future: The Revolutions of 1989 and Their Aftermath*, ed. Vladimir Tismaneanu and Antohi Sorin [Budapest: Open University Press, 2000], §36, https://books.openedition.org/ceup/1880).
74. Zhidong Hao, *Intellectuals at a Crossroads* (Albany: State University of New York Press, 2003), 138–139. See also a selection of articles from *Orient* (*Dongfang*) edited by Carine Defoort in *Contemporary Chinese Thought* 29, no. 2 (1997).
75. *The Golden Age* was published in 1992 first in Hong Kong, then in Taiwan, and was first published in China in 1994: *Huangjin shidai*, in *Wang Er fengliu shi* (The romantic adventures of Wang Er) (Hong Kong: Fan In, 1992); *Huangjin niandai*, (Taipei: Lianjing, 1992); and *Huangjin shidai* (Guangzhou: Huaxia, 1994).
76. Geremie Barmé mentions Wang Xiaobo in passing in the last chapter of *In the Red: On Contemporary Chinese Culture* (New York: Columbia University Press, 1999), 352, which suggests that Wang's significance only became apparent in later years. Barmé also notes elsewhere that Wang, "perhaps more than any other 1990s writer, represented the urbane skepticism of people both weary and wary of that abiding afflatus of China's chattering classes" ("The Revolution of Resistance," 296).
77. Xie Yong and Ding Dong, "Wang Xiaobo: Yiwei zhishifenzi he yige shidai" (Wang Xiaobo: An intellectual and an era) (1997), in *Wang Xiaobo yanjiu ziliao*, ed. Han Yuanhong, 1:134, 136.
78. Wang Xiaobo, "Chenmo de daduoshu," 10.
79. Wang Xiaobo, "Chenmo de daduoshu," 11.
80. Interestingly, Konrád and Szelényi had already pointed to the political dangers posed by an alliance between intellectuals in the technocracy and the "silent majority" in 1970s Hungary and the need for the ruling elite to take countermeasures: "Thus the ruling elite is reinforcing its supporters in the technocracy with the silent majority of the middle strata and with an ever-growing labor aristocracy, cutting across class lines to create, within every class, strata whose interests tie them to the ruling elite as much as to their own class" (*Intellectuals on the Road to Class Power*, 217).
81. Yang Guobin, "China's Other Revolution," reply to Edward Steinfeld, *Boston Review*, July 13, 2011, http://bostonreview.net/yang-social-empowerment.
82. Yue Wencheng, *Wang Xiaobo zhuan* (A biography of Wang Xiaobo) (Hangzhou: Zhejiang University Press, 2013), 131.
83. Ding Dong, "Xiaobo de rensheng xuanze—yu Li Yinhe nüshi tan Wang Xiaobo" (Xiaobo's life choices—discussing Wang Xiaobo with Ms. Li Yinhe, 1997), in *Wang Xiaobo yanjiu ziliao*, ed. Han Yuanhong, 1:270.
84. Ding Dong, "Xiaobo de rensheng xuanze," 1:264.
85. Wang Xiaobo, "Chenmo de daduoshu," 11.
86. Zeng Jinyan, "Duoyu de ren de xiaoshi" (The extinction of superfluous men), in *Zhongguo nüquan*, 235.

87. Ding Dong, "Xiaobo de rensheng xuanze," 265.
88. Dai Jinhua, "Zhizhe xixue—du Wang Xiaobo" (Banter of the cognoscenti—reading Wang Xiaobo) (1998), in *Wang Xiaobo yanjiu ziliao*, ed. Han Yuanhong, 1:292.
89. Wendy Larson, "Intellectuals, Sex, and Time in Wang Xiaobo's *The Golden Years*," in *From Ah Q to Lei Feng: Freud and Revolutionary Spirit in 20th Century China* (Stanford, Calif.: Stanford University Press, 2009), 148.
90. For example, Zhidong Hao believes that intellectuals in today's China may become the organic intellectuals of a more contentious working class (*Intellectuals at a Crossroads*, 307). This in a way is the aspiration of the New Left intellectuals in China who, despite professing their sympathy with the working class, still usually hope to play their traditional guiding role in harmony with the leadership.
91. Jan-Werner Müller, "European Intellectual History as Contemporary History," *Journal of Contemporary History* 46, no. 3 (2011): 574–590.
92. In this spirit and to facilitate further engagement with the ideas discussed later, I have tried to refer to existing English translations of quoted text whenever possible. When only the Chinese source is quoted, the translation is my own.

1. GRASSROOTS INTELLECTUALS: THEORETICAL AND HISTORICAL PERSPECTIVES

1. The noun *intellectuel* became popular in France in conjunction with Émile Zola's intervention into the Dreyfus Affair in 1898, at first as a pejorative term but subsequently reclaimed by the defenders of Dreyfus to highlight the writer's role as the proponent of Enlightenment rationality in the public sphere (see Christophe Charle, *Naissance des "intellectuels" 1880–1900* [Paris: Minuit, 1990]). However, the figure of the intellectual is generally considered to predate Zola's intervention. The Russian term *intelligentsia* appeared in the mid-nineteenth century (possibly originating in Poland) (Andrzej Walicki, "Polish Conceptions of the Intelligentsia and Its Calling," *Slavica Lundensia*, no. 22 [2005]" 1–22). Zygmunt Bauman identifies the "intellectual" with the Enlightenment *philosophe* who appeared in the eighteenth century (*Legislators and Interpreters: On Modernity, Post-modernity, and Intellectuals* [Ithaca, N.Y.: Cornell University Press, 1987], 21).
2. A good recent overview is provided in Christian Fleck, Andreas Hess, and E. Stina Lyon, eds., *Intellectuals and Their Publics: Perspectives from the Social Sciences* (New York: Routledge, 2009), in particular the introduction.
3. Lloyd Kramer, "Habermas, Foucault, and the Legacy of Enlightenment Intellectuals," in *Intellectuals and Public Life: Between Radicalism and Reform*, ed. Leon Fink, Stephen Leonard, and Donald Reid (Ithaca, N.Y.: Cornell University Press, 1996), 37, 38.
4. Kramer, "Habermas, Foucault, and the Legacy of Enlightenment Intellectuals," 42, 44.
5. Kramer concludes that "there is, finally, a commitment to criticism and even to rationality in Foucault's work which take it closer to Habermas than the dichotomies of contemporary intellectual life may suggest. The experts, after all, are still subjected to criticism; and the critics still make their cases with the learning and knowledge of experts" ("Habermas, Foucault, and the Legacy of Enlightenment Intellectuals," 47).

6. Antonio Gramsci, *The Gramsci Reader: Selected Writings 1916–1935* (New York: New York University Press, 2000), 303, 306.
7. Pierre Bourdieu, "The Intellectual Field: A World Apart" (1985), in *In Other Words: Essays Towards a Reflexive Sociology* (Stanford, Calif.: Stanford University Press, 1990), 145, 144.
8. "Sociology must take as its object, rather than being caught up in it, the struggle for the monopoly of legitimate representation of the social world" (Pierre Bourdieu, *Leçon sur la leçon* [Paris: Minuit, 1982], 13–14; translations of French-language texts are the author's unless otherwise noted).
9. Pierre Bourdieu, "Pour un corporatisme de l'universel" (1989), in *Les règles de l'art* (Paris: Seuil, Points, 1998), 547. This is why Bourdieu advocates a "corporatism of the universal": intellectuals should strengthen their autonomy within their field to speak out beyond their area of expertise.
10. Pierre Bourdieu, "Le fonctionnement du champ intellectuel," *Regards Sociologiques*, no. 17–18 (1999): 20.
11. Bourdieu, "The Intellectual Field," 146.
12. Michel Foucault, "La fonction politique de l'intellectuel" (1976), in *Dits et écrits*, 4 vols. (Paris: Gallimard, 1994), 3:109.
13. Foucault, "La fonction politique de l'intellectuel," 3:109, 110.
14. Foucault, "La fonction politique de l'intellectuel," 3:112.
15. Foucault, "La fonction politique de l'intellectuel," 3:113.
16. Gisèle Sapiro, "Modèles d'intervention politique des intellectuels," *Actes de la Recherche en Sciences Sociales*, nos. 176–177 (2009): 14. Table 1.1 in this chapter is a simplified version of Sapiro's model. In fact, Sapiro proposes a three-dimensional model that measures the intellectual's degree of universality versus specificity (Bourdieu's writer versus Foucault's expert), degree of autonomy versus heteronomy (proximity to power), and degree of domination within the field. She thus comes up with eight categories of intellectuals (corresponding to different historical situations and roles). She finds that the more dominant an intellectual is within a field, the more universalized and depoliticized his or her interventions are. Table 1.1 also has some similarities with Zhidong Hao's typology of Chinese intellectuals in *Intellectuals at a Crossroads* (Albany: State University of New York Press, 2003), 70, which proposes to measure the degree of loyalty to power (organic/unattached-neutral/critical) versus profession (humanistic/technical). The latter distinction is not unlike the one between universal and specialized. In Zhidong Hao and Zhengyang Guo, "Professors as Intellectuals in China: Political Identities and Roles in a Provincial University," *China Quarterly*, no. 228 (December 2016): 1039–1060, the typology is further refined to include three categories, now defined as "roles" rather than types: establishment/organic, nonestablishment/professional, contraestablishment/critical.
17. Intellectuals in totalitarian contexts have been studied mainly in the traditional author-by-author approach: for example, Mark Lilla, *The Reckless Mind: Intellectuals in Politics* (New York: New York Review of Books, 2001) and Joachim Fest, "Die Intellektuellen und die totalitäre Epoche: Gedanken zu einer Geschichte der Täuschungen und Enttäuschungen," in *Bürgerlichkeit als Lebensform: Späte Essays* (Reinbek bei Hamburg: Rowohlt, 2007), 163–190. More sociological approaches include George Konrád and

Iván Szelényi, *Intellectuals on the Road to Class Power* (New York: Harcourt, 1979), and Vladimir Shlapentokh, *Soviet Intellectuals and Political Power: The Post-Stalin Era* (Princeton, N.J.: Princeton University Press, 1990).

18. Stefan Auer notes that dissident intellectuals in central and eastern Europe were often less sanguine about their own role than were their counterparts in more liberal societies ("Public Intellectuals, East and West," in *Intellectuals and Their Publics*, ed. Fleck, Hess, and Lyon, 89–106). See also Václav Havel, "The Power of the Powerless," trans. Paul Wilson, in *The Power of the Powerless: Citizens Against the State in Central-Eastern Europe*, ed. John Keane (Armonk, N.Y.: M. E. Sharpe, 1985), 23–96, with the reference to "living in truth" on 39–44.
19. Czeslaw Milosz, *The Captive Mind* (New York: Vintage, 1990), 8, 11.
20. Konrád and Szelényi, *Intellectuals on the Road to Class Power*, 1, 32, 12, 222. See also Milovan Djilas, *The New Class: An Analysis of the Communist System* (New York: Harcourt Brace and Jovanovich, 1957).
21. In connection with China, Konrád and Szelényi note, "When Liu Shao-chi advocated an extension of rational redistribution on the Stalinist model, which would have resulted in a rapid growth of the Chinese working class and urban population, he was in fact advancing a class program for the intelligentsia, even though on the ideological plane he and his supporters had to come forward as spokesmen for industrialization and the working class" (*Intellectuals on the Road to Class Power*, 59). It is therefore consistent with their framework to see intellectuals' role as a possible leading class reasserted in China in the 1980s under Deng Xiaoping (as Liu Shaoqi's heir).
22. Miklós Haraszti, *The Velvet Prison: Artists Under State Socialism* (New York: Basic Books, 1987), 92.
23. Geremie Barmé, *In the Red: On Contemporary Chinese Culture* (New York: Columbia University Press, 1999).
24. Zygmunt Bauman, *Legislators and Interpreters: On Modernity, Post-modernity, and Intellectuals* (Ithaca, N.Y.: Cornell University Press, 1987), 1–7.
25. Bauman, *Legislators and Interpreters*, 175.
26. Edward Said, *Representations of the Intellectual* (New York: Pantheon Books, 1994), xvi–xviii.
27. Said, *Representations of the Intellectual*, xvii.
28. Said, *Representations of the Intellectual*, 64.
29. An excellent synthetic overview of the role of intellectuals in twentieth-century China is provided in Timothy Cheek, "Citizen Intellectuals in Historical Perspective: Reflections on Callahan's 'Citizen Ai,'" *Journal of Asian Studies* 73, no. 4 (2014): 921–925, and *The Intellectual in Modern Chinese History* (Cambridge: Cambridge University Press, 2016).
30. Yü Ying-shih, "Zhongguo zhishifenzi de bianyuanhua" (The marginalization of Chinese intellectuals), *Ershiyi Shiji* 6 (August 1991): 15–25. See also Jerome Grieder, *Intellectuals and the State in Modern China: A Narrative History* (New York: Free Press, 1981), 2.
31. The first is usually attributed to Fan Zhongyan (989–1052), the second to a gloss of Fan Zhongyan by Wang Fuzhi (1619–1692), and the third to Zhou Dunyi (1017–1073). The first two translations are borrowed from Perry Link, *Evening Chats in Beijing: Probing China's Predicament* (New York: Norton, 1992), 12.

32. Link, *Evening Chats in Beijing*, 12.
33. C. T. Hsia, "Obsession with China: The Moral Burden of Chinese Literature," in *A History of Modern Chinese Fiction*, 3rd ed. (Bloomington: Indiana University Press, 1999), 533–554; C. T. Hsia, *Zhongguo xiandai xiaoshuoshi* (A history of modern Chinese fiction) (Hong Kong: Chinese University of Hong Kong Press, 2001). More recently, scholars have taken issue with Hsia's own translation of "obsession with China" as *gan shi you guo*, and rephrased it as *zhimi Zhongguo*. See Wang Dewei, "Xiandai Zhongguo xiaoshuo yanjiu zai xifang" (Research on modern Chinese fiction in the West), *Zhongguo wenzhe yanjiu tongxun* 1, no. 3 (1991): 34.
34. Andrew Nathan, *Chinese Democracy* (New York: Knopf, 1985), 225–226.
35. Benjamin Schwartz, "The Intelligentsia in Communist China: A Tentative Comparison," *Daedalus*, no. 89 (1960): 611. By contrast, Timothy Cheek argues that the unifying theme of intellectual pursuits in the twentieth century has been "the self-appointed task and widely held social expectation of thinkers and writers in China to serve the public good" (rather than the state) (*The Intellectual in Modern Chinese History*, xii).
36. See, for example, Lu Xun, "Guanyu zhishi jieji" (On the intelligentsia), November 13, 1927, in *Jiwaiji shiyi bubian* (Addenda to the supplements to the uncollected essays), vol. 8 of *Lu Xun quanji* (Lu Xun: Complete Works), 18 vols. (Beijing: Renmin wenxue: 2005), 8:223–231, and Lu Xun, "Wenyi yu zhengzhi de qitu" (The branching paths of literature and politics), December 21, 1927, in *Jiwaiji* (Uncollected essays), in *Lu Xun quanji*, 7:115–123.
37. He Baogang, "Chinese Intellectuals Facing the Challenges of the New Century," in *Chinese Intellectuals Between State and Market*, ed. Edward X. Gu and Merle Goldman (London: Routledge, 2004), 267.
38. The term *zhishifenzi* displaced *zhishi jieji* (intellectual class), which, according to Lydia Liu was the first term borrowed from Japanese to translate the Russian term *intelligentsia* (*Translingual Practice: Literature, National Culture, and Translated Modernity—China, 1900–1937* [Stanford, Calif.: Stanford University Press, 1995], 302). In his famous essay "Lun zhishi jieji" (On the intellectual class, 1947), Fei Xiaotong still used the older term (see Eddy U, "Reifications of the Chinese Intellectual," *Modern China* 35, no. 6 [2009]: 604–631). U's argument that intellectuals were "reified" under Mao seems to mean that their social category was progressively reconstructed in Marxist terms against their own self-definition.
39. In "The Making of *Zhishifenzi*," *China Quarterly*, no. 173 (2003): 100–121, Eddy U shows how the registration process in the early 1950s drew a social boundary around a category of intellectuals very broadly defined as "mid and low-level white-collar workers" (120), with an education level of junior high school or higher, and at the same time institutionalized the CCP's distrust of them. U argues against the elitist bias in studying intellectuals and for a better recognition of the historically variable borders of this group in China. While the present study precisely seeks to redefine a category of "grassroots intellectuals," this category cannot be coterminous with Mao's "knowledge workers," which was an ideological rather than an analytical concept.
40. See various contributions in Timothy Cheek and Carol Lee Hamrin, eds., *China's Establishment Intellectuals* (Armonk, N.Y.: M. E. Sharpe, 1986), which discuss intellectuals' engagement with the PRC state despite the persecutions they encountered after 1949.

41. Timothy Cheek, "Deng Tuo: A Chinese Leninist Approach to Journalism," in *China's Establishment Intellectuals*, ed. Cheek and Hamrin, 92–123. See also Timothy Cheek, *Propaganda and Culture in Mao's China: Deng Tuo and the Intelligentsia* (Oxford: Clarendon Press, 1997).
42. Merle Goldman and Timothy Cheek, "Uncertain Change," in *China's Intellectuals and the State: In Search of a New Relationship*, ed. Merle Goldman and Timothy Cheek (Cambridge: Council on East Asian Studies, 1987), 3.
43. Yang Kuisong, *Renbuzhu de guanhuai: 1949 nian qianhou de shusheng yu zhengzhi* (Unbearable solicitude. Scholars and politics before and after 1949) (Guilin: Guangxi Normal, 2013), 106.
44. See Jean-François Billeter, "The System of Class Status," in *The Scope of State Power in China*, ed. Stuart Schram (London: School of Oriental and African Studies, University of London, 1985), 127–169, and James Watson, ed., *Class and Social Stratification in Post-revolution China* (Cambridge: Cambridge University Press, 1984). Therefore, although Eddy U is right to point out that after 1949 intellectuals were redefined in a nonelite manner, this redefinition did not necessarily prevent elitism from being reconfigured and practiced in new ways.
45. Lynn White, "Thought Workers in Deng's Time," in *China's Intellectuals and the State*, ed. Goldman and Cheek, 254.
46. Michel Bonnin and Yves Chevrier, "The Intellectual and the State: Social Dynamics of Intellectual Autonomy During the Post-Mao Era," *China Quarterly*, no. 127 (September 1991): 571–572.
47. Teresa Wright, "Intellectuals and the Politics of Protest: The Case of the China Democratic Party," in *Chinese Intellectuals Between State and Market*, ed. Gu and Goldman, 176.
48. Maurizio Marinelli, "Jiang Zemin's Discourse on Intellectuals: The Political Use of Formalised Language and the Conundrum of Stability," *Journal of Current Chinese Affairs* 42, no. 2 (2013): 119. See also Deng Xiaoping, "Zai quanguo kexue dahui kaimushi shang de jianghua" (Address at the opening ceremony of the national science conference), March 18, 1978, in *Deng Xiaoping Wenxuan* (Selected works of Deng Xiaoping), 2 vols. (Beijing: Renmin, 1983), 2:105.
49. For example, Yan Jiaqi became the youngest institute director at the Academy of Social Sciences when he took over the new institute of political science. See Carol Lee Hamrin, "Conclusion: New Trends Under Deng Xiaoping and His Successors," in *China's Intellectuals and the State*, ed. Goldman and Cheek, 300.
50. See Edward X. Gu, "Non-establishment Intellectuals, Public Space, and the Creation of Non-government Organizations in China," *China Journal* 39 (1998): 39–58.
51. Bonnin and Chevrier, "The Intellectual and the State," 569.
52. Bonnin and Chevrier, "The Intellectual and the State." See also Edward X. Gu, "Social Capital, Institutional Change, and the Development of Non-governmental Intellectual Organizations in China," in *Chinese Intellectuals Between State and Market*, ed. Gu and Goldman, 21–42. More generally, see Andrew Walder, *Communist Neo-traditionalism: Work and Authority in Chinese Industry* (Berkeley: University of California Press, 1986).
53. John Burns, "China's Governance," *China Quarterly*, no. 119 (September 1989): 503.
54. He Baogang, "Chinese Intellectuals Facing the Challenges of the New Century," in *Chinese Intellectuals Between State and Market*, ed. Gu and Goldman, 264.

55. Craig Calhoun, *Neither Gods nor Emperors: Students and the Struggle for Democracy in China* (Berkeley: University of California Press, 1994), 187.
56. He Baogang, "Chinese Intellectuals Facing the Challenges of the New Century," 266.
57. Timothy Cheek, "From Priests to Professionals: Intellectuals and the State Under the CCP," in *Popular Protest and Political Culture in Modern China*, ed. Jeffrey N. Wasserstrom and Elizabeth J. Perry (Boulder, Colo.: Westview Press, 1994), 184–205.
58. Joseph Fewsmith, *China Since Tiananmen*, 2nd ed. (New York: Cambridge University Press, 2008), 115.
59. See Yü Ying-shih, "Dai cong tou, shoushi jiu shanhe" (A new start, collecting the pieces of the old land), *Ershiyi Shiji*, no. 2 (December 1990): 5–7; "Zai lun Zhongguo xiandai sixiang zhong de jijin yu baoshou: Da Jiang Yihua xiansheng" (Further discussion of radicalism and conservatism in modern Chinese thought: A reply to Mr. Jiang Yihuah), *Ershiyi Shiji*, no. 10 (April 1992):143–149; and "The Radicalization of China in the Twentieth Century," *Daedalus* 122, no. 2 (1993): 125–150. See also Fewsmith, *China Since Tiananmen*, 91–92.
60. Chen Pingyuan, "Xueshushi, zhishifenzi, Minzuzhuyi" (History of scholarship, intellectuals, and nationalism), *Xiandai yu Chuantong*, no. 7 (1993): 27–35. See also Gloria Davies, *Worrying About China: The Language of Chinese Critical Inquiry* (Cambridge, Mass.: Harvard University Press, 2007), 213–214.
61. Jean-Philippe Béja, "The Role of Intellectuals in the Reform Process," *Contemporary Chinese Thought* 34, no. 4 (2003): 23.
62. Jiang Zemin's report to the Fourteenth Party Congress in 1992 stressed the importance of "reform of the cultural system" (*wenhua tizhi gaige*) See Kong Shuyu, *Consuming Literature: Best Sellers and the Commercialization of Literary Production in Contemporary China* (Stanford, Calif.: Stanford University Press, 2005), 28–29.
63. Zha Jianying, *China Pop* (New York: New Press, 1996). For a systematic study of the impact of marketization on the literary and cultural field, see Kong Shuyu, *Consuming Literature*.
64. He Baogang, "Chinese Intellectuals Facing the Challenges of the New Century," 270.
65. On the debate, see Barmé, *In the Red*, 283–301; Xu Jilin, "The Fate of an Enlightenment: 20 Years in the Chinese Intellectual Sphere," *East Asian History* 20 (2000): 181–184; Wang Chaohua, "Minds of the Nineties," in *One China, Many Paths*, ed. Wang Chaohua (London: Verso, 2003), 17–22; Davies, *Worrying About China*, 87–105; Jason McGrath, "Ideologies of Popular Culture: The 'Humanist Spirit" Debate," in *Postsocialist Modernity: Chinese Cinema, Literature, and Criticism in the Market Age* (Stanford, Calif.: Stanford University Press, 2008), 25–58; and Giorgio Strafella, *Intellectual Discourse in Reform Era China: The Debate on the Spirit of the Humanities in the 1990s* (London: Routledge, 2017).
66. Xu Jilin, "The Fate of an Enlightenment."
67. Xu Jilin, "Cong teshu zouxiang pubian" (From specific to universal), in *Gonggongxing yu gonggong zhishifenzi* (Publicness and public intellectuals) (Nanjing: Jiangsu Remin, 2003). In this chapter, Xu clearly takes the side of Habermas's endorsement of universality and enlightenment against what he sees as Foucault's relativism. See also Davies's discussion of Xu's position in her book *Worrying About China*, 104–105. Xu Jilin's more wide-ranging discussion in *Qimeng ruhe qi si huisheng: Xiandai Zhongguo zhishifenzi de sixiang*

kunjing (How enlightenment rose, died, and was reborn: The dilemmas of modern Chinese intellectuals) (Beijing: Peking University Press, 2010) includes a revised version of the original article (119–152).

68. Xu Jilin, Liu Qing, Luo Gang, and Xue Yi, "In Search of a Third Way: A Conversation Regarding 'Liberalism' and the 'New Left Wing,'" trans. Geremie Barmé, in *Voicing Concerns: Contemporary Chinese Critical Inquiry*, ed. Gloria Davies (Lanham, Md.: Rowman and Littlefield, 2001), 199–226.

69. Xu Jilin, "Zixu" (Preface), in *Ling yizhong qimeng* (Another kind of enlightenment) (Guangzhou: Huacheng, 1999), 14, and Cheek, *The Intellectual in Modern Chinese History*, 294.

70. Wang Chaohua, "Minds of the Nineties," 16–17. The name "New Left" was coined in January 1996 by the Hong Kong periodical *Mingpao Monthly* to refer mainly to four scholars: Wang Shaoguang and Hu Angang, who called for the reinforcement of "state capacity"; Cui Zhiyuan, who called for a "second emancipation" from liberalism and transition theory as well as for a return to the "institutional innovations" of Mao's regime; and Gan Yang, who argued for China's unique modernization path without urbanization and proletarianization. Wang Hui was initially quite critical of these four scholars, as illustrated in the essays written between 1996 and 1999 that are collected in *Sihuo chong wen* (Rekindling a dead fire) (Beijing: Renmin Wenxue, 2000). See also Lei Yi's critique of the New Left, "Beijing yu cuowei—ye tan Zhongguo de hou zhimin yu hou xiandai" (Background and misplacement—also on China's postcolonialism and postmodernism), *Dushu*, no. 4 (1995): 16–20.

71. See Fewsmith, *China Since Tiananmen*, 113–131; Kalpana Misra, "Neo-Left and Neo-Right in Post-Tiananmen China," *Asian Survey* 43, no. 5 (2003): 717–744; Xudong Zhang, *Postsocialism and Cultural Politics: China in the Last Decade of the Twentieth Century* (Durham, N.C.: Duke University Press, 2008), 78–101; Davies, *Worrying About China*, 72–86.

72. This debate was initiated by the senior journalist Zhou Ruijin, who under the collective name "Huang Fuping" published four commentaries supporting Deng in the Shanghai newspaper *Liberation Daily* from February to April 1991 (see Fewsmith, *China Since Tiananmen*, 49–50). These commentaries triggered a series of rebuttals, beginning with the article "Gaige kaifang keyi bu wen xing 'she' xing 'zi' ma?" (Is it possible not to ask whether Reform and Opening are surnamed C or S?) *Dangdai Sichao*, no. 2 (April 20, 1991): "Even as the wave of liberal thinking flooded everything, a catchphrase became fashionable 'don't ask if the surname is C or S.' . . . As a result, some people successfully guided reforms toward the evil road of capitalism. . . . Under this popular catchphrase, proponents of privatizing and marketizing the economy, establishing a multiparty system, a parliamentary regime, and pluralizing thinking have already pushed the socialist policy of Opening and Reforms into a blind alley" (quoted in Liu Qingsong, "Xing She haishi xing Zi?" [Is the surname S or C?], in *Zhen hua: 1978–2008 Zhongguo zhuangyu* [True words: Hyperbole in China 1978-2008] [Beijing: Jiuzhou, 2009], http://data.book.hexun.com/chapter-5196-3-26.shtml).

73. For a version of this view, see Zhu Xueqin, "For a Chinese Liberalism," in *One China, Many Paths*, ed. Wang Chaohua, 106–107. Jiang Zemin did not oppose this narrative: he continued to rely on a group of elite reformers in academia, couching his ideas in

"heart-to-heart" talks with twelve CASS scholars published in the fall of 1996 and later wooing the academic constituency in his famous speech for the one hundredth anniversary of PKU in 1998 (Fewsmith, *China Since Tiananmen*, 207–208).

74. In 1997, Wang Hui published his well-known essay "Xiandai Zhongguo de sixiang zhuangkuang yu xiandaixing wenti," *Tianya*, no. 5 (September–October 1997): 133–150; translated as "Contemporary Chinese Thought and the Question of Modernity," trans. Rebecca Karl, in Wang Hui, *China's New Order. Society, Politics, and Economy in Transition* (Cambridge, Mass.: Harvard University Press, 2003), 139–187. In it, he drew inspiration from non-Marxist critics of capitalism such as Karl Polanyi and Fernand Braudel and took to task the "simplistic" views of the "New Left" thinkers who did not understand the systemic nature of Max Weber's "crisis of modernity." He further argued that Mao provided an alternative "nonmodern modernity."

75. See Davies, *Worrying About China*, 72–86, and Wang Chaohua, "Minds of the Nineties," 22–26.

76. The earliest occurrence of the expression "crony capitalism" in the CNKI database is a brief piece by Wu Jinglian that compares China to Russia: "'Quangui ziben zhuyi' weihai yanzhong" (The danger of 'crony capitalism' is severe), *Lingdao Juece Xinxi*, no. 13 (April 2001): 17. Wu Jinglian lists three factions in the policy debate: believers in the market, believers in the planned economy, and proponents of crony capitalism. Qin Hui previously used the term *quangui* in his contribution to a discussion with journalist He Qinglian about her book *Zhongguo de xianjing* (China's trap) (Hong Kong: Mingjing, 1997; republished on the mainland one year later as *Xiandaihua de xianjing* [Modernization's trap] [Beijing: Jinri Zhongguo, 1998]), which exposed systemic corruption and social inequalities. See Qin Hui, "Shehui gongzheng yu xueshu liangxin" (Social justice and academic conscience), *Tianya*, no. 4 (1997): 4–9. Interestingly, although He Qinglian was criticized by liberal economists Fan Gang and Wang Shuguang, she was not endorsed by the Left but rather by critical liberals such as Qin Hui. See Wang Chaohua, "Minds of the Nineties," 30–33, and He Qinglian, "A Listing Social Structure," in *One China, Many Paths*, ed. Wang Chaohua, 163–188.

77. See Qin Hui, "Dividing the Big Family Assets," in *One China, Many Paths*, ed. Wang Chaohua, 148–149.

78. Some thinkers identified with the New Left have expressed satisfaction with the state-led capitalism pursued by the Chinese government since the late 1990s, and many "liberals" have criticized the cronyism, corruption, and inequalities resulting from it. As Jase Short writes about the New Left, "An assumption among many thinkers in this camp holds that China's bureaucratic state represents the interests of the vast majority, and that without its monopoly on political power neoliberal reforms would savage the population. That the Party's own reforms have savaged the population is apparently lost on those who hold this view, a view common enough among some sectors of the Western left who erroneously claim China to represent a kind of alternative to Western capitalism, rather than an example of neo-liberal capitalism" ("Review of *China's Rise: Strength and Fragility* by Au Loong-yu," *International Viewpoint*, March 23, 2015).

79. See Wang Chaohua, "Minds of the Nineties," 34–35.

80. See Sebastian Veg, "The Rise of China's 'Statist' Intellectuals: Law, Sovereignty, and 'Repoliticization,'" *China Journal*, forthcoming.

81. See, for example, Ge Zhaoguang, "Yi xiang tian kai: Jinnianlai dalu xin Ruxue de zhengzhi suqiu" (Indulging in wild fantasies: Political claims of New Confucians from mainland China in recent years), July 1, 2017, http://www.aisixiang.com/data/104951.html. Xu Xiliang similarly argues for distinguishing between a few Confucian democrats such as Sheng Hong and a majority of *guoxue* scholars whose main goal is to prevent political reforms ("Guoxue guoran shi yige yinmou" [Of course national studies are a conspiracy], *Caijing*, May 18, 2010).
82. Frederic Wakeman sets out five possible traditional roles: the policy maker, the practical reformer, the ethical idealist, the aesthete, and the eremite ("The Price of Autonomy: Intellectuals in Ming and Ch'ing Politics," *Daedalus* 101, no. 2 [1972]: 35–70).
83. Zhidong Hao, *Intellectuals at a Crossroads*, 56.
84. Merle Goldman, *China's Intellectuals: Advise and Dissent* (Cambridge, Mass.: Harvard University Press, 1981).
85. Goldman and Cheek, "Uncertain Change," 1.
86. Li Zehou, "Qimeng yu jiuwang de shuangchong bianzou" (Enlightenment and saving the nation: Variations on a duet), in *Zhongguo xiandai sixiangshi lun* (On modern Chinese intellectual history) (Beijing: Dongfang, 1987), 7–49. The article was originally published in the inaugural issue of *Zouxiang Weilai* (Toward the future) in 1986.
87. Zi Zhongyun, "Zhishifenzi dui daotong de chengzai yu shiluo" (Intellectuals' continuation and abandonment of the orthodoxy), *Caijing*, September 13, 2010.
88. Timothy Cheek, "The End of Intellectuals," in *The People's Republic of China at 60: An International Assessment*, ed. William Kirby (Cambridge, Mass.: Asia Center, Harvard University, 2011), 340. These roles are basically the same three discussed by Goldman and Cheek in "Uncertain Change": "service" refers to the role as ideological spokesperson, "subversion" to the role as moral critic, and "selling" to the professional elite. In a chapter on the 1996–2015 period in his most recent study, Cheek distinguishes between intellectuals in the establishment, in the academy, and in civil society (*The Intellectual in Modern Chinese History*, 262–319).
89. Cheek, "The End of Intellectuals," 353, 351.
90. He Li, *Political Thought and China's Transformation: Ideas Shaping Reform in Post-Mao China* (New York: Palgrave Macmillan, 2015). See also Ma Licheng, *Leading Schools of Thought in Contemporary China*, trans. Jing L. Liu (Singapore: World Scientific, 2013).
91. Zhang Boshu, *Gaibian Zhongguo: Liusi yilai de Zhongguo zhengzhi sichao* (Changing China: Trends in political thought in China since June Fourth) (Hong Kong: Fountainhead Books, 2015).
92. See Perry Link, *The Uses of Literature: Life in the Socialist Literary System* (Princeton, N.J.: Princeton University Press, 2000).
93. See, for example, Perry Link, "Politics and the Chinese Language," *China File*, December 26, 2012.
94. Gu and Goldman, *Chinese Intellectuals Between State and Market*.
95. Gu, "Social Capital, Institutional Change, and the Development of Non-governmental Intellectual Organizations in China," 21–42.
96. Zhidong Hao, *Intellectuals at a Crossroads*, 129–130. Prominent examples of semi-independent journals include *Xueren* (The scholar, edited by Chen Pingyuan), *Zhongguo Shehui Kexue Jikan* (China social science quarterly, edited by Deng Zhenglai), *Yuan Dao*

(Original way, edited by Chen Ming), *Res Publica* (*Gonggong Luncong*, edited by Liu Junning, 1994–2000), *Shijie* (Horizons, edited by Li Tuo), *Strategy and Management* (*Zhanlüe yu Guanli*, edited by Qin Zhaoying, closed down over a foreign-policy article in 1998), *Orient* (*Dongfang*, edited by Zhong Peizhang, 1993–1996, closed down over a Cultural Revolution issue), *Dushu* (Reading, edited by Huang Ping and Wang Hui, 1995–2007), *Tianya* (Horizon, edited by Han Shaogong and Jiang Zidan), *Yanhuang Chunqiu* (Annals of the Yellow Emperor, 1991–2016), as well as press enterprises supported by financial technocrats like *Caijing* (Finance and economics). Hao also lists a number of new television programs providing a newfound public space, in particular *Jiaodian fangtan* (Focus interview) and *Dongfang Shikong* (Eastern moment).

97. Zhidong Hao, *Intellectuals at a Crossroads*, 224. This view seems somewhat judgmental. First, it is not clear that all the people moving into commercial professions in the 1990s were previously universalistic, disinterested humanists in the 1980s. Many of them were no doubt "cogs and screws" (*luosiding*) in the post-Maoist state before they entered the market. Second, the rise of specialization has not only produced cash-hungry experts but also, as argued later, created the condition for a new type of critical autonomy.
98. Haraszti, *The Velvet Prison*, 157–158.
99. Barmé, *In the Red*, 12.
100. This policy is discussed through the example of the Chinese Academy of Social Sciences in Margaret Sleeboom-Faulkner, "Regulating Intellectual Life in China: The Case of the Chinese Academy of Social Sciences," *China Quarterly*, no. 189 (March 2007): 83–99.
101. Maurizio Marinelli, "Jiang Zemin's Discourse on Intellectuals: The Political Use of Formalised Language and the Conundrum of Stability," *Journal of Current Chinese Affairs* 42, no. 2 (2013): 122.
102. Jason McGrath, *Postsocialist Modernity: Chinese Cinema, Literature, and Criticism in the Market Age* (Stanford, Calif.: Stanford University Press, 2008), 13–18. It should be noted that "socialism" is still the official doctrine of the PRC, enshrined in its constitution, so using the term "postsocialism" also requires some care.
103. Jiemuxun (Fredric Jameson), *Houxiandaizhuyi yu wenhua lilun* (Postmodernism and cultural theory), trans. Tang Xiaobing (Xi'an: Shaanxi Shifan Daxue, 1986). See also Arif Dirlik and Zhang Xudong, "Postmodernism in China," and Wang Ning, "The Mapping of Chinese Postmodernity," *boundary 2* 23, no. 3 (1997): 1–18, 19–40. Wang Ning outlines various literary trends of the 1980s he sees as examples of postmodernism: avant-garde fiction, new realism, market literature (Wang Shuo), historical novels, literary criticism, and postcolonial discourse.
104. See Wang Chaohua, "Minds of the Nineties," 21–22.
105. This typology is inspired by Antoine Compagnon, *The Five Paradoxes of Modernity* (New York: Columbia University Press, 1994), 143–175.
106. See Thomas Epstein, introduction to Mikhail Epstein, Alexander Genis, and Slobodanka Vladiv-Glover, *Russian Postmodernism: New Perspectives on Post-Soviet Culture*, trans. Slobodanka Vladiv-Glover (New York: Berghahn Books, 1999), vii–xii. Conceptualism is cited as an example of exposing "the illusions of the self, the over-determinations of ideology and monological discourse, thereby opening Soviet-Russian culture to the experience of silence" (viii).

107. Davies, *Worrying About China*, 84.
108. Jing Wang, *High Culture Fever: Politics, Aesthetics, and Ideology in Deng's China* (Berkeley: University of California Press, 1996), 2–3.
109. Xudong Zhang, "The Return of the Political: The Making of the Post-Tiananmen Intellectual Field," in *Postsocialism and Cultural Politics*, 76. It is unfortunate that much of Zhang's argument is formulated in aggressively normative terms, which cast him as a partisan participant in the sterile factional debates of China's academic elite rather than as an even-minded observer. See, for example, his discussion of liberal theorists in the 1990s, where he refers to "the utterly pre-theoretical, uncritical and ahistorical argument of the 'liberal discourse' betrayed by Xu [Youyu] and Ren [Jiantao]'s writing" (55).
110. Xudong Zhang, "Introduction: The Cultural Politics of Postmodernism," in *Postsocialism and Cultural Politics*, 19–20.
111. See Xu Jilin, "The Fate of an Enlightenment," 183. Wang Shuo resisted being labeled an intellectual for many years, before he ultimately "recanted," as Barmé notes, ironically recognizing that "years of writing have turned me, also, into one of them, an intellectual" (Wang Shuo, preface to *Zixuanji* [Self-selected writings] [Beijing: Huayi, 1998], 4, quoted in Barmé, *In the Red*, 358).
112. Davies, *Worrying about China*, 15–18. Whether the notion of *youhuan* does carry such connotations is in fact the crux of the matter: in Joseph Levenson's perspective, the premodern notion of *youhuan* would have universal, ethical (rather than patriotic) value, and only its modern derivate after the demise of the Confucian order acquired a nationalist valence (*Confucian China and Its Modern Fate*, 3 vols. [London: Routledge, 1958–1965]).
113. Henry Zhao wrote in 1997: "Post-modernism has actually turned itself into a conformist theory in China which serves to justify the institutionalized mainstream culture" ("Post-ism and Chinese New Conservatism," *New Literary History* 28 [1997]: 42).
114. Wang Hui, "Contemporary Chinese Thought and the Question of Modernity," 170.
115. This argument echoes the conclusions of an earlier study by Ben Xu, *Disenchanted Democracy: Chinese Cultural Criticism After 1989* (Ann Arbor: University of Michigan Press, 1999), esp. chap. 3, 88–128.
116. For example, the academician system, reinstated in 1991, has resisted political intervention on at least two important occasions by invoking academic norms. See Richard Suttmeier and Cong Cao, "China's Technical Community: Market Reforms and the Changing Policy Cultures of Science," in *Chinese Intellectuals Between State and Market*, ed. Gu and Goldman, 138–157.
117. Davies, *Worrying About China*, 232. See also Rogier Creemers's notion of "monism" in intellectual inquiry in China in "Why Marx Still Matters: The Ideological Drivers of Chinese Politics," *China File*, December 16, 2014.

2. WANG XIAOBO AND THE SILENT MAJORITY: REDEFINING THE ROLE OF INTELLECTUALS AFTER TIANANMEN

1. *Huangjin shidai* (The golden age) was first published in a slim collection in Hong Kong, *Wang Er fengliu shi* (Hong Kong: Fan In, 1992), and subsequently in Taiwan under the title *Huangjin niandai* (Taipei: Lianjing, 1992).

2. See Wang Xiaobo, "Cong *Huangjin shidai* tan xiaoshuo yishu" (Discussing the art of fiction through *The Golden Age*), *Chuban Guang Jiao* 5 (1997), in *Wode jingshen jiayuan* (My spiritual home) (Kunming: Yunnan Renmin, 2006), 63–64.
3. Ai Xiaoming, "Shiji zhi jiao de wenxue xinling" (A literary soul at the turn of the century) (1997), in *Wang Xiaobo yanjiu ziliao* (Materials for research on Wang Xiaobo), 2 vols., ed. Han Yuanhong (Tianjin: Tianjin Renmin, 2009), 1:140–156.
4. Li Jing, Wang Xiaobo's first editor at *Beijing Wenxue*, has written about the huge difficulties involved in getting Wang's first pieces of fiction through the censorship system. See Li Jing, "Wang Xiaobo tuigao ji" (The story of Wang Xiaobo's rejected manuscripts), *Shucheng*, May 2014, 35–40.
5. See Ying Xia, Bing Guan, and Gong Cheng, "Power Structure and Media Autonomy in China: The Case of *Southern Weekend*," *Journal of Contemporary China* 26, no. 104 (2017): 233–248.
6. Wang Xiaobo, "Chenmo de daduoshu" (The silent majority), in *Siwei de lequ* (The pleasure of thinking) (Kunming: Yunnan Renmin, 2006), 10.
7. As formulated by Wang Fuzhi; see chapter 1, note 31.
8. Wang Xiaobo, "Siwei de lequ" (The pleasure of thinking), in *Siwei de lequ*, 19.
9. Wang Xiaobo, "Lunzhan yu daode" (Word fights and morals), *Dongfang*, no. 4 (1994), in *Siwei de lequ*, 56.
10. Wang Xiaobo, "Zhongguo zhishifenzi yu zhonggu yifeng" (Chinese intellectuals and their medieval ways), *Dongfang*, no. 3 (1994), in *Siwei de lequ*, 23–24.
11. Wang Xiaobo, "Zhongguo zhishifenzi yu zhonggu yifeng," 26.
12. See Yang Jiang, *Xizao* (Shower) (Hong Kong: Sanlian, 1988), and Yang Jiang, *Baptism*, trans. Judith Amory and Yaohua Shi (Hong Kong: Hong Kong University Press, 2007).
13. Wang Xiaobo, "Zhishifenzi de buxing" (The misfortune of intellectuals), *Dongfang*, no. 2 (1996), in *Siwei de lequ*, 29.
14. Wang Xiaobo, "Zhishifenzi de buxing," 30.
15. Wang Xiaobo, "Zhishifenzi de buxing," 32. Yao Wenyuan (1931–2005) was originally a literary critic who became a member of the radical Gang of Four in the 1970s.
16. Wang Xiaobo, "Wo kan guoxue" (My view of national studies), *Zhongguo Qingnian Yanjiu*, no. 2 (1995), in *Siwei de lequ*, 82.
17. Wang Xiaobo, "Jiushi qingjie yu bairimeng" (The save-the-world complex and dreaming wide awake), *Nanfang Zhoumo*, August 23, 1996, in *Siwei de lequ*, 95.
18. Wang Xiaobo, "Renxing de nizhuan" (Reversing humanity), in *Siwei de lequ*, 108.
19. Wang Xiaobo, "Renxing de nizhuan," 111.
20. Wang Xiaobo, "Renxing de nizhuan," 113.
21. Wang Xiaobo, "Tiyan shenghuo" (Experiencing life), *Sanlian shenghuo zhoukan*, no. 13 (1996), in *Siwei de lequ*, 140.
22. Wang Xiaobo, "Wo kan lao san jie" (My view of the three old cohorts), *Zhongguo Qingjian Yanjiu*, no. 6 (1995), in *Wode jingshen jiayuan*, 15.
23. Wang Xiaobo, "Daode duoluo yu zhishifenzi" (Moral collapse and intellectuals), in *Siwei de lequ*, 52.
24. In this vein, the historian Yang Zao points out that although Wang Shuo uses lowbrow vulgarity (*disu*) to unmask the hypocrisy of what writers in the 1980s idealized as the

"sublime" (*chonggao*), Wang Xiaobo counters the coercion of power with a form of carnivalesque that is not simply cynical. See Yang Zao, "Yi fei Wang Xiaobo de fangshi jinian Wang Xiaobo, tai kebeile" (Commemorating Wang Xiaobo in an un-Wang-Xiaobo-like way is too sad), *Dajia*, April 18, 2017.

25. Wang Xiaobo, "Huangdi zuo xiti" (The emperor does exercises), *Nanfang Zhoumo*, March 28, 1997, in *Siwei de lequ*, 142.
26. Wang Xiaobo, "Lixiangguo yu zherenwang" (The ideal republic and the philosopher-king), in *Siwei de lequ*, 94.
27. Quoted in Wang Xiaobo, "Zhihui yu guoxue" (Knowledge and national studies), *Dushu*, no. 11 (1995), in *Siwei de lequ*, 87.
28. Wang Xiaobo, "Kexue de meihao" (The beauty of science), *Jinqiu Ke Yuan* (Autumn World of Science), no. 1 (1997), in *Siwei de lequ*, 174.
29. Wang Xiaobo, "Kexue de meihao," 175.
30. Wang Xiaobo, "Zixu" (Author's preface) (June 1995), in *Siwei de lequ*, 1.
31. Wang Xiaobo, "Xu" (Preface) (March 20, 1997), in *Wode jingshen jiayuan*, 1.
32. Wang Xiaobo, "Xu," in *Wode jingshen jiayuan*, 3.
33. Wang Xiaobo, "Siwei de lequ," 16.
34. Wang Xiaobo, "Wenhua zhi zheng" (Culture wars), in *Siwei de lequ*, 67–70.
35. Wang Xiaobo, "Zhihui yu guoxue," 86.
36. Wang Xiaobo, "Chenmo de daduoshu," 4. The five red categories were revolutionary cadres, martyrs, workers, soldiers, and peasants; the five black ones were landlords, rich peasants, counterrevolutionaries, "bad elements," and rightists.
37. Wang Xiaobo, "Chenmo de daduoshu," 3, 8.
38. Wang Xiaobo, "Chenmo de daduoshu," 8.
39. A similar idea is expressed in *The Golden Age*, when the main character, Wang Er, initially refuses to confess because he will not adopt the language of the party cadres and finally only agrees to write a confession as a form of fictional writing, which he uses to mock them. The notion of "youth without regrets" emerged during the wave of nostalgia among former sent-down youths in the early 1990s.
40. At this time, Foucault was hardly known in China. On Foucault's reception in the late 1990s and the PKU Foucault reading club, see Zhang Xu, "Women wei shenme name milian Fuke?" (Why were we so infatuated with Foucault?), *Pengpai*, December 30, 2014, http://www.guancha.cn/zhangxu/2014_12_30_304850.shtml.
41. Wang Xiaobo directly criticizes educated youth literature in "The Courage to Admit," an essay he wrote after watching *The Passing of Years* (*Nianlun*, 年輪), a famous television series on the rustication movement: "Authors of educated youth literature always deal with issues in this way: the times left no choice, history left no choice. It seems that one has no responsibility when one makes a fool of oneself" ("Chengren de yongqi" [The courage to admit], in *Wode jingshen jiayuan*, 140).
42. Wang Xiaobo, "Chengren de yongqi," 140–141.
43. Wang Xiaobo, "Chengren de yongqi," 142.
44. See the interview of Ai Xiaoming by Song Hua and Wang Xiaoping, "Chengzhang suiyue" (The years of growing up) (2007), in *Wang Xiaobo yanjiu ziliao*, ed. Han Yuanhong, 1:165–166.

45. Wang Xiaobo, "Wo wei shenme yao xiezuo" (Why I decided to write), *Xianggang Wenxue*, no. 111 (March 1994), in *Wode jingshen jiayuan*, 52.
46. Wang Xiaobo, "Siwei de lequ," 15. Sir Thomas More is often quoted in China as a precursor of socialism.
47. Wang Xiaobo, "Lixiangguo yu zherenwang," 91–92.
48. Wang Xiaobo, "*Daijia lun*, wutuobang, shengren" (*The Theory of the Price to Pay*, utopia, sages), *Bolan Qunshu*, no. 5 (1997), in *Siwei de lequ*, 196.
49. Wang Xiaobo, "*Daijia lun*, wutuobang, shengren," 196.
50. Wang Xiaobo, "Lixiangguo yu zherenwang," 93.
51. Wang Xiaobo, "Lixiangguo yu zherenwang," 94.
52. Wang Xiaobo, "Siwei de lequ," 17–18.
53. Wang Xiaobo, "Shenghuo he xiaoshuo" (Life and fiction), in *Wode jingshen jiayuan*, 11.
54. Li Jing, "Yige zuojia de jingshen shiye—chongdu Wang Xiaobo zawen" (A writer's spiritual perspective—rereading Wang Xiaobo's essays), *Nanfang Wentan*, no. 2 (2008), in *Wang Xiaobo yanjiu ziliao*, ed. Han Yuanhong, 2:655. Fang Wei also makes this point, underscoring that although Wang Xiaobo was reimagined as a "cultural hero of liberalism," he opposed the cultural elitism of the enlightenment of the 1980s (*Wenhua beilun yu wenxue chuangxin: shijiemo wenhua zhuanxing zhong de Wang Xiaobo yanjiu* [Cultural paradox and literary creation: Wang Xiaobo research in the fin-de-siècle cultural transition] [Shanghai: Shanghai Sanlian, 2010], 170).
55. Wang Xiaobo, "Yang guizi yu Gu Hongming" (The foreign devil and Gu Hongming), *Sanlian Shenghuo Zhoukan*, no. 15 (1996), in *Siwei de lequ*, 79.
56. Wang further compares the sadomasochistic relation between intellectuals and the Maoist state to the adventures of a "sadist bisexual foreign devil" who visits the court of the Qing emperor: "When he heard that a vassal must salute the emperor by kneeling three times and kowtowing nine times, he immediately had an emperor dream: playing such an amusing sexual game every day would be worth dying for. Overall, in his eyes, the Chinese political system of the time was a delicious sexual game and sexual ceremony; unfortunately he was a foreign devil and could only watch, not play" ("Yang guizi yu Gu Hongming," 78).
57. Wang Xiaobo, "Jingxi xia'ai minzuzhuyi de guhuo xuanchuan" (Raise our guard against the poisonous propaganda of narrow nationalism), *Sanlian Shenghuo Zhoukan*, no. 22 (1996), in *Siwei de lequ*, 102.
58. Wang Xiaobo, "Duzi li de zhanzheng" (War in the belly), *Sanlian Shenghuo Zhoukan*, no. 9 (1997), in *Siwei de lequ*, 127–128.
59. Wang Xiaobo, "Jiduan tiyan" (Extreme experience), *Nanfang Zhoumo*, October 11, 1996, in *Siwei de lequ*, 76.
60. Wang Xiaobo, "Xu," in *Wode jingshen jiayuan*, 2. See also Song Qiang, Zhang Cangcang, and Qiao Bian, *Zhongguo keyi shuo bu: Hou lengzhan shidai de zhengzhi yu qinggan jueze* (China can say no: Political and emotional choices in the post–Cold War era) (Beijing: Zhonghua Gongshang Lianhe, 1996).
61. Xu Jilin, "Ta si gu ta zai: Wang Xiaobo de sixiang shijie" (He thinks, therefore he is: Wang Xiaobo's intellectual world), *Shanghai Wenxue*, no. 12 (1997), in *Wang Xiaobo yanjiu ziliao*, ed. Han Yuanhong, 2:581.

62. Dai Jinhua, "Zhizhe xixue—du Wang Xiaobo" (Banter of the cognoscenti—Reading Wang Xiaobo) (1998), in *Wang Xiaobo yanjiu ziliao*, ed. Han Yuanhong, 1:298.
63. Wang Xiaobo, "Wo kan wenhua re" (My view of cultural fever), *Nanfang Zhoumo*, July 12, 1996, in *Siwei de lequ*, 65.
64. Dai Jinhua, "Zhizhe xixue," 1:290.
65. Wang Xiaobo, "Xie gei xin de yinian (1997 nian)" (Written for the new year 1997), *Guangming Ribao*, January 3, 1997, in *Wode jingshen jiayuan*, 218–219.
66. Li Yinhe, "Langman qishi, xingyin shiren, ziyou sixiangjia—dao Wang Xiaobo" (Romantic knight, humming poet, free thinker: Mourning Wang Xiaobo) (1998), in *Wang Xiaobo yanjiu ziliao*, ed. Han Yuanhong, 1:160.
67. Ding Dong, "Xiaobo de rensheng xuanze," interview with Li Yinhe, in *Wang Xiaobo yanjiu ziliao*, ed. Han Yuanhong, 1:271.
68. Qin Hui, "Liushui qianbo huan houbo—lun Wang Xiaobo yu dangdai piping xianshizhuyi wenxue de mingyun" (A first wave announces a groundswell—on Wang Xiaobo and the fate of critical realism in contemporary literature) (1998), in *Wang Xiaobo yanjiu ziliao*, ed. Han Yuanhong, 1:321.
69. Wang Xiaobo, "Jiji de jielun" (A positive conclusion), *Zhongguo Qingnian Yanjiu*, no. 4 (1994), in *Siwei de lequ*, 40–41.
70. Wang Xiaobo, "Chenmo de daduoshu," 12.
71. For example, a chronological search in the CNKI database suggests that, apart from a few isolated articles in biology (referring to "weak" groups of mice or other test animals), the first articles that substantively use the term *ruoshi qunti* appeared in 1997, the year following the publication of "The Silent Majority." Two representative early articles are: Ureltu (Wure'ertu), "Ruoshi qunti de xiezuo" (Vulnerable group literature), *Tianya*, no. 2 (1997): 26–30 (an essay by a writer of the Evenki ethnic group who discusses Ralph Ellison's novel *Invisible Man*), and Song Xiuqing, "Ji xu guanzhu de shehui ruoshi qunti: Chengshi pinkun renkou" (A vulnerable group in society that urgently needs attention: The urban poor), *Baike Zhishi*, no. 7 (1997): 41–42, a short article by a PKU sociologist. Sun Wanning considers the term *diceng* the Chinese equivalent of "subaltern"; she further discusses the notion of the "subaltern in China" but refers only to Western scholarship (*Subaltern China: Rural Migrants, Media, and Cultural Practices* [Lanham, Md.: Rowman and Littlefield, 2014], 11, 32–41). See also the double special issue "Class and Class Consciousness in China" of *Journal of Contemporary China* 21, nos. 77–78 (2012).
72. Author's interview with Li Yinhe, Beijing, July 12, 2017.
73. The terms *youshi* (dominant) and *ruoshi* (dominated) can be found in Chinese translations of certain texts by Marx; for example, *youshi* appears in *German Ideology* to refer to "dominant countries."
74. Havel's essay first received attention in China when Leo Ou-fan Lee published a Chinese review of its English translation in the inaugural issue of *Twenty-First Century* in 1990. See Li Ou-fan, "Haweier de qishi" (The lessons from Havel), *Ershiyi Shiji*, no. 1 (October 1990): 48–53. It is quite possible that Wang Xiaobo obtained a copy of this important inaugural issue, which also contained an article by his teacher Hsu Cho-yun. Cui Weiping published an underground collection of Havel's writings in 1994. See Wen

Hai, *Fangzhu de ningshi: Jianzheng Zhongguo duli jilupian* (The banished gaze: Chinese independent documentary) (Taipei: Tendency, 2016), 32 n. 5. See also Cui Weiping, "Hawei'er yu dangdai Zhongguo zhishifenzi" (Havel and contemporary Chinese intellectuals), interview by Shen Shan, *Ai Sixiang*, December 19, 2011. Havel became more widely known in China through an essay by Li Shenzhi, "Wuquanzhe de quanli he fanzhengzhi de zhengzhi: Hou jiquanzhuyi shidai de rensheng zhexue" (The power of the powerless and antipolitical politics: The life philosophy of a post-totalitarian time), *Guancha Wencong*, no. 1 (January 1999). It is included in a later version of Cui's collection on the Chinese community website Boxun, http://blog.boxun.com/sixiang/haweier/index.htm. *Beijing Literature* ran a special feature on Havel in February 1999 (6–24), including Xu Youyu's essay "Cunzai de yiyi he daode de zhengzhi" (The meaning of existence and the politics of morality), Cui's essay "Xinyang Shenghuo" (Believing in life), and extracts from "Power of the Powerless."

75. David Goodman, *Class in Contemporary China* (Cambridge: Polity Press, 2014), 14. For a comprehensive discussion, see also James Watson, ed., *Class and Social Stratification in Post-revolution China* (Cambridge: Cambridge University Press, 1984).

76. Goodman, *Class in Contemporary China*, 9. In the 1970s, the two classes, workers and peasants, were complemented by adding one "stratum," intellectuals.

77. "Resolution on Certain Questions in the History of Our Party Since the Founding of the People's Republic of China," June 27, 1981, https://www.marxists.org/subject/china/documents/cpc/history/01.htm.

78. In parallel to the orthodox view of class according to ideology, Lu Xueyi developed a typology of class (strata) by occupation. Drawing on Anthony Giddens's notion of occupational class, he derived ten strata from surveys of working population. See Lu Xueyi, *Dangdai Zhongguo jieceng yanjiu baogao* (Report on social classes in contemporary China) (Beijing: Shehui Kexue Wenxian, 2002). Although the relation between the notions of class and stratum remained ambiguous, the strata were supposed to support the notion of an olive-shaped society with a large middle class advocated by Jiang Zemin. See also Alvin So, "The Changing Pattern of Classes and Class Conflict in China," *Journal of Contemporary China*, no. 33 (2003): 363–376; Iván Szelényi, "A Theory of Transitions," *Modern China*, no. 34 (2008): 165–175; and Pun Ngai and Chris Chan, "The Subsumption of Class Discourse in China," *boundary 2* 35, no. 2 (2008): 84.

79. See Sally Sargeson, "The Demise of China's Peasantry as a Class," *Asia Pacific Journal* 14, no. 13 (2016), http://apjjf.org/2016/13/Sargeson.html. Of course, the notion of *nongmin* (peasant) was a Communist construction. Myron T. Cohen argues that the most common premodern words for "farmer" were *nongfu* and *zhuanghu* ("Cultural and Political Inventions in Modern China: The Case of the Chinese 'Peasant,'" in "China in Transformation," special issue of *Daedalus* 122, no. 2 [1993]: 151–170).

80. See Lin Chun, "Qingxing de shaoshu" (The lucid minority), *Dushu*, no. 5 (1998): 51–55.

81. Wang Xiaobo, "Zhongguo zhishifenzi yu zhonggu yifeng," 21.

82. He Qinglian, "Dangqian Zhongguo shehui jiegou yanbian de zongtixing fenxi" (General analysis of the changes in current Chinese society), *Shuwu*, March 2000. See also He Qinglian, "A Listing Social Structure," in *One China, Many Paths*, ed. Wang Chaohua (London: Verso, 2003), 163–188; Qin Hui, "Fin de Siècle China: Economic Transition, Social Justice, and Democracy," *The Chinese Economy* 38, no. 5 (2005): 3–54.

83. He Qinglian, "A Listing Social Structure," 177.
84. Wang Xiaobo, "Daode baoshouzhuyi ji qita" (Moral conservatism and other things), *Dongfang*, no. 5 (1994), in *Siwei de lequ*, 63.
85. Wang Xiaobo, "You yu wu" (To have and have not), in *Siwei de lequ*, 187.
86. See Sebastian Veg, "Utopian Fiction and Critical Examination: The Cultural Revolution in Wang Xiaobo's *The Golden Age*," *China Perspectives*, no. 4 (2007): 75–87.
87. Wang Xiaobo, "Yizhi teli duxing de zhu" (An unconventional, independent pig), *Sanlian Shenghuo Zhoukan*, no. 11 (1996), in *Siwei de lequ*, 130, 131.
88. Wang Xiaobo, "Li Yinhe de *Zhongguoren de xing'ai yu hunyin*" (Li Yinhe's *Sex and Marriage Among the Chinese*), in *Wode jingshen jiayuan*, 29.
89. Wang Xiaobo, "Li Yinhe de *Zhongguoren de xing'ai yu hunyin*," 31.
90. In 1997, "hooliganism" was decriminalized; in 2001, homosexuality was removed from the list of mental diseases.
91. Wang Xiaobo, "Guanyu tongxinglian wenti" (On the problem of homosexuality), *Zhongguo Qingnian Yanjiu*, no. 1 (1994), in *Wode jingshen jiayuan*, 37. See also Li Yinhe, *Tamen de shijie: Zhongguo nan tongxinglian qunluo toushi* (Their World: Perspectives on the community of China's male homosexuals) (Taiyuan: Shanxi Renmin, 1992).
92. Wang Xiaobo, "Youguan tongxinglian de lunli wenti" (On the ethical problem of homosexuality), in *Wode jingshen jiayuan*, 39.
93. Wang Xiaobo, "*Tamen de shijie* xu" (Preface to *Their World*) (November 1992), in *Wode jingshen jiayuan*, 43.
94. The term *bentu* refers both to the grassroots nature of the investigation and to the "indigenization" of sociological methods as advocated by Fei.
95. Wang Xiaobo, "Kaowen shehuixue" (Putting sociology to the test), *Fangfa*, no. 12 (1997), in *Wode jingshen jiayuan*, 50.
96. Charles Taylor developed the notion of "equal dignity" in *Multiculturalism and the Politics of Recognition* (Princeton, N.J.: Princeton University Press, 1992).
97. Wang Xiaobo, "Geren zunyan" (Personal dignity), *Sanlian Shenghuo Zhoukan*, no. 5 (1995), in *Wode jingshen jiayuan*, 176.
98. Wang Xiaobo, "Yinshi weisheng yu zunyan" (Food hygiene and dignity), *Liaoning Qingnian*, no. 3 (1996), in *Wode jingshen jiayuan*, 186.
99. Wang Xiaobo, "Juzhu huanjing yu zunyan" (Living environment and dignity), *Liaoning Qingnian*, no. 2 (1996), in *Wode jingshen jiayuan*, 183.
100. Wang Xiaobo, "Junzi de zunyan" (The dignity of the gentleman), *Sanlian Shenghuo Zhoukan*, no. 5 (1995), in *Wode jingshen jiayuan*, 180.
101. Wang Xiaobo, "Wenhua de yuandi" (The garden of culture), *Sanlian Shenghuo Zhoukan*, no. 17 (1996), in *Wode jingshen jiayuan*, 171–172.
102. Wang Xiaobo, "Xie gei xin de yinian (1996)" (For the new year 1996), in *Wode jingshen jiayuan*, 216.
103. Li Yinhe, Han Yuanhong, and Zang Ce, "Guanyu Wang Xiaobo de duihua" (A dialogue on Wang Xiaobo), in *Wang Xiaobo yanjiu ziliao*, ed. Han Yuanhong, 1:2.
104. Ai Xiaoming, "Bu xu cisheng" (A life not lived in vain), in *Wang Xiaobo yanjiu ziliao*, ed. Han Yuanhong, 1:277.
105. Yi Hui, "Kuangye manyou" (Flaneur in the wilderness), in *Dangdai wenxue guankui* (A peek at contemporary literature) (Beijing: Wenhua Yishu, 2014), 168.

106. Sun Yu, "Wang Xiaobo yimo" (Wang Xiaobo's posthumous manuscripts), *Shouhuo*, June 2010.
107. Wang Xiaobo, "Chenmo de daduoshu," 11.
108. Li Jing, "Yige zuojia de jingshen shiye," 2:653.
109. Wang Xiaobo, "Chenmo de daduoshu," 12.
110. Wang Xiaobo, "Xiaoshuo de yishu" (The art of fiction), *Bolan Qun Shu*, no. 3 (1996), in *Wode jingshen jiayuan*, 61.
111. Wang Xiaobo, "Yishu yu guanhuai ruoshi qunti" (Art and caring for vulnerable groups), *Zhonghua Dushubao*, February 28, 1996, in *Wode jingshen jiayuan*, 150.
112. Wang Xiaobo, "Cong *Huangjin shidai* tan xiaoshuo yishu," 63–64.
113. Chen Xiaoming, *Biaoyi de jiaolü: Lishi qumei yu dangdai wenxue biange* (Ideographic anxieties: Historical exorcism and contemporary literary transformation) (Beijing: Zhongyang Bianyi, 2001), 321, quoted and translated in Jason McGrath, *Postsocialist Modernity: Chinese Cinema, Literature, and Criticism in the Market Age* (Stanford, Calif.: Stanford University Press, 2008), 78.
114. Zhu Wen, "Duanlie: Yifen wenjuan he 56 fen dajuan" (Rupture: 1 questionnaire and 56 responses), *Beijing Wenxue*, no. 10 (1998): 19–47. A book version later appeared under the title: *Duanlie: Shijimo de wenxue shigu. Ziyou zuojia fangtanlu* (Rupture: A fin de siècle literary incident. Interviews with freelance writers), ed. Wang Jifang (Nanjing: Jiangsu Wenyi, 2000). For further discussion of Duanlie, see Kong Shuyu, *Consuming Literature: Best Sellers and the Commercialization of Literary Production in Contemporary China* (Stanford, Calif.: Stanford University Press, 2005), 34. Geremie Barmé notes the irony of publishing this manifesto in a leading official magazine ("Time's Arrow: Imaginative Pasts and Nostalgic Futures," in *Voicing Concerns: Contemporary Chinese Critical Inquiry*, ed. Gloria Davies [Lanham, Md.: Rowman and Littlefield, 2001], 238). Jason McGrath espouses Chen Xiaoming's argument that the significance of the Rupture writers lies in their turn to "the details of daily life[, which] now become magnified to the point of achieving an estranging perspective that gives the stories a modernist sensibility despite their relative lack of formal experimentation" (*Postsocialist Modernity*, 79). Wu Yiqin argues that Duanlie marked the beginning of the "new generation fiction [*xin shengdai xiaoshuo*]" (*Ziyou yu juxian: Zhongguo dangdai xinshengdai xiaoshuojia lun* [Freedom and constraints: On contemporary China's new generation fiction writers] [Beijing: Renmin Wenxue, 2010], 8–10). Julia Lovell places Murong Xuecun and Xu Zechen among the contemporary heirs to the "contrarian" writing of the Rupture authors ("Finding a Place: Mainland Chinese Fiction in the 2000s," *Journal of Asian Studies* 71, no. 1 [2012]: 20–23).
115. Zhu Wen, "Duanlie: Yifen wenjuan he 56 fen dajuan" (Rupture: 1 questionnaire and 56 responses), in *Duanlie*, ed. Wang Jifang, 267–271.
116. Han Dong, "Beiwang: Youguan 'Duanlie' xingwei de wenti huida" (Memo: About the answers to the questions in the "Rupture" action), in *Duanlie*, ed. Wang Jifang, 309.
117. Han Dong, "Beiwang," 310, 311.
118. Quoted in Eric Abrahamsen, "Broken," *Words Without Borders*, August 2008, http://www.wordswithoutborders.org/article/broken.
119. The title *Tamen* is rendered as *They* on the cover, although it is originally a translation of the title of Joyce Carol Oates's novel *Them*. See Maghiel van Crevel, *Chinese Poetry in*

Times of Mind, Mayhem, and Money (Leiden: Brill, 2008), 72. *Tamen* has continued to be published online since 2002. For a complete discussion of Han Dong and Yu Jian, see Maghiel van Crevel, "Desecrations: Han Dong's and Yu Jian's Explicit Poetics," in *Chinese Poetry*, 365–397.

120. This is my reformulation of van Crevel's typology in *Chinese Poetry*, 25.
121. Van Crevel, *Chinese Poetry*, 365, 409. Yu Jian's essay "Chuanyue Hanyu de shige zhi guang" (The light of poetry: Cutting through the Chinese language) was published in *1998 Zhongguo xinshi nianjian* (1998 yearbook of China's New Poetry), ed. Yang Ke (Guangzhou: Huacheng, 1999), 1–17.
122. Han Dong, "Lun minjian" (On *minjian*), in *1999 Zhongguo shi nianxuan* (Selected Chinese poems of 1999), ed. He Xiaozhu (Xi'an: Shaanxi Normal University, 1999), 1–18.
123. Of course, some writers of literature also continue to produce critical works on the margins, although they no longer enjoy the same position of cultural authority they had in the 1980s.
124. The list is reprinted in Nicolai Volland, "Fifty Influential Public Intellectuals," revised May 16, 2014, Heidelberg University, http://www.zo.uni-heidelberg.de/boa/digital_resources/dachs/special_collections/fipi_en.html. Other deceased emeriti listed are the liberal thinker Yin Haiguang 殷海光 (1919–1969), the economist Gu Zhun (1915–1974), the *People's Daily* vice editor Wang Ruoshui 王若水 (1926–2002), the economist and critic of the Cultural Revolution Yang Xiguang 楊曦光 (1948–2004), and the hydrologist and dam critic Huang Wanli 黃萬里 (1911–2001).
125. Jia Zhangke, "Building a Public Consciousness," interview by Sebastian Veg, *China Perspectives*, no. 1 (2010): 60.
126. For an overview of how literary practice in the 2000s branched out into the new directions of "underclass literature" and "workers' literature" as well as Internet literature and fantasy, see Shao Yanjun, *Xin shiji di yige 10 nian xiaoshuo yanjiu* (Research on fiction in the first decade of a new century) (Beijing: Peking University, 2016).
127. Ji Fangping, "Touguo biaoxiang kan shizhi: Xi 'gonggong zhishifenzi' lun" (Discerning the substance behind the idea: An analysis of "public intellectuals"), *Jiefang Ribao*, November 15, 2004, reprinted in *People's Daily*, November 25, 2004. The intellectuals on the list were also singled out for the elitism displayed in their claim to be "custodians of public interests and public conscience" and "guardians of social fairness and moral conscience" (Wang would probably not have recognized himself in this role).
128. Yuan Peng, "Zhongguo zhenzheng de tiaozhan zai nali?" *People's Daily* (Overseas Edition), July 31, 2012, http://paper.people.com.cn/rmrbhwb/html/2012-07/31/content_1090137.htm, translated as "The Five Vermin Threatening China," trans. Geremie Barmé, *The China Story*, November 4, 2012.

3. *MINJIAN* HISTORIANS OF THE MAO ERA: COMMEMORATING, DOCUMENTING, DEBATING

1. *Zhonggong zhongyang pizhun "Guanyu quanbu zhaidiao 'youpai' fenzi maozi de qingshi baogao" tongzhi* (Notice on approval by Party Central of the "Report and request for instructions on completely removing the 'rightist' hat"), Zhongfa Document no. 11, April 5, 1978; *Pizhun Zhonggong zhongyang Zuzhibu, Xuanchuanbu, Tongzhanbu, Gong'anbu, Minzhengbu*

guanche Zhongyang guanyu quanbu zhaidiao youpai fenzi maozi jueding de shishi fang'an (Approbation of the proposal by the Organization Department, the Propaganda Department, the United Front Department, the Ministry of Public Security, and the Ministry of Civil Affairs for implementing Party Central's decision to completely remove the rightist hat), Zhongfa Document no. 55, September 17, 1978.

2. Niu Han and Deng Jiuping, eds., *Jiyi zhong de fan youpai yundong* (Memories of the Anti-Rightist Movement), vol. 1: *Yuan shang cao* (Weeds on the steppe); vol. 2: *Liu yue xue* (Snow in June), vol. 3: *Jingji lu* (A thorny road) (Beijing: Jingji Ribao, 1998). This collection of writings from PKU in 1957 includes the personal testimonies of several well-known intellectuals (Nie Gannu 聶紺弩, Ding Ling 丁玲, Chen Qixia 陳企霞, Wang Meng).

3. PKU literature professor He Guimei 賀桂梅, whose research has dealt mainly with propaganda fiction from the socialist period, provided the earliest round-up of these publications, describing the wave as the expression of a "fin-de-siècle nostalgia." She argued that, for liberal intellectuals who had been rehabilitated and had collaborated with the state in the 1980s, these memoirs and studies represented a turn against the state, whose economic reforms were depriving them of social influence. See He Guimei, "Shijimo de ziwo jiushu zhilu—1998 nian 'fanyou' shuji re de wenhua fenxi" (The road to fin-de-siècle self-redemption—a cultural analysis of the 1998 'Anti-Rightist' book fever), *Shanghai Wenxue*, April 2000, 71–76.

4. Early versions of several chapters of *Zui hou de guizu* (The last aristocrats) were published in the semiofficial journal *Old Photos* in 2002 and 2003; the first book version was subsequently published in China as *Wang shi bing bu ru yan* (The past is not like smoke) (Beijing: Renmin Wenxue, 2004); it quickly became a best seller before being banned and republished in Hong Kong as *The Last Aristocrats* (Hong Kong: Oxford University Press, 2004). The uncensored Hong Kong edition circulated in China in official, pirated, and electronic versions. Zhang's subsequent book, *Ling ren wang shi* (Past stories of stars of Peking opera) (Changsha: Hunan Wenyi, 2006), was also banned, together with a set of eight other books in 2007, and Zhang was informed that she could no longer publish in China. In 2010, she began publishing in Hong Kong a series of fictional portraits of women prisoners inspired by her own ten-year imprisonment during the Cultural Revolution (four have been published to date), illustrating how elite intellectuals moved from commemorating "the last aristocrats" to attempting to rethink history from a subaltern viewpoint.

5. Dai Huang, *Jiu si yi sheng* (Nine deaths, one life) (Beijing: Zhongyang bianyi, 1998; reprint, Shanghai: Xuelin, 2000). Extracts are translated as "The Killing Field," *EastSouthWestNorth* blog, March 24, 2007, http://www.zonaeuropa.com/20070324_1.htm. For more examples of rightist memoirs in translation, see also Yin Shuping, *Qiu wang* (Autumn hope), and Kong Lingping, *Xue ji* (Blood chronicle), translated by David Cowhig on his blog, https://gaodawei.wordpress.com.

6. See, for example, Dai Weiwei's memories of her mother published on the Universities Service Center for China Studies, Chinese University of Hong Kong, special website Minjian Memory: "Xuanxudiao" (Recitative), n.d., http://mjlsh.usc.cuhk.edu.hk/Book.aspx?cid=4&tid=1206.

7. Qian Liqun, "Bu rong mosha de sixiang yichan—chongdu *Beijing Daxue youpai fenzi fandong yanlun huiji, Xiao nei wai youpai yanlun huiji*" (An intellectual heritage that should not be erased—re-reading *A Collection of PKU Rightists' Reactionary Theories* and *A Collection of Rightist Theories from Inside and Outside the University*), in *Jujue yiwang: 1957 nian xue yanjiu biji* (Refusing to forget: Notes for "1957 studies") (Hong Kong: Oxford University Press, 2007), 1–15.
8. Qian Liqun, "Xie zai qianmian" (Foreword), *Jujue yiwang*, 17.
9. Qian Liqun, "Xie zai qianmian, "18.
10. Qian Liqun, *Jujue yiwang*, 496.
11. One such grassroots activist in Chengdu, Ran Yunfei, set out to investigate the ninety-six rightists in Sichuan rumored not to have been rehabilitated in 1978, mainly former "bad elements" and victims of the socialist education campaign that followed the Anti-Rightist Movement. See Ran Yunfei, "Cong guanfang shiliao kan yige sheng de fanyou yundong" (Understanding the Anti-Rightist Movement in one province from official documents), *Initium*, July 10, 2015. An important role was also played by the 1957 Studies Society, based in Hong Kong.
12. For example, the documentary film *PKU 5.19* (*Beida 5.19*, 2013) by Han Song, which triggered the shutdown of the Beijing Independent Film Festival in Songzhuang in 2014.
13. See, for example, a contribution by Chen Tushou (editor of *Beijing Youth Daily*'s cultural supplement): "Beijing gaoxiao 50 niandai dui jiaoshou rudang de taidu" (The attitude of universities in Beijing in the 1950s toward professors applying for party membership), *Nanfang Zhoumo*, December 6, 2011. See also Chen Tushou, *Ren you bing, Tian zhi fou* (When people feel such pain, does heaven know?) (Beijing: Renmin Wenxue, 2000). On Ma Li, see "Fangtan Ma Li: Zai yiding de chicun shang reshao" (Interviewing Ma Li: Burning to a certain degree), December 8, 2013, *Fangtanjia*, no. 1 (2016), http://cul.qq.com/a/20170615/004737.htm.
14. "Resolution on Certain Questions in the History of Our Party Since the Founding of the People's Republic of China," June 27, 1981, https://www.marxists.org/subject/china/documents/cpc/history/01.htm.
15. Ba Jin, "Jinian" (Remembering), in *Suixianglu xuanji* (Selected random thoughts) (Beijing: Sanlian, 2003), 53.
16. Liu Zaifu, "Xinshiqi wenxue de tupo he shenhua" (Breakthrough and deepening accomplishments of the new era literature), *Renmin Ribao*, September 8, 1986. The full text was later published as "Wenxue yu chanhui yishi: Du Ba Jin de *Suixianglu*" (Literature and repentance: Reading Ba Jin's *Random Thoughts*) (December 1986), in *Liu Zaifu Ji* (Harbin: Heilongjiang Jiaoyu, 1988), 313–326.
17. Liu Xiaobo, "Weiji! Xin shiqi wenxue mianlin de weiji" (Crisis! The literature of the new era faces a crisis), *Shenzhen Qingnianbao*, October 3, 1986. See also the French translation "Crise! La littérature de la nouvelle époque est entrée en crise," trans. Sebastian Veg, in Liu Xiaobo, *La philosophie du porc et autres essais*, (Paris: Gallimard "Bleu de Chine," 2011), 57–87, esp. 64–70.
18. Yan Jiaqi and Gao Gao, *Zhongguo "Wen ge" shinian shi* (Hong Kong: Ta Kung Pao She, 1986), translated as *Turbulent Decade: A History of the Cultural Revolution*, trans. Danny Kwok (Honolulu: Hawai'i University Press, 1996). In particular, the authors identify

the "despotic political system" as a key factor in the "colossal catastrophe" of the Cultural Revolution (*Turbulent Decade*, 3, 529).

19. See Xu Youyu, ed., *1966: Women na yidai de huiyi* (1966: The memories of our generation) (Beijing: Wenlian, 1998), and Xu's study on Red Guard activism, *Xingxing sese de zaofan* (Rebellion of all shapes and colors) (Hong Kong: Chinese University of Hong Kong Press, 1999).
20. Wang Shuo, "Dongwu xiongmeng" (Animals are wild), *Shouhuo*, no. 6 (1991): 130–169.
21. See Wendy Larson, "Okay, Whatever: Intellectuals, Sex, and Time in Wang Xiaobo's *The Golden Years*" and "As You Wish It: *In the Heat of the Sun*," in *From Ah Q to Lei Feng: Freud and Revolutionary Spirit in 20th Century China* (Stanford, Calif.: Stanford University Press, 2009), 132–153, 157–183; Sebastian Veg, "Utopian Fiction and Critical Examination: The Cultural Revolution in Wang Xiaobo's *The Golden Age*," *China Perspectives*, no. 4 (2007): 75–87.
22. Zhi Liang, *Ji'e de shancun* (A starving mountain village) (Guilin: Lijiang, 1994). Extracts are published as *Hungry Mountain Village*, trans. Andrew Endrey, *Renditions*, no. 68 (2007): 112–142.
23. Wang Xiaobo, "Chenmo de daduoshu" (The silent majority), in *Siwei de lequ* (The pleasure of thinking) (Kunming: Yunnan Renmin, 2006), 3.
24. In its general approach, this chapter draws inspiration from a book-length collection on the topic I recently edited: *Popular Memories of the Mao Era: From Critical Debate to Reassessing History* (Hong Kong: Hong Kong University Press, 2019).
25. See Jonathan Unger, ed., *Using the Past to Serve the Present: Historiography and Politics in Contemporary China* (Armonk, N.Y.: M. E. Sharpe, 1993); Ching Kwan Lee and Guobin Yang, eds., *Re-envisioning the Chinese Revolution: The Politics and Poetics of Collective Memories in Reform China* (Washington, D.C.: Woodrow Wilson Center Press, 2007).
26. See Susanne Weigelin-Schwiedrzik, "Trauma and Memory: The Case of the Great Famine in the People's Republic of China (1959–1961)," *Historiography East and West* 1, no. 1 (2003): 41–67; Felix Wemheuer, "Der Weg in die Hungersnot: Erinnerungen chinesischer Intellektueller an den ländlichen 'Großen Sprung nach vorne' (1958–1961)" (The path to famine: Memories of Chinese intellectuals about the rural "Great Leap Forward" [1958–1961]), *Asien*, no. 25 (2005): 25–41; Sun Liping, "Qingting 'bei geming juanruzhe' de xinling" (Listening to the souls of those "caught up in the revolution"), preface to Guo Yuhua, *Shoukuren de jiangshu: Jicun lishi yu yizhong wenming de luoji* (Narratives of the sufferers: The history of Jicun and the logic of civilization) (Hong Kong: Chinese University of Hong Kong Press, 2013), xv–xix.
27. Rubie Watson, "Memory, History, and Opposition Under State Socialism: An Introduction," *Memory, History, and Opposition Under State Socialism*, ed. Rubie Watson (Santa Fe, N.M.: School of American Research, 1994), 10–12.
28. See Peng Lingfan, "Wo de jiejie Lin Zhao" (My older sister Lin Zhao) (November 1998), *Ai Sixiang*, April 29, 2006. On Lin Zhao, see also the recent study by Lian Xi, *Blood Letters: The Untold Story of Lin Zhao, a Martyr in Mao's China* (New York: Basic Books, 2018).
29. Jie Li, "Virtual Museums of Forbidden Memories," *Public Culture* 21, no. 3 (2009): 541.
30. Ian Johnson, "China's Invisible History: An Interview with Filmmaker and Artist Hu Jie," *New York Review* blog, May 27, 2015, https://www.nybooks.com/daily/2015/05/27/chinas-invisible-history-hu-jie/.

31. Fu Guoyong, "Du Lin Zhao shisiwan yan shu" (Reading Lin Zhao's 140,000 character letter), *Nanfang Zhoumo*, May 1, 2008.
32. More than one hundred mourners (as well as two hundred police officers) joined the commemoration in 2013, by which time the police had already installed a camera near Lin Zhao's grave and state security had visited local volunteer guides (Patrick Boehler, "Remembrance of Dissident Lin Zhao Obstructed on 45th Execution Anniversary," *South China Morning Post*, April 29, 2013). By 2015, Radio Free Asia was reporting that thousands of riot police had cordoned off access to Mt. Lingyan, and several dozen activists were arrested on the date of Lin's execution.
33. Peng Lingfan, "Wo fumu he Lin Zhao de mudi" (My parents and Lin Zhao's grave), *Nanfang Zhoumo*, December 2, 2013. Peng Lingfan confesses to letting her imagination conjure up a scene in which Lin Zhao's soul meets Chiang Kai-shek in the Hoover Archive, telling him "my mother knew you."
34. Ai Xiaoming, "Lin Zhao yigao yanjiu zhi yi" (Research on Lin Zhao's posthumous manuscripts, one), *Dongfang Lishi Pinglun*, February 25, 2014. See also the collection: Fu Guoyong, ed., *Lin Zhao zhi si: 40 nian ji* (In Memoriam: On the 40th anniversary of Lin Zhao's death) (Hong Kong: Kaifang, 2008). An online version of Lin's writings was also published in 2008.
35. See Jean-Philippe Béja, "Writing About the Past, an Act of Resistance: An Overview of Independent Journals and Publications About the Mao Era," in *Popular Memories of the Mao Era*, ed. Veg, 21–42.
36. Tan Chanxue, *Qiusuo: Lanzhou da xue "youpai fan'geming jituan an" jishi* (Searching: Records of the Lanzhou University "Rightist Antirevolutionary Clique") (Hong Kong: Hong Kong Tianma, 2010), 13.
37. Tan Chanxue, *Qiusuo*, 14.
38. Qian Liqun, "Xin shi chandongde, xue shi rede, linghun shi shengjiede" (The heart is quivering, the blood is hot, the soul is pure), preface to Tan Chanxue, *Qiusuo*, 2.
39. Qian Liqun, "Xin shi chandongde," 7.
40. Hu Jie's film *Spark* (2013) further contributed to kindling interest in and discussion of the Spark group, whose members had noted many failings in the system that remain relevant to the system today.
41. The first edition of He's book *Jingli: Wo de 1957* (Experience: My 1957) was published in 2001 (Lanzhou: Dunhuang Wenyi). Other significant memoirs dealing with Jiabiangou include the one by the philosophy scholar Gao Ertai 高爾泰 and the former local cadre Xing Tongyi 邢同義. See Gao Ertai, *Xunzhao jiayuan* (In search of my homeland) (Guangzhou: Huacheng, 2004), translated as *In Search of My Homeland: A Memoir of a Chinese Labor Camp*, trans. Robert Dorsett and David Pollard (New York: Harper Collins, 2009); and Xing Tongyi, *Huang ruo ge shi: Huimou Jiabiangou* (Like another world: Remembering Jiabiangou) (Lanzhou: Lanzhou Daxue, 2004). For an overview of Jiabiangou memoirs, see Huang Yong, "Jiabiangou youpai laojiao wenxue shuxie" (Literary narratives of the Jiabiangou rightist reeducation camp), *Ershiyi Shiji*, no. 102 (August 2007): 118–126.
42. Qian Liqun, *Jujue Yiwang*; Shi Tao, "Huyu jinkuai jianli 'Jiabiangou jinianguan'" (Call to establish a "Jiabiangou memorial" as soon as possible), Boxun, September 15, 2002, http://blog.boxun.com/hero/shitao/45_1.shtml.

43. Shao Yanjun, "Wenxue, zuowei yizhong zhengyan—Yang Xianhui fangtanlu" (Literature as a kind of testimony—a discussion with Yang Xianhui), *Shanghai Wenxue*, no. 12 (2009): 94.
44. Shao Yanjun, "Wenxue," 94.
45. See a more detailed discussion in Sebastian Veg, "Testimony, History, and Ethics: From the Memory of Jiabiangou Prison Camp to a Reappraisal of the Anti-Rightist Movement in Present-Day China," *China Quarterly*, no. 218 (June 2014): 514–539.
46. Seven stories were published in 2002 under the title *Jiabiangou jishi* (Chronicles of Jiabiangou) (Tianjin: Tianjin Guji); then nineteen were included in a second edition in 2003 under the title *Gaobie Jiabiangou* (Farewell to Jiabiangou) (Shanghai: Shanghai Wenyi), which was reprinted in 2008 under the original title *Jiabiangou jishi* (Chronicles of Jiabiangou) (Guangzhou: Huacheng). A partial English translation by Wen Huang is published under the title *Woman from Shanghai* (New York: Pantheon Books, 2009). On the ban, see Solidot, "*Chronicles of Jiabiangou* and Other Works Removed from Electronic Bookstores Within China," *China Digital Times*, July 16, 2017, http://chinadigitaltimes.net/chinese/2017/07/solidot| 《夹边沟记事》等多部书籍从国内电子商务网/.
47. See also Wang Bing's review of Yang Xianhui's third book, *Gannan jishi*: "Liangzhi, zeren yu wenxue de zhenshixing" (Moral conscience, responsibility, and the authenticity of literature), *Nanfang Renwu Zhoukan*, no. 13 (April 22, 2012): 109.
48. For a more detailed discussion of these two films, see Veg, "Testimony, History, and Ethics," and Sebastian Veg, "The Limits of Representation: Wang Bing's Labor Camp Films," *Journal of Chinese Cinemas* 6, no. 2 (2012): 173–187.
49. "'Youpai' laogaiying 50 nian" (The Rightist Labor Camp: 50 Years), *Nandu Zhoukan*, December 3, 2010, https://news.qq.com/a/20101203/000777.htm or http://news.sina.com.cn/c/sd/2010-11-26/152021539314.shtml.
50. Ian Johnson, "The People in Retreat: An Interview with Ai Xiaoming," *New York Review of Books Daily*, September 8, 2016.
51. See Judith Pernin, "Filmed Testimonies, Archives, and Memoirs of the Mao Era: Staging Unofficial History in Chinese Independent Documentaries," in *Popular Memories of the Mao Era*, ed. Veg, 137–160. See also Zhang Xianchi, *Laogai huiyilu* (Memories of labor camp) (Taipei: Xiuwei, 2013).
52. Liu Yangshuo, "Chongfan Dabao 1960 shaonian laojiao wangshi" (Returning to the forgotten events of the Dabao Youth Labor Camp in 1960), *Nanfang Renwu Zhoukan*, no. 30 (September 2, 2013), 12, http://www.nfpeople.com/story_view.php?id=4781.
53. See Wu Hongfei, "Shen Zhihua: Zhongjin souji Sulian dang'an" (Shen Zhihua: Using a lump of money to collect Soviet archives), *Nanfang Renwu Zhoukan*, no. 18 (June 21, 2008): 70–73.
54. Cao, originally a historian of population and epidemics, published a book on the Great Famine in Hong Kong in 2005 and articles on the Anti-Rightist Movement in several Chinese academic journals. See Cao Shuji, *Dajihuang: 1959–1961 nian de Zhongguo renkou* (The Great Famine: China's population 1959–1961) (Hong Kong: Xianggang Shidai Guoji, 2005).
55. See Yang Kuisong's unusual essay on Mao published in English in which he dwells at length on Mao's advocacy of Hunan independence in the 1920s: "Mao's Winding Road to Socialism," *Caixin*, January 18, 2015. Shen Zhihua's intervention on North Korea

policy in the summer of 2017 is another example. Another historian who regularly intervenes in public is Yuan Weishi (Sun Yat-sen University, Guangzhou), whose columns are collected in *Zuotian de Zhongguo* (Yesterday's China) (Hangzhou: Zhejiang University, 2012).

56. See Shen Zhihua, "Chaoxian zhanzheng de qiyuan" (The origins of the Korean War), lecture organized by the journal *Dongfang Lishi Pinglun*, April 13, 2013, Beijing, and his book *Mao, Stalin, and the Korean War: Trilateral Communist Relations in the 1950s*, trans. Neil Silver (London: Routledge, 2012).
57. Wang Hui, "Ershishiji Zhongguo lishi shiye xia de kang Mei yuan Chao zhanzheng" (The war to resist America and support Korea in the lens of twentieth century Chinese history), *Wenhua Congheng*, no. 6 (December 2013): 78–100.
58. Yang Kuisong, "Yi lun dai shi de ganga" (The embarrassments of history led by theory), *Dongfang Zaobao*, December 29, 2013.
59. Yang Kuisong, "Ye tan 'quzhengzhihua' wenti" (Also on the problem of depoliticization), *Dongfang Zaobao*, January 19, 2014.
60. See Gao Hua, *Hong Taiyang shi zenyang shengqi de* (Hong Kong: Chinese University of Hong Kong Press, 2000), translated as *How the Red Sun Rose: The Origin and Development of the Yan'an Rectification Movement, 1930–1945*, trans. Stacy Mosher and Guo Jian (Hong Kong: Chinese University of Hong Kong Press, 2018). See also David Chang, review of *How the Red Sun Rose*, *China Review International* 15, no. 4 (2008): 515–521. According to the publisher, Gao's book is currently (2018) in its nineteenth printing in Chinese.
61. Gao Hua, "Youguan Mao Zedong yanjiu de jige wenti" (A few questions related to research on Mao Zedong), lecture at East China Normal University, Shanghai, October 18, 2002, available, for example, via http://book.ifeng.com/shupingzhoukan/special/duyao67/wenzhang/detail_2012_02/24/12762728_0.shtml.
62. Weigelin-Schwiedrzik, "Trauma and Memory."
63. Yang Jisheng, *Mubei* (Hong Kong: Cosmos, 2008), 5–26, translated as *Tombstone: The Great Chinese Famine, 1958–1962*, trans. Stacy Mosher and Guo Jian (London: Penguin, 2013), 3–22.
64. Yan Lianke, *Si shu* (The four books) (Hong Kong: Mingpao, 2010). See also Sebastian Veg, "Creating a Literary Space to Debate the Mao Era: The Fictionalization of the Great Leap Forward in Yan Lianke's Four Books," *China Perspectives*, no. 4 (2014): 7–16.
65. Yu Hua, "China Waits for an Apology," *New York Times*, April 9, 2014, https://www.nytimes.com/2014/04/10/opinion/yu-hua-cultural-revolution-nostalgia.html.
66. Parts of this section have previously appeared in Sebastian Veg, "Literary and Documentary Accounts of the Great Famine: Challenging the Political System and the Social Hierarchies of Memory," in *Popular Memories of the Mao Era*, ed. Veg, 115–136.
67. Ian Johnson, "Finding the Facts About Mao's Victims," interview with Yang Jisheng, *New York Review of Books Daily*, December 20, 2010, http://www.nybooks.com/blogs/nyrblog/2010/dec/20/finding-facts-about-maos-victims/.
68. Yang Jisheng, *Tombstone*, 17.
69. Yang Jisheng, *Tombstone*, 21, 49.
70. Editorial Board, "Yi chengshi he liangzhi jidian jihuang" (Commemorating the famine with sincerity and a conscience), in "Da Jihuang" (The Great Famine), special issue of *Nanfang Renwu Zhoukan*, no. 16 (May 21, 2012): 35.

71. Xie Yihui also made a documentary about Li Shengzhao: *Rightist Li Shengzhao's Famine Report* (*Youpai Li Shengzhao de ji'e baodao*, 2012).
72. See also the analysis of this phenomenon on Weibo by Jun Liu and Hui Zhao: "Social Media and Collective Remembrance," *China Perspectives*, no. 1 (2015): 41–48.
73. Quoted in Jun Liu, "Contested Past: Social Media and the Production of Historical Knowledge of the Mao Era," in *Popular Memories of the Mao Era*, ed. Veg, 66. The controversy was reignited when Lin Zhibo was appointed head of the Journalism School at Lanzhou University in July 2014.
74. See Wendy Qian, "In *Going Back to 1942*, Chinese Film Director Takes Subtle Aim at Communist Party," *Atlantic*, March 28, 2013. See also Liu Zhenyun's op-ed "Memory, Loss," *New York Times*, November 30, 2012, http://www.nytimes.com/2012/11/30/opinion/global/why-wont-the-chinese-acknowledge-the-1942-famine.html.
75. Xu Youyu, "Wei 3600 wan jifu li mubei" (Erecting a tombstone for 36 million corpses), *Open Magazine*, October 2008.
76. Yang Jisheng, "Bo esi sanqianwan shi yaoyan" (Rebutting the claim that 30 million starvation deaths is mere rumor), *Yanhuang Chunqiu*, December 2013.
77. See Anthony Garnaut, "The Mass Line on a Massive Famine," *The China Story*, October 8, 2014, https://www.thechinastory.org/2014/10/the-mass-line-on-a-massive-famine/.
78. See Wu Si, "*Annals of the Yellow Emperor*: Reconstructing Public Memory of the Mao Era," trans. Stacy Mosher, in *Popular Memories of the Mao Era*, ed. Veg, 43–60.
79. Yang Jisheng, speech written for the reception of the Louis Lyons Award for Conscience and Integrity in Journalism, March 10, 2016, transcript, http://nieman.harvard.edu/awards/louis-lyons-award/yang-jisheng-speech-transcript/.
80. See Bérénice Reynaud, "Translating the Unspeakable: On-Screen and Off-Screen Voices in Wu Wenguang's Documentary Work," in *The New Chinese Documentary Film Movement: For the Public Record*, ed. Chris Berry, Xinyu Lu, and Lisa Rofel (Hong Kong: Hong Kong University Press, 2010), 157–176. On the Village Documentary Project, see Huang Xuelei, "Murmuring Voices of the Everyday: Jia Zhitan and His Village Documentaries," *Journal of Chinese Cinemas* 10, no. 2 (2016): 166–186.
81. See also Paul Pickowicz, "A Hundred Years Later: Zou Xueping's Documentaries and the Legacies of China's New Culture Movement," *Journal of Chinese Cinemas* 10, no. 2 (2016): 187–201.
82. Wu Wenguang, "Opening the Door of Memory with a Camera Lens: The Folk Memory Project and Documentary Production," trans. Stacy Mosher, *China Perspectives*, no. 4 (2014): 47. See also Wu Wenguang, "'Minjian jiyi jihua' zhong de dajihuang jilupian" (Famine documentaries in the Folk Memory Project), *Ershiyi Shiji*, no. 142 (April 2014): 104–113.
83. Wu Wenguang, "Opening the Door of Memory," 37.
84. Wu Wenguang, "Opening the Door of Memory," 41.
85. For example, Guo Rui took her film to the First Annual Convention of Chinese Historians in Suzhou in November 2013.
86. Luo Bing's films are *Luo Village: Me and Ren Dingqi* (*Luojiawu: Wo he Ren Dingqi*, 2011); *Luo Village: A Ruthless World* (*Luojiawu: Tiandi wu qing*, 2012); and *Luo Village: Farewell, Luojiang Bridge* (*Luojiawu: Yongbie Luojiang qiao*, 2013). Ren Dingqi is reminiscent of the "village

intellectual" whom Paul Pickowicz describes in "Memories of Revolution and Collectivization in China: The Unauthorized Reminiscences of a Rural Intellectual," in *Memory, History, and Opposition*, ed. Watson, 127–148.

87. Gail Hershatter's study *The Gender of Memory: Rural Women and China's Collective Past* (Berkeley: University of California Press, 2011), published in China as *Jiyi de xingbie: Nongcun funü he Zhongguo jitihua lishi*, trans. Zhang Yun (Beijing: Renmin, 2017), has also been influential in this regard.
88. Guo Yuhua, *Qingting diceng: Women ruhe jiangshu kunan* (Listening closely to the lowest level: How we describe suffering) (Guilin: Guangxi Imaginist, 2011).
89. See, for example, Guo Yuhua, "Quanli ruhe yange women de lishi jiyi" (How power amputates our historical memory), *Xiandai Daxue Zhoubao*, December 15, 2015, transcript of a public talk.
90. Guo Yuhua, "'Ruozhe de wuqi' yu 'yincang de wenben': Yanjiu nongmin fankang de diceng shijiao" (*Weapons of the Weak* and *Hidden Transcripts*: Researching a subaltern viewpoint of peasant resistance), *Dushu*, no. 7 (2002): 11–18.
91. Guo Yuhua, *Shoukuren de jiangshu*, 2.
92. Sun Liping, "Qingting 'bei geming juanruzhe' de xinling," xix.
93. Guo Yuhua, *Shoukuren de jiangshu*, 13, 27, 23.
94. Quoted in Guo Yuhua, *Shoukuren de jiangshu*, 155.
95. Guo Yuhua, *Shoukuren de jiangshu*, 164.
96. See the overview in Béja, "Writing About the Past."
97. Wu Si, "*Annals of the Yellow Emperor*," 47. See also Mary G. Mazur, "Public Space for Memory in Contemporary Civil Society: Freedom to Learn from the Mirror of the Past?" *China Quarterly*, no. 160 (December 1999): 1019–1035, esp. 1027–1032.
98. Jiang Xun, "Dujia zhuanfang *Yanhuang Chunqiu* zazhishe shezhang Du Daozheng—Zhongguo minzhu manbu qianjin tupo," *Yazhou Zhoukan*, no. 22, June 10, 2007, translated as "Du Daozheng: Democracy Moves Ahead and Breaks Through Slowly in China," *EastSouthWestNorth* blog, http://www.zonaeuropa.com/20070604_1.htm.
99. Zi Zhongyun, "Gexin Zhongguo chuantong lishiguan" (Renewing China's traditional view of history), *Yanhuang Chunqiu*, July 2014.
100. See Wu Si, "*Annals of the Yellow Emperor*," 48.
101. Ding Dong, "*Old Photos* and Historical Memory," *Chinese Cross-Currents*, April–June 2006, 96 (the last sentence has been retranslated from Chinese; both versions are printed in the journal).
102. Another example of a semiofficial magazine is *Kan Lishi* (Looking at history), published in Chengdu (first as *Xianfeng Guojia Lishi* [Avant-garde national history]) with support from a commercial publisher (Chengdu Xianfeng Wenhua Chuanmei) from 2007 to February 2013, when it was shut down over an issue dealing with Taiwan and reorganized as a purely commercial magazine.
103. Jean-Philippe Béja quotes the statement of purpose given in the first issue of *Tiny Scars*: "We, who have reached a ripe old age, have always wanted to write accounts of the small and great facts of our experience for everyone (including ourselves) in a spirit of frankness, realism and objectivity in order to restore historical truth and to show the goodness and beauty of the human heart. With this, we want to encourage the living, and warn the future generations" (quoted in Béja, "Writing About the Past," 32). See also

Chris Buckley, "Conviction for Memoirs Is Reminder of Mao Era," *New York Times*, February 25, 2015.

104. See Ian Johnson, "China's Brave Underground Journal," *New York Review of Books*, December 4, 2014.
105. See the self-description on the Minjian History website of the Universities Service Centre for China Studies at the Chinese University of Hong Kong: "This is a website for the history of ordinary people, we invite readers to send letters, manuscripts and to recommend publications, to participate. Regarding possible errors in commemorative manuscripts, we also welcome readers to send letters to correct them" (http://mjlsh.usc.cuhk.edu.hk/default.aspx).
106. Wuzala.Di, "Cong guanfang dao minjian—Wang Nianyi de daolu yu yiyi" (From official to *minjian*—Wang Nianyi's path and its meaning), *Jiyi*, no. 1 (September 2013): 15–17. See also Wang Nianyi, *Da dongluan de niandai* (The age of the great turmoil) (Zhengzhou: Henan Renmin, 1988).
107. Qizhi (Wu Di), "*Jiyi* zhubian gao duzhe" (From the chief editor of *Remembrance* to readers), *Jiyi*, no. 92 (January 2013): 148.
108. Qizhi (Wu Di), "*Jiyi* zhubian gao duzhe," 148.
109. Qizhi (Wu Di), "*Jiyi* zhubian gao duzhe," 150.
110. According to Wu Di, Wang Youqin (a PKU graduate in Chinese literature who now teaches at the University of Chicago and edits the online Memorial to the Victims of the Cultural Revolution, which was published in book form in 2004) demanded that *Remembrance* reprint in full a text by her that had already been published rather than excerpts, as the magazine editors had suggested. When the editors refused, she accused them of taking money from Song Binbin to publish her version of the "August 5th incident" (1966). Wu Di also points out problems in Wang's scholarship—for example, no acknowledgment that the statistics she uses for the deaths during "Red August" in Beijing in 1966 are taken from Yin Hongbiao's work ("*Jiyi* zhubian gao duzhe," 150).
111. Other documentaries devoted to victims of Red Guard violence include Zhang Ke, *Youth Cemetery* (*Qingchun muyuan*, 2005), devoted to the Chongqing Red Guard cemetery; and two films by Xu Xing, *A Chronicle of My Cultural Revolution* (*Wo de Wenge biannianshi*, 2007) and *Summary of Crimes* (*Zuixing zhaiyao*, 2013).
112. Qizhi (Wu Di), "*Jiyi* zhubian gao duzhe," 151.
113. Jonathan Kaimann, "China Cracks Down on Social Media with Threat of Jail for 'Online Rumours'?" *Guardian*, September 10, 2013, https://www.theguardian.com/world/2013/sep/10/china-social-media-jail-rumours.
114. Jiao Guobiao, "Fakanci" (opening editorial), *Hei Wu Lei Yijiu*, no. 1 (July 30, 2010): 2–3.
115. The first such essay was by Wang Keming, "Wo da Gu Zhiyou" (I beat up Gu Zhiyou), *Yanhuang Chunqiu*, no. 5 (2008): 64, which inaugurated what became the regular column "Chanhui lu" (Confessions). Wang Keming and Song Xiaoming published a book with the same title, *Women Chanhui* (We confess) (Beijing: Zhongxin, 2014).
116. Song Binbin, "40 nian lai, wo yizhi xiang shuo de hua" (For 40 years, here's what I've been wanting to say), *Jiyi*, no. 80 (February 4, 2012), http://news.qq.com/a/20140113/001794_all.htm. *Remembrance* devoted many special issues to the Song Binbin case: numbers 47, 49, 80, and most recently number 112.

117. The contents of the commemorative issue of *Orient* were censored, but the cover was not changed, revealing the original table of contents; officials subsequently closed down the journal. See Edward X. Gu, "Social Capital, Institutional Change, and the Development of Non-governmental Intellectual Organizations in China," in *Chinese Intellectuals Between State and Market*, ed. Edward X. Gu and Merle Goldman (London: Routledge, 2004), 35–37.
118. Wang Meng, "Fansi Wenge ze wu pang dai" (Reflecting on the Cultural Revolution is a responsibility that cannot be shirked), *Yanhuang Chunqiu*, March 2016, http://www.yhcqw.com/html/qsp/2016/39/1639224332EKECH10107383HJ162KAI3H3B.html.
119. Wang Haiguang, "Cong 'chedi fouding' dao 'chedi fansi'" (From "completely negate" to "completely reflect"), *Yanhuang Chunqiu*, May 2016, http://www.yhcqw.com/html/qsp/2016/39/1639225449J5FH6101080228KBKC96C7BAG.html. This paragraph is adapted from Sebastian Veg, "Debating the Memory of the Cultural Revolution in China Today," *Modern Chinese Literature and Culture*, August 2016, http://u.osu.edu/mclc/online-series/veg2/ .
120. Ma Yong, "Jintian gai ruhe fansi Wenge" (How we should reflect on the Cultural Revolution today), *Fenghuang Pinglun*, February 17, 2016.
121. Hu Ping, "Dali tuijian Yang Jisheng xiansheng xin zhu *Tiandi fanfu—Zhongguo wenhua dageming shi*" (Strongly recommend Mr. Yang Jisheng's new work *Overthrowing Heaven and Earth—a History of China's Great Cultural Revolution*), *Human Rights in China*, February 5, 2017, https://www.hrichina.org/chs/zhong-guo-ren-quan-shuang-zhou-kan/hu-ping-da-li-tui-jian-yang-ji-sheng-xian-sheng-xin-zhu-tian-di.
122. Yang Jisheng, "Daolu, lilun, zhidu: Wo dui Wenhua dageming de sikao" (A road, a theory, and a system: My thoughts on the Cultural Revolution), *Jiyi*, no. 104 (November 30, 2013): 18, 22.
123. Qin Hui, "Women gai zenyang fansi wenge" (How should we remember the Cultural Revolution?), in *Wenti yu Zhuyi: Qin Hui wenxuan* (Problems and isms: Selected essays by Qin Hui) (Changchun: Changchun Press, 1999), 10–12. In another article, Qin Hui compares economic inequalities under Mao to a caste system. See Qin Hui, "Fin de Siècle China: Economic Transition, Social Justice, and Democracy," *The Chinese Economy* 38, no. 5 (2005): 3–54.
124. He Shu, "Zhong xi benyong hui jiang hai: Wenge yanjiu lushang 20 nian suozhi suogan" (All torrents converge toward the sea: What I have learned and felt over 20 years of Cultural Revolution research), *Zuotian*, no. 77 (September 30, 2016), supplement: 60.
125. The questions raised about the status of intellectuals in this discussion echoed the general trend away from the elite perspective, although the specific accusations against Yang Jiang were somewhat unreasonable. See Veg, "Debating the Memory of the Cultural Revolution in China Today."
126. Jack Hu, "Chinese Lawmakers Seek to Protect Dead Communist Heroes with New Law," *Global Voices*, March 25, 2017, https://www.hongkongfp.com/2017/03/25/chinese-lawmakers-seek-protect-dead-communist-heros-new-law/.
127. Zi Zhongyun, "Gexin Zhongguo chuantong lishiguan."

4. INVESTIGATING AND TRANSFORMING SOCIETY FROM THE MARGINS: THE RISE AND FALL OF INDEPENDENT CINEMA

1. Cui Weiping, "Zhongguo dalu duli zhizuo jilupian de shengzhang kongjian" (A space for the growth of China's independently produced documentaries), *Ershiyi Shiji*, no. 77 (June 2003): 92, 94. The First Independent Film Festival was interrupted by the authorities halfway through. Lin Xudong notes that Du Haibin's film *Along the Railroad* received the first prize.
2. Yangzi, "Minjian de hanyi" (The meaning of *minjian*), *Nanfang Zhoumo*, September 30, 2001. On Yangzi (b. 1973), see Wen Hai, *Fangzhu de ningshi: Jianzheng Zhongguo duli jilupian* (The banished gaze: Chinese independent documentary) (Taipei: Tendency, 2016), 77.
3. Yangzi, "Minjian de hanyi."
4. Seio Nakajima, "Film as Cultural Politics," in *Reclaiming Chinese Society: The New Social Activism*, ed. You-tien Hsing and Ching Kwan Lee (New York: Routledge, 2009), 159–183.
5. For example, *Nanfang Zhoumo* organized a DV competition, "Quanmin luan pai—yingxiangli" (Everyone madly filming—influence), which supported ten film projects every quarter. The first call took place in 2007 on the theme "family" (*jiazu*). See, for example, the Douban page for the competition: "Quanmin luan pai—yingxiangli: *Nanfang Zhoumo* DV xingdong zhengji qishi" (Everyone madly filming—influence: Call for entries to *Southern Weekly*'s DV happening), November 1, 2007, https://www.douban.com/group/topic/2143419/.
6. Lü Xinyu, "Zai wutuobang de feixu shang—xin jilu yundong zai Zhongguo" (On the ruins of Utopia: The new documentary movement in China, 2001), in *Jilu Zhongguo: Dangdai Zhongguo xin jilu yundong* (Documenting China: The New Documentary Movement in contemporary China) (Beijing: Sanlian, 2003), 4.
7. Chris Berry effectively highlights the "June Fourth issue" as "the structuring absence at the heart" of the early New Documentaries in his article "Getting Real," in *The Urban Generation: Chinese Cinema and Society at the Turn of the Twenty-First Century*, ed. Zhang Zhen (Durham, N.C.: Duke University Press, 2007), 119.
8. For example, Paola Voci argues that the independent filmmakers emphasize visuality (visual wandering) over discourse (verbal dissent): "Verbal dissent (e.g. *River Elegy*) openly claims to be the force that can mobilize people and inspire and even organize revolutions. Visual wanderers almost never turn their criticism into a pragmatic project; however, their uncompromising resistance to being appropriated by ideologies and instead showing 'some authentic things' demands our attention" ("From the Center to the Periphery: Chinese Documentary's Visual Conjectures," *Modern Chinese Literature and Culture* 16, no. 1 [2004]: 105). See also Luke Robinson's argument contrasting teleological time in *River Elegy* versus time as contingency in independent films (*Independent Chinese Documentary: From the Studio to the Street* [New York: Palgrave Macmillan, 2013], 74–84).
9. Lü Xinyu, "Zai wutuobang de feixu shang," 5. *The Other Shore* (*Bi'an*) was a play by Gao Xingjian that director Mou Sen used for an experimental theater performance, which was in turn filmed by independent documentary director Jiang Yue. See also Yu Jian,

"Xin xiju: Mou Sen de *Bi'an*," in *Yu Jian ji* (The collected works of Yu Jian), vol. 5: *Jujue yinyu* (Kunming: Yunnan Renmin Wenxue, 2004), 176–182. Huang Wenhai (Wen Hai) takes issue with Lü's interpretation, arguing that Jiang Yue was actually trying to make a case for the utopian optimism of the actors in the play but that Lü's stance was typical of the cynicism of post-1989 intellectuals (Wen Hai, *Fangzhu de ningshi*, 37).

10. Lü Xinyu writes, "The meaning of the New Documentary Movement for today's China is that it established a channel for a bottom-up perspective. In the present socioeconomic situation, it illuminates the survival claims and feelings of people from different social strata; it supplements and corrects the mainstream ideology; it makes history open and spacious; it promises everyone the possibility to enter history; it creates history; it is the expression of a democratic society" ("Zai wutuobang de feixu shang," 23).
11. Zhang Yuan and Zhu Wen were close to Wang Xiaobo and Li Yinhe. Wang cowrote the screenplay for *East Palace, West Palace* based on his story "Tender as Water" ("Sishui rouqing") and on his and Li's study on homosexuality *Their World* (*Tamen de shijie*). See chapter 2 in this volume and Chris Berry, "Staging Gay Life in China: Zhang Yuan and *East Palace, West Palace*," in *Chinese Connections: Critical Perspectives on Film, Identity, and Diaspora*, ed. Tan See-kam, Peter X. Feng, and Gina Marchetti (Philadelphia: Temple University Press, 2009), 165–176.
12. Jia Zhangke, "Wo bu xiangxin ni neng caidui women de jieju," *Nanfang Zhoumo*, July 21, 2010, translated as "I Don't Believe You Can Predict Our Ending," *dGenerate Films*, November 10, 2010, http://dgeneratefilms.com/academia/full-translation-of-jia-zhangkes-essay-on-sixth-generation-cinema-now-available/.
13. See Lin Xudong, "Documentary in Mainland China," Yamagata International Documentary Film Festival Publications, 2005. *Bumming in Beijing* was also shown in several foreign festivals, including the Hong Kong International Film Festival and Yamagata in 1991.
14. For two attempts at compiling a comprehensive filmography, see *From Underground to Independent: Alternative Film Culture in Contemporary China*, ed. Paul Pickowicz and Zhang Yingjin (Lanham, Md.: Rowman and Littlefield, 2006), 209–244 and 245–248, and Judith Pernin, *Pratiques indépendantes du documentaire en Chine: Histoire, esthétique et discours visuels (1990–2010)* (Rennes, France: PUR, 2015), 263–280.
15. Parts of the section "Independent Directors as *Minjian* Intellectuals," are adapted from Sebastian Veg, "Opening Public Spaces," in "Filming in the Space of the People," ed. Judith Pernin and Sebastian Veg, special issue of *China Perspectives*, no. 1 (2010): 4–10.
16. *Avant-garde Today* was a journal/book series edited by Peking Normal University professor Jiang Yuanlun and Wang Meng. Published from 1994 by Sanlian, then from 2000 by the Tianjin Academy of Sciences, it included seventeen issues up to 2013. Another journal, *Xianfeng Yicong* (Collection of avant-garde translations), published from 2000, also paid attention to independent cinema. Its first five issues were on "rock and culture," "queer theory," "the Sixties" "TV and power," and "the soul of the Internet." Later issues focused on experimental theater, experimental architecture, and experimental film (issue 9).
17. Jia Zhangke, "Wode jiaodian" (My focal point), *Jinri Xianfeng*, no. 5 (1997), in *Jia xiang* (Jia's thoughts) (Beijing: Peking University Press, 2009), 18.

18. Jia Zhangke, "Yeyu dianying shidai jijiang zaici daolai" (The age of amateur cinema is about to return), *Nanfang Zhoumo*, November 13, 1998, in *Jia xiang*, 35.
19. Jia Zhangke, "Youle VCD he shuma shexiangji yihou" (Now that we have VCDs and digital cameras), in *Jia xiang*, 37, 38. "Internal reference screenings" of foreign films were sometimes organized by work units for leading officials but were not open to the general public.
20. Jia Zhangke, "Yige laizi Zhongguo jiceng de minjian daoyan" (An unofficial director from China's grass roots), interview by Lin Xudong, *Jintian*, no. 3 (June 1998), in *Jia xiang*, 46, 69. For an elaboration on this topic, see also Leung Yee-man, "Cong bianyuan dao *Shijie* de minjian shishi" (A folk/*minjian* epic from the margins to *The World*), in *All About the World of Jia Zhangke* (Hong Kong: Hong Kong Arts Centre, 2005), 18–20.
21. Jia Zhangke has repeatedly underlined that his use of the word "amateur" refers to a mindset in approaching his subject matter, not to the technical quality (or lack thereof) of the films gathered under this label. However, the "impossible ideal of art not made by artists" can be challenging to realize (Valerie Jaffee, "'Every Man a Star': The Ambivalent Cult of Amateur Art in New Chinese Documentaries," in *From Underground to Independent*, ed. Pickowicz and Zhang, 103).
22. Ji Dan, director's statement for *When the Bough Breaks* (Wei chao, 2010), in *5th Yunfest Catalogue* (Kunming: Yunnan Meishu, 2011), 29.
23. Jia Zhangke, "Building a Public Consciousness," interviewed by Sebastian Veg, *China Perspectives*, no. 1 (2010): 62.
24. Jia Zhangke, "Building a Public Consciousness," 62.
25. *Still Life* won a prize in Venice but was deemed "without love, not worth watching" by Zhang Hongsen, the head of the State Administration of Press, Publication, Radio, Film, and Television. See Guo Qiang, "Film Chief Chides 'Cold Hearted' Director," *China Daily*, March 26, 2007. Local languages are generally frowned upon in approved films and actually also banned in the case of important political characters such as Mao. See Dali Yang, "Language and the Politics of Identity in China in the Age of Globalization," in *Is There a Greater China Identity? Security and Economic Dilemma*, ed. I Yuan (Taipei: National Chengchi University, 2007), 159–172. For a full discussion of the use of local languages, see Liu Jin, "The Rhetoric of Local Languages as the Marginal: Chinese Underground and Independent Films by Jia Zhangke and Others," *Modern Chinese Literature and Culture* 18, no. 2 (2006): 163–205.
26. Jia Zhangke, "Building a Public Consciousness," 64.
27. Jia Zhangke, "Wo bu shihua ziji de jingli" (I don't poeticize my experience) (1998), in *Jia xiang*, 30.
28. In Zhang Yimou's film *Qiu Ju*, the protagonist, as has been remarked, is not an individual, but the "larger-than-life icon of the repressed peasant woman," whereas the migrant worker, "unlike the timeless cipher of Gong Li, is hardly an icon for a 'national cinema'" (Zhang Zhen, "Introduction. Bearing Witness: Chinese Urban Cinema in the Era of 'Transformation' [Zhuanxing]," in *The Urban Generation*, ed. Zhang Zhen, 6).
29. Jia Zhangke, "Yige laizi Zhongguo jiceng," in *Jia xiang*, 55
30. Jia Zhangke refers to a conversation between Wang Xiaobo and Hsu Cho-yun about how art can establish a more fruitful relationship between individuals and society ("Building a Public Consciousness," 60).

31. Jia Zhangke, "Building a Public Consciousness," 61–62.
32. Jia Zhangke, "Building a Public Consciousness," 60.
33. See Wu Wenguang, "DV: Yige ren de yingxiang," in *Jingtou xiang ziji de yanjing yiyang* (The camera is just like my own eyes) (Shanghai: Shanghai Wenyi, 2001), 256–263, translated as "DV: Individual Filmmaking," trans. Cathryn Clayton, in *The New Chinese Documentary Film Movement: For the Public Record*, ed. Chris Berry, Xinyu Lu, and Lisa Rofel (Hong Kong: Hong Kong University Press, 2010), 51.
34. Wu Wenguang, "DV," 49, 54.
35. Wu Wenguang, "*Xianchang*: He jilu fangshi youguan de shu" (*Document*: A book related to a style of documentation), *Xianchang* 1 (2000): 274–275, quoted and translated in Luke Robinson, "From 'Public' to 'Private': Chinese Documentary and the Logic of *Xianchang*," in *The New Chinese Documentary Film Movement*, ed. Berry, Lü, and Rofel, 180.
36. Wu Wenguang, "2017: Leng nuan wenti" (2017: Problems of warmth and coldness), Caochangdi Public WeChat Account, December 31, 2017, http://www.ifuun.com/a201801068649526/.
37. Luke Robinson, "Contingency and Event in China's New Documentary Film Movement," Nottingham University, 2007, 27, http://eprints.nottingham.ac.uk/546/. See also Luke Robinson, *Independent Chinese Documentary: From the Studio to the Street* (New York: Palgrave Macmillan, 2013), 30.
38. Quoted in Robinson, "From 'Public' to 'Private,'" 180, 188. Hu Xinyu is in fact echoing an earlier manifesto by Yu Jian in favor of *minjian* poetry. See Yu Jian, "Jujue yinyu" (Rejecting metaphor) (August 1995), in *Yu Jian ji*, 5:125–136, and chapter 1 in this book.
39. In this sense, one might argue that certain works of independent cinema are perhaps more indebted to the formal experiments of the Soviet avant-garde than to Italian neorealism. See also my discussion in "From Documentary to Fiction and Back: Reality and Contingency in Wang Bing's and Jia Zhangke's Films," *China Perspectives*, no. 3 (2007): 136.
40. Jia Zhangke notes the inspiration he took for the execution scene in *Xiao Wu* from Lu Xun's novella *The True Story of Ah Q* (1921). See Michael Berry, *Jia Zhangke's Hometown Trilogy: "Xiao Wu," "Platform," "Unknown Pleasures"* (Houndmills, U.K.: Palgrave Macmillan on behalf of the British Film Institute, 2009), 46–47. Jia has also repeatedly highlighted in interviews that ordinary spaces are a kind of matrix for his films, including their most "unrealistic" aspects. See "*Gonggong changsuo* zishu" (My account of *In Public*) in *Jia xiang*, 107.
41. In this perspective, Zhang Zhen's characterization of independent filmmakers as "the urban generation" may be somewhat problematic: not only were urban settings not new (many "urban" films were already made by the Fifth Generation), but also most independent films are set in rural county towns. As Zhang suggests, the urban paradigm is better understood as "a critical category that places film practice right in the middle of a living, if often agitated, social, cultural, and political experience," which brings it very close to the meaning of *xianchang* (introduction to *The Urban Generation*, ed. Zhang Zhen, 8).
42. Wu Wenguang, "Filmer l'imprévisible," interview by Judith Pernin, *Monde chinois*, no. 14 (October 2008): 32, author's translation.

43. Ai Xiaoming, "Caméra-stylo, pour un réquisitoire social," interview by Judith Pernin, *Monde chinois*, no. 14 (October 2008): 37, author's translation. Margherita Viviani argues for a redefinition of "independent" in the sense of "a clear direction towards social involvement and forms of civic engagement" ("Chinese Independent Documentary Films: What Role in Contemporary China?" paper presented at the Asian Studies Association of Australia biennial conference, July 5–8, 2010, Adelaide).
44. See Paul Pickowicz, "Social and Political Dynamics of Underground Filmmaking in China," in *From Underground to Independent*, ed. Pickowicz and Zhang, 1–21. See also Valerie Jaffee, "Bringing the World to the Nation: Jia Zhangke and the Legitimation of Chinese Underground Film," *Senses of Cinema*, no. 32 (July–September 2004), http://sensesofcinema.com/2004/feature-articles/chinese_underground_film/.
45. Cui Weiping, "Zhongguo dalu duli zhizuo jilupian de shengzhang kongjian."
46. Li Xiaoshan quoted in Lü Xinyu, "Bei faxian de nüxing shijiao—guanyu jilupian *Huidao Fenghuang qiao* fang Li Hong, Li Xiaoshan" (The female gaze discovered—interview with Li Hong and Li Xiaoshan about the documentary *Back to Fenghuang Bridge*), *Jintian*, no. 3 (2001): 53, in *Jilu Zhongguo*, 204.
47. Cui Weiping, "Zhongguo dalu duli zhizuo jilupian de shengzhang kongjian," 84.
48. Cheng Qingsong and Huang Ou, *Wode sheyingji bu sahuang: Xianfeng dianyingren dang'an—shengyu 1961–1970* (My camera doesn't lie: Archives of avant-garde film people born in the 1960s) (Beijing: Zhongguo Youyi Chuban Gongsi, 2002; reprint, Beijing: Shandong Huabao Chubanshe, 2010). This book includes interviews with Zhang Ming, Jiang Wen, Zhang Yuan, Wang Chao, Lu Xuechang, Lou Ye, Wang Xiaoshuai, and Jia Zhangke.
49. Mei Bing and Zhu Jingjiang, "Qianyan" (Preface), in *Zhongguo duli jilupian dang'an* (Archives of China's independent documentaries), ed. Mei Bing and Zhu Jingjiang (Xi'an: Shaanxi Normal University, 2004), 2.
50. Zhu Jingjiang, "Daolun: Xunzhao de niandai—Zhongguo duli jilupian de qianshi jinsheng" (Introduction: Years of searching—the past and present of independent Chinese documentary), in *Zhongguo duli jilupian dang'an*, ed. Mei Bing and Zhu Jingjiang, 6–7. Zhu also notes that the habit of showing ordinary people was popularized by new types of television shows (8).
51. Zhu Jingjiang, "Daolun," 12.
52. Yangzi, "Sikao de dianying yu xiangxiang minjianhua—Yangzi fangtan" (Films that think and the *minjian* turn of imagination—an interview with Yangzi), in *Zhongguo duli jilupian dang'an*, ed. Mei Bing and Zhu Jingjiang, 53.
53. Zhu Rikun and Wan Xiaogang, "Xu" (Foreword), in *Yingxiang Chongdong: Duihua Zhongguo Xinrui Daoyan* (Subtitle: The image is excited), ed. Zhu Rikun and Wan Xiaogang (Fuzhou: Haixia Wenyi, 2005), 1.
54. Cui Weiping, "Zhongguo dalu duli zhizuo jilupian de shengzhang kongjian."
55. Zhang Xianmin and Zhang Yaxuan, eds., *Yige ren de yingxiang: DV wanquan shouce* (Subtitle: All about DV: Works, making, creation, comments) (Beijing: Zhongguo qingnian, 2003), which includes discussion of four foreign documentaries; four Chinese films—Zhu Wen's *Seafood* (*Haixian*, 2001), Jia Zhangke's *In Public*, Du Haibin's *Along the Railway*, Ying Weiwei's *The Box* (*Hezi* , 2001)—profiles of a dozen documentary directors, technical advice on shooting in DV, and a series of essays.

56. Lü Xinyu, "Zai wutuobang de feixu shang," 13. Wu Wenguang has expressed doubts about the relevance of designating such a disparate body of films as a movement: he views it as simply a group of friends who shared some ideas and a new way of making documentaries, which began before DV cameras appeared ("Filmer l'imprévisible," 33).
57. Lü Xinyu, "Zai wutuobang de feixu shang," 16. Overseas scholars have persistently questioned the "independence" of this set of films. For example, Zhang Yingjin writes: "What is meant by 'independence' when they take orders from, and report directly to, overseas funding agencies, be they international film festivals, private foundations or television stations?" ("Thinking Outside the Box: Mediation of Imaging and Information in Contemporary Chinese Independent Documentary," *Screen* 48, no. 2 [2007]: 19). Jason McGrath notes that "the sensationalised marketing in the West of independent Chinese cinema as 'banned in China!' is an undeniable phenomenon symptomatic of a lingering cold war cultural discourse" ("The Independent Cinema of Jia Zhangke: From Postsocialist Realism to a Transnational Aesthetic," in *The Urban Generation*, ed. Zhang Zhen, 108). By contrast, Lü Xinyu's study shows that the origins of the new documentary movement are quite "local," with foreign interest appearing only later.
58. Lü Xinyu, "Xin Jilu yundong de li yu tong" (The power and pain of the New Documentary Movement), *Dushu*, no. 5 (2006): 12–22.
59. In Jia's words: "Fiction is also a bridge to authenticity [*zhenshi*]. Including our understanding of it—how it happens, how it becomes real; what are its levels? Authenticity itself is a kind of experience, a kind of judgment, not a style of documentary-making. That is why, in my documentaries there are many arranged shots, I make up a lot, and I use actual people to act" ("Jia Zhangke vs. Du Haibin," *Mingpao Weekly*, November 28, 2009).
60. Wang Xiaolu, "'Zhuti' jian xian: Ershi nian Zhongguo duli jilupian de guancha" (The "subject" gradually appears: An investigation of twenty years of independent film in China), *Dianying Yishu*, no. 6 (June 2010): 72–78, also in *Jintian huo huangjin shidai* (Today or the golden age), ed. Yi Sicheng (Kunming: Yunfest Internal Publication, 2011), 169, 174.
61. Lü Xinyu, "Ruins of the Future: Class and History in Wang Bing's *Tiexi District*," *New Left Review*, no. 31 (January–February 2005): 127, 132, 136. See also Lü Xinyu, "*Tiexi qu*: Lishi yu jieji yishi" (*West of the Tracks*: History and class consciousness), *Dushu*, no. 1 (2004): 3–15.
62. The discussion, bringing together Li Tuo, Cui Weiping, Jia Zhangke, Xi Chuan, Ouyang Jianghe, and Wang Hui, was published in *Dushu*, no. 2 (2007): 3–31, and as "*Sanxia hao ren*: Guli, bianqian yu Jia Zhangke de xianshizhuyi" (*Still Life*: Hometown, change, and Jia Zhangke's realism), in *Zhongguo duli jilupian: Fangtan lu* (Chinese independent cinema: A collection of interviews), ed. Ouyang Jianghe (Hong Kong: Oxford University Press, 2007), 240–275.
63. Wang Hui, "Jia Zhangke's World and China's Great Transformation: A Revised Version of a Speech Given at 'The *Still Life* Symposium' at Fenyang High School," trans. Nathaniel Proctor, *positions* 19, no. 1 (2011): 228, For the Chinese original, see "Jia Zhangke de *Shijie* yu Zhongguo de da zhuanxing," *Renwen yu Shehui*, February 5, 2007, http://wen.org.cn/modules/article/view.article.php/article=152.

64. This tension between Marxist and post-Marxist views of the subaltern is very similar to the one expressed in Lin Chun's critical discussion of Wang Xiaobo's notion of the "silent majority" (see chapter 2).
65. Wang Bing, *Alors, la Chine*, interview by Emmanuel Burdeau and Eugenio Renzi (Paris: Les Prairies Ordinaires, 2014), 92, author's translation.
66. The discussion of the forum relies on Ying Qian, "Just Images: Ethics and Documentary Film in China," *China Heritage Quarterly*, no. 29 (March 2012), http://www.chinaheritagequarterly.org/scholarship.php?searchterm=029_qian.inc&issue=029.
67. Independent Chinese filmmakers have increasingly sought to take back control of theoretical discourse from critics. A significant endeavor in this regard is the collectively edited unofficial journal published as a pdf under the title *Film Auteur* (*Dianying Zuozhe*). The collective was formed in June 2012 by a dozen members at director Mao Chenyu's home in Hunan, arguing that "independent film as a whole, in order to be seen as one of the subjective languages of contemporary culture and recognized collectively, needs a gathering of forces and a collective symbol" (Mao Chenyu, "Ci han geming haishi qingnian ren zai yinyu" [Words calling for revolution or young people using metaphors?], preface to *Dianying Zuozhe*, no. 1 [2012]: [p. i]). The manifesto "Shamanism-Animal" was posted to a wall during the China Independent Film Festival (CIFF) in Nanjing in 2011. It can be found online: "Saman-dongwu: Dui 2011 nian 10 yue 31 ri CIFF jilupian luntan de huiying" (Shamanism-animal: A reply to the Documentary Forum at CIFF on October 31, 2011), *Douban*, https://site.douban.com/129499/widget/notes/5494326/note/181581347/.
68. Dan Edwards and Marina Svensson, "Show Us Life and Make Us Think: Engagement, Witnessing, and Activism in Independent Chinese Documentary Today," in a special issue of *Studies in Documentary Film* 11, no. 3 (2017): 164. Ai's approach is further documented in the other articles of this special issue.
69. Ouyang Jianghe, "Bianzhe qianyan" (Editor's introduction), in *Zhongguo duli jilupian: Fangtan lu*, ed. Ouyang Jianghe, viii–x.
70. Ouyang Jianghe, "Bianzhe qianyan," ix.
71. Zeng Jinyan, "Dang women tanlun duli dianying shi, women tanlun shenme" (What are we talking about when we discuss independent film?), in Wen Hai, *Fangzhu de ningshi*, 9–23.
72. An earlier version of this section appeared in Chinese in an internal publication of Yunfest.
73. Yi Sicheng, "A Window to Our Times: China's Independent Film Since the Late 1990s," Ph.D. diss., University of Kiel, 2006, 38.
74. Judith Pernin counts less than ten independent documentaries per year in the 1990s but between twenty and fifty a year now, with about fifty active directors, for a total of about five hundred films (*Pratiques indépendantes du documentaire en Chine*, 10). She singles out four important aspects for discussion: the use of space, the attitude of participant observation, unofficial memory, and the representation of catastrophe. Ying Qian suggests another loose typology structured around six thematic categories: vagabond artists, state power, intimate films, demolition, activist films, and testimony ("Power in the Frame: China's Independent Documentary Movement," *New Left Review*, no. 74

[March–April 2012]: 105–123). Marina Svensson and Dan Edwards argue that independent documentary shows things that are generally hidden in mainstream images: people and identities, events and situations, memories and historical experiences ("Show Us Life and Make Us Think: Engagement, Witnessing, and Activism in Independent Chinese Documentary Today," *Studies in Documentary Film* 11, no. 3 [2017]: 164).

75. Wen Hai, "Zha gen: Yige Zhongguo duli jilupianren de zibai" (Putting down roots: The monologue of an independent Chinese documentary director), in *Fangzhu de ningshi*, 333.
76. Ying Qian, "Power in the Frame," 105.
77. For this understanding of trains and the railways in China, see, for example, Emma Yu Zhang, "Socialist Builders on the Rails and Road: Industrialization, Social Engineering, and National Imagination in Chinese Socialist Films, 1949–1965," *Twentieth Century China* 42, no. 3 (2017): 255–273.
78. Sidney Leng, "Why a Chinese State Media Journalist Gave Up His Career to Become an Independent Filmmaker," interview, *South China Morning Post*, July 9, 2017, http://www.scmp.com/news/china/article/2101845/filmmaker-recalls-chinas-golden-age-documentaries.
79. Ning Ying, "My Motivation Is to Depict People I Can Identify With," interview by S. Louisa Wei, *China Perspectives*, no. 1 (2010): 66.
80. Jia Zhangke, "Building a Public Consciousness," 61. Of course, the theme of trains and travel also evokes fantasies of emancipation and escape from the bleak towns of Shanxi, a metaphorical role played by the train in Jia's feature *Platform* (*Zhantai*, 2000).
81. Jia Zhangke, "*Gonggong changsuo* daoyan de hua" (Director's statement on *In Public*), in *Jia xiang*, 105. Jia Zhangke says in another interview: "It's very obvious that I have an affection for trains. The train stands for hope and the future. The motif of the train is very well integrated into *Platform*. It is really very special. Personally, when I learned how to ride the bicycle, the first thing I did was to peddle to a distant place to look at a train because I had never seen a train. I was already in my teens" (Stephen Teo, "Cinema with an Accent—Interview with Jia Zhangke, Director of *Platform*," *Senses of Cinema*, July 2001, http://sensesofcinema.com/2001/feature-articles/zhangke_interview/).
82. One might say that this cinema's aesthetic fascination with ruins reveals its Benjaminian affinities, wherein it is prone to contemplating the past as a growing mountain of ruins as the camera, like Klee's angel, continues to be blown forward.
83. Lü Xinyu, "Ruins of the Future," 128.
84. Jia Zhangke, "Qiyu de dou shi chenmo," in *Zhongguo gongren fangtanlu* (Records of interviews with China's working class) (Jinan: Shandong Huabao, 2009), translated as "What Remains Is Silence," *China Perspectives*, no. 1 (2010): 55.
85. See also Pernin, *Pratiques indépendantes du cinéma documentaire*, 226–234. Marina Svensson argues that the documentaries devoted to the earthquake marked an evolution from the approach of bearing witness to a more engaged or confrontational approach ("Digitally Enabled Engagement and Witnessing: The Sichuan Earthquake on Independent Documentary Film," *Studies in Documentary Film* 11, no. 3 [2017]: 200–216).
86. Yu Jian, "Jingtou houmian de chanhui" (The confessions behind the camera), in *Jintian huo huangjin shidai*, ed. Yi Sicheng, 3.

87. "Fly on the Wall: Interview with Liu Jiayin, Director of *Oxhide & Oxhide II*," *Artspace China* (University of Sydney), June 3, 2011, http://blogs.usyd.edu.au/artspacechina/2011/06/the_universal_in_particular_in.html.
88. Jie Li, "Filming Power and the Powerless," *China Perspectives*, no. 1 (2010): 41.
89. Zhao Liang, interview in *Liang You* (Companion), February 1, 2010, trans. Yan Yuqian, *dGenerate Films*, http://dgeneratefilms.com/critical-essays/zhao-liang-interviewed-about-petition.
90. Zhao Liang, "I'm More Concerned with Elegance of Expression," *Phenomena*, May 4, 2009, http://zhaoliangstudio.com/work/petition.
91. "Jilupian yu shehui xianshi" (Documentary film and social reality), *Fanhall Film*, July 24, 2009.
92. Ying Qian, "Power in the Frame," 108.
93. Zhang Xianmin, "Questioning and Understanding: On the Chinese Free Documentary Movement Since 2000," in *Asian Documentary Today*, ed. Jane H. C. Yu (Busan: Busan International Film Festival, 2012), 58–59. Zhang quotes the example of the Qifang Cinephile Collective, which has been active since 2011,with branches in sixteen cities, and was developed out of social media.
94. Lin Xudong, "Documentary in Mainland China." The six films, screened in the New Asian Currents category, were: Wu Wenguang, *1966 My Time in the Red Guards* (which received the Shinsuke Ogawa Prize); SWYC Group, *I Graduated* (*Wo biye le*, 1992); Hao Zhiqiang, *Big Tree County* (*Da shu xian*, 1992); Wen Pulin, *The Sacred Site of Asceticism* (*Qingpu: Kuxiuzhe de shengdi*, 1992); Jiang Yue, *Catholicism in Tibet* (*Tianzhu zai Xizang*, 1992); and Fu Hongxing, *Tibetan Opera Troupe in Khams* (*Ganzi Zangxi tuan*, 1992).
95. A connection thus developed between the new generation of film directors and Hong Kong (where Jia Zhangke set up his production company X-Stream). See Li Cheuk-to, Wong Ain-ling, and Jacob Wong, "New Chinese Cinema at the HKIFF: A Look Back at the Last 20 Years," *China Perspectives*, no. 1 (2010): 79. This connection is somewhat similar to Hong Kong's role in book publishing.
96. See Jia Zhangke, "Youle VCD he shuma shexiangji yihou," and Seio Nakajima, "Film Clubs in Beijing: The Cultural Consumption of Chinese Independent Films," in *From Underground to Independent*, ed. Pickowicz and Zhang, 161–188. Beijing's first "arthouse cinema" was opened in the MOMA complex by the Hong Kong–based Broadway circuit in early 2010.
97. Wen Hai, *Fangzhu de ningshi*, 75.
98. Chris Berry and Lisa Rofel, introduction to *The New Chinese Documentary Film Movement*, ed. Berry, Lu, and Rofel, 3–13.
99. Shu Kewen, "Lao Li qianshi" (The prehistory of Mr. Li), *Sanlian Shenghuo Zhoukan*, no. 43 (November 18, 2008), http://lifeweek.com.cn/2008/1118/23320.shtml. According to Li Xianting, Yuanmingyuan began in 1986 with the artist Tian Bin. It offered cheap housing and cheap food at university canteens nearby, making it ideal for graduated students who didn't want to enter the system. Both Zhao Liang and Hu Jie made films about Yuanmingyuan and its destruction: Hu Jie, *The Artists of Yuanmingyuan* (*Yuanmingyuan de yishujia*, 1995), and Zhao Liang, *Farewell to Yuanmingyuan* (*Gaobie Yuanmingyuan*, 1995/2006). See also Zheng Kuo, *The Cold Winter* (*Nuandong* [lit., Warm winter], 2011), which documents the struggle against the expropriation of artists in District 798.

100. Sun Meng, "The Production of Art Districts," Ph.D. diss., University of Chicago, 2010. At this time, Songzhuang village was classified as a rural area, meaning the land was collectively owned by the village. When artists "bought" plots of land, they acquired only what is known as "minor property rights" (*xiao chanquan*), in contrast with urban land, which is owned by the state and can be "sold" to private owners (usually in the form of seventy-year renewable government leases). This means that when rural land is rezoned as urban and appropriated by the local government for development and sale, holders of "minor property rights" are not entitled to specific compensation for anything they have built on the land but must take whatever the government offers them for the plot and leave. Several famous artists, such as Huang Rui in Caochangdi, have been trapped in this legal conundrum. See also "Zhuming xuezhe Yu Jianrong gongzuoshi mianlin chaiqian" (Famous schloar Yu Jianrong's workshop faces demolition), *Mingpao*, May 23, 2017, https://news.mingpao.com/pns17052414955623549 87.
101. Meng Jing, "Xiaopu dili" (The geography of Xiaopu), *Sanlian Shenghuo Zhoukan*, no. 43 (November 18, 2008), http://lifeweek.com.cn/2008/1118/23318.shtml.
102. Zeng Yan, "Wanwu shengzhang" (All things grow), *Sanlian Shenghuo Zhoukan*, no. 43 (November 18, 2008), http://lifeweek.com.cn/2008/1118/23321.shtml, including quotation from Li Xianting.
103. Yu Jianrong, "Songzhuang wenhua: Dangdai Zhongguo beifang nongcun shehui bianqian" (The culture of Songzhuang: Changes in present-day northern Chinese villages), *Dongshufang* (Yu Jianrong's WeChat account), February 6, 2014.
104. Shu Kewen, "Li Xianting de cunzhuang shi" (Li Xianting's village history), *Sanlian Shenghuo Zhoukan*, no. 43 (November 18, 2008), http://lifeweek.com.cn/2008/1118/23322.shtml.
105. Yue Zhang, "Governing Art Districts: State Control and Cultural Production in Contemporary China," *China Quarterly*, no. 219 (September 2014): 838.
106. Yue Zhang, "Governing Art Districts," 840.
107. Sun Meng, "The Production of Art Districts," 176–209.
108. 798 Factory, which had become an art district in the 1990s, was dismantled and privatized in 2000. In 2003, the owner, Seven Stars Group, stopped issuing leases and prepared for demolition to build a high-tech park. In 2004, academics tabled a motion with the municipal government to preserve the district. In 2006, 798 District was officially designated a Cultural Creative Industry Cluster, although the government shut down the Dashanzi Art Festival. Leases increased sevenfold in five years, and the number of galleries went from 22 in 2003 to 398 in 2008. Commercial activities blossomed, and 798 subsequently became a tourist hotspot (Yue Zhang, "Governing Art Districts," 835).
109. Yue Zhang, "Governing Art Districts," 829.
110. See Wen Hai, *Fangzhu de ningshi*, 80, 82.
111. Author's interview with Li Xianting, Songzhuang, July 11, 2015.
112. According to the respective program catalogs, Zhou Chunya sponsored the fourth BIFF in 2009; Oriental Group's Xu Xiaoping supported the fifth BIFF in 2010; designer Ding Yong the seventh DOChina in 2010; and Zeng Fanzhi the ninth BIFF in 2012.
113. Yomi Braester discusses "independent film schools" (Li Xianting and Caochangdi) in "Film Schools in the PRC: Professionalization and Its Discontents," in *The Education of*

the Filmmaker in Europe, Australia, and Asia, ed. Mette Hjort (New York: Palgrave Macmillan, 2013), 214–215. Braester notes that the success of LXT Film School was correlated with growing government control of Beijing Film Academy (Cui Zi'en was barred from teaching, Cui Weiping was increasingly sidelined until her retirement in 2011, and Zhang Xianmin avoided sensitive subjects).

114. See Li Xianting, "We Just Want to Make the Films We Like," October 5, 2011, in *Catalogue of the 6th BIFF* (N.p.: publisher not listed, 2011). From 2008, Zhu began publishing a yearly report on the Fanhall website as well as the journal *Zhongguo duli yingxiang* (China independent images).
115. Wen Hai, *Fangzhu de ningshi*, 92.
116. Zhu Rikun, "Preface," trans. J. P. Sniadnecki, in *Catalogue of the 4th Beijing Independent Film Festival* (N.p: publisher not listed, 2009), unpaginated.
117. See also Abe Markus Nornes's ethnography of the BIFF in 2009: "Bulldozers, Bibles, and Very Sharp Knives," *Film Quarterly*, Fall 2009, 50–55.
118. Wen Hai, *Fangzhu de ningshi*, 266.
119. See Wang Hongwei and Qiu Jiongjiong, "Jijin, xuexiao, dianyingjie" (A foundation, a school, and a film festival), *Film Auteur*, no. 6 (2014): 197. Around the same time, Ying Liang was forced to leave China and settled in Hong Kong after being prevented from showing his film *When Nights Falls* (*Wo haiyou hua yao shuo*, 2012) on the Shanghai Yang Jia stabbing case (the state tried to buy up all the rights to the film).
120. In 2011, several films were devoted to sensitive historical themes—for instance, Wang Bing's *The Ditch* (*Jiabiangou*) and Hu Jie's *Wang Peiying*.
121. Li Xianting, "We Just Want to Make the Films We Like," unpaginated.
122. Wen Hai, *Fangzhu de ningshi*, 272.
123. Li Xianting, "Combining Efforts to Build 'Small Environments,'" August 10, 2012, trans. Qian Ying, in *Catalogue of the 9th Beijing Independent Film Festival* (N.p.: publisher not listed, [2012]), unpaginated.
124. According to Zeng Jinyan, 1,522 films were confiscated ("Dang women tanlun duli dianying shi women tanlun shenme," 10).
125. Wang Hongwei and Qiu Jiongjiong, "Jijin, xuexiao, dianyingjie," 200.
126. Wang Hongwei, "Mu'er de gushi/A story of black ear-fungus," in *Catalogue of the 11th Beijing Independent Film Festival* (N.p.: n.p., 2014), 2.
127. Similar events occurred in the village of Picun, a little farther north, where the Workers' Museum (Gong You Zhi Jia, established in 2002) was forced to move in 2016.
128. Wang Hongwei and Qiu Jiongjiong, "Jijin, xuexiao, dianyingjie," 201.
129. Yi Sicheng, preface to the *5th Yunfest Catalogue*, unpaginated.
130. Yi Sicheng, preface to the *5th Yunfest Catalogue*.
131. Wen Hai, *Fangzhu de ningshi*, 273, 275.
132. See Lü Xinyu, "Xin Jilu yundong de li yu tong."
133. Ou Ning, "Interview about the Notebook Project Bishan Commune," in *Bishan Commune: How to Start Your Own Utopia* ([Copenhagen]: Ovopress, 2015), 14. See also Ou Ning, "Social Change and Rediscovering Rural Reconstruction in China," in *New Worlds from Below: Grassroots Networking and Informal Life Politics in Twenty-First Century East Asia*, ed. Tessa Morris-Suzuki (Canberra: Australian National University Press, 2017), 37–50.

134. See Calum Macleod, "Crushed Dreams of Utopia in Rural China," *Times* (London), May 2, 2016.
135. For example, Tang Xiaobing formulates a "dissidence hypothesis" according to which Western scholars are interested only in what is marginalized or forbidden in China while ignoring the mainstream (*Visual Culture in Contemporary China* [Cambridge: Cambridge University Press, 2015], 199).
136. Ying Zhu and Seio Nakajima "The Evolution of Chinese Film as an Industry," in *Art, Politics, and Commerce in Chinese Cinema*, ed. Ying Zhu and Stanley Rosen (Hong Kong: Hong Kong University Press, 2010), 29.
137. For example, Gu Changwei's film *Love for Life* (*Zui Ai*, 2011).
138. Quoted in "Lights, Camera, Redaction: China Sets New Rules for Filmmakers," *Wall Street Journal*, November 19, 2016, http://www.wsj.com/articles/lights-camera-redaction-china-sets-new-rules-for-filmmakers-1479466803.
139. Quoted in "China Passes Restrictive New Film Law," Radio Television Hong Kong, November 7, 2016, http://news.rthk.hk/rthk/en/component/k2/1295250-20161107.htm.
140. Yiwen Cai, "Less Censorship Could Make Independent Films Suffer," *China Film Insider*, November 9, 2016, http://chinafilminsider.com/less-censorship-make-independent-film-productions-suffer.
141. See the translation of the draft Film Industry Promotion Law, November 7, 2016, http://www.chinalawtranslate.com/2016年电影产业促进法/, and Sidney Leng, "Indie Filmmakers Struggle to Rewrite the Script in Chinese Cinemas," *South China Morning Post*, October 8, 2017, http://www.scmp.com/news/china/society/article/2114377/indie-filmmakers-struggle-rewrite-script-chinese-cinemas.
142. In this sense, although allowing for some films to be "absorbed" within the system, the system continues to repress the very idea of "independent" films. Chris Berry argues that, despite the pressure, independent cinema can survive in new niches ("The Death of Chinese Independent Cinema?" *Asia Dialogue*, July 3, 2017, http://theasiadialogue.com/2017/07/03/the-death-of-chinese-independent-cinema/).

5. PROFESSIONALS AT THE GRASSROOTS: RIGHTS LAWYERS, ACADEMICS, AND PETITIONERS

1. Eva Pils notes June Fourth's "formative significance" on the *weiquan* movement ("The Practice of Law as Conscientious Resistance," in *The Impact of China's 1989 Tiananmen Massacre*, ed. Jean-Philippe Béja [London: Routledge, 2011], 109).
2. Many thanks to Eva Pils for pointing this out and for her close reading of the entire chapter.
3. See Eva Pils, *China's Human Rights Lawyers: Advocacy and Resistance* (London: Routledge, 2015), 39. Pils also notes that the Administrative Procedure Law adopted in 1989 already allowed for litigation against the state. Fu Hualing details the strategic use of public-interest litigation in nonsensitive cases in the 1990s ("Developing Rule of Law Through Public Interest Litigation," in *A Sword and a Shield: China's Human Rights Lawyers*, ed. Stacy Mosher and Patrick Poon [Hong Kong: China Human Rights Lawyers Concern Group, 2009], 129–140). Pils further argues that early reformers did not understand the threat to the party-state inherent in legal reforms before 2003 or 2004 (the

year "human rights" were written into the Constitution). In her view, Hu Jintao's "Three Supremes" (December 2007) mark the state's reply ("The Dislocation of the Chinese Human Rights Movement," in *A Sword and a Shield*, ed. Mosher and Poon, 141–159). For a full list of the laws enacted in the 1990s that brought about the professionalization of the legal sector, see Hualing Fu and Richard Cullen, "*Weiquan* (Rights Protection) Lawyering in an Authoritarian State: Building a Culture of Public-Interest Lawyering," *China Journal*, no. 59 (January 2008): 123.

4. Pils, *China's Human Rights Lawyers*, 49.
5. Teng Biao, "What Is Rights Defense?" in *A Sword and a Shield*, ed. Mosher and Poon, 122–123.
6. Pils, *China's Human Rights Lawyers*, 50, in which the term "vernacularize" is borrowed from Sally Engle-Merry, *Human Rights and Gender Violence* (Chicago: Chicago University Press, 2006).
7. He Weifang, "The Nascence and Growing Pains of a Professionalized Legal Class," *Columbia Journal of Asian Law* 19 (2005): 138–152.
8. Yu Xingzhong, "Judicial Professionalism in China: From Discourse to Reality," in *Prospects for the Professions in China*, ed. William Alford, Kenneth Winston, and William Kirby (London: Routledge, 2009), 78–108. See also Pils, *China's Human Rights Lawyers*, 48.
9. "Bei shourongzhe Sun Zhigang zhi si" (The death of custody and repatriation victim Sun Zhigang), *Nanfang Dushi Bao*, April 24, 2003.
10. Teng Biao, "The Sun Zhigang Incident and the Future of Constitutionalism: Does the Chinese Constitution Have a Future?," occasional paper, Centre for Rights and Justice, Chinese University of Hong Kong Faculty of Law, December 30, 2013, 1. See also Pils, *China's Human Rights Lawyers*, 49. The open letter "Proposal on Reviewing the *Measures for Internment*" was followed by another letter signed by He Weifang and four other scholars demanding an inquiry into the Sun Zhigang case. See also Keith Hand, "Using a Law for a Righteous Purpose: The Sun Zhigang Incident and Evolving Forms of Citizens' Action in China," *Columbia Journal of Transnational Law* 45 (2007): 114–159, reprinted in *Building Constitutionalism in China*, ed. Stéphanie Balme and Michael Dowdle (Paris: Sciences Po, 2009), 221–242.
11. Xu Zhiyong, "Sun Zhigang zhisi: Gongmin jianyi" (Sun Zhigang's death: A citizen proposal), in *Tangtang zhengzheng zuo gongmin: Wo de ziyou Zhongguo* (To be a citizen: A free China) (Hong Kong: New Century, 2014), 27. This essay provides an account of the Sun Zhigang incident as well as a copy of the original letter (39–40).
12. Teng Biao, "The Sun Zhigang Incident," 5. Teng makes similar points in "What Is Rights Defense?" in *A Sword and a Shield*, ed. Mosher and Poon, 122–128. In particular, he notes that in the 1980s it was difficult to tie the notions of freedom and democracy to issues directly affecting people's lives (123). By contrast, he argues, in the 2000s "grassroots elites" have come to support human rights (128).
13. Teng Biao, "Gongmin weiquan yu shehui zhuanxing" (Citizen rights defense and social transition), Boxun, June 26, 2010, https://blog.boxun.com/hero/201007/wqgc/2_1.shtml. In another article, Teng mentions the influence of liberalism and Václav Havel on the movement. For him, the five decisive factors in the rights-defense movement's rise were the development of the legal profession and the rise of rights consciousness among

citizens; the development of new media and smartphones that citizen journalists could use to directly post information to the Internet; the development of the market economy; the feeling of disenfranchisement of the middle class; and the return of liberalism and the resilience of the democracy movement. See Teng Biao, "Rights Defence (*Weiquan*), Microblogs (*Weibo*), and Popular Surveillance (*Weiguan*): The Rights Defence Movement Online and Offline," *China Perspectives*, no. 3 (2012): 29–39.

14. Xu Zhiyong references this use of *minquan* by Sun Yat-sen, for example, in "Yisheng weile yige mengxiang" (My whole life for a dream), in *Tangtang zhengzheng zuo gongmin*, 7. Ironically, Xu was born in a district in Henan named Minquan, a town developed under the republican government. He also attended Minquan High School.
15. Teng Biao, "Who Is Xu Zhiyong?" *China Change*, April 10, 2014, See also the original issue of *Yazhou Zhoukan*, no. 52 (December 25, 2005) at http://yzzk.com/cfm/content_archive.cfm?id=1367556872793&docissue=2005-52.
16. Kevin O'Brien, "Rightful Resistance," *World Politics* 49, no. 1 (1996): 33.
17. Pils, *China's Human Rights Lawyers*, 66.
18. Anthony Spires, "Contingent Symbiosis and Civil Society in an Authoritarian State: Understanding the Survival of China's Grassroots NGOs," *American Journal of Sociology* 117, no. 1 (2011): 1–45.
19. Eva Pils argues, "Compared to the June Fourth movement, the protagonists of today's human rights movement are [more] professionally sophisticated in their use of the law. They are also able to appeal to principles of legality that the state has by now propagated for nearly three decades. The mindset that insists on 'keeping to the rules,' on legality, on rejecting bribes, rule circumvention, and informal deals, is not exclusive to *weiquan* lawyers" ("The Practice of Law as Conscientious Resistance," 113).
20. Pils, *China's Human Rights Lawyers*, 236. Pils notes that this strategy was contested by younger lawyers. See also her discussion of Ding Zilin's critique of Gao Zhisheng in "Rights Activism in China: The Case of Lawyer Gao Zhisheng," in *Building Constitutionalism*, ed. Balme and Dowdle, 256–259.
21. Teng Biao, "Gongmin weiquan yu shehui zhuanxing."
22. Quoted in Teng Biao, "89 minzhu yundong yu gongmin weiquan yundong" (The 1989 democracy movement and the rights defense movement), May 2014, copy in the author's files.
23. See Teng Biao, "Speech During the June Fourth Vigil in Victoria Park in Hong Kong," *China Change*, June 5, 2014.
24. Jerome A. Cohen, "China Human Rights Lawyers' Current Challenges and Prospects," in *A Sword and a Shield*, ed. Mosher and Poon, 38–43. When Gao Zhisheng proposed in 2006 that *weiquan*, although remaining nonviolent, should become more politicized, more organized, and more street oriented, he provoked a heated discussion among lawyers (see Teng Biao, "89 minzhu yundong").
25. Fu and Cullen, "*Weiquan* (Rights Protection) Lawyering in an Authoritarian State," 122.
26. Rachel Stern, "Activist Lawmakers in Post-Tiananmen China," *Law and Social Inquiry* 42 (Winter 2017): 238.
27. Author's interview with Teng Biao, Hong Kong, June 11, 2014.
28. Teng Biao, "Rights Defence (*Weiquan*), Microblogs (*Weibo*), and Popular Surveillance (*Weiguan*)."

29. Ai Xiaoming was born in Wuhan in 1954; she moved to Beijing in 1985 to enroll in a Ph.D. program in literature at Beijing Normal University (where Liu Xiaobo was just finishing his degree). She was skeptical about the Tiananmen movement and watched the students from a distance. In the early 1990s, she developed a strong interest in Wang Xiaobo's writing and corresponded with him. She left Beijing in 1994 to take up a teaching position at Sun Yat-sen University in Guangzhou. In 1999, she spent a year at the University of the South in Tennessee and increasingly paid attention to civil rights activism. She retired in 2014 at the age of sixty and has pursued citizen activities, especially documentary film, since the early 2000s.
30. Huang Jing, a twenty-one-year-old primary-school teacher was found dead and naked in her school dormitory in Xiangtan, Hunan, on February 24, 2003. The authorities first tried to suppress the case, but public pressure through online petitions and mobilizations resulted in reopening the case and reforming judicial procedures for investigating suspected rape cases. For the larger background, see Pauline Stoltz, Marina Svensson, Sun Zhongxin, and Qi Wang, eds., *Gender Equality, Citizenship, and Human Rights: Controversies and Challenges in China and the Nordic Countries* (London: Routledge, 2010).
31. Ian Johnson, "The People in Retreat: An Interview with Ai Xiaoming," *New York Review of Books Daily*, September 8, 2016.
32. Ai Xiaoming, "The Citizen Camera," interview by Ying Qian and Chang Tieh-chih, *New Left Review*, no. 72 (November–December 2011): 67–69. Ai notes: "His [Hu Jie's] opinion was different from mine—at one point he told me he couldn't work on the film any more, since he didn't believe it was rape. We argued a lot about this" (69).
33. Johnson, "The People in Retreat."
34. Ai Xiaoming, "The Citizen Camera," 75–76.
35. Johnson, "The People in Retreat."
36. Johnson, "The People in Retreat."
37. Zeng Jinyan, "Daolun" (Introduction), in *Zhongguo nüquan: Gongmin zhishifenzi de dansheng* (Chinese feminism: The birth of a citizen intelligentsia) (Hong Kong: City University Press, 2016), 4; Zeng Jinyan, "The Politics of Emotion in Grassroots Feminist Protests: A Case Study of Xiaoming Ai's Nude Breasts Photography Protest Online," *Georgetown Journal of International Affairs*15, no. 1 (2014): 31–42.
38. Xu Zhiyong, "Gongmeng," in *Tangtang zhengzheng zuo gongmin*, 101; Teng Biao, "Who Is Xu Zhiyong?" According to Teng Biao, Zhang Xingshui withdrew after 2006.
39. Author's interview with Teng Biao, June 11, 2014; Xu Zhiyong, "Gongmeng," 105. Other legal NGOs such as the Transition Institute and China Against the Death Penalty all registered as commercial enterprises (Pils, *China's Human Rights Lawyers*, 248).
40. Xu Zhiyong, "Zhe 10 nian" (These ten years), in *Tangtang zhengzheng zuo gongmin*, 170.
41. Teng Biao, "Who Is Xu Zhiyong?"
42. The inaugural editorial of *Citizen Monthly* in March 2007 highlighted the importance of being citizens rather than subjects or "commoners" (*laobaixing*) and that the journal welcomed participation from all citizens. See "Guanyu *Gongmin Yuekan*" (On *Citizen Monthly*), *Gongmin Yuekan*, March 2007, https://cncitizens.wordpress.com/about-2/.
43. Teng Biao, "Who Is Xu Zhiyong?"
44. These structures can be considered NGOs: among NGOs in China, the vast majority pursue "service delivery." Gongmeng falls into the category of "advocacy in sensitive

areas," the type of NGO most likely to become a target for the authorities. See Fengshi Wu and Kinman Chan, "Graduated Control and Beyond: The Evolving Government-NGO Relations," *China Perspectives* 3 (2012): 9–17.

45. See Edward X. Gu, "Social Capital, Institutional Change, and the Development of Non-governmental Intellectual Organizations in China," in *Chinese Intellectuals Between State and Market*, ed. Edward X. Gu and Merle Goldman (London: Routledge, 2004), 40. The latter arrangement is known as a "second-order affiliation" (*erji guakao*).
46. Mao Yushi, "Zhuanfang Mao Yushi: Tianzesuo 23 nian, he zhe sannian, 'cuozhe shidai'" (Feature interview with Mao Yushi: Twenty-three years of Unirule and the "setback period" in the last three years), interview by Xiao Shu, *Initium*, October 4, 2016.
47. Mao Yushi, "Ba Mao Zedong huanyuan cheng ren" (Return Mao to the world of humans), *Caixin*, April 26, 2011 (removed from the Internet), translated as "Judging Mao as a Man," *Wall Street Journal*, July 6, 2011.
48. See Wendy Wu and Jane Cai, "Beijing Internet Censors Close Websites of Liberal Economic Think Tank," *South China Morning Post*, January 22, 2017.
49. See Sheng Hong, "Unirule Announcement on the Website Incident," Atlas Network, January 24, 2017, https://www.atlasnetwork.org/assets/uploads/misc/20170124_Unirule_announcement_on_website_incident.pdf (published on the website of Unirule's global partner network).
50. Lu Jun, "One More Law Won't Make Us Helpless," *China Digital Times*, July 16, 2015.
51. Zeng Jinyan, "Guo Yushan and the Predicament of NGOs in China," *Probe International*, May 2, 2015, https://journal.probeinternational.org/2015/05/21/guo-yushan-and-the-predicament-of-ngos-in-china/.
52. Zeng Jinyan, "Guo Yushan and the Predicament of NGOs." Guo's views are quoted from Zhao Sile, "Zhuanfang Beijing Chuanzhixing chuangbanren Guo Yushan: Baozhi juewang zitai zuo zhuanye de weiquan" (Interview with Beijing Transition Institute founder Guo Yushan: Doing professional rights defense while keeping a hopeless mindset), *iSun Affairs*, December 17, 2012.
53. See Xiao Shu, "Just Man Guo Yushan," *China Change*, November 9, 2014. According to Xiao Shu, Guo is a deep believer in Confucian "humanity" (*ren*).
54. Xu Zhiyong, "Yisheng weile yige mengxiang," 20–21. The Tieling local authorities approached PKU directly and also pulled strings at the Ministry of Public Security, which put pressure on PKU through the Ministry of Education. Xu was saved from expulsion by his supervisor, Zhu Suli, despite their political differences.
55. Xu Zhiyong, "Yisheng weile yige mengxiang," 12, 15.
56. Xu Zhiyong, "Xiangcun zhi xing: *Zhongguo gaige* nongcun ban de rizi" (My days at *China Reform*, village edition), in *Tangtang zhengzheng zuo gongmin*, 24.
57. Teng Biao, "Who Is Xu Zhiyong?"
58. Xu Zhiyong, "Women zai yiqi: Zoujin shangfangcun" (Together: Entering a petitioner village), in *Tangtang zhengzheng zuo gongmin*, 92.
59. Teng Biao, "Who Is Xu Zhiyong?"
60. The fullest timeline of these cases is "Gongmeng nianjian" (Annals of Gongmeng), n.d., https://xgmyd.com/archives/29099.
61. Teng Biao, "Defense in the Second Trial of Xia Junfeng's Case," originally translated at the Seeing Red in China website, https://seeingredinchina.com/2013/02/18/teng-biao

-defense-in-the-second-trial-of-xia-junfeng-case/, now defunct. The essay is still available on other websites, such as China Change: https://chinachange.org/2013/02/18/teng-biao-defense-in-the-second-trial-of-xia-junfeng-case/. Xia was executed on September 25, 2013, after two appeals were denied. See also Teng Biao, "Politics of the Death Penalty in China," *China Change*, January 16, 2014.

62. Since the All-China Bar Association became the main gatekeeper to the profession, disbarring lawyers and threatening law firms that did not fire rights lawyers, demanding an election was a way of resisting within the system.

63. Andrew Nathan, introduction to Xu Zhiyong, *To Build a Free China: A Citizen's Journey* (Boulder, Colo.: Lynne Rienner, 2016), ix. Some other legal clinics appeared at the same time (e.g., in Tsinghua University).

64. Teng Biao describes Gongmeng's stance as "we do not oppose for the sake of opposing" ("Who Is Xu Zhiyong?"). Xu Zhiyong recalls he believed the report should consist of one-third achievements, one-third criticism, and one-third recommendations, and Teng Biao argued that the citizen standpoints should be critical (Xu Zhiyong, "Pipingzhe," in *Tangtang zhengzheng zuo gongmin*, 151).

65. *Zhongguo xinfang baogao 2004–2007* (China Letters and Visits report) (Beijing: Gongmeng, 2008).

66. Teng Biao, "Who Is Xu Zhiyong?"

67. Xu Zhiyong, "Zhe shi nian," in *Tangtang zhengzheng zuo gongmin*, 173.

68. See "Open Letter," *Chinese Law and Government* 46, nos. 5–6 (2013): 61–62.

69. Foreword to Gongmeng Law Research Center, *Zangqu 3.14 shijian shehui jingji chengyin diaocha baogao* (Investigation of the social and economic causes of the March 14 incident in Tibetan areas) (Beijing: Gongmeng, 2008), https://docs.google.com/Doc?id=df4nrxxq_91ctcf6sck. The version on Woeser's blog (http://woeser.middle-way.net/2009/05/314.html) also contains appendix 1, which is missing on the Google site. An English translation was prepared by the International Campaign for Tibet but is marred by several elementary translations errors (such as "ethnic state" rather than "nation-state" for *minzu guojia*; the first author is given as Li Kun rather than Fang Kun; and so on). See Gongmeng, "An Investigative Report Into the Social and Economic Causes of the 3.14 Incident in Tibetan Areas," Save Tibet, n.d., http://www.savetibet.org/bold-report-by-beijing-scholars-reveals-breakdown-of-chinas-tibet-policy/.

70. By contrast, Wang Hui, for example, highlighted the following points: Western Orientalism, the wish to reduce the world to nation-states, the significance of the Chinese autonomy status, the end of class politics and the return of religion, conflicts between modernization and traditional lifestyle, and the dilemma of how to give "recognition" to vulnerable groups, which he views as part of the general crisis of postsocialism throughout China. He concludes by endorsing the *minjian* China expressed in his view in the patriotic student movement to defend the Olympic flame. See Wang Hui, "Dongfang zhuyi, minzu quyu zizhi yu zunyan zhengzhi—guanyu 'Xizang wenti' de yidian sikao" (Orientalism, self-rule of ethnic areas, and the politics of dignity—a few thoughts about the "Tibet problem"), *Tianya*, no. 4 (July 2008): 173–191, and the discussion in Sebastian Veg, "Tibet, Nationalism, and Modernity: Two Chinese Contributions," *China Perspectives*, no. 3 (2009): 98–107.

71. Xu Zhiyong, "Gongmeng," 109.

72. Gongmeng, *Zangqu 3.14 shijian*, sec. I.2.[2].
73. Gongmeng, *Zangqu 3.14 shijian*, sec. VI.
74. Xu Zhiyong, "Gongmeng," 105.
75. Eva Pils and Joshua Rosenzweig, "Beijing Confronts a New Kind of Dissident," *Wall Street Journal*, January 26, 2014.
76. Christoph Steinhardt, "State Behavior and the Intensification of Intellectual Criticism in China: The Social Stability Debate," *Modern China* 42, no. 3 (2016): 300–336. Steinhardt highlights the growing echo—at least up to 2013—of discourses critical of "stability maintenance" among intellectuals.
77. Pils, *China's Human Rights Lawyers*, 259. The umbrella company (registered as a business) continued to operate but could no longer access foreign funding.
78. Teng Biao, "Who Is Xu Zhiyong?"
79. Xu Zhiyong, "Gongmeng," 110.
80. Author's interview with Teng Biao, June 11, 2014. The name "Gongmin" was originally deemed too sensitive to be used openly. See Xu Zhiyong, "Gongmeng," 111.
81. Xu Zhiyong, "On the New Citizens' Movement," *China Digital Times*, May 13, 2013.
82. An institutional blueprint appears as "Zhi Zhongguo gongmin shu" (A letter to Chinese citizens), in Xu Zhiyong, *Tangtang zhengzheng zuo gongmin*, 176–255. In December 2013, a group of lawyers publicly called for a constitutional court (Pils, *China's Human Rights Lawyers*, 65).
83. A list of forty-five Chinese human rights lawyers' names appears on the first few pages of *A Sword and a Shield*, ed. Mosher and Poon. Pils suggests there may be around two hundred.
84. This chronology was proposed by Ying Xing. See Zhao Ling, "China's First Report on Petitions Attracts High-Level Attention," originally published in Chinese in *Nanfang Zhoumo*, November 4, 2004, translated by Stacy Mosher in *Contemporary Chinese Thought* 46, no. 1 (2014): 58.
85. Carl Minzner, "*Xinfang*, an Alternative to Formal Chinese Legal Institutions," *Stanford International Law Journal*, no. 103 (2006): 105.
86. Isabelle Thireau and Hua Linshan, *Les ruses de la démocratie* (Paris: Le Seuil, 2010), 215–219.
87. Pils, *China's Human Rights Lawyers*, 319.
88. Thireau and Hua, *Les ruses*, 250.
89. Pils, *China's Human Rights Lawyers*, 115–118.
90. Pils, *China's Human Rights Lawyers*, 82.
91. Eva Pils and Marina Svensson, "Yu Jianrong, from Concerned Scholar to Advocate for the Marginalized," *Contemporary Chinese Thought* 46, no. 1 (2014): 12. See also Eva Pils, "Taking *Yuan* Seriously," *Temple International and Comparative Law Journal*, no. 25 (2011): 285, 316–321 (on the use of judicial psychiatry). See also Yu Jianrong, "Jingshenbingxue zhuanjia Sun jiaoshou de pai naodai xueshu" (Mental illness expert Professor Sun's head-banging scholarship), *Nanfang Dushi Bao*, April 6, 2009.
92. In their model, bureaucratic absorption is one of three kinds of absorption used by the state, along with commodification and clientelism. See Ching Kwan Lee and Yonghong Zhang, "The Power of Instability: Unraveling the Microfoundations of Bargained Authoritarianism in China," *American Journal of Sociology* 118, no. 6 (2013): 1475–1508. See

also William Hurst, Mingxing Liu, Yongdong Liu, and Ran Tao, "Reassessing Collective Petitioning in Rural China: Civic Engagement, Extra-state Violence, and Regional Variation," *Comparative Politics* 46, no. 4 (July 2014): 459–478, where the authors find that, with the exception of Fujian (where some tolerance for civic organizations limits petitioning), contentious protests by petitioners are often repressed by an "insidious symbiosis" of local states and crime syndicates.

93. See Li Lianjiang, Liu Mingxing, and Kevin O'Brien, "Petitioning Beijing: The High Tide of 2003–2006," *China Quarterly* 210 (June 2012): 313–334.
94. Pils, *China's Human Rights Lawyers*, 50.
95. Pils, *China's Human Rights Lawyers*, 47, 29.
96. See Li Lianjiang, "The Magnitude and Resilience of Trust in the Center in Contemporary China: Evidence from Interviews with Petitioners in Beijing and a Local Survey in Rural China," *Modern China* 39, no. 1 (2013): 3–36.
97. Pils "Taking *Yuan* Seriously," 302.
98. Thireau and Hua, *Les ruses*, 431–435.
99. On the report prepared by Yu's institute at CASS, *Xinfang de zhiduxing queshi jiqi zhengzhi weihai* (The systemic shortcomings of the Letters and Visits system and its political harm), see Yu Jianrong, "Dui xinfang zhidu gaige zhenglun de fansi" (Reflections on the controversy surrounding the Letters and Visits system), *Zhongguo Dangzheng Ganbu Luntan*, May 2005, reproduced in *People's Daily Online*, http://theory.people.com.cn/GB/40540/3409533.html, and Zhao Ling, "China's First Report on Petitions Attracts High-Level Attention," 57.
100. Yu Jianrong, *Xinfang zhidu diaocha ji gaige silu* (Report on the Letters and Visits system and ideas for reform) (Beijing: Chinese Academy of Social Sciences, 2004). See also Zhao Ling, "China's First Report on Petitions Attracts High-Level Attention," 62–63.
101. Yu Jianrong, "Dui xinfang zhidu gaige zhenglun de fansi."
102. Minzner, "Xinfang," 178, 134.
103. See, for example, Yu Jianrong, "Zhongguo xinfang zhidu de kunjing he chulu" (The problems and way forward for China's Letters and Visits system), *Ai Sixiang*, November 23, 2012.
104. See Yu Jianrong, "Wo weishenme zhuzhang feichu Xinfang zhidu" (Why I advocate abolishing the Letters and Visits system), May 2, 2016 (originally published on Yu's WeChat account, available via *Ai Sixiang* and other websites), and "The Two Stages of the Re-education Through Labour System: From Tool of Political Struggle to Means of Social Governance," *China Perspectives*, no. 2 (2010): 66–72.
105. Eva Pils and Marina Svensson, "From Nonperson to Public Intellectual: The Life and Works of Yu Jianrong. Guest Editors' Introduction," *Contemporary Chinese Thought* 45, no. 4 (2014): 9.
106. He Xiongfei, "Houji," in Yu Jianrong, *Diceng lichang* (Shanghai: Shanghai Sanlian, 2010), 297.
107. See Liu Yinfeng, "Prof. Yu Jianrong Receives Petitioners, Says He Wishes to Speak Out for His Own Class," originally published in Chinese in *Xinjingbao*, November 3, 2010, translated by Stacy Mosher in *Contemporary Chinese Thought* 45, no. 4 (2014): 53–57. The situation gave rise to a particularly painful episode when at age six Yu was dragged out of the classroom, and his only jacket was torn.
108. Quoted in Liu Yinfeng, "Prof. Yu Jianrong Receives Petitioners," 56.

109. Published as *Yue cun zhengzhi* (The politics of Yue village) (Beijing: Commercial Press, 2001).
110. Yu Jianrong, "Zhongguo de diceng shehui: Wode yanjiu he lichang" (China's lower-strata society: My research and posture), lecture at the People's University, July 29, 2008, translated as "China's Underclass," *Contemporary Chinese Thought* 45, no. 4 (2014): 19. The translators of Yu's essay translate *diceng* as "underclass," whereas I generally render it as "lower strata."
111. Yu Jianrong, "China's Underclass," 28. There was a tradition of intellectuals speaking out on "rural issues"; however, Yu Jianrong's stance is theoretically quite different from previous interventions (e.g., Chen Guidi and Chun Tao, *Zhongguo Nongmin diaocha* [An investigation of China's peasants] [Beijing: Renmin wenxue, 2004], translated as *Will the Boat Sink the Water? The Life of China's Peasants*, trans. Zhu Hong [New York: Public Affairs, 2006]).
112. Yu Jianrong, "China's Underclass," 31–33.
113. Yu Jianrong also argues that, among these groups, "law-based resistance" is more developed than "principle-based rights defense" ("Jiejue Zhongguo nongmin wenti xuyao xin siwei—Yu Jianrong duihua," Gongshiwang, January 20, 2010, translated as "Solving China's Peasant Issues Requires a New Way of Thinking," *Contemporary Chinese Thought* 46, no. 1 [2014]: 24–25). Yu agrees with Elizabeth Perry that the "awareness of rules" outweighs the "awareness of rights" (Elizabeth Perry, "A New Rights Consciousness?" *Journal of Democracy* 20, no. 3 [July 2009]: 17–20).
114. Pun Ngai and Chris Chan, "The Subsumption of Class Discourse in China," *boundary 2* 35, no. 2 (2008): 88.
115. Yu Jianrong, "China's Underclass," 36.
116. Yu Jianrong, "China's Underclass," 40, 41.
117. Zhang Xiong, "Yu Jianrong hongle," *Nandu Zhoukan*, December 2010, translated as "Yu Jianrong Is All the Rage," *Contemporary Chinese Thought* 45, no. 4 (2014): 72.
118. Yu Jianrong, "Nongmingong yanglao baoxian xuyao zhidu chuangxin" (Retirement pensions for migrant workers requires systemic innovation), *Xinjingbao*, April 18, 2005.
119. Yu Jianrong, "Yi zhiduxing anpai baozhang nongmin de tudi quanli" (Create a system to guarantee peasants land rights), *Nanfang Zhoumo*, September 14, 2006, and "Tudi chengbao jingyingquan liuzhuan de zhuti shi nongmin" (The subject of transmittable land lease-management rights are the peasants), *Zhongguo Jingmao Daokan*, no. 23 (2008): 25. On the intense debate surrounding privatization of land, see Sally Sargeson, "The Demise of China's Peasantry as a Class," *Asia Pacific Journal* 14, no. 13 (2016), http://apjjf.org/2016/13/Sargeson.html.
120. Yu Jianrong, "Yao zhongshi nongcun jiceng gan-qun guanxi zhong de xinren weiji" (We should take seriously the crisis of confidence between cadres and masses at the village grassroots), *Renmin Luntan*, no. 18 (2008): 40–41.
121. Yu Jianrong, "Zai Diceng faxian zhengzhi" (Discovering politics at the grass roots), *Chengshi Zhongguo*, no. 38 (2009), in *Diceng lichang*, 253.
122. Yu Jianrong, "Diceng shehui de quanli luoji" (The power logic of lower-tier society), *Nanfeng Chuang*, no. 5 (2008): 22–23.
123. Yu Jianrong, "Gangxing wending: Zhongguo shehui xingshi de yige jieshi kuangjia," Yanshan Lecture no. 31, May 9, 2009, translated as "Rigid Stability: An Explanatory

Framework for China's Social Situation," *Contemporary Chinese Thought* 46, no. 1 (2014): 78–81.

124. Yu Jianrong, "30 nian lai Zhongguo gongmin quanli yishi de bianqian" (Changes in rights consciousness among Chinese citizens in the past 30 years), *Banyuetan*, no. 5 (2008), in *Diceng lichang*, 280.
125. Yu Jianrong, "Maintaining a Baseline of Social Stability," PRC Ministry of Finance, December 26, 2009, published in *China Digital Times*, March 6, 2010, https://chinadigitaltimes.net/2010/03/yu-jianrong-maintaining-a-baseline-of-social-stability-part-i/. Yu argues that "mass incidents" can be divided into three types: defending rights, venting, and rabble-rousing.
126. Yu Jianrong, "Gongmeng de kunjing shi women shehui de beiyuan" (The difficulties of Gongmeng are the tragedy of our society), in *Diceng lichang*, 286.
127. Quoted in Zhang Xiong, "Yu Jianrong Is All the Rage," 79–80.
128. Yu Jianrong, "Everyone has a microphone," *China Digital Times*, 20 December 2010; see also the translation in Zhang Xiong, "Yu Jianrong Is All the Rage," 81.
129. Editor's note in "Selection of Postings from Yu Jianrong's Sina Weibo Account," *Contemporary Chinese Thought* 45, no. 4 (2014): 58. Yu's WeChat account was closed in late 2016, but his Weibo account remained open as of January 2018.
130. Quoted in Zhang Xiong, "Yu Jianrong Is All the Rage," 77–78.
131. Quoted in Pils and Svensson, "From Nonperson to Public Intellectual," 14.
132. Yu Jianrong, "Zeren yu liangzhi: Zhongguo xuezhe 30 nian" (Responsibility and conscience: 30 years of Chinese scholars), *Renmin luntan*, no. 4 (2008), in *Diceng lichang*, 296.
133. Yu Jianrong, "Zeren yu liangzhi," in *Diceng lichang*, 296.
134. See Liao Yiwu, *Zhongguo diceng fangtanlu* (Interviews with the underclass) (Wuhan: Changjiang Wenyi, 2001; Taipei: Maitian, 2002). Selections were published in English translation as *The Corpse Walker*, trans. Wen Huang (New York: Anchor Books, 2009). See also Lu Yuegang, "Guanyu *Zhongguo diceng fangtanlu* de duihua" (Dialogue about *Interviews with the Underclass*), interview of Lao Wei [Liao Yiwu], *Nanfang Zhoumo*, April 19, 2001. Liao claimed that three top editors were fired because of his story (see for example "Zhuanfang jinshu zuojia Liao Yiwu" [Interview with banned author Liao Yiwu], Voice of America, April 23, 2011, https://www.voachinese.com/a/article-20110423-china-writer-120531854/780956.html; Shen Lizhi, "Shiren Liao Yiwu yu *Nanfang Zhoumo* da dizhen" [Poet Liao Yiwu and the big earthquake at *Southern Weekly*], June 2001, http://www.angelfire.com/sk/jiuxin/backyard/plagiarist48.htm). However, the generally accepted reason for their being fired is that they were punished for a sensationalistic report on a gang murder. See Cho Li-Fung, "The Development of Investigative Reporting and Journalistic Professionalism in *Southern Weekend*," in *Chinese Investigative Journalists' Dreams: Autonomy, Agency, Voice*, ed. Marina Svensson, Elin Sæther, and Zhi'an Zhang (Lexington, Ky.: Lexington Books, 2014), 191.
135. Hu Ping, preface to Liao Yiwu, *Zhongguo shangfang cun* (China's petitioner village) (New York: Mirror Books, 2005), 2.
136. Liao Yiwu, *Zhongguo shangfang cun*, 39.
137. A major academic conference on *diceng wenxue* was held in 2006. See, for example, "Wenxue ruhe miandui diceng," *Zonghe Xinwen*, May 16, 2006. By contrast, what critics have been eager to assert as "New Left literature" (with the novella *There* [*Na'r*] by Cao

Zhenglu as its poster piece) inevitably focuses on reform of state-owned enterprises rather than on what Wang Xiaobo envisaged as "vulnerable groups." See chapters by Zhong Xueping and Jie Lu on *diceng wenxue* in Wang Ban and Jie Lu, eds., *China and New Left Visions: Political and Cultural Interventions* (Lexington, Ky.: Lexington Books, 2012).

138. Jessica Teets, "Let Many Civil Societies Bloom: The Rise of Consultative Authoritarianism in China," *China Quarterly* 213 (March 2013): 19–38. In this article, written shortly before Xi Jinping took office, Teets considers an evolution toward "consultative democracy" (a term she borrows from CCP official Li Junru), in which the party-state builds consensus by consulting with civil society. This now seems unlikely. By contrast, in the same issue of *China Quarterly* Patricia Thornton points out the growing role of the CCP within grassroots NGOs, creating "PONGOs": "The Advance of the Party: Transformation or Takeover of Urban Grassroots Society?" *China Quarterly*, no. 213 (March 2013): 1–18.

139. Carl Minzner, "The Turn Against Legal Reform," *Journal of Democracy* 24, no. 1 (2013): 69. In Minzner's view, this evolution led to the "end of reforms" under Xi Jinping: "Political stability, ideological openness, and rapid economic growth were the hallmarks of China's reform era. But they are ending. China is entering a new era, the age after reform" ("China After the Reform Era," *Journal of Democracy* 26, no. 3 [2015]: 140).

140. See Feng Chongyi, "Charter 08 Framer Liu Xiaobo Awarded Nobel Peace Prize: The Troubled History and Future of Chinese Liberalism," *Asia-Pacific Journal* 8, no. 2, (2010), https://apjjf.org/-Feng-Chongyi/3285/article.html.

141. Yu Jianrong, "Qing zhen yi qie: yong bie" (With affection and concern: Farewell), July 13, 2017, https://www.bannedbook.org/bnews/renquan/minyun/20170713/790871.html.

142. Qin Hui, "Zhongguo geng xuyao minzhu taolun yu chongxin qimeng," Boxun, March 1, 2009, https://news.boxun.com/news/gb/pubvp/2009/03/200903011250.shtml. Translated as "Qin Hui's Critique of Charter 08: Democratic Debate and Renewed Enlightenment Is More Necessary for China," Boxun, May 29, 2009.

143. Qin Hui, "The Common Baseline of Modern Thought," in a special issue on Qin Hui, *The Chinese Economy* 38, no. 4 (2005): 20, emphasis in David Kelly's translation.

144. For example, Qin Hui has discussed China's economic model and growth performance ("Command vs. Planned Economy" and "China's Economic Development Performance Under the Pre-reform System," *The Chinese Economy* 38, no. 4 [2005]: 23–60 and 61–85); socioeconomic inequalities in historical perspective ("Fin de Siècle China: Economic Transition, Social Justice, and Democracy," *The Chinese Economy* 38, no. 5 [2005]: 3–54); reform of state-owned enterprises ("The Dialectic of 'Downsizing' and 'Prioritizing Employment': Techniques for How to Subtract Value from State-Owned Assets," *The Chinese Economy* 38, no. 5 [2005]: 66–69); tax reform ("Tax and Fee Reform, Village Autonomy, and Central and Local Finance: Historical Experience and Realistic Options," *The Chinese Economy* 38, no. 6 [2005]: 3–35); and urban slums and migrant workers ("Chengshihua yu pinmin quanli—jindai geguo dushi xiaceng shequ bianqianshi" [Urbanization and the rights of the poor: A comparative history of changes in poor urban neighborhoods in modern times], *Nanfang Dushi Bao*, April 13, 2008, http://www.aisixiang.com/data/18345.html).

145. Qin Hui, "Power, Responsibility, and Constitutional Politics: State 'Size' in Theory and History," *The Chinese Economy* 38, no. 6 (2005): 75–76.

146. Teng Biao, "Who Is Xu Zhiyong?"
147. Teng Biao, "Who Is Xu Zhiyong?"
148. See "Gongmin chengnuo," Tiger Temple Blog, June 17, 2010, translated as "The Citizen Pledge," *Chinageeks*, June 20, 2010, https://chinageeksarchive.wordpress.com/2010/06/20/xu-zhiyong-et-al-the-chinese-citizens-pledge/.
149. Pils, *China's Human Rights Lawyers*, 232. At the same time, a specific role for lawyers on the basis of their professional knowledge and ethics is also desirable (Pils, *China's Human Rights Lawyers*, 274).
150. The fullest account and discussion to date of the New Citizen Movement, including its origins in the Sun Zhigang case and Gongmeng is Eva Pils, "From Independent Lawyer Groups to Civic Opposition: The Case of China's New Citizen Movement," *Asian-Pacific Law and Policy Journal* 19, no. 1 (2017): 110–152.
151. Xu Zhiyong, "China Needs a New Citizens' Movement," July 23, 2012, http://www.hrichina.org/en/print/crf/article/6205. See also the version of this article in "The Rights Defense Movement in China," ed. Teng Biao, special issue of *China Law and Government* 46, nos. 5–6 (2013): 4–12.
152. Xu Zhiyong, "China Needs a New Citizens' Movement."
153. Eva Pils argues that Xu's manifesto does not call for civil disobedience but for correctly implementing the Constitution (*China's Human Rights Lawyers*, 260).
154. Xu Zhiyong, "Gongmin Xu Zhiyong guanyu yuemo gongmin tongcheng jucan he xiao quanzi chabie de shuoming" (Citizen Xu Zhiyong's explanation about end-of-month meal gatherings in cities and differences between small circles), May 6, 2013, translated in Eva Pils, *China's Human Rights Lawyers*, 263–264.
155. Xu Zhiyong, "Transcript of Comments at a Civic Meal Meeting on Christmas Eve 2012," *Gongmin Zhuankan*, no. 8, 78, quoted in Pils, *China's Human Rights Lawyers*, 255 (year not identified in Pils's citation).
156. Xu Zhiyong, "Gongmin zimian: Fuwu, dandang, fangxia," April 23, 2013, in *Tangtang zhengzheng zuo gongmin*, 278, translated as "Citizen Self-Encouragement—Service, Duty, Letting Go," *China Digital Times*, May 13, 2013, http://chinadigitaltimes.net/2013/05/xu-zhiyong-on-the-new-citizens-movement/.
157. Xu Zhiyong, "Zhi Xi Jinping xiansheng de gongkai xin" (Open letter to Mr. Xi Jinping), November 15, 2012, in *Tangtang zhengzheng zuo gongmin*, 307.
158. Josh Chin, "Chinese Activists Challenge Beijing by Going to Dinner Over Unassuming Meals," *Wall Street Journal*, November 7, 2013: Pils, "From Independent Lawyer Groups to Civic Opposition," 134.
159. Xu Zhiyong, "Citizen Self-Encouragement."
160. Xu Zhiyong, "Shei ba ziyou, zhengyi, ai dangcheng diren, yiding shi Zhonghua minzu de diren" (Whoever takes freedom, righteousness, and love as enemies is surely an enemy of the Chinese nation), *Gongmin Zhuankan*, no. 8, quoted in Pils, *China's Human Rights Lawyers*, 261.
161. Teng Biao, "Beyond Stability Maintenance—from Surveillance to Elimination," *China Change*, June 22, 2014, https://chinachange.org/2014/06/22/beyond-stability-maintenance-from-surveillance-to-elimination/.
162. Xu Zhiyuan, "Xu Zhiyong zaoyu de huangdan" (The absurdity of Xu Zhiyong's misfortunes), *Yazhou Zhoukan*, no. 30 (2013), http://yzzk.com/cfm/blogger3.cfm?id=1374723647400.

163. Xu Zhiyong, "Fating de zuihou chenshu: Weile ziyou, gongyi, ai," January 22, 2014, in *Tangtang zhengzheng zuo gongmin*, 334, translated by China Change as "For Freedom, Justice, Love: Xu Zhiyong's Final Statement to Court," *China File*, January 26, 2014, http://www.chinafile.com/freedom-justice-and-love.
164. Xu Zhiyong, "Fating de zuihou chenshu," 338.
165. Xu Zhiyong, "Fating de zuihou chenshu," 339, 341, 342.
166. See Tom Philips, "Pu Zhiqiang Given Three-Year Suspended Sentence," *Guardian*, December 22, 2015, https://www.theguardian.com/world/2015/dec/22/pu-zhiqiang-chinese-human-rights-lawyer-sentenced-to-three-years. Ilham Tohti is an Uyghur academic who was sentenced to life in prison for "separatism" in 2014.
167. See Zeng Jinyan, "China's Feminist Five: 'This Is the Worst Crackdown on Lawyers, Activists, and Scholars in Decades,'" *Guardian*, April 17, 2015, https://www.theguardian.com/lifeandstyle/2015/apr/17/chinas-feminist-five-this-is-the-worst-crackdown-on-lawyers-activists-and-scholars-in-decades; Leta Hong Fincher, "China's Feminist Five" *Dissent*, Fall 2016, https://www.dissentmagazine.org/article/china-feminist-five.
168. See "A Café Chat with Li Tingting" *China Change*, July 26, 2016, https://chinachange.org/2016/07/27/a-cafe-chat-with-li-tingting/.
169. Fengrui's website (no longer available) described its mission as follows: "Impactful public interest litigation and legal aid to vulnerable citizens is the genuine contribution of Fengrui lawyers to modern civil society and the development of rule of law" (quoted in Sui-Lee Wee, "How Support for a Chinese Rights Lawyer Could Have Led to Crackdown," Reuters, July 13, 2015).
170. See "This Morning in Beijing, One Lawyer Gone Missing, Another Lawyer Kidnapped, and Fengrui Law Office Visited by Police," *China Change*, July 9, 2015, https://chinachange.org/2015/07/09/breaking-this-morning-in-beijing-one-lawyer-gone-missing-another-lawyer-kidnapped-and-fengrui-law-office-visited-by-police/.
171. Yaqiu Wang, "Wu Gan the Butcher," *China Change*, July 22, 2015.
172. See Pils, "From Independent Lawyer Groups to Civic Opposition," 130.
173. Pils, *China's Human Rights Lawyers*, 94.
174. Chaohua Wang, "I'm a Petitioner—Open Fire!" *London Review of Books*, November 5, 2015.

6. JOURNALISTS, BLOGGERS, AND A NEW PUBLIC CULTURE

1. Robert Barnett provides the following estimates for deaths during the protests: 2 security personnel, 18 civilian bystanders, between 30 and 219 protesters killed by security ("The Tibet Protests of Spring 2008," *China Perspectives*, no. 3 [2009]: 12).
2. Created by a young Tsinghua graduate named Rao Jin, Anti-CNN was renamed April Media in 2009 and continued to play a role in criticizing Western media and governments. See Rebecca MacKinnon, *Consent of the Networked: The Worldwide Struggle for Internet Freedom* (New York: Basic Books, 2012), 34–40. It is an interesting question to what extent nationalist groups such as April Media can be considered *minjian*. MacKinnon notes that April Media's exposure of Ambassador John Huntsman's presence on Wangfujing Street in Beijing in 2011 at the time when "Jasmine Revolution" activists congregated was not state directed but a product of the "nationalist commons."

However, Rao Jin was immediately co-opted into the state media system and appeared frequently on CCTV in the aftermath of the Tibet protests, which sets him apart from most *minjian* intellectuals, who do not have access to such a forum. Members of April Media present themselves as "diverse" but united by a concern with Western media. See an article by one of the group's founders: Hu Yinan, "Forget About 'Rising China,'" *Financial Times*, September 20, 2013.

3. See, for example, "Chinese Demand Carrefour Boycott for Tibet Support," Reuters, April 15, 2008, https://www.reuters.com/article/us-china-tibet-carrefour/chinese-demand-carrefour-boycott-for-tibet-support-idUSPEK24412820080415.
4. Of course, as discussed in chapter 5, some traditional universal intellectuals also intervened in this debate, such as Wang Hui, but their intervention was to an extent driven by the journalists' and bloggers' positions.
5. Chang Ping, "Xizang: Zhenxiang yu minzuzhuyi qingxu" (Tibet: Truth and nationalist sentiment), *FTChinese*, April 3, 2008, http://www.ftchinese.com/story/001018387, translated as "Where Does the Truth About Lhasa Come From?" trans. Stephen Soong, *EastSouthWestNorth* blog, http://www.zonaeuropa.com/200804061.htm.
6. Chang Ping, "Xizang."
7. Wen Feng, "Zaoyao ziyou de Nandu Chang Ping" (Southern Metropolis Chang Ping's freedom to rumor-monger), *Beijing Wanbao*, April 14, 2014, http://news.21cn.com/today/zhuanlan/2008/04/14/4592381.shtml, translated as "The Internet Wages War on the Liberal Media," trans. Joel Martinsen, *Danwei*, April 14, 2008, http://www.danwei.org/internet/southern_metropolis_chang_ping.php. The expression *danghong zhaziji* is a Cantonese-inflected term used by the Hong Kong media to refer to entertainment stars; its use here also contains implicit critiques of both capitalist entertainment media and foreign influence channeled through Hong Kong (*zhaziji* is a type of Cantonese roast chicken specialty and should not be rendered as "spicy chicken").
8. Several English-language media began offering Chinese-language reporting—both original and translated from English—in the 2000s: the *Financial Times* in 2005 (hitting 2 million registered users in 2013), the *Wall Street Journal* in 2010, and the *New York Times* in 2012. See "*FTChinese* Names Editor in Chief," *Marketing Interactive*, February 25, 2015, http://www.marketing-interactive.com/ftchinese-names-editor-in-chief/. The latter two were blocked in China in 2013, but *FTChinese* is still operating after it was briefly blocked in 2017.
9. Han Han, "Gan ji" (Going to market), April 20, 2008, http://blog.sina.com.cn/s/blog_4701280b010092vq.html, translated as "Market Day for Patriots," in Han Han, *This Generation: Dispatches from China's Most Popular Literary Star (and Race Car Driver)*, ed. and trans. Allan H. Barr (London: Simon and Schuster, 2010), 34–35.
10. Han Han, "Huida aiguozhe de wenti" (Replying to patriots' questions), April 23, 2008, http://blog.sina.com.cn/s/blog_4701280b0100945n.html, translated as "Q and A with Chinese Nationalists," in *This Generation*, 36–40.
11. Discussing the tension around the Diaoyu/Senkaku Islands in 2010, Han Han argues that the Chinese people are in the role of the tenant whose landlord is in a dispute with his neighbor over a tile blown into the next garden. He also highlights the double standards for authorizing protest: "If a nation cannot take part in a peaceful demonstration for domestic matters, any demonstration for foreign matters loses its value, it

simply becomes a group dance" ("Youxing de yiyi" [The meaning of demonstrations], Gongshiwang, September 18, 2010, translated as "Should We or Shouldn't We?" in *This Generation*, 187–188).

12. "In my early twenties I supported a boycott of Japanese goods. I was a nationalist. But in 2008, I opposed the Carrefour boycott. When I was younger, I advocated war and the retaking of Taiwan, but now I'm embarrassed even to admit it. When I was 17 or 18, I boasted: 'Out of all the essay writers alive, I'm second best.' How this makes me blush now! But I blush even harder when I remember that I thought Li Ao was the best" (Han Han, "For Every Self" [April 2012], in *The Problem with Me: And Other Essays About Making Trouble*, ed. and trans. Alice Xin Liu and Joel Martinson [London: Simon and Schuster, 2016], 108).
13. Han Han often discusses double standards and the need for "higher standards" in China: "If China is to win respect, we must create better products and set higher standards—and not just for cars" ("My Feelings About the Recent Anti-Japanese Protests," *South China Morning Post*, September 28, 2012).
14. Han Han, "Bu yao dongbudong jiu juguo baonu" (We shouldn't systematically throw a fit about the nation), June 4, 2008, translated as "Let's Not Get in a Rage so Easily," in *This Generation*, 51.
15. Han Han, "Let's Not Get in a Rage so Easily," 48.
16. For a history of the debate on popular culture and consumerism, see Jing Wang, ed., "Chinese Popular Culture and the State," special issue of *Positions: East Asia Cultures Critique* 9, no. 1 (2001), and Michel Hockx and Julia Strauss, introduction to "Culture in the Contemporary PRC," ed. Michel Hockx and Julia Strauss, special issue of *China Quarterly*, no. 183 (September 2005): 523–531.
17. Quoted in Li Pei-fen, "Chang Ping daodi shuole shenme?" (What did Chang Ping say after all?), *Mingpao Sunday*, March 30, 2011.
18. Qian Gang and David Bandurski, "China's Emerging Public Sphere," in *Changing Media, Changing China*, ed. Susan Shirk (New York: Oxford University Press, 2011), 40.
19. Zha Jianying, *China Pop: How Soap Operas, Tabloids, and Bestsellers Are Transforming a Culture* (New York: New Press, 1996). Yu Pun Hoi's latest ventures are Duowei News and HK01.
20. Zhao Yuezhi, "Underdogs, Lapdogs, and Watchdogs: Journalists and the Public Sphere Problematic in China," in *Chinese Intellectuals Between State and Market*, ed. Edward X. Gu and Merle Goldman (London: Routledge, 2004), 43–74.
21. "Jiu xinwen zhenshixing wenti: zhi zuozhe" (The issue of fact-based news reporting: To writers), *Nanfang Zhoumo*, November 5, 1993, discussed in Cho Li-Fung, "The Development of Investigative Reporting and Journalistic Professionalism in *Southern Weekend*," in *Chinese Investigative Journalists' Dreams: Autonomy, Agency, and Voice*, ed. Marina Svensson, Elin Sæther, and Zhi'an Zhang (Lexington: Lexington Books, 2014), 185. See also Zuo Fang, *Gangtie shi zenyang lianbuchengde* (How steel was not tempered) (Hong Kong: Cosmos, 2014), 238–253; Ying Xia, Bing Guan, and Gong Cheng, "Power Structure and Media Autonomy in China: The Case of *Southern Weekend*," *Journal of Contemporary China* 26, no. 104 (2017): 233–248.
22. Cho Li-Fung, "The Development of Investigative Reporting," 181; Zuo Fang, *Gangtie*, 238.

23. Qian and Bandurski, "China's Emerging Public Sphere," 42.
24. "Rang wulizhe you li, rang beiguanzhe qianxing" (Give strength to the weak, help the pessimists move forward) (editorial), *Nanfang Zhoumo*, January 1, 1999, http://news.sina.com.cn/m/2013-01-04/114025952416.shtml. Qian Gang and David Bandurski also quote another editorial, which advocated: "Show care for the weak, give strength to the powerless" ("Yinwei women shi jizhe" [Because we are journalists], *Nanfang Zhoumo*, November 8, 2000, quoted in "China's Emerging Public Sphere," 57). After Jiang Yiping and Qian Gang were fired in June 2001, the new editor of *Southern Weekly*, Xiang Xi, advocated the slogans "More knowledge is more power" and "Read us to understand China" (Cho Li-Fung, "The Development of Investigative Reporting," 192).
25. In the aftermath of the events of 2013, Sina.com compiled a full set of *Southern Weekly* New Year editorials from 1997 to 2013. See http://news.sina.com.cn/m/2013-01-04/122825952555.shtml.
26. Xiao Shu, "Zou ziji de lu, rang bieren shuoqu ba" (Take our own path, and let other people say what they want), *Nanfang Zhoumo*, April 17, 2008.
27. Chang Ping, "The Fate of Press Freedom in China," ChinaChange.org, December 15, 2016, https://chinachange.org/2016/12/15/the-fate-of-press-freedom-in-chinas-era-of-reform-and-opening-up-an-interview-with-chang-ping/.
28. Li Pei-fen, "Chang Ping daodi shuole shenme?"
29. Chang Ping, "The Fate of Press Freedom in China," The other articles were reports on the Red Guard cemetery in Chongqing, an explosion in Shijiazhuang, and a commentary on the Middle East linking dictatorships to oil resources. In the Zhang Jun case, the notion that a crime could have social causes and ultimately be attributable to certain official policies proved unacceptable to the authorities.
30. Because the Hong Kong government stalled his work visa application for two years, Chang Ping had to work from overseas.
31. The publisher of *iSun Affairs*, Chen Ping, was a former member of Zhao Ziyang's team in the 1980s who had invested in a lucrative satellite broadcaster (iSun TV) in Hong Kong. Under Chang Ping as chief editor and Cheng Yizhong as managing editor and with reporters such as Zhang Jieping, who reported on the Wukan events of 2010, and Zhao Sile, who reported on NGOs in China, the Hong Kong weekly continued the best tradition of the Chinese independent journalism for eighteen months, until it ended its publication in early 2013.
32. According to his official biography, Cai Hua (b. 1977 in Fujian) graduated from China University of Law and Politics and then earned a J.D. from Stanford. He initially worked for the Supreme People's Court (1997–2003) before setting up as a corporate lawyer in Hong Kong, where he specialized in technology deals. Despite being rapidly blocked in China, *Initium* reached 2 million unique visitors a month. See Shai Oster, "Internet Media Start-ups Fight China's Censorship Crackdown," *Bloomberg/Taipei Times*, April 30, 2016, http://www.taipeitimes.com/News/editorials/archives/2016/04/30/2003645141/1. However, in April 2017, *Initium* announced it was downsizing and moving to a pay-for-view business model.
33. See also Zhai Minglei, "The Kou Yanding I Knew," *China Change*, February 5, 2015, https://chinachange.org/2015/02/05/the-kou-yanding-i-know/. Zhai later published several

books in Hong Kong documenting the evolution of the media over this period. See, for instance, Zhai Minglei, *Chu da shi le: Xin meiti shidai de tufa shijian yu gongmin xingdong* (Big problem! Sudden incidents and citizen mobilization in the era of new media) (Hong Kong: Cosmos, 2013).

34. Wang Boming is a Columbia graduate in finance and the son of a vice minister of foreign affairs. The Stock Exchange Executive Council, founded in March 1989, included people such as Wang Qishan and Zhou Xiaochuan. *Caijing* was supervised by the All-China Federation of Industry and Commerce, which gave it relative freedom from political intervention. Wang Boming encountered some trouble in 2015 when *Caijing* journalist Wang Xiaolu had to publicly apologize over reporting on the falling stock market.
35. For example, in the Lu Liang case in February 2001 Lu was accused of manipulating share prices. *Caijing*'s mission determined its registration with the All-China Federation of Industry and Commerce.
36. Cheng Yizhong is quoted in Evan Osnos, "The Forbidden Zone," *New Yorker*, July 20, 2009.
37. Zhao Yuezhi, "Underdogs, Lapdogs, and Watchdogs," 60–62.
38. See Jonathan Ansfield, "Editor Departs China Magazine After High-Profile Tussle," *New York Times*, November 9, 2009, http://www.nytimes.com/2009/11/10/business/global/10mag.html.
39. On the rise of investigative journalism in China, see David Bandurski and Martin Hala, eds., *Investigative Journalism in China: Eight Cases in Chinese Watchdog Journalism* (Hong Kong: Hong Kong University Press, 2010). Jonathan Hassid classifies Chinese journalists into four categories (Communist professionals, workaday reporters, American-style journalists, and advocacy professionals) in *China's Unruly Journalists: How Committed Professionals Are Changing the People's Republic* (London: Routledge, 2016).
40. Quoted in Qian and Bandurski, "China's Emerging Public Sphere," 71. Qian and Bandurski also note that the notion of "professionalism" (*zhuanye zhuyi*) appeared in the 1990s. For a broader overview of the major figures of journalism, see also Qian Gang and Ying Chan, eds., *Zhongguo chuanmei rui si lu: 13 wei Xianggang daxue fangwen xuezhe de yanjiang* (Records of cutting-edge ideas in Chinese media: Talks by 13 visiting scholars at Hong Kong University) (Hong Kong: Cosmos, 2012), with talks by Dai Qing, Lu Yuegang, Yang Hengjun, Chen Ping, Wu Si, Zhou Duo, Xiong Peiyun, Xiao Shu, Yu Jianrong, Cheng Yizhong, Zhai Minglei, Zhang Ming, and Ran Yunfei.
41. Zhao Yuezhi, "Underdogs, Lapdogs, and Watchdogs," 69–70.
42. Liu Qing and Barrett McCormick, "The Media and the Public Sphere in Contemporary China," *boundary 2* 38, no. 1 (2011): 125.
43. Liu and McCormick, "The Media and the Public Sphere," 124. Liu and McCormick also argue that even if this plural sphere is oriented toward consumption and commodification, it still plays a liberalizing political role in creating a space that is outside the reach of the state and the unifying ideology and is antagonistic to Leninism. However, it should also be noted that the party strives to use this pop culture to promote its own messages (for example, by cultivating a group of "patriotic" pop stars), thus conveying its ideology in a less obtrusive and probably more effective manner.

44. "Gaige gongshi changyi shu" (Proposal for a consensus on reforms), Radio France Internationale, December 26, 2012, http://cn.rfi.fr/中国/20121226-中国70多位知名学者联名推出《改革共识倡议书》.
45. See Qian Gang, "Why *Southern Weekly* Said No" and "Why *Southern Weekly*," *China Media Project*, January 11 and February 18, 2013; David Bandurski, "A New Years' Greeting Gets the Axe in China," *China Media Project*, January 3, 2013 (which includes the original editorial); and Xia, Guan, and Cheng, "Power Structure and Media Autonomy in China."
46. See He Weifang, "Zhongguo xianzheng zhi lu" (China's path to constitutionalism), October 4, 2013; a three-part recording of the talk is available on YouTube, https://www.youtube.com/watch?v=5WrGY9TpXQo.
47. Rogier Creemers, "China's Constitutionalism Debate: Content, Context, and Implications," *China Journal*, no. 74 (July 2015): 91–109.
48. See Steven Millward, "China Now Has 731 million Internet Users, 95% Access from Their Phones," *Tech in Asia*, January 23, 2017, https://www.techinasia.com/china-731-million-internet-users-end-2016.
49. PKU's forum Yita Hutu was shut down in 2004.
50. For a fuller presentation, see Yang Guobin, *The Power of the Internet in China: Citizen Activism Online* (New York: Columbia University Press, 2009), esp. chap. 2, "The Politics of Digital Contention," 44–63.
51. Zhai Minglei, ed., *Zhongguo mengbo: Xin meiti shidai de minjian huayu liliang* (China's bold [awesome] blogs: The power of *minjian* discourse in the era of new media) (Hong Kong: Cosmos Books, 2009).
52. Ying Chan, "Xu" (Preface), in *Zhongguo mengbo*, ed. Zhai Minglei, 5.
53. Ying Chan, "Xu" (Preface), in *Zhongguo mengbo*, ed. Zhai Minglei, 6.
54. Zhai Minglei, *Zhongguo mengbo*.
55. See Christoph Steinhardt and Fengshi Wu, "In the Name of the Public: Environmental Protest and the Changing Landscape of Popular Contention in China," *China Journal*, no. 75 (January 2016): 61–82.
56. Rebecca MacKinnon, "Chinese Censorship 2.0: How Companies Censor Bloggers," *First Monday* 14, no. 2 (2009), http://journals.uic.edu/ojs/index.php/fm/article/view/2378/2089.
57. Sina recruited Ai Weiwei in this manner. See the introduction to Ai Weiwei, *Ai Weiwei's Blog: Writings, Interviews, and Digital Rants, 2006–2009*, ed. and trans. Lee Ambrozy (Cambridge, Mass.: MIT Press, 2011), xxi.
58. For a study on censorship of public WeChat accounts, see Jason Q. Ng, "Politics, Rumors, and Ambiguity: Tracking Censorship on WeChat's Public Accounts Platform," *Citizen Lab*, July 20, 2015, https://citizenlab.org/2015/07/tracking-censorship-on-wechat-public-accounts-platform/. See also Eric Harwit, "WeChat: Social and Political Development of China's Dominant Messaging App," *Chinese Journal of Communication* 10, no. 3 (2017): 312–327.
59. Yang Guobin, *The Power of the Internet in China*, 215.
60. Rebecca MacKinnon, "China's 'Networked Authoritarianism,'" *Journal of Democracy* 22, no. 2 (2011): 32–46. Of course, this debate between techno-optimists and techno-pessimists has played out on a much larger scale between scholars such as Larry Diamond, Clay Shirky, and W. Lance Bennett and Alexandra Segerberg, on the one hand, and Manuel Castells and Nicholas Carr, on the other.

61. Yang Guobin, "The Internet and the Rise of a Transnational Chinese Cultural Sphere," *Media Culture and Society* 25, no. 4 (2003): 469–490.
62. Zhou Zhixing, "Wo de siwei laoshi" (My four teachers), in *Wo chuangbanle Gongshiwang* (I established Consensus Net) (Phoenix: Nanjing, 2015), 79–97.
63. Zhou Zhixing, "Zhe yichuan jiaoyin" (This series of footprints), in *Wo chuangbanle Gongshiwang*, 238.
64. Zhou Zhixing, "Wu nian kanke lu, yishou zhengqi ge—wo chuangbanle Gongshiwang" (Five years of bumpy road, one upright song—I established Consensus Net), in *Wo chuangbanle Gongshiwang*, 219. Consensus Net also published a three-volume collection of selected articles as an internal document: *Gongshi wenji: Guoshi gengyin shuo, Gaige gengyin shuo, Sichao xinmao shuo* (Consensus Net collection: National history 2010, Reforms 2010, Thought trends 2011) (Beijing: Shijie Huawen, 2010).
65. Zhou Zhixing, "Gongshi xuyao gaige; ye xuyao tuoxie" (Consensus needs reforms; it also needs compromise), in *Wo chuangbanle Gongshiwang*, 269.
66. William Callahan, "Citizen Ai: Warrior, Jester, and Middleman," *Journal of Asian Studies* 73, no. 4 (2014): 914. Callahan expands on this category of "citizen intellectual," including not only Jia Zhangke, who indeed makes for a good point of comparison, but also the nationalistic retired officer Liu Mingfu 劉明福 and the party academic Pan Wei 潘維 (916–917), which suggests that Callahan's definition of the category of "citizen intellectual" may be overly broad.
67. See Ai Weiwei, "A Word of Thanks," February 14, 2008, in *Ai Weiwei's Blog*, 143–144. See also Philip Tinari, "A Kind of True Living: The Art of Ai Weiwei," *Artforum International* 45, no. 10 (2007): 453–459, and Bei Ling, ed., *Qiao: Ai Weiwei* (Look: Ai Weiwei) (Taipei, Tendency, 2011).
68. See Ai Weiwei, "My Regards to Your Mother," February 27, 2009, in *Ai Weiwei's Blog*, 207.
69. Ai mocks the idea that his role was to introduce "Chinese elements" into the design of the Bird's Nest ("On the Bird's Nest," July 9, 2008, in *Ai Weiwei's Blog*, 163).
70. Ai Weiwei, "Architecture and Space," January 13, 2006, trans. Philip Tinari, in *Ai Weiwei's Blog*, 8–9.
71. Tinari, "A Kind of True Living." See also a classic argument connecting the post-Communist avant-garde and the democracy movement: Ralph Crozier, "The Avant-Garde and the Democracy Movement: Reflections on Late Communism in the USSR and China," *Europe-Asia Studies* 51, no. 3 (1999): 483–513.
72. Ai Weiwei, "Different Worlds, Different Dreams," September 5, 2006, trans. Eric Abrahamsen, in *Ai Weiwei's Blog*, 98.
73. Ai Weiwei, "Different Worlds, Different Dreams," 100.
74. Ai Weiwei, "*Shanzhai* Ideals," January 4, 2009, in *Ai Weiwei's Blog*, 192. Ai further elaborates on this issue in his discussion of fake milk powder, concluding that the China miracle is based on selling fake products (193).
75. For example, Ai writes in one blog post, "And then they [officials] emphasize the different architectural standards and earthquake defenses in different eras. The dead perished under institutional rules, and no one will take the blame. What they haven't clarified is, among those buildings that toppled, which structures reflect the standards of what era. Is this really that complicated?" ("These Days I Can't Believe Anything You Say," May 7, 2009, in *Ai Weiwei's Blog*, 220).

76. Ai Weiwei, "Does the Nation Have a List?" July 28, 2008, in *Ai Weiwei's Blog*, 178.
77. Callahan, "Citizen Ai," 905.
78. Ai Weiwei, "Citizen Investigation," March 20, 2009, in *Ai Weiwei's Blog*, 209.
79. Ai Weiwei, "Guests from All Corners of the Earth," March 24, 2009, in *Ai Weiwei's Blog*, 214.
80. Giorgio Strafella and Daria Berg, "The Making of an Online Celebrity: A Critical Analysis of Han Han's Blog," *China Information* 29, no. 3 (2015): 353.
81. "Dalu xinshengdai zuojia Han Han zhuanfang: 'Shanghai shi maoxianji de leyuan, que shi renmin de diyu'" (Exclusive interview with new-generation writer Han Han: "Shanghai is an adventurer's paradise, but the people's hell"), *Tianxia*, March 2010.
82. Han Han, "Let's Do Away with Student Essays," June 15, 2007, in *This Generation*, 24.
83. Evan Osnos, "The Han Dynasty," *New Yorker*, July 4, 2011.
84. Wu Chen, "Han Han: Finding Happiness by Being Different," *China Daily*, September 30, 2009.
85. In Strafella and Berg's words, Han Han's "moderate and pragmatic" approach, his "mainstream and common-sense views" ("The Making of an Online Celebrity," 358).
86. William Callahan, "Shanghai's Alternative Futures: The World Expo, Citizen Intellectuals, and China's New Civil Society," *China Information*, no. 26 (2012): 268.
87. Quoted in Strafella and Berg, "The Making of an Online Celebrity," 359 n. 79.
88. In 2008, Han Han was awarded a prize by Gongmeng, and Xu Zhiyong described him as a "typical citizen" (Osnos, "The Han Dynasty"). See also Chen Sihe, "Han Han rangren kuangre" (Han Han makes people go crazy), *Sina*, April 24, 2009.
89. Xu Zhiyuan, "Yongzhong de shengli," (The victory of the *Vulgum pecus*), *Phoenix Weekly*, May 11, 2010. In fact, Han Han's readers may be more elitist than Xu suggests.
90. In "Shanghai's Alternative Futures," Callahan argues that Han Han is neither inside nor outside the system. This argument is somewhat unpersuasive: although in a sense Han Han is of course within the (global) capitalist system, he is quite independent from Chinese institutions, probably more so than any other *minjian* intellectual discussed in this book. Conversely, Callahan's conclusion that places Han Han in the wake of Havel and describes him as "the most notable example of a citizen intellectual who works to build civil society through the parallel society of the Internet" (268) is also exaggerated. Blog posts are not a sufficient condition for advancing civil society, as the crackdown on the Chinese Internet since 2012 has amply demonstrated.
91. On the day the award was announced, Han Han posted an entry on his blog composed of a set of quotation marks framing three dots. The post drew one and a half million hits and more than twenty-eight thousand comments (Osnos, "The Han Dynasty").
92. For example, in Han Han's novel *1988*, one of the main characters pulls out a gun and says, "I wanted this model; it's the June Fourth [6.4] type [*liu si shi*]" (*1988: Wo xiang he zhege shijie tantan* [Hong Kong: Mingpao, 2010], 249; translated as *1988: I Want to Talk with the World*, trans. Howard Goldblatt [Seattle: AmazonCrossing, 2013]). In Hong Kong, when asked whether the verdict on June Fourth should be revised, Han Han replied, "Every cultured person will give you the same answer: of course" (quoted in Zhang Jieping and Li Meng, "Dang Han Han yujian Xianggang" [When Han Han meets Hong Kong], *Yazhou Zhoukan*, August 3, 2008).

93. Strafella and Berg, "The Making of an Online Celebrity," 358. Strafella and Berg rightly point out that cultural nationalism and antiradicalism are positions Han Han shares with establishment intellectuals.
94. Strafella and Berg, "The Making of an Online Celebrity," 357.
95. Han Han, "Wo meiyou lichang: Zhi fen duicuo" (I have no stance: I just differentiate right and wrong), interview by Zhang Jieping, *Yazhou Zhoukan* 24, no. 1 (2010), http://yzzk.com/cfm/content_archive.cfm?id=1365137135416&docissue=2010-01.
96. "Why have our politicians been able to pump up their chests on the world stage . . .? It's because of you, China's cheap labor: you are China's gambling chips, hostage to GDP. Whether it is socialism with Chinese characteristics of capitalism with feudal characteristics, in the next ten years there is no way out for these young people. This is so sad: young blood that should be coursing through veins—spilled on the ground, instead" (Han Han, "Youth," May 28, 2010, in *This Generation*, 173).
97. "The people who are in the direst need of all most likely are quite unable to appeal" (Han Han, "Letters from Strangers," April 2010, in *This Generation*, 144).
98. "Poor children, it's you who are poisoned by the tainted milk powder, you who are harmed by the faulty vaccine, you who are crushed by the earthquake, you who are burned by the fire. Even if it's in the adult world that things go wrong, you're the ones on whom the adults seek to exact vengeance. . . . Your elders have failed in their duty, but I hope that when you grow up you can do better, not just protecting your own children, but making society protect *all* its children" (Han Han, "Children, You're Spoiling Grandpa's Fun," May 2, 2010, in *This Generation*, 160, emphasis added in the translation).
99. Chen Ling, "Yuedu Han Han: Huigui shuohua de yishu" (Reading Han Han: Back to the art of speaking), *Mingpao Sunday*, July 25, 2010. Chen Ling also praises Han's style as natural and completely free from the shadow of "Mao-style."
100. Another writer who became increasingly vocal after direct confrontations with censorship is Murong Xuecun, who at the peak of his fame had 8.5 million followers on Weibo. See Murong Xuecun, "Absurdities of China's Censorship System," *Time*, February 22, 2011 (a speech he gave after he was awarded a prize for a nonfiction book on pyramid schemes, *Zhongguo shaole yiwei yao* [China is missing one medical ingredient] [Beijing: Zhongguo Heping, 2010]). Murong is earnest where Han Han is flippant and repeatedly highlights his constitutional right to express himself. Ultimately, all of Murong's social media accounts were closed. See Verna Yu, "Changing Faces," *South China Morning Post*, July 12, 2015.
101. Zhang Jieping and Li Meng, "Dang Han Han yujian Xianggang" (When Han Han meets Hong Kong), *Yazhou Zhoukan*, August 3, 2008.
102. Priscilla Jiao, "Writer Walks Tightrope of the Censors in Magazine," *South China Morning Post*, August 24, 2010.
103. Han Han, "Gediao bu gao zenme ban?" (What do you do if it's too downbeat?), November 2, 2011, in *This Generation*, 223.
104. Han Han, "Suowei wenhua daguo" (So-called cultural superpower), speech given at Xiamen University, February 1, 2010.
105. "Dalu xinshengdai zuojia Han Han zhuanfang."
106. Han Han, "Taipingyang de feng," May 11, 2012, translated as "The Pacific Wind," in *The Problem with Me*, 164–165.

107. "Dalu xinshengdai zuojia Han Han zhuanfang."
108. In the chapter text, I use my own translations of the titles of these three essays rather than the translations used in *This Generation*.
109. Han Han, "Tan Geming," December 23, 2011, translated as "Speaking of Revolution," in *This Generation*, 232, 233, 235. See also Han Han's satirical description of the Chinese Internet becoming an intranet: "Wo zhishi zai caixiang" (Only Guessing), January 17, 2010, originally posted on Han Han's Sina blog (no longer available).
110. Han Han, "Speaking of Revolution," 236, 237, 238.
111. "Gongdi Han Han" (Public Enemy Han Han), interview, *Nandu Zhoukan*, January 16, 2011, translated by Roland Soong on the *EastSouthWestNorth* blog, http://www.zonaeuropa.com/20120111_1.htm.
112. Han Han, "Shuo minzhu," December 24, 2011, translated as "Talking About Democracy," in *This Generation*, 240, 242.
113. In another interview, Han Han further points out the danger of populism that would arise if a popular vote were dependent on the choice of 800 million "peasants" (*nongmin*), who could be promised social security that would result in taxing the middle class ("Xuehui zai tuoxie zhong zhuiqiu" [I learned how to keep up my quest in the midst of compromises], *Nanfang Renwu Zhoukan*, January 14, 2012).
114. Han Han, "Talking About Democracy," 243.
115. Han Han, "Yao ziyou," December 26, 2011, translated as "Pressing for Freedom," in *This Generation*, 245.
116. Han Han, "Pressing for Freedom," 247.
117. See Han Han, "Just Testing," January 15, 2010, in *This Generation*, 123.
118. "Gongdi Han Han."
119. Li Chengpeng, "Shuohua: Beida yanjiang lu" (Speaking out: Record of PKU speech), November 16, 2012, in *Quan shijie renmin dou zhidao* (The people in the whole world know) (Beijing: Xinxing, 2012), 191–197. This collection of essays covers very similar issues to Han Han's posts, ranging from mass protests to environmental degradation, residency of migrant workers, nationalism and double standards, delayed democracy, and the Taiwan experience. The book sold more than seven hundred thousand copies in a little less than a year before it was banned.
120. Han Han, "This Last Year of Mine," January 8, 2012, in *This Generation*, 253–254.
121. See Han Han's essay on the village chief Qian Yunhui: "Do We Need the Truth, or Just the Truth That Fits Our Needs?" in *This Generation*, 189. In another interview, he accepts that these fact-bending liberals are mainly "pub-ints" (public intellectuals) ("Xuehui zai tuoxie zhong zhuiqiu").
122. "Gongdi Han Han."
123. See, for example, Fang Zhouzi, "'Han san pian' wei Han Renjun suoxie de tiezheng" (Iron-clad proof that the 'three Han essays' were written by Han Renjun), *Caijing*, November 19, 2012, http://blog.caijing.com.cn/expert_article-151278-43833.shtml, and Han Han, "For Every Self," April 2012, in *The Problem with Me*, 107.
124. Xiao Ying, "'Tiancai Han Han' shi dangdai wentan de zuida chouwen: *Houhui wuqi* he Han Han xianxiang" (The "genius Han Han" is the biggest scandal on the contemporary literary scene: *We Won't Meet Again* and the Han Han phenomenon), *Zhongguo Qingnianbao*, August 19, 2014, http://opinion.people.com.cn/n/2014/0819/c1003-25496316.html.

125. Han Han, "I Still Want to Be a Stinking Public Intellectual," March 2012, in *The Problem with Me*, 117–118.
126. See Jin Yixiang, "Shaoshupai Xu Zhiyuan" (Minority faction Xu Zhiyuan), *Wenyi Meixuewang*, WeChat public account, September 6, 2017, via Sohu, http://www.sohu.com/a/190055603_707966. See also Xu Zhiyuan, *Naxie youshang de nianqingren* (All the sad young men) (Haikou: Hainan Press, 2001).
127. Xu Zhiyuan, "Zixu: 46 nian zhihou" (Preface: In 46 years), in *Naxie youshang de nianqingren*, http://www.tzytxt.com/read/19795_1.html.
128. Quoted in Dong Meiqi, "Danxiangjie: Yijia shudian de shangye nixi" (One-way Street: A bookstore's commercial turn), *Shangye Jiazhi*, December 1, 2014, http://www.tmtpost.com/173843.html.
129. Dong Meiqi, "Danxiangjie."
130. Dong Meiqi, "Danxiangjie."
131. Xu Zhiyuan, "Women zhe yi dai" (Our generation), January 27, 2014, in *Jiquan de youhuo* (The totalitarian temptation) (Taipei: Baqi Wenhua, 2010), 247–248.
132. Xu Zhiyuan, "Yiqie dou shi keyi jiaohuan de" (Everything can be traded), *FTChinese*, May 24, 2007, http://www.ftchinese.com/story/001011551, translated as "Trading on Heritage," trans. Geremie Barmé, *China Heritage Quarterly*, no. 18 (June 2009), http://www.chinaheritagequarterly.org/articles.php?searchterm=018_tradingheritage.inc&issue=018.
133. "Danxiangjie Xu Zhiyuan: 'Wo haishi jizhe ba, dan bushi hao jizhe'" (One-Way Street's Xu Zhiyuan: "I'm still a journalist, but not a good journalist"), iCenr WeChat, August 20, 2014, http://www.tmtpost.com/132130.html.
134. Xu Zhiyuan, "Collective Amnesia," June 12, 2010, in *Paper Tiger: Inside the Real China*, trans. Michelle Deeter and Nicky Harman (London: Zeus, 2015), 99.
135. Xu Zhiyuan, "The Victory of the Masses," May 10, 2010, in *Paper Tiger*, 31–33. In the essay "The Anxiety of the Youths in the Outer Provinces" (September 11, 2011, in *Paper Tiger*, 59–61), Xu voices similar doubts about the entire "Internet generation" and its ability to transform China.
136. Xu Zhiyuan, "From Instant Gratification to Instant Forgetfulness," October 19, 2008, in *Paper Tiger*, 166.
137. Xu Zhiyuan, "Neizai de ziyou" (Inner freedom), July 2010, in *Shidai de daocaoren* (A scarecrow of the times) (Guilin: Guangxi Imaginist, 2013), 215.
138. The Imaginist series was the result of a creative endeavor typical of the Chinese publishing environment: under its publisher He Linxia, Guangxi Normal Press set up a private company (named BBT for "Be Better"), which published the Imaginist/Lixiangguo series under the editorship of Liu Ruilin ("Lixiangguo" refers to the Chinese translation of Plato's *Republic*). The series published several sensitive titles, including a posthumous collection of essays by the historian Gao Hua (who had published *How the Red Sun Rose* in Hong Kong) and one of Zhang Yihe's novellas on the Cultural Revolution. Many people believed that this was the reason why Liu was forced to resign and He Linxia was arrested in the spring of 2016. See, for example, "Guangxi shida chubanshe jituan yuan dongshizhang He Linxia she shouyu beibu" (Former CEO of Guangxi Normal Press arrested under suspicion of corruption), *Initium*, May 24, 2016, https://theinitium.com/article/20160524-dailynews-helinxia/.

139. Xu Zhiyuan, "Weizai, Danxiangjie, dou shi wo zui timian de shengyi, shangye yu zuojia ye keyi xiang'an wushi" (Both WeZeit, One-Way Street are dignified forms of business, both business and writers can put their hearts at ease), May 7, 2016, https://www.huxiu .com/article/149056.html.
140. Dong Meiqi, "Danxiangjie."
141. See the interview with Yu Wei: "Danxiangjie shudian: Yinwei gao zujin chedian, xian cheng Zhongguo wenyi dibiao, bei dichanshang feng wei zuoshang bin" (One-Way Street bookstore: Closing store because of high rent, it becomes a culture label and is wooed by mall operators), July 21, 2016, https://read01.com/JmADM5.html#.Wid5 GDPpMkg.
142. Xu Zhiyuan, "Weizai, Danxiangjie, dou shi wo zui timian de shengyi."
143. Xu Zhiyuan, "Wo dangran shi gonggong zhishifenzi" (Of course I'm a public intellectual), *Bowang* blog, May 20, 2016, http://www.bowangzhi.com/2016/05/20/xuzhiyuan2/.
144. Xu Zhiyuan, "Wo dangran shi gonggong zhishifenzi."
145. See Xu Zhiyuan, *Jiquan de youhuo* (The totalitarian temptation); *Zuguo de moshengren* (Stranger in the motherland) (Taipei: Baqi, 2011); and *Kangzhengzhe* (Rebels) (Taipei: Baqi, 2013).
146. Xu Zhiyuan, "Shidai de daocaoren" (A scarecrow of the times), July 2011, in *Shidai de daocaoren*, 242.
147. Xu Zhiyuan, "Zixu: Shidai de xuanxiao" (Preface: The commotion of the times), May 27, 2012, in *Shidai de daocaoren*, ii–iii.
148. Xu Zhiyuan, "Dang jiquan cong panxuan touding de jumang biancheng lingren mamu de daxiang" (When totalitarianism changes from a coiled-up anaconda to a numbing elephant), *Initium*, January 12, 2016, https://theinitium.com/article/20160112-opinion -totalitarianism-of-china-xuzhiyuan/, translated as "The Anaconda and the Elephant," trans. Callum Smith, *China Heritage*, June 27, 2017, http://chinaheritage.net/journal/ elephants-anacondas/. The anaconda metaphor is from Perry Link's article "The Anaconda in the Chandelier," *New York Review of Books*, April 11, 2002.
149. Xu Zhiyuan, "The Difficulty of Defending Legal Rights," August 5, 2010, in *Paper Tiger*, 197–198.
150. Xu Zhiyuan, "Women zhe yi dai" (Our generation), *FTChinese*, August 7, 2009, in *Jiquan de youhuo*, 244–245.
151. Xu Zhiyuan, "Xu Zhiyong zaoyu de huangdan" (The absurdity of Xu Zhiyong's misadventure), *Yazhou Zhoukan*, August 4, 2013.
152. Xu Zhiyuan, "The Anaconda and the Elephant."
153. Xu Zhiyuan, "The Anaconda and the Elephant."
154. Rogier Creemers, "The Pivot in Chinese Cybergovernance," *China Perspectives*, no. 4 (2015): 5.
155. See "Chinese Internet: A New Censorship Campaign Has Commenced," *Guardian*, May 15, 2013.
156. Creemers, "The Pivot in Chinese Cybergovernance," 10.
157. Creemers, "The Pivot in Chinese Cybergovernance," 9–10 (Creemers notes that Weibo use dropped from its peak in 2012).
158. See, for example, Patrick Gorman, "Red Guard 2.0: Nationalist Flesh Search in China," *Journal of Contemporary China* 26, no. 104 (2017): 83–98.

159. Zeng Jinyan, "Chongguo huanxiang" (Rebuilding illusions), *New York Times Chinese*, September 29, 2016, https://cn.nytimes.com/opinion/20160929/letter-zengjinyan-hanhan-response/zh-hant/.

CONCLUSION

1. Mischa Gabowitsch, *Protest in Putin's Russia* (Cambridge: Polity, 2017).
2. John Runciman, "China's Challenge to Democracy," *Wall Street Journal*, April 26, 2018.
3. Andrew Nathan, "The Puzzle of the Chinese Middle Class," *Journal of Democracy*, April 2016, 5–19.
4. As Brantley Womack argues, Mao's campaign against social science and broader anti-intellectualism was based on the notion that the education system was controlled by the elite and opinions were dictated by interests rather than by knowledge ("From Urban Radical to Rural Revolutionary: Mao From the 1920s to 1937," in *A Critical Introduction to Mao*, ed. Timothy Cheek [Cambridge: Cambridge University Press, 2010], 61–86).
5. Gloria Davies, "Knowing How to Be: The Dangers of Putting (Chinese) Thought Into Action," in *Chinese Thought as Global Theory: Diversifying Knowledge Production in the Social Sciences and Humanities*, ed. Leigh Jenco (Albany: State University of New York Press, 2016), 51. Davies sees the "unbroken tradition of truth," expressed for example in the continuity between Confucian and Marxian epistemology, as the main obstacle to a stronger global presence of Chinese thinkers and social scientists. While it is certainly desirable for more discourses produced in China to circulate among the international public, the present study concurs that such circulation can take place only on the condition that a greater plurality of discourses can be sustained within China.
6. See Daniel Drezner, *The Ideas Industry* (Oxford: Oxford University Press, 2017).

Index

1957 Studies, 86, 289n7, 289n11
798 Art district, 154, 157, 306n99, 307n108
Academy of Social Sciences: Chinese Academy of Social Sciences (CASS), 43, 101, 106, 156, 183, 185, 188, 156, 259, 273n49, 276n73, 278n100, 316n100; Shanghai Academy of Social Sciences, 37; Tianjin Academy of Social Sciences, 299n16; Yunnan Academy of Social Sciences, 154, 160, 258; Zhengzhou Academy of Social Sciences, 175
activism, 1, 4, 9–11, 13, 23–24, 38, 51, 82–83, 137, 141, 165, 167, 169, 170, 172, 174, 176, 183, 185, 191–192, 195–196, 199, 201–203, 208, 219, 224–225, 247, 250, 255–259, 263n23, 263n27, 264n33–36, 289n11, 290n19, 291n32, 298n4
Administrative Procedure Law, 309n3
Ai Weiwei, 9, 24, 107, 148, 171, 217, 220–225, 227, 246, 255, 326n57, 327n67–70, 327n72–76, 327n78–79
Ai Xiaoming, 4, 10, 23, 52, 77, 93, 97, 99, 135, 140, 147, 170, 248, 249, 255, 262n11, 280n3, 281n44, 285n104, 291n34, 292n50, 302n43, 312n29, 312n31–32, 312n34
All Sages bookstore, 235
amateur, 2, 33, 67, 81–82, 89, 94, 101, 104, 116, 121, 124, 128–131, 133, 141, 150, 202, 214, 248, 250, 253, 257n8, 300n18, 300n21
American Civil Liberties Union, 172, 179
Anti-CNN (also April Media), 204, 321n2
Anti-Rightist Movement, 55, 71, 73, 94, 96–98, 100, 102, 121, 190, 258, 288n2–3, 289n11, 292n45, 292n54; fortieth anniversary, 28, 84–86, 90, 92, 248, 257
archive, 92, 98, 101, 103, 105, 108, 116–117, 121, 136, 154, 156–157, 160, 257, 291n33, 292n51, 292n53, 302n48–49
artist (visual), 1, 5, 8, 12, 28–29, 45–46, 80, 107, 125, 132, 134, 141, 144, 171, 191, 220–221, 224, 255–256, 271n22, 290n30, 300n21, 304n74, 306n99, 307n100
artist village, 3, 16–17, 25, 123, 125, 127, 154–163, 248–249, 306n99, 307n100
authoritarian, 31–33, 40–41, 44, 53, 74, 125, 192, 196–197, 230, 244, 267n72, 310n3, 311n18, 311n25, 315n92, 319n138, 326n60; neoauthoritarian, 44, 52, 53; antiauthoritarian, 77, 82, 196
Avant-garde Today (*Jinri Xianfeng*), 128, 135, 299n16

Ba Jin, 17, 87, 289n15–16
Back Window Films, 123, 154
Barmé, Geremie, 32, 46, 263n23, 264n38, 268n76, 268n79, 271n23, 274n65, 275n68, 278n99, 279n111, 286n114, 287n128, 331n132
Bauman, Zygmunt, 6, 32, 33, 56, 253, 269n1, 271n24–25
Bei Dao, 80–81, 135
Beijing Bar Association, 177

Beijing Evening News (*Beijing Wanbao*), 206, 322n7
Beijing Film Academy (BFA), 123, 128, 136, 154, 308n113
Beijing Independent Film Festival (BIFF), 143, 154, 157–160, 289n12, 307n112, 308n114, 308n116–117, 308n123, 308n126
Beijing Literature (*Beijing Wenxue*), 79, 81, 280n4, 284n74, 286n114
Beijing Normal University, 52, 117, 157, 256, 312n29
Beijing Youth Daily (*Beijing Qingnianbao*), 87, 289n13
Benjamin, Walter, 235, 305n82
Bentham, Jeremy, 27, 32
Bian Zhongyun, 92, 117
biaotai (expressing a stance), 20, 54, 62
Big V, 190, 218, 233, 244, 246
Bingdian (Freezing point), 214
Bishan Commune, 161, 308n133
black jails, 176, 182, 200
blog, blogger, 1, 3, 8, 16, 23–25, 108, 170, 189, 204–209, 213, 216–217, 221, 225, 233, 235, 238, 245–246, 249, 254–55, 259, 263n27, 265n48, 311n13, 311n28, 314n69, 322n4, 326n51, 326n56–57, 327n75, 328n80, 328n90–91
Bo Xilai, 105–106
Bonnin, Michel, 37, 273n46, 273n51
bookstore, 98, 219, 234–236, 238–239, 246, 249, 258, 292n46, 331n128, 332n141
Bourdieu, Pierre, 12–13, 15, 26, 28–31, 33, 45, 253, 265n49, 267n62–63, 270n7–11, 270n16
Box Bar, 154
Bund Illustrated (*Waitan Huabao*), 213
Burns, John, 37, 273n53
Busan International Film Festival, 128, 154, 306n93

Cai Hua (Will Cai), 213, 324n32
Cai Yuanpei, 190
Caijing (Finance and economics), 213–214, 216, 277n81, 277n87, 278n96, 325n34–35, 330n123
Caixin (Financial news), 18, 173, 175, 214, 261n2, 292n55, 313n47
Calhoun, Craig, 38, 274n55
Callahan, William, 9, 220, 226, 263n30, 264n31, 271n29, 327n66, 328n77, 328n86, 328n90
Cao Shuji, 102, 292n54
Caochangdi, 3, 107–111, 220–221, 248, 258, 301n36, 307n100, 307n113
capitalism, 18, 32, 40–41, 47, 49, 65, 71, 138–139, 145, 148, 161, 207, 210, 229, 230, 252, 275n72, 276n74, 276n76, 276n78, 322n7, 328n90, 329n96; crony capitalism, 41, 71, 276n76, 276n78
Carrefour boycott, 24, 204, 206–207, 322n13, 323n12
censorship, 47, 53, 122, 124, 131, 168, 218, 226–227, 232, 234, 238, 244, 280n4, 288n4, 297n117, 309n140, 313n48, 324n32, 326n56, 326n58, 329n100, 329n102, 332n155; self-censorship, 32, 45, 104, 210, 242–243
Central Committee (of the CCP), 4, 287n1; Third Plenum of the Eleventh Central Committee, 87; Fourth Plenum of the Sixteenth Central Committee, 217
Central Document number 29 (2004), 4
Central Document number 9 (2013), 122, 216, 244
Cha, Louis (Jin Yong), 210
Chan Koonchung, 39, 210, 235
Chan, Chris, 186, 252, 284n78, 317n114
Chan, Ying, 217, 325n40, 326n52–53
Chang Ping, 204–209, 212–213, 217, 219, 249, 255, 322n5–7, 323n18, 324n27–31
chanhui (confession and repentance), 87, 89, 118, 289n16, 296n115, 305n86
Charter 08, 168, 181, 188, 192–195, 267n61, 319n140, 319n142
Cheek, Timothy, 36, 38, 43–44, 261n1, 266n52, 267n66, 267n68, 271n29, 272n35, 272n40, 273n41–42, 273n45, 273n49, 274n57, 275n69, 277n85, 277n88–89, 333n4
Chen Guangcheng, 175–177

Chen Ping, 213, 324n31, 325n40
Chen Pingyuan, 39, 274n60, 277n96
Chen Sihe, 11, 225, 265n43, 265n88
Chen Xiaolu, 118
Chen Xiaoming, 47, 79, 286n113–114
Chen Yi, 118
Chen Yinke, 79
Chen Zonghai, 99
Cheng Yizhong, 166, 176, 212, 214, 324n31, 325n36, 325n40
Chengdu, 24, 80, 100, 114, 144, 147, 158, 191, 224, 227, 289n11, 295n102
chengguan, 176, 197
Chevrier, Yves, 37, 273n46, 273n51–52
China Business Times (*Zhonghua Gongshang Shibao*), 210, 213
China Can Say No, 68, 282n60
China Central Television (CCTV), 125, 152, 213, 219, 322n1
China Independent Film Archive (Beijing), 154
China Independent Film Festival (Nanjing), 154, 304n67
China Reform (*Zhongguo Gaige*), 175, 313n56
China Village Documentary Project, 107, 294n80
China Youth Daily (*Zhongguo Qingnianbao*), 52, 214, 233, 262n12
Chinese Communist Party (CCP), 4–5, 17–18, 36–37, 40–42, 44, 47, 49–50, 62, 65, 71, 83–84, 87, 89, 91, 94–95, 98–100, 102–103, 105–106, 113, 115, 119, 121–122, 151, 165, 166, 169, 182, 185–186, 189, 194, 197–198, 209–211, 215–216, 219, 230–231, 266n52, 272n39, 274n57, 287n1, 289n13–14, 294n74, 319n138, 325n43, 327n66; party-state, 44, 96, 192, 216, 252, 267n69, 309n3, 319n138; Thirteenth Congress, 210; Fourteenth Congress, 274n62; Fifteenth Congress, 6, 84; Eighteenth Congress, 106, 198
Chinese People's Political Consultative Conference (CPPCC), 220
Chinese Social Sciences Today (*Zhongguo Shehui Kexuebao*), 106
Cho, Li-fung, 211, 318n134, 323n21–22, 324n24
Chomsky, Noam, 328
Citizen Monthly (*Gongmin Yuekan*), 172, 312n42
citizen, 2, 7, 8–11, 16–17, 44, 70, 75–76, 91, 117, 135, 142, 165, 169, 171–172, 178, 180–182, 192, 195–200, 202, 212, 219–220, 224, 226, 233, 243, 246–247, 252, 254, 258, 263n27, 263n29–30, 264n33, 264n36, 268n73, 271n29, 310n10, 310n13, 312n29, 312n30, 312n32, 312n42, 314n64, 315n81–82, 318n124, 320n148, 320n150–156, 321n169, 325n33, 327n66, 328n88, 328n90; citizen meals, 198–199, 202; citizenship, 9, 181, 195, 199, 200, 251, 312n30; Citizens' Commitment Pledge, 195
civil rights, 166–167, 171, 257–259, 312n29
civil society, 8–9, 17, 31, 37, 100, 168, 192, 199, 220, 243, 251, 263n21, 263n26, 264n30–32, 267n72, 277n88, 295n97, 311n18, 319n138, 321n169, 328n86, 328n90; civil society organizations, 7, 242
class: class consciousness, 95, 186, 283n71, 303n61; class labels, 71–72; class identity, 186; class status, 273n44; class structure, 252–253; class struggle, 57, 71, 102, 176, 252; dominant class, 15, 27–28, 31, 72, 90; intellectual class, 32, 272n38; lower class, 89, 185, 192, 228, 265n42; Marxist class, 21, 32, 72, 75; middle class, 31, 72, 186, 221, 229, 252, 284n78, 311n13, 330n113, 333n3; ruling class, 31, 45, 51, 185, 186, 214; social class, 70, 144, 234, 284n78; underclass, 15, 185, 187, 191, 266n59, 267n63, 287n126, 317n110–116, 318n134; working class, 4, 21, 28–30, 32, 37, 55, 64, 70, 72, 83, 138–139, 144–145, 176, 185–186, 252, 269n90, 271n21, 305n84
Cohen, Jerome, 169, 311n24
commemoration: 15, 84–85, 89–101, 105, 110, 113, 117–121, 148, 169, 224, 288n4, 291n32, 296n105, 297n117
Confucianism, 2, 19, 20, 35–38, 42, 44, 52, 54, 55–57, 59–60, 76, 88, 183, 209, 247, 264n35, 277n81, 279n112, 313n53, 333n5

Consensus Net (Gongshi wang), 122, 216, 219–220, 327n62–65
Constitution (of the PRC), 44, 166, 172–173, 188, 200, 215, 231, 233, 242, 250, 278n102, 310n3, 329n100
constitutionalism, 166–169, 176, 181, 192–198, 200, 215–216, 220, 248–249, 257, 310n10, 315n82, 320n153, 326n46–47
consumerism, 16, 33, 39, 47–50, 146, 157, 159, 207–209, 217, 226, 229, 234, 243, 251, 323n16
Cosmos (publisher), 119, 219
Creemers, Rogier, 216, 244, 279n117, 326n47, 332n154, 332n156–157
Cui Dabo, 155
Cui Weiping, 136–137, 283n74, 298n1, 302n45, 302n47, 302n54, 303n62, 308n113
Cui Zhiyuan, 40, 275n70
cultural fever, 57, 63, 68, 279n108, 283n63
Cultural Revolution, 11, 15, 18–19, 56–58, 62-67, 71, 78, 80, 84, 87–91, 96, 101, 103, 107, 113–122, 148, 184, 222, 233, 258, 267n64, 278n96, 285n86, 287n124, 288n4, 289n18, 290n21, 296n110–111, 297n117, 297n119–125, 331n138
custody and repatriation (system), 164, 166, 310n9

Dabao Labor Camp (Sichuan), 100, 292n51–52
Dai Huang, 85, 115, 288n5
Dai Jinhua, 22, 68, 269n88, 283n62, 283n64
Dai Weiwei, 85, 115–116, 288n6
Dai Zhiyong, 215
Dali (Yunnan), 161
Dan Du (Reading alone), 239–240
Danxiangjie (One-way street), 235–239, 331n128–130, 331n133, 332n139–142
Davies, Gloria, 28, 48–51, 190, 264n38, 266n58, 267n64, 274n60, 274n65, 274n67, 275n68, 275n71, 276n75, 279n107, 279n112, 279n117, 286n114, 333n5
death penalty, 176, 312n39, 314n61
democracy movement (1989), 1–2, 35, 38, 39–40, 46–48, 81, 113, 125, 164, 167–168, 181, 202, 209–210, 247, 265n44, 267n61, 274n55, 309n1, 311n13, 311n22, 312n29, 327n71,
democracy, 2, 3, 7, 14–15, 35–36, 38, 40–41, 44, 48, 94, 125, 151, 161, 167–168, 175, 193–197, 200–201, 223, 229–233, 242, 257, 272n34, 279n115, 284n82, 295n98, 297n123, 310n12, 319n138, 319n144, 330n112–114, 330n119, 333n2
Deng Liqun, 101
Deng Rong, 219
Deng Tuo, 36, 209, 273n41
Deng Xiaoping, 37, 39–40, 48, 52, 56, 84, 209, 219, 252, 271n21, 273n48–49
Deng Yujiao, 201
Derrida, Jacques, 50
Diao Dou, 80
diceng (lower strata, underclass),14, 20, 94, 111, 125, 127, 133, 185, 187, 191–192, 265n47, 266n59, 267n63, 283n71, 295n88, 295n90, 316n106, 317n110, 317n121–122, 318n124, 318n134; *diceng wenxue* (lower-class literature), 192, 318n137. *See also* class; subaltern
digital video (DV), 1, 16, 127, 129, 133, 136–138, 298n5, 301n33–34, 302n55, 303n56
Ding Dang, 80
Ding Dong, 114, 268n77, 268n83–84, 269n87, 283n67, 295n101
Ding Zilin, 311n20
dissident, 17, 23, 31, 38, 46, 80, 83, 228, 242–243, 251, 268n73, 271n18, 291n32, 309n135, 315n75
Djilas, Milovan, 31, 271n20
DOChina Festival, 154, 157–159, 307n112
documentary film, 3, 10, 14–15, 81–82, 87, 100, 104, 107, 109, 121, 133, 135–137, 140, 142, 147, 149, 154, 157, 170, 202, 250, 252–253, 255–259, 289n12, 294n80, 299n13, 301n33, 301n35, 301n37, 302n43, 304n66, 301n68, 305n74, 305n85, 306n91 306n98, 312n29; documentary film movement, 137–138, 299n10, 303n57–58, 304n74, 306n93

Douban (social media), 154, 298n5
Du Haibin, 127, 134, 143, 148, 198n1, 302n55, 303n59
Du Yinghua, 96
Duan Jinchuan, 136
Dushu (Reading), 11, 53, 65, 71, 79, 111, 139, 264n38, 265n45–47, 267n63, 275n70, 278n96, 281n27, 284n80, 295n90, 303n58, 303n61–62

eastern Europe, 31–32, 268n73, 271n18
Economic Observer (*Jingji Guanchabao*), 235
educated (rusticated) youth (*zhiqing*), 18, 57–58, 63, 65–66, 71–72, 74, 78, 82, 88, 95, 97, 281n41
Einstein, Albert, 3
enlightenment, 2–3, 7, 10, 16, 18, 22, 27, 30–33, 40, 43, 48–51, 54, 65–69, 73, 82, 220, 237, 241, 262n13, 265n42, 269n1, 269n3–5, 274n65–67, 275n69, 277n86, 282n54, 319n142
environment (issue), 170, 174, 197, 218, 263n27, 326n55, 330n219
equality, 13, 25, 41, 60, 129, 144, 169–170, 174, 193, 196, 199, 259, 312n30
Eslite bookstore, 238, 240
exile, 10, 23, 33–34, 38, 135, 220
expert, 3, 5, 13–14, 17–18, 24, 26–28, 30–33, 40, 59, 149, 165, 179, 247, 253, 254, 264n33, 269n5, 270n9, 270n16, 278n97, 315n91

Falungong, 165, 191
Fan Gang, 173, 276n76
Fan Zhongyan, 56, 271n31
Fang Kun, 178, 314n69
Fang Lijun, 155, 160
Fang Lizhi, 13, 84
Fang Zhouzi, 225, 233, 330n123
Fanhall Café (Songzhuang), 152, 157–158, 259, 306n91, 308n114
Fei Xiaotong, 75, 272n38
feminism (women's rights), 4, 10, 52, 170–171, 255 264n36–37; feminist five, 201, 321n167
Feng Xiaogang, 106
Fengrui Law Firm, 201, 321n169–170
feudalism, 54, 66
Fewsmith, Joseph, 38, 262n10, 267n65, 274n58–59, 275n71–73
film (independent), 1, 16, 23–24, 107, 123–163, 248, 256, 264n37, 289n12, 298n1, 298n8, 300n25, 301n41, 303n60, 304n67, 304n71, 304n73, 305n78, 306n93, 306n96, 306n113, 308n116, 308n123, 308n126, 309n140, 309n142
Film Auteur, 304n67, 308n119
Film Bureau, 124, 131, 163; Film and Television Bureau, 162. *See also* State Administration of Radio, Film and Television
film director (filmmaker), 2–3, 10, 14–16, 23–24, 81–82, 104, 106, 121, 126, 127, 129, 136, 139–142, 150, 152, 154, 159, 161–163, 202, 227, 248, 250, 253, 255–259, 262n11, 290n30, 298n8, 301n41, 304n67, 305n78, 306n95, 309n138; Fifth Generation of, 87, 138–141, 301n41; Sixth Generation of, 126–127, 139, 140
film festival, 23, 100, 110, 123, 128, 143, 154–159, 163, 248, 254, 256, 258, 259, 289n12, 298n1, 299n13, 303n57, 304n67, 306n93, 308n116, 308n119, 308n123, 308n126
Film Industry Promotion Law, 162, 309n141
five black categories, 62, 64, 70, 83, 115, 117–118, 120
Folk Memory Project (Minjian Jiyi Jihua), 107, 108, 258, 294
Foucault, Michel, 3, 13, 18–20, 22, 25, 27, 29–34, 50–51, 53, 62–63, 67–69, 79, 253, 261n4, 266n50, 266n53, 269n3–5, 270n12–16, 274n67; PKU Foucault Reading Club 281n40
freelance, 19, 52, 78, 90, 125, 247–248, 257, 286n114
Freud, Sigmund, 58, 269n89, 290n21
Friends of Nature, 7, 173
FTChinese, 204, 206, 213, 235, 255, 258, 322n5, 322n8, 331n132, 332n150
Fu Guoyong, 93, 291n31, 291n34

Gan Yang, 11, 40, 265n44, 275n70
Gandhi, Mahatma, 175
Gang of Four, 15, 280n15
Gao brothers, 191
Gao Ertai, 291n41
Gao Gao, 88, 289n18
Gao Hua, 102–103, 293n60–61, 331n138
Gao Xingjian, 10, 34, 298n9
Gao Zhisheng, 311n20, 311n24
Ge Zhaoguang, 277n81
gender, 10, 19, 30, 54, 74, 111, 141, 170–171, 186, 201, 236, 248–149, 256, 265n39, 295n87, 312n30; gender studies, 248, 255, 259
General Administration of Press and Publications (GAPP), 210
Golden Shield project, 217
Goldman, Merle, 15, 18, 43, 45, 266n61, 267n68, 267n70, 273n42, 277n84–85, 277n88, 277n94
Gongmeng (later Gongmin), 171–181, 183, 188, 194–195, 198, 202, 225, 243, 256–258, 312n38–39, 312n44, 313n60, 314n64–65, 314n69, 314n71, 315n72–74, 315n79–80, 318n126, 320n150n 328n88
Gramsci, Antonio, 14, 27–29, 54, 70, 111, 141, 266n59, 270n6
Grand Master (*Dajia*), 81
Great Famine (1959-1961), 62, 82, 88–90, 94, 96–97, 99, 101–113, 121, 232, 248, 250, 258, 290n26, 292n54, 293n63, 293n66, 293n70, 294n71, 294n77, 294n82
Great Firewall, 217
Great Leap Forward, 62, 88, 103, 112, 290n26, 293n64
Green Dam (Lüba), 218
Gu Changwei, 309n137
Gu Zhun, 79, 86, 265n47, 287n124
Gu, Edward X., 18, 45, 263n25, 267n70, 273n50, 273n52, 297n117, 313n45
Guan Hu, 126
Guan Jinwen, 99
Guangzhou, 5, 8, 24, 52, 101, 154, 164, 166, 210, 213–214, 255, 263n27, 293n55, 312n29
Guo Jingming, 225
Guo Rui, 107, 294n85
Guo Yuhua, 15, 82, 104, 111–112, 248–249, 256, 266n59, 267n63, 290n26, 295n88–95
Guo Yushan, 10, 174–177, 256, 313n51–53

Habermas, Jürgen, 27, 32–33, 269n3–5, 274n67
Han Dong, 79–81, 286n116–117, 287n119, 287n122
Han Han, 16–17, 24, 206–209, 217, 225–234, 237–238, 244–246, 248–250, 256, 267n69, 322n9–323n15, 328n80–92, 329n93–106, 330n 107–124, 331n125
Han Jie, 140
Han Renjun, 233, 330n123
Han Shaogong, 53, 79, 278n96
Hao Zhidong, 18, 43, 45, 252, 268, 269n90, 270n16, 277n83, 277n96, 278n97
Hao Zhiqiang, 136, 306n94
Haraszti, Miklós, 32, 46, 238, 271n22, 278n98
Havel, Václav, 31, 32, 70, 192, 200, 229, 263n30, 271n18, 283n74, 283n74, 310n13, 328n90; and Charter 77, 192–193
He Baogang, 36, 38, 272n37, 273n54, 274n56, 274n64
He Fengming, 86, 97–98, 149, 291n41
He Guimei, 288n3
He Qinglian, 72, 276n76, 284n82, 285n83
He Shu, 115, 120, 297n124
He Weifang, 216, 310n7, 310n10, 326n46
He Xuefeng, 106
He Yuan, 160
Hegelian, 14, 50, 68, 145
Hei Wu Lei Yijiu (Remembering the five black categories), 115, 117–118, 296n114
Heine, Heinrich, 27, 32
historian (amateur), 81, 94, 101–112, 202, 214, 248, 250, 253, 257, 258
historical nihilism, 121–122
history (oral), 87, 90, 101, 104–105, 111–112, 115, 120–121, 134, 248, 256
Hitler, Adolf, 67
HIV, AIDS epidemic, 2, 226, 255
homosexual, 20, 69, 71–72, 74, 256, 285n90–92, 299n11

Hong Kong International Film Festival, 154, 299n13
Hong Kong, 17, 39, 52, 87–88, 93, 100, 103, 106, 111, 115, 118–119, 133, 135, 147, 154, 167, 169, 199, 207, 210, 213, 219, 226–228, 235, 242–243, 258–259, 268n75, 275n70, 279n1, 288n4, 288n6, 289n11, 292n54, 296n105, 299n13, 306n95–96, 308n119, 311n23, 322n7, 324n30–33, 328n92, 329n101, 331n138
Hong Zhenkuai, 106, 122
Honglou (Red building), 91
household registration (*hukou*), 70–71, 109, 142, 180, 184, 193, 218
Hsia, C. T., 35, 272n33
Hsing, You-tien, 9, 264n34
Hsu Cho-yun, 63, 74, 300n30
Hu Angang, 41, 216, 275n70
Hu Feng, 65, 86
Hu Jia, 218, 259
Hu Jie, 92–93, 100, 117, 155, 170, 248, 256, 290n30, 291n40, 306n99, 308n120, 312n32
Hu Jintao, 41, 117, 210, 217–218, 244, 310n3
Hu Kuan, 79
Hu Ping, 85, 119, 169, 191, 297n121, 318n135
Hu Shi, 53
Hu Shuli, 18, 213–214
Hu Xinyu, 134, 301n38
Hu Yaobang, 113–114
Huang Jing (rape and murder case), 170, 255, 312n30
Huang Ping, 53, 278n96
Huang Rui, 307n100
Huang Wanli, 287n124
Huang Wenhai (also: Wen Hai), 10, 141–143, 264n37,298n2, 299n9, 305n75, 306n97, 307n110, 308n115, 308n118, 308n122, 308n131
humanist spirit (debate), 39–40, 46–47, 49, 55, 59, 68, 274n65
Hundred Flowers, 257
Hung Huang, 235

Imaginist (series published by Guangxi Normal Press), 239–240, 331n138
Initium (*Duan*), 213, 219, 324n31–32
intellectual history, 12, 19, 24–26, 29, 50, 183, 249, 265n45, 269n91, 277n86
intellectual: businessman-intellectual, 240; establishment intellectual, 34, 36, 38, 45, 209, 225, 272n40, 273n41, 273n50, 329n93; grassroots intellectual, 8, 10, 12, 23, 26, 52, 59, 68, 121, 248–249, 262n11, 272n39; Marxist intellectual, 186; May Fourth intellectual, 2, 35; media intellectual, 4, 16–17, 40, 250; *minjian* intellectual, 7, 10, 13, 19, 21, 23–2534, 82, 90–91, 95, 97, 103, 111, 116, 121, 124–127, 130, 139, 141, 149, 156, 161, 164–165, 171, 176, 184–185, 189–190, 201–202, 207–210, 221, 225, 230, 233, 237, 245–247, 251, 253, 254, 322n2, 328n90; normative/realist definition, 26–34, 37, 44, 50; public intellectual, 3–9, 15–16, 34, 82, 83, 143, 190, 217, 225, 234, 240, 243, 261n1, 261n5, 261n7, 261n9, 261n14,263n21, 263n29, 264n33, 266n61, 271n18, 274n67, 287n124, 287n127, 316n105, 330n121, 331n125, 332n143; organic intellectual, 27–29, 176, 249, 252, 269n90; postmodern intellectual, 32, 33, 49; regime intellectual, 31; role as moral critic, 5, 36, 43–44, 277n88; role as expert (see: expert); traditional intellectual, 27, 249, 254; specific intellectual, 3, 13, 30–31, 34, 121, 165, 189, 214, 220, 232, 253, 268n73; universal intellectual, 3, 13, 22, 29, 30, 59, 189, 247, 270n9, 322n4; *zhishifenzi*, 36–37, 39
intelligentsia, 10, 36, 141, 264n36, 269n1, 271n21, 272n35–36, 272n38, 273n41, 312n37
Internet, 1, 3, 16, 21, 23–24, 60, 83, 104, 106, 114 ,117, 120, 124, 161, 168, 170–171, 180, 181, 195, 204, 209, 216–234, 236, 238, 244–246, 249, 262n18, 264n36, 287n126, 311n13, 313n48, 321n2, 322n7, 324n32, 326n48, 326n50, 326n59, 327n61, 328n90, 330n109, 331n135, 332n155
iSun Affairs (*Yangguang Shiwu*), 213, 219, 313n52, 324n31

Jameson, Fredric, 47, 278n103
Ji Dan, 130, 140, 253, 256, 300n22
Jia Jia, 10, 264n36
Jia Pingwa, 39, 55, 79, 207
Jia Zhangke, 9, 82, 124, 126–128, 130–132, 134–135, 138–140, 144–145, 147, 154, 158, 248, 256, 287n125, 299n12, 299n17, 300n18–21, 300n23–27, 300n29–30, 301n31–32, 301n39–40, 302n44, 302n48, 302n55, 303n57, 303n59, 303n62–63, 305n80–81, 305n84, 306n95–96, 327n66
Jia Zhitan, 107, 294n80
Jiabiangou, 91, 96–101, 257–258, 291n41–42, 292n45–46, 308n120
Jiang Mianheng, 216
Jiang Wen, 88, 302n48
Jiang Yiping, 211, 324n24
Jiang Yue, 136, 298n9, 306n94
Jiang Zemin, 6, 41, 47, 85, 165, 210, 216, 262n12, 273n48, 274n62, 275n73, 278n101, 284n78
Jiang Zidan, 53, 278n96
Jiao Guobiao, 115, 117, 296n114
Jifeng bookstore, 235
Jin Guowang, 155
journalist, 1–2, 5, 10, 12, 14–16, 18, 24, 40, 51, 72, 101, 103, 114, 121, 135, 162, 172, 176, 184, 191, 204–217, 235, 237, 245–246, 249, 255, 257–258, 263n27, 267n71, 275n72, 276n76, 305n78, 311n13, 322n4, 323n20–21, 324n24, 325n34, 325n39, 331n133; investigative journalist: 18, 105, 204, 210–211, 214, 255–256, 314n69, 323n21–22, 324n24, 325n39
June Fourth. *See* democracy movement

Kan Lishi (Looking at History), 295n102
Kang Jianning, 134
Kant, Immanuel, 10
Ke Qingshi, 93
Kelly, David, 9, 13, 261n5, 263n29, 266n55–56, 319n143
King, Martin Luther, Jr., 175
knowledge, 4, 6, 12–14, 23–24, 26–27, 29, 30–34, 45, 53, 56, 59–62, 66, 73–74, 77, 90, 113, 121–122, 127, 142, 161–162, 165–166, 172, 187, 189, 191, 194, 202–203, 219–220, 224, 226–227, 230, 233, 238, 240, 245, 247–248, 251–254, 269n5, 272n39, 281n27, 294n73, 320n149, 324n24, 333n4–5
Konrád, György, 31–32, 46, 266n52, 268n80, 270n17, 271n20–21
Korean War, 102, 147, 293n56–57
Kramer, Lloyd, 27, 32–34, 269n3–5
Kunming, 24, 80, 124–125, 148, 154, 160

Lanzhou, 91, 93–95, 97–98, 149, 291n36, 294n73
Lanzmann, Claude, 98
Lao She, 65, 88
Larson, Wendy, 22, 269n89, 290n21
Law on Lawyers, 165
Law on Legislation, 166
Law on Regional National Autonomy, 179
lawyers (grassroots), 1–3, 9, 14–15, 24, 30, 81, 83, 164–181, 183, 188, 192, 195, 199, 201–202, 214, 242, 250, 257–259, 263n23, 263n27, 309n3, 310n10, 311n19–20, 311n24–25, 314n62, 315n82–83, 320n149–150, 320n158, 321n167, 321n169, 321n170
Leader (*Lingdaozhe*), 118, 219
Lee Ou-fan, Leo, 283n74
Lee, Ching Kwan, 9, 182, 264n34, 290n25, 315n92
Legal Daily (*Fazhi Ribao*), 166
Lei Yi, 275n70
Leninism, 36, 212, 273n41, 325n43
letters and visits (also *xinfang*): 152, 176–177, 182–184, 191, 314n65, 315n85, 316n99–104. *See also* petitioners
Leung Man-tao, 219, 225
Levenson, Joseph, 247, 279n112
LGBT, 201, 256
Li Chengpeng, 232, 330n119
Li Datong, 214
Li Hongqi, 140
Li Hsiao-t'i, 10–11, 265n40, 265n42
Li Jing, 66, 77, 280n4, 282n54, 286n108
Li Rui, 113

Li Shengzhao, 105, 294n71
Li Shenzhi, 284
Li Tingting, 201, 321n168
Li Tuo, 278n96, 303n62
Li Xianting, 153, 155–159, 256, 306n99, 307n102, 307n104, 307n111, 308n114, 308n121, 308n123; Li Xianting Film Fund and Film School, 157–158, 160, 307n113
Li Xiaoshan, 136, 302n46
Li Xinmin, 107
Li Yang, 140
Li Yifan, 147
Li Yinhe, 19–22, 54, 63, 68, 70, 73, 76, 82, 126, 248–249, 256–257, 268n83, 283n66–67, 283n72, 285n88, 285n88–89, 285n91, 285n103, 299n11
Li Yu, 140
Li Zehou, 43, 277n86
Li, He, 44, 277n90
Li, Jie, 92, 151, 290n29, 306n88
Lian Yue, 217
Liang Congjie, 7, 173, 263n21
Liang Qichao, 35, 229, 240
Liao Bokang, 105
Liao Yiwu, 15, 82, 191, 318n134–136
liberalism, 4–5, 10, 14, 16, 36–37, 40–44, 48–49, 53, 65–66, 68, 83, 85, 92–93, 105, 113, 124, 136, 166–167, 169, 177, 180, 183–184, 188, 192–193, 197, 220, 225–226, 230, 233, 250–251, 254, 264n32, 271n18, 275n68, 275n70, 275n72–73, 276n76, 276n78, 279n109, 282n54, 287n124, 288n3, 310n13, 319n140, 322n7, 330n121
Liberation Daily (*Jiefang Ribao*), 4, 275n72
Lin Bai, 80
Lin Biao, 11, 69, 117
Lin Chun, 71, 252, 284n80, 304n64
Lin Xiling, 86, 99
Lin Xudong, 130, 298n1, 299n13, 300n20, 306n94
Lin Zhao, 86, 91–96, 100, 114, 170, 232, 248, 290n28, 291n31–34
Lin Zhibo, 106, 294n73
Link, Perry, 35, 44, 263n24, 271n31, 277n92–93, 332n148
literary youth (*wen qing*), 6, 235
literati, 2, 7, 34–37, 42–43, 49–51, 76, 80, 209, 230, 247, 253
Little Red Book, 57, 73
Liu Binyan, 17, 43, 84
Liu Guangji, 99
Liu Jiayin, 149, 306n87
Liu Junning, 53, 278n96
Liu Mingfu, 327n66
Liu Qidi, 86
Liu Qing, 214, 275n68, 325n42
Liu Shaoqi, 219, 271n21
Liu Suli, 235
Liu Wai-tong, 235
Liu Xiaobo, 88, 192–193, 226, 238, 289n17, 312n29, 319n139
Liu Xinwu, 79
Liu Zaifu, 87, 289n16
Liu Zhende, 219
Liu Zhenyun, 79, 106, 294n74
Lou Ye, 124, 126, 140, 302n48
Lu Jinbo, 233
Lu Jun, 174, 313n50
Lu Wei, 244
Lü Xinyu, 125, 136–139, 145–146, 154, 252–253, 298n6, 298n8, 299n10, 302n46, 303n56–58, 303n61, 303n83, 308n132
Lu Xueyi, 71, 186, 284n78
Lu Xun, 36, 39, 77, 79, 93, 226, 292n36, 301n40
Lu Yuegang, 191, 318n134, 325n40
Lukács, 139, 141, 145
Lung Ying-tai, 62, 219
Luo Bing, 107, 110, 294n86
Luo Yonghao, 217
Lushan Conference (1959), 96

Ma Jian, 80
Ma Li (documentary filmmaker), 153, 248–249, 257
Ma Li (poet, journalist), 87, 289n13
Ma Yong, 119, 239, 297n120
Ma Yuan, 79
Ma, Pony, 230

MacKinnon, Rebecca, 219, 321n2, 326n56, 326n60
mangliu (drifter), 125, 155
Mao Chenyu, 304n67
Mao era, 11–12, 15, 23, 34, 36–37, 41, 44, 50, 55–56, 64, 70–72, 76, 80–81, 84–122, 131, 139, 149, 161, 168, 214, 252, 255–257, 265n47, 272n38, 290n24, 291n35, 292n51, 293n64, 293n66, 294n73, 294n78, 295n103, 297n123
Mao Yushi, 115, 173, 262n10, 313n46–47
Mao Zedong, 5, 36, 65–67, 69, 71, 85, 95, 106, 113, 119, 131, 138, 173, 252, 276n74, 292n55, 293n56, 293n61, 300n25, 313n47, 333n4; Mao Zedong thought, 20, 60; Maoism, 2, 15, 19–20, 22, 34, 41, 44, 52, 54, 57, 63, 66–67, 69, 74–75, 87–80, 95, 98, 106, 121, 138, 282n56
market reforms, 1, 7, 16–17, 23, 37–40, 44–47, 51, 75, 165, 173, 209, 252, 272n63, 279n116, 288n3
Marx, Karl, 11, 14, 16, 21–22, 32, 54, 70, 72, 75, 96, 106, 112, 132, 138–139, 142–143, 145, 186–187, 198, 202, 249–250, 252–254, 266n59, 272n38, 276n74, 279n117, 283n73, 304n64, 333n5
May Fourth (New Culture) Movement, 2, 4, 5, 11–13, 19, 35–36, 43, 50, 60, 92, 95, 125, 249, 294n81
McCormick, Barrett, 214, 325n42–43
McGrath, Jason, 47, 274n65, 278n102, 286n113–114, 303n57
media (commercial), 1, 3, 7, 24, 104, 177, 180, 208–216, 246, 248
Mei Ninghua, 206
memory, 23, 48, 89–91, 100–101, 104, 107–108, 111, 136, 148, 222, 258, 288n6, 290n26–27, 292n45, 293n62, 293n66, 294n74, 294n78, 294n82–86, 295n87–89, 295n97, 295n101, 297n119, 297n125, 304n74
Mencius, 59–60
Mian Mian, 80
microblog (*weibo*), 3, 16, 106, 189–190, 208, 218, 239, 254, 294n72, 311n13, 311n28, 318n129, 329n100, 332n157
migrant worker (*nongmingong*), 2–3, 15, 17, 41, 71, 75, 82, 108, 134, 136, 143–144, 155–156, 164, 174, 176, 180, 187, 194, 200, 221, 226, 256, 258, 300n28, 317n118, 319n144, 330n119
Milosz, Czeslaw, 31, 271n19
Mingpao, 210, 226, 275
minjian intellectual. *See under* intellectual
minjian society, 9, 15, 19, 160, 192, 214, 250, 254, 263n26, 265n44, 265n48; vs. *guanfang* (official), 7, 183, 296n106
Minzner, Carl, 182, 192, 315n85, 316n102, 319n139
Misty poets, 81
Mo Shaoping, 168
Mo Yan, 79, 235
Mo Zhixu, 245
mobilization, 6–7, 35, 138, 167, 182, 185–186, 192, 201, 221, 226, 229, 247, 253, 298n8, 312n30, 325n33
Modern People (*Xiandairen Bao*), 210
modernization, 2–3, 36, 40, 49, 112, 146–147, 151, 178–179, 253, 275n70, 276n76, 314n70
More, Thomas, 65, 282n46
Mou Sen, 298n9
Müller, Jan-Werner, 25, 269n91
Murong Xuecun, 244, 286n114, 329n100

Nathan, Andrew, 35, 177, 272n34, 314n63, 333n3
National People's Congress (NPC), 164, 166
national studies (*guoxue*), 57, 68, 277n81, 280n16, 281n27, 281n35
nationalism, 48, 50, 67, 68, 177, 204–207, 221, 227, 230, 241, 245–246, 249, 274n60, 282n57, 314n70, 329n93, 330n119
neutrality (axiological), 13, 53–54, 72–74, 82, 253
New Citizen Movement, 180, 192, 196–202, 258, 315n81, 320n150–152
New Left, 10, 11, 16, 40–42, 44, 48, 67–68, 169, 250, 269n90, 275n68, 275n70, 276n74, 276n78, 318n137
Nietzsche, Friedrich, 66
Ning Ying, 144, 305n79
Niu Ben, 105

nongovernmental organizations (NGOs), 1, 3, 7, 10, 17–18, 23–25, 51, 75, 168, 170, 172–174, 192, 213–214, 235, 256–258, 263n25, 267n72, 311n18, 312n39, 312n44, 313n51–52, 319n138, 324n31

Office 101, 154
Ogawa Shinsuke, 128, 133, 306n94
Old Photos (*Lao Zhaopian*), 114, 288n4, 295n101
Olympics: 6, 148, 151, 176–177, 192, 204, 249–250, 314n70
One Man's Journal (*1 Bao*), 213
One-Way Street, later One-Way Space (Danxiang), 234–240, 246, 249, 258, 331n128, 331n133, 332n139, 332n141
Oppenheimer, J. Robert, 13
oral history. *See* history
Orient (*Dongfang*), 2, 18, 53, 59, 73, 113, 119, 268n74, 278n96, 297n117
Oriental History Review (*Dongfang Lishi Pinglun*), 93, 239, 258
Ou Ning, 161, 308n133
Ouyang Jianghe, 140, 303n62, 304n69–70

Pan Jianlin, 148
Pan Shiyi, 118
Pan Wei, 327n66
Pang Ho-cheung, 227
Peking University (PKU), 12, 19, 22, 39, 64, 75, 85–86, 91–92, 94–95, 101, 115, 132, 155, 157, 166, 175, 177–178, 182, 232–233, 256–257, 276n73, 281n40, 283n71, 288n2–3, 289n7, 289n12, 296n110, 313n54, 330n119
Pema Tseden, 127, 140
Peng Lingfan, 92, 290n28, 291n33
People's Commune, 95–96, 108, 112
People's Daily (*Renmin Ribao*), 4, 83, 87, 93, 106, 209–210, 215, 262n9, 287n124, 287n127–128
People's Liberation Army, 53, 92, 256
People's Literature (*Renmin Wenxue*), 21
People's Republic of China (PRC); 3, 7, 12, 37, 43, 70, 84, 87, 90, 94, 102–103, 110, 147, 166, 169, 248, 250, 252, 272n40, 278n102, 284n77, 289n14, 290n26; foundational period of the PRC (1949-1966), 84, 88
People's University, 11, 19, 52, 64–65, 317n110
petitioners, 2, 15, 16, 21, 41, 54, 71–72, 150–153, 156, 167, 172, 175–177, 180–192, 201–202, 226, 242, 248–249, 257–259, 313n58, 316n92, 316n96, 316n107–108, 318n135, 321n174; petitioners' village, 150–153, 175–177, 191, 313n58, 318n135
Phoenix (TV, Weekly), 219
Pils, Eva, 166, 180, 183–184, 195, 202, 264n32, 309n1–3, 310n4, 310n6, 310n8, 310n10, 311n17, 311n19–20, 312n39, 315n75, 315n77, 315n82–83, 315n87, 315n89–91, 316n94–95, 316n97, 316n105, 320n149–150, 320n153–155, 320n158, 320n160, 321n172–173
Plato, 66, 331n138
popular culture, 11, 16, 47, 48, 50, 130, 183, 209, 221, 263n24, 265n42, 274n65, 323n16
Posner, Richard, 3, 261n5
postmodernism, 17, 32–33, 39, 42, 47–51, 68, 190, 275n70, 278n103, 278n106, 279n110
postsocialism, 9, 47–48, 253, 278n102, 314n70
Practice Society (Shijian She), 123, 136–137
press. *See* media
profession, 12, 127–128, 150, 156, 166, 190, 217, 231–232, 270n16, 310n13, 314n62; professional, 178, 195, 202, 205, 207–208, 211–212, 214–215, 232, 246, 251 270n16, 277n88, 313n52, 320n149; professional ethos, 102, 116, 154, 165, 202, 205, 207–208, 211–212, 214–215, 232, 246; professionalism, 18, 212, 310n8, 318n134, 323n21, 325n40
progress, 14, 50, 76, 129, 134, 147, 200, 236, 238
proletariat,11, 29–30, 32–33, 72, 95, 132, 253, 275
Propaganda Department (of the CCP), 113, 206, 211, 216, 225, 288n1
Pu Zhiqiang, 201, 321n166
public culture, 24, 154, 246
public opinion, 166, 177, 180, 183, 191, 201, 209–210, 238, 244; opinion leaders, 218, 234
public sphere, 12–13, 16–17, 23, 27, 34–35, 100, 104–105, 107, 180, 187, 189, 214–215, 218, 225, 227, 267n66, 267n71, 269n1, 323n18, 323n20, 324n23–24, 325n40, 325n42–43

publishing sector, 3, 16, 53, 219, 225, 306n95, 331n138
Pun Ngai, 186, 252, 263n22, 263n78, 317n114

Qian Gang, 211, 219, 323n18, 324n24, 325n40, 326n45
Qian Liqun, 12, 37, 85, 93, 97, 100, 193, 257, 265n47–48, 289n7–10, 291n38–39, 291n42
Qian Ying (Minister of Supervision), 99
Qian Zhongshu, 120
Qian, Ying (scholar), 142, 153, 304n66, 304n74, 305n76, 306n92, 308n123, 312n32
Qianliexian, 217
Qin Hui, 4, 6, 13, 15, 41, 69, 120, 193–195, 250, 257, 263n19, 266n54–57, 267n61, 267n64, 276n76–77, 283n68, 284n82, 297n123, 319n142–145
Qingming (Tomb-sweeping) Festival, 100
Qingnian Zazhi / La Jeunesse, 35
Qiu Jiongjiong, 100, 308n119, 308n125, 308n128
Qiu Zhijie, 17, 267n67

Ran Yunfei, 217, 289n11, 325n40
Rao Jin, 321n2
Red Guards, 56, 88–89, 92, 117–118, 250, 290n19, 296n111, 306n94, 324n29
Reeducation Through Labor, 91, 95–96, 100, 172–173, 184, 291n41
Reform and Opening (*gaige kaifang*), 11, 34, 119, 165, 186, 265n48, 275n72
religion, 1, 9, 60, 83, 314n70
Remembrance (*Jiyi*), 85, 115–119, 257, 296n107, 296n110, 296n116
Ren Dingqi, 110, 294n86
Res Publica (*Gonggong luncong*), 53, 278n96
Resolution on Certain Questions in the History of our Party (1981), 71, 87–89, 284n77, 289n14
rightful resistance, 167, 311n16
rights-defense (*weiquan*), 3, 16, 165–170, 180–181, 183, 186, 200–202, 309n1, 310n3 310n5, 310n12–13, 311n19, 311n21–22, 311n24–25, 311n28, 313n52, 317n113
River Elegy, 125, 298n8
Robinson, Luke, 133, 298n8, 301n35, 301n37, 301n38
roots literature, 11
Rupture (Duanlie) questionnaire and group, 79, 81, 286n114–116
Russell, Bertrand, 3, 57, 58, 60–61, 65–66, 68

Said, Edward, 33, 141, 206, 217, 271n26–28
salon, 37, 172, 234–236, 239
Sanlian Shenghuo Zhoukan (Sanlian life weekly), 21, 53, 156, 211, 280n21, 282n55, 282n57–58, 285n87, 285n97, 285n100–101, 306n99, 307n101–102
Sanwei Teahouse, 234
Sapiro, Gisèle, 31, 270n16
Sartre, Jean-Paul, 28
scar literature, 15, 64, 66, 79, 87–88
scholar-official, 34, 56. *See also* literati
Schwartz, Benjamin, 36, 272n35
science, 2, 22, 26–27, 37, 43, 47, 50, 56, 59–61, 65, 70, 73–75, 78, 190, 233, 252, 254, 273n48–49, 279n116, 281n28, 333n4
Scott, James, 111–112, 188
sex worker, 15, 20, 41, 71–72, 82, 201, 226
Shanghai Literature (*Shanghai Wenxue*), 98, 225, 265n43, 282n61, 288n3, 292n43
Shanghai, 4, 11, 24, 37, 49, 92–93, 98, 102, 119, 137, 148, 154, 210, 213–214, 224–225, 228, 235, 256, 264n30, 275n72, 293n61, 308n119, 328n81, 328n86, 328n90
Shaw, George Bernard, 61
Shen Changwen, 53
Shen Zhihua, 101, 248, 257, 292n53, 292n55, 293n56
Sheng Hong, 173, 277n81, 313n49
Shenzhen Youth Daily (*Shenzhen Qingnianbao*), 88, 289n17
Shenzhen, 101, 161
Shi Jian, 136
Shi Yong, 5, 262n16, 262n18, 263n20
Shi Zhi, 79
Shi, Nansun, 210
Shouhuo (Harvest), 79, 286n106, 290n20
Shu Qiao, 107
Shu Ting, 79

Si Jicai, 97
Sichuan, 100, 105, 144, 289n11; *Sichuan Daily*, 114; Sichuan earthquake, 24, 147–148, 170, 192, 208, 220–221, 223, 249, 255, 305n85
silent majority, 2, 18–22, 52, 54, 61–62, 70–71, 77, 83, 88, 112, 118, 137, 139, 141, 143–144, 162, 176, 180–181, 191–192, 241–243, 247, 249–252, 261n3, 268n78–80, 268n85, 280n6, 281n36–38, 283n70–71, 286n107, 286n109, 290n23, 304n64
sinophone (transnational) public sphere, 12, 17, 219, 327n61
social democracy, 14, 44, 257
social media, 185, 189, 208, 216, 234, 245–246, 249–251, 294n72–73, 296n113, 306n93, 329n100
socialism, 7, 11, 32–33, 40, 44, 46–49, 65, 88–89, 96, 131, 134, 143–146, 148, 162, 169, 194, 223, 201, 251, 271n22, 275n72, 277n92, 278n102, 282n46, 288n3, 289n11, 290n27, 292n55, 305n77, 329n96
sociology, 13, 15, 19–20, 24, 26–28, 30, 37, 44, 53, 63–64, 69–71, 73, 75, 82, 87, 104, 111–112, 142, 156, 185–186, 212, 248, 256, 259, 270n8, 270n17, 283n71, 285n94–95
Socrates, 60
Solzhenitsyn, Aleksandr, 106
Song Binbin, 117, 118, 296n110, 296n116
Songzhuang, 3, 124–125, 127, 137, 152, 154–158, 160–161, 183, 185, 187, 193, 199, 201, 248, 256–257, 259, 289n12, 307n100, 307n103, 307n111
Sontag, Susan, 4
South Reviews (*Nanfeng Chuang*), 5, 262n12–16, 317n122
Southern Film Forum, 154
Southern Inspection (1992), 40
Southern Media Group, 3, 16, 53, 166, 206, 213, 255
Southern Metropolis Daily (*Nanfang Dushi Bao*), 164, 166, 204, 211–213, 310n9, 315n91, 319n144
Southern Metropolis Weekly (*Nandu Zhoukan*), 99, 264n38, 292n49, 317n117, 322n7, 330n111
Southern People Weekly (*Nanfang Renwu Zhoukan*), 3–4, 16, 82–83, 105–106, 261n7, 262n10, 292n47, 292n52–53, 293n70, 330n113
Southern Weekly (*Nanfang Zhoumo*), 53, 210, 280n5, 318n134, 323n21
Soviet, Soviet Union, 44, 47–48, 96, 101–103, 147,149, 240, 257, 262n12, 271n17, 278n106, 292n53, 301n39
Spark (Xinghuo) group and journal, 91–96, 103, 110, 112, 291n40
specialization, 2, 14, 31, 33, 37, 172, 187, 202, 248n97
Spires, Anthony, 168, 267n72, 311n18
Spivak, Gayatri Chakravorty, 14, 70, 111, 266n59
Stalin, 31–32, 62, 271n17, 271n21, 293n56
Stars exhibition (1979), 136
State Administration of Radio, Film, and Television (SARFT), 124, 162; later State Administration of Press, Publication, Radio, Film, and Television (SAPPRFT), 162, 300n25
State Council, 166, 182–183
state-owned enterprise (SOE), 7, 113, 127, 146–147, 175, 186, 194, 222, 257, 318n137, 319n144
statist (neostatist), 41, 44, 276n80
Steinhardt, Christoph, 180, 315n76, 326n55
Stern, Rachel, 169, 311n26
Stone, Sharon, 208
Stop Domestic Violence Network, 170
Strafella, Giorgio, 225–226, 274n65, 328n80, 328n85, 328n87, 329n93–94
Strategy and Management (*Zhanlüe yu Guanli*), 53, 278n96
Su Tong, 21
subaltern, 10, 14–16, 19, 27, 34, 70, 86, 89, 93, 103, 111, 121, 127, 130, 132–133, 139, 141, 143, 187, 190–191, 202, 214, 220–221, 247–251, 266n59, 283n71, 288n4, 295n90, 304n64
subordinated, 14, 17, 43
Sun Dongdong, 182
Sun Jingxian, 106
Sun Liping, 111, 187, 290n26, 295n92

Sun Tzu, 220
Sun Yat-sen University (Guangzhou), 52, 213–214, 255, 293n55, 312n29
Sun Yat-sen, 167, 197, 311n14
Sun Yu, 11, 77, 265n46, 286n106
Sun Zhigang, 4, 24, 164–167, 170–171, 176, 202, 212, 217, 257–258, 310n9–12, 320n150
Supreme People's Court, 244–245, 324n32
Svensson, Marina, 140, 184, 304n68, 305n74, 305n85, 312n30, 315n91, 316n105, 318n131, 318n134, 323n21
Szelényi, Iván, 31, 46, 266n52, 268n80, 271n17, 271n20–21, 284n78

Ta Kung Pao, 36, 87–88, 289n18
Taiping Uprising, 229
Taishicun (Guangdong), 135, 170
Taiwan, 17, 52, 62, 131, 219, 227–228, 238, 240, 268n75, 279n1, 295n102, 323n12, 330n119
Tamen, 79–80, 286n119
Tan Chanxue, 93–94, 291n36–38
Tan Tianrong, 86, 265n47
Tan Zuoren, 224
Tang Shouning, 173
Taylor, Charles, 75, 285n96
Teets, Jessica, 192, 319n138
television, 39, 124–126, 128, 131, 137–138, 162, 219, 278n96, 281n41, 302n50, 303n57
Teng Biao, 166–170, 172, 174–177, 194, 248, 257–258, 310n5, 310n10, 310n12–13, 311n15, 311n21–24, 311n27–28, 312n38–39, 312n41, 312n43, 313n57, 313n59, 313n61, 314n64, 314n66, 315n78, 315n80, 320n146–147, 320n151, 320n161
Teng, Teresa, 131
third sector, 13, 17–18, 162
Thireau, Isabelle, 182–183, 315n86, 315n88, 316n98
Three Antis Movement, 65
Three Gorges Dam, 147, 174
Three Represents, 262n12
Tian Han, 43
Tian Zhuangzhuang, 87
Tiananmen. *See* democracy movement
tianxia, 17, 62, 247; *yi tianxia wei ji ren*, 20, 35, 54
Tianya (Horizon), 53, 276n74, 276n76, 278n96, 283n71, 314n70
Tibet, 176, 256, 306n94; Tibet protests (14 March 2008), 177–180, 192, 204, 206, 208, 212–213, 249, 255, 314n69–70, 321n1, 322n2–3, 322n5
Tie Liu, 114–115
Tiger Temple (Laohumiao), 320n148
Time-News (*Shidai Zhoubao*), 8
Tinari, Philip, 222, 327n67, 327n71
tizhinei, *tizhiwai* (inside/outside the system), 7, 8, 37, 211, 262n15
Tocqueville, Alexis de, 34, 168
Today (*Jintian*), 11, 79, 81, 130, 135, 140, 300n20, 302n46
Tohti, Ilham, 201, 321n166
totalitarianism, 31, 63, 67, 102, 104–106, 240, 270n17, 284n74, 331n131, 332n145, 332n148
Transition Institute (Chuanzhixing), 174–175, 256, 312n39, 313n52
Tsinghua University, 69, 104, 111, 115, 117, 256–257, 264n33, 314n63, 321n2
Tuo Zhen, 215
Twenty-First Century (Ershiyi Shiji), 135–136, 271n30, 274n59, 283n74, 291n41, 294n82, 298n1

U, Eddy, 272n38–39, 273n44
Umbrella Movement, 243
underground (journals, films), 11, 48, 83, 91, 94, 135, 158, 161, 220, 283n74, 296n104, 299n14, 302n44, 306n296
Unirule Institute (Tianzesuo), 45, 173, 258, 313n46, 313n49
United Daily News (*Lianhebao*), 52
United Front, 94, 102, 151, 288n1
Ürümqi protests (2009), 214, 218
utopia, 6, 54, 62, 65–66, 81–82, 110, 112, 125, 138–139, 146, 154, 156, 186, 235, 239, 262n17, 264n35, 282n48, 285n86, 290n21, 298n6, 299n9, 308n133, 309n134

Van Crevel, Maghiel, 80–81, 286n119, 287n120–121
velvet prison, 32, 46, 271n22, 278n98
victims of Maoism, 2, 15, 58, 63–64, 71, 82, 84, 86–92, 96, 98, 100, 103, 105–106, 118, 121, 250, 258, 289n11, 293n67, 296n110–111
video compact disc (VCD), 128–129, 300n19, 306n96
vulnerable groups, 2–3, 6–7, 13–15, 20, 41, 52, 54, 69, 71–72, 78, 82–83, 118, 127, 136, 164, 169, 174–175, 181, 186, 188, 192–193, 197–198, 200, 202, 212, 221, 225, 231, 242–243, 245, 248, 257, 283n71, 286n111, 314n70, 319n137, 321n169. *See also ruoshi qunti*, 2, 14, 20–21, 52, 69, 70–71, 83, 121, 169, 193, 266n59, 283n71, 286n111

Walder, Andrew, 45, 273n52
Wang Bing, 98, 127, 138–139, 143, 145–147, 149, 157–158, 252, 257, 292n47–48, 301n39, 303n61, 304n65, 308n120
Wang Boming, 214, 325n34
Wang Chao, 127, 140, 302n48
Wang Chaohua, 40, 202, 274n65, 275n70, 276n75–76, 276n79, 278n104
Wang Fuzhi, 271n31, 280n7
Wang Gongquan, 181, 195, 199
Wang Hai'an, 107
Wang Haiguang, 119, 297n119
Wang Hongwei, 131, 158, 160, 308n119, 308n125–126, 308n128
Wang Hui, 139, 252, 264n38, 275n70, 276n74, 278n96, 279n114, 293n57, 303n62–63, 314n70, 322n4
Wang Jingchao, 97
Wang Kang, 149
Wang Libo, 147
Wang Lixiong, 59, 178
Wang Meng, 43, 48, 79, 88, 119, 288n2, 297n118, 299n16
Wang Nianyi, 115, 296n106
Wang Ruoshui, 287n124
Wang Shaoguang, 40–41, 216, 275n70
Wang Shiwei, 65
Wang Shuo, 19, 39, 46, 48–49, 59, 79, 88, 207, 278n103, 279n111, 280n24, 290n20
Wang Tiancheng, 168
Wang Xiaobo, 2, 8, 10, 12–14, 18–19, 21–23, 34, 51, 52–83, 88, 93, 116, 118–119, 126, 132, 139, 141, 158, 170, 176, 192, 231–232, 235, 240, 248, 252–253, 256–257, 261n3, 263n19, 268n76–79, 268n82–83, 268n85, 269n88–89, 280n2–4, 280n6, 280n8–11, 280n13–23, 281n24–38, 281n41–44, 282n45–61, 283n62–63, 283n65–70, 283n74, 284n81, 285n84–89, 285n91–93, 285n95, 285n97–104, 286n106–107, 286n109–112, 290n21, 290n23, 299n11, 300n30, 304n64, 312n29, 319n137
Wang Xiaolu, 138, 303n60, 325n34
Wang Xiaoming, 49
Wang Xiaoshuai, 124, 126, 131, 302n48
Wang Yang, 106
Wang Yi, 262n10
Wang Youqin, 116–118, 296n110
Wang Yu, 201
Wang Yunsheng, 36
Wang, Jing, 48, 279n108, 323n16
Wangshi weihen (Tiny scars of the past), 114
Wangxinban (Office for Cybersecurity and Informatization), 244
Weber, Max, 53, 276n74
WeChat (Weixin), 106, 208, 218, 239, 245, 301n36, 307n103, 316n104, 318n129, 326n58, 331n126, 331n133
Wei Hui, 80
Weibo. *See* microblog
Weigelin-Schwiedrzik, Susanne, 103, 290n26, 293n62
welfare state, 41, 194
Wen Hui, 107
Wen Pulin, 136, 306n94
Wen Qiang, 213
Wiseman, Frederick, 133
Woeser, 314n69
Women's Federation (All-China), 170

women's rights. *See* feminism
work unit (*danwei*), 2, 7, 12, 19, 23, 45, 71, 75, 84, 98, 113, 116, 125, 138, 155, 300n19
Workers' Daily (*Gongren Ribao*), 213
World Economic Herald (*Shijie Jingji Daobao*), 37, 210
Writers' Association, 2, 17, 79–80, 225, 232, 267n69
Wu Di, 115–117, 257, 296n107–110, 296n112
Wu Gan, 201, 321n171
Wu Jinglian, 4, 41, 276n76
Wu Qi, 239
Wu Si, 113, 118, 258, 294n78, 295n97, 295n100, 325n40
Wu Wenguang, 88, 104, 107, 110, 121, 124–125, 133–136, 157, 220, 248, 258, 294n80, 294n82–84, 301n33–36, 301n42, 303n56, 306n94
Wukan (Guangdong), 6, 213, 324n31

Xi Chuan, 303n62
Xi Jinping, 117–118, 121, 198, 215–216, 233, 243–245, 319n138–139, 320n157
Xia Junfeng, 176, 313n61
xianchang (aesthetics of liveness), 133–135, 301n41
Xianchang (Document), 133, 301n35
Xiang Chengjian, 94–95
Xiao Gongqin, 41
Xiao Ke, 53, 113
Xiao Shu, 212, 313n46, 313n53, 324n26, 325n40
Xiao Ying, 233, 330n124
Xie Yihui, 100, 170, 294n71
Xie Yong, 19, 268n77
Xin Ziling, 115
Xing Tongyi, 291n41
Xinhai Revolution (1911), 34
Xinhua (New China news agency), 92, 103, 256, 258
Xu Ben, 23, 47, 279n115
Xu Jilin, 4–5, 39, 68, 261n1, 262n15, 274n65–67, 275n68–69, 279n111, 282n61
Xu Xiao, 11, 265n46
Xu Youyu, 88, 106, 284n74, 290n19, 294n75
Xu Zhiyong, 166, 172, 175–181, 188, 194, 196–197, 199–200, 217, 225, 242–243, 248, 258, 310n11, 311n14–15, 312n38–41, 312n43, 313n54–59, 314n63–64, 314n66–67, 314n71, 315n74, 315n78–82, 320n146–147, 320n151–152, 320n154–157, 320n159–160, 320n162, 321n163–165, 328n88, 332n151
Xu Zhiyuan, 93, 199, 206, 225–226, 235, 237–244, 246, 249, 258, 320n162, 328n89, 331n126–127, 331n131–137, 332n139, 332n142–153
Xue Manzi, Charles, 244
Xueren (The Scholar), 39, 277n96

Yamagata (Documentary Film Festival), 133, 154, 299n13
Yan Geling, 235
Yan Jiaqi, 88, 273n49, 289n18
Yan Lianke, 82, 103, 235, 293n64
Yan Yu, 147
Yan'an, 65; Yan'an Rectification Movement, 102–103, 293n60
Yang Fudong, 5, 262n17
Yang Guobin, 7, 21, 219, 262n18, 263n21, 268n81, 326n50, 326n59, 327n51
Yang Jiang, 10, 56, 120, 280n12, 297n125
Yang Jisheng, 16, 103–104, 106–107, 113, 119, 122, 219, 248, 258, 293n63, 293n67–69, 294n76, 294n79, 297n121–122
Yang Kuisong, 36, 102, 273n43, 292n55, 293n58–59
Yang Shangkun, 105
Yang Weidong, 8, 263n28
Yang Xianhui, 97–99, 258, 292n43, 292n47
Yang Xiguang, 287
Yangzi, 123, 137, 298n2–3, 302n52
Yanhuang Chunqiu (Annals of the Yellow Emperor), 103, 106, 113, 118–119, 122, 216, 248, 258, 278n96, 294n76, 294n78, 295n97–100, 296n115, 297n118–119
Yao Renjie, 86
Yao Wenyuan, 57, 67, 280n15

Yazhou Zhoukan (Asia news weekly), 167, 199, 226, 235, 258, 295n98, 311n15, 320n162, 328n92, 329n95, 329n101, 332n151
Ye Haiyan, 10
Ye Shengtao, 240
Yen, James (Yan Yangchu), 161, 175
Yesterday (*Zuotian*), 115, 120, 297n124
Yi Hui, 77, 285n105
Yi Sicheng, 141, 160–161, 258, 303n60, 304n73, 305n86, 308n129–130
Yin Haiguang, 287n124
Ying Weiwei, 302n55
Yirenping, 174, 201
Yu Hua, 21, 79, 103, 293n65
Yu Jian, 79–81, 148, 248, 259, 287n119, 298n9, 301n38, 305n86
Yu Jiang, 166
Yu Jianrong, 13, 54, 153, 156, 181–191, 193, 202, 249, 252–254, 259, 265n47, 266n59, 307n100, 307n103, 315n91, 316n99–101, 316n103–108, 317n110–113, 317n115–123, 318n124–130, 317n132–133, 319n141, 325n40
Yu Luoke, 114, 265n47
Yu Pun Hoi, 39, 210, 323n19
Yu Wei, 235, 238–239, 332n141
Yu Xiaowei, 79
Yü Ying-shih, 38–39, 271n30, 274n59
Yu Zhaoyuan, 99
yuan (grievance), 183, 315n91, 316n97
Yuan Weishi, 293
Yuanmingyuan, 125, 155–157, 221, 235, 256, 306n99
Yue Minjun, 155
Yunfest, 141, 154, 160–161, 258–259, 300n22, 303n60, 304n72, 308n129–130
Yunnan, 19, 58, 63, 73, 82, 107, 124, 154, 160, 258–259

zawen (essay), 52, 77, 282n54
Zeng Jinyan, 10, 22, 141, 174, 218, 245, 249, 259, 264n36–37, 265n39, 268n86, 304n71, 308n124, 312n37, 313n51, 313n52, 321n167, 333n159
Zha Jianying, 39, 274n63, 323n19
Zhai Minglei, 212–213, 217, 324n33, 325n40, 326n51, 326n54
Zhai Yongming, 80
Zhang Aiping, 113
Zhang Bojun, 85
Zhang Boshu, 44, 277n91
Zhang Chengzhi, 49
Zhang Chunyuan, 95
Zhang Jieping, 213, 324n31, 328n92, 329n95, 329n101
Zhang Jun (scandal), 213, 255, 324n29
Zhang Mengqi, 107, 110
Zhang Ming (film director), 140, 149, 302n48
Zhang Naiqi, 114
Zhang Shuguang, 173
Zhang Wei, 49, 79
Zhang Xianchi, 86, 100, 292n51
Zhang Xianliang, 87–88
Zhang Xianmin, 137, 154, 302n55, 306n93, 308n113
Zhang Xingshui, 171, 312n38
Zhang Xudong, 48, 275n71, 278n103, 279n109–110
Zhang Yaxuan, 137, 157, 302n55
Zhang Yihe, 85, 91, 114, 331n138
Zhang Yimou, 300n28
Zhang Yiwu, 47
Zhang Yuan, 126, 131, 135–136, 299n11, 302n48
Zhang Yuanxun, 91
Zhang Zhongxiao, 86
Zhang Zuhua, 192
Zhao Liang, 127, 150–152, 155, 248, 306n89–90, 306n99
Zhao Yuezhi, 18, 210, 214, 252, 323n20, 325n37, 325n41
Zhao Ziyang, 210, 324n31
Zhao, Henry Yiheng, 47, 49, 279n113
Zhi Liang, 88, 290n22
Zhou Dunyi, 271n31
Zhou Enlai, 131
Zhou Ruijin, 275n72
Zhou Shifeng, 201
Zhou Yunpeng, 227

Zhou Zhixing, 219, 327n62–65
Zhu Jingjiang, 137, 302n49–52
Zhu Rikun, 152, 157–158, 160, 259, 302n53, 308n116
Zhu Rongji, 41, 85, 117
Zhu Wen, 79–80, 140, 248, 286n114–115, 299n11, 302n55
Zhu Xi, 61
Zhu Xueqin, 11, 37, 265n45, 275n73
Zhu Zheng, 85
Zi Zhongyun, 43, 113, 122, 277n87, 295n99, 297n127
Žižek, Slavoj, 50
Zola (blogger), 218
Zola, Emile, 28, 269n1
Zou Xueping, 107, 110, 294n81
Zuo Fang, 210–211, 323n21–22
Zuo Jing, 161

GPSR Authorized Representative: Easy Access System Europe, Mustamäe tee 50, 10621 Tallinn, Estonia, gpsr.requests@easproject.com

www.ingramcontent.com/pod-product-compliance
Lightning Source LLC
Chambersburg PA
CBHW020916110726
47900CB00001B/164

9780231191418